CONTEMPORARY SOUTHERN POLITICAL ATTITUDES AND BEHAVIOR

CONTEMPORARY SOUTHERN POLITICAL ATTITUDES AND BEHAVIOR

Studies and Essays

Edited by
Laurence W. Moreland
Tod A. Baker
Robert P. Steed

Introduction by Numan Bartley

PRAEGER

PRAEGER SPECIAL STUDIES • PRAEGER SCIENTIFIC

Library of Congress Cataloging in Publication Data
Main entry under title:

Contemporary Southern political attitudes and
    behavior.

    Bibliography: p.
    1. Southern States — Politics and government —
1951-   . I. Moreland, Laurence W.   II. Baker,
Tod A.   III. Steed, Robert P.
JK2408.C628   320.975   81-15694
ISBN 0-03-060424-9   AACR2

JK
2408
.C628
1982

Published in 1982 by Praeger Publishers
CBS Educational and Professional Publishing
a Division of CBS, Inc.
521 Fifth Avenue, New York, New York 10175 U.S.A.

© 1982 by Praeger Publishers

23456789   145   987654321

Printed in the United States of America

ACKNOWLEDGMENTS

This volume was developed from the second Citadel Symposium on Southern Politics, held at The Citadel on March 27-29, 1980. With the exception of the general introduction and three chapters which were prepared especially for the volume; each of the studies which follow was originally presented as a scholarly paper at the conference. The Symposium itself, directed by the editors of this volume, was facilitated by the efforts of a number of persons associated with The Citadel. These included Professor S. A. Arcilesi, head of the Department of Political Science, who willingly shouldered many of the administrative burdens related to the conference. Both Maj. Gen. James A. Grimsley, Jr., President of The Citadel, and Brig. Gen. George F. Meenaghan, Vice President for Academic Affairs, not only have worked to enhance the kind of intellectual atmosphere in which such a conference might succeed, but also have consistently supported and encouraged the Symposium on Southern Politics itself. Funding for the Symposium was generously provided by The Citadel Development Foundation, and we are grateful for their ongoing support and interest.

In relation to the development of the manuscript of *Contemporary Southern Political Attitudes and Behavior* we wish to thank the discussants at the 1980 Symposium whose commentaries proved very useful in selecting and editing the papers which comprise the volume. We are especially pleased that Professor Numan G. Bartley, a leading historian of the South, so graciously agreed to provide a general introductory essay. Our editors and production coordinators at Praeger, Betsy N. Brown, Tina Nimmons, and, especially, Marina Psaltoudis, have smoothed the publication process in ways too numerous to mention, and we thank them and Praeger for their invaluable assistance.

Finally, we wish to acknowledge our debt to Professor William C. Havard, a preeminent scholar of southern politics, who has enthusiastically supported the idea of the Symposium from its inception and who has encouraged the development of the Symposium publications.

CONTENTS

LIST OF TABLES

GENERAL INTRODUCTION

Numan V. Bartley

For the better part of a century Mississippi was among the most Democratic states in the Union. Nine out of ten voters normally endorsed the Democratic ticket in presidential elections, and, more often than not, Democratic candidates in state elections faced no opposition at all. Mississippi voters neared the ultimate in one-party politics in 1944, when the state's "yaller dawg" Democrats — the Democrats who would vote for a yellow dog if the party nominated one — marked 98 percent of their ballots for the Democratic presidential candidate. Twenty years later in the 1964 presidential election, almost 90 percent of Mississippians pulled the Republican lever, thereby making Mississippi the most Republican state in the nation and to some extent justifying the remark by a bemused observer that "Mississippi believes in the two-party system; it just believes in having them one at a time." In 1968 Mississippi cast almost two-thirds of its popular vote for George C. Wallace's third party ticket; in 1972 just under 80 percent of Mississippi voters supported Richard M. Nixon and the Republican party; in 1976 a slim majority of Mississippi voters joined the almost solid Democratic South in support of a Deep South native son; and in 1980 a plurality of Mississippi voters, like those in all but one other southern state, rejected Jimmy Carter and endorsed the Republican ticket. By 1980 Mississippi had a Republican Senator, and two (of five) Republican Representatives in Congress. Rarely in the history of electoral politics have there been such violent shifts in partisan voting patterns.

Mississippi is not the South, of course. As V. O. Key noted: "Northerners, provincials that they are, regard the South as one large Mississippi. Southerners, with their eye for distinction, place Mississippi in a class by itself."[1] Yet Mississippi exemplified, in somewhat exaggerated form, the general post-World War II political upheaval in the once Solid South. More than two decades of political strife marked the disruption of a political system, the origins of which stretched far back into the southern past.

Throughout its history the South has experienced difficulty finding a place in American partisan politics. Only once before has the region been fully integrated into a national two-party system. During the 1840s and early 1850s, Whigs and Democrats competed on approximately equal terms both within and outside the South. In the mid-1850s, however, growing sectional controversy over slavery undermined this system. The bulk of southern whites moved into the Democratic party in opposition to the antislavery threat embodied in the

Republican party, and for the most part they have been Democratic ever since, at least until very recent years.

The traumatic impact of the Civil War and Reconstruction generated social and ideological conflict too intense to be contained by normal political processes. Electoral fraud and violence became standard as newly freed blacks, declining yeomen, Bourbon planters, and New South would-be industrialists struggled for political dominance. The Populists' revolt of the 1890s broke apart the tottering one-party edifice erected by the Democrats following the political wars of Reconstruction. Bourbon planters and New South businessmen joined forces in opposition to the Populist challenge and established the social and political institutions that were to stabilize southern politics for half a century.

During the late nineteenth and early twentieth century, Democratic elites codified de jure white supremacy with the enactment of a bewildering variety of segregation laws and ordinances. Democratic white primary elections both circumscribed political participation by black southerners and entrenched the one-party system. Disfranchisement measures — poll taxes, literacy tests, and similar requirements — drove blacks and most lower income whites from the polls and ensured "responsible" government by effectively limiting electoral participation to a broadly based oligarchy. As the twentieth century progressed, growing legislative malapportionment ensured that state government in an urbanizing region would remain attentive to rural interests. As a study of Virginia politics reported, "the reforms undertaken in the Old Dominion during the progressive era returned the state to a political and social system as stable and resistant to innovation as any that had existed prior to the Civil War."[2]

Low levels of political participation and one-party politics became hallmarks of southern electoral behavior. The high voter turnout that characterized the politics of the middle and late nineteenth century plummeted around the turn of the twentieth century. In 1900, for the first time since 1836, a majority of potential voters in the former Confederate states failed to appear at the polling places in a presidential election. By the 1924 general election the average turnout in the 11 southern states had dropped to 17 percent of the potential electorate. Turnout in Democratic primary elections varied from state to state but in any case was on the average only marginally higher than participation in presidential elections. Throughout the region political elites well insulated from mass pressures could provide "responsible" government without the annoying distractions of popular democracy.

One-party politics thrived on electoral decimation. Those Mississippians who rallied around the Democratic presidential candidate with 98 percent of their votes in 1944 represented 15 percent of the potential electorate in the state. In 1924, when the Republican candidate for president received just over 2 percent of the popular vote in South Carolina, Senator Coleman L. Blease declaimed: "I do not know where he got them. I was astonished to know that they were cast and shocked to know that they were counted."[3] The Democratic monolith confined electoral competition to Democratic primary elections, where transitory and often nebulous factions rarely possessed the discipline or longevity to carry through meaningful legislative programs (as an essay by Earl Black and Merle Black in this volume documents). It is little wonder that V. O. Key concluded in 1949: "The South may not be the nation's number one political problem, as some northerners assert, but politics is the South's number one problem."[4]

One result of Democratic domination in the South was southern white domination of the national Democratic party. By the early 1880s southern Democrats normally comprised a majority of all Democrats in both houses of Congress. In 1896 the national party convention repudiated the northeastern oriented Grover Cleveland to nominate William Jennings Bryan, the champion of southern and western agrarians. Thereafter, for a generation, the national party remained anchored to the South. Even though the Democrats were usually in the minority, control of one of the major parties placed southerners in a strategic position to defend white supremacy and other peculiarly white southern interests. In Congress, southern Democrats with their numbers, their seniority, and their committee positions dominated the party caucuses, and in presidential politics the two-thirds requirement for nominations at the national conventions gave southern political elites a veto over the party's candidates.

This situation changed abruptly in the 1930s with the coming age of the ethnic and religious minorities in the northern cities, the Great Depression, the New Deal, the emergence of large-scale organized labor, and the shift of black voters from the party of Lincoln into the Democratic party. These groups — the well-known New Deal coalition — fundamentally changed the mass base of the Democratic party. When combined with the intellectual liberals attracted by the idealism of the New Deal, they also profoundly altered the party's policy objectives. Now, rather than being dependent on rural or small town white southern voters, the national Democratic party relied on northern, urban, minority voters. The repeal of the two-thirds rule at the 1936 national party convention recognized the new alignment of electoral forces.

Similarly, the nonsouthern Democrats arriving in Congress swamped the southern delegation. Professor David M. Potter observed: "In congressional elections from 1896 through 1930, the South and Border states together chose about two-thirds of all the Democrats elected. But in the seven Democratic Congresses between 1932 and 1946, the South and Border states elected fewer than half of all Democratic members."[5] This percentage continued to decline. In 1959, the former Confederate states elected 35 percent of House Democrats; in 1967 they chose 33 percent. The southern congressional delegation — the "Dixieland Band" as its critics were wont to term it — retained formidable power, particularly because of its seniority and its near monopoly of important committee chairmanships. Yet, however one measures the various factors, by the mid-1930s the Democratic party had become a different party, and the South's place in it had dropped precipitously.

At first, during the early 1930s, the stress of the Great Depression encouraged Democrats generally to rally around the president in time of crisis. But during the mid-1930s the New Deal shifted left, toward greater concern for social welfare and organized labor. Southern Democrats became increasingly restive. One reason for this, to be sure, was the fact that the political South — based on disfranchisement, the one-party system, legislative malapportionment, and an overriding commitment to protect segregation — was more conservative than the southern population in general. By the late 1930s, southern Democrats were joining northern Republicans in an informal but effective anti-New Deal coalition. The emergence of this coalition protected southern influence in Congress, but it also laid the foundation for an escalating sectional conflict within the Democratic party. Northern liberals persistently searched for ways to extend the liberal-labor-minority coalition into the South and thereby to transform southern politics. At the same time, southern political elites, while entrenched in Congress, fretted over liberal control of presidential politics and sought to restore their influence in national party affairs. This struggle between the northern liberal-labor-minority coalition and the Solid Democratic South was a crucial factor in American politics from the mid-1930s until the mid-1960s.

Open conflict began in 1938. Roosevelt attempted to "purge" some of the more reactionary southern congressional Democrats. The president campaigned against three leading southern Senators but this initial attempt to reform the Democratic party failed when all three senators were renominated and reelected. Shortly afterward, northern congressional liberals launched a sustained though temporarily unsuccessful drive for anti-poll tax legislation. The United States Supreme Court, reconstituted into a New Deal court following the court-packing fight of 1937, declared the southern white primary unconstitutional (*Smith v. Allwright*, 1944). During these years, the Congress of Industrial Organizations created its Political Action Committee (CIO-PAC) and endeavored to extend both its organizational and political influence into the South. Leading civil rights organizations adopted "A Declaration by Negro Voters," and the National Association for the Advancement of Colored People pushed its judicial war against the southern caste system. Somewhat later, the intellectual liberals created the Americans for Democratic Action. These organizations espoused various programs, but one aim of each was the reform of the wicked — and politically conservative — South. The efforts to defeat conservative southern Senators, to organize southern blue collar workers, to use CIO-PAC financial resources to support southern liberal politicians, and to expand black voting were all aimed toward extending the northern liberal-labor-minority coalition into the South.

Southern political elites struck back. In 1943, southern Democrats joined with Republicans to pass the Smith-Connally Act (a wartime measure sharply curtailing labor union organizational and political activities) and to override President Roosevelt's veto of the bill. Following the war the conservative coalition enacted the even more stringently anti-labor Taft-Hartley Act, and passed it over President Harry S Truman's veto. When the CIO launched its massive southern organizational drive — termed Operation Dixie — and the American Federation of Labor initiated a competing effort, southern states blunted the drives by enacting "Right to Work" laws permitted by the Taft-Hartley act. Similarly, several southern states strengthened voter registration barriers in the wake of the *Smith* v. *Allwright* decision.

The coming of the civil rights movement further exacerbated sectional divisions within the Democratic party. In February 1948, Truman asked Congress to abolish the poll tax and to enact other antidiscrimination legislation. Later in the year the national Democratic convention endorsed Truman's civil rights program and made "the right of full and equal political participation" a part of its platform.[6]

Outraged southern conservatives responded with the formation of the States' Rights Democratic party. The Dixiecrat revolt was an elite movement; southern voters held to their traditional loyalty to the Democratic party. The goal of the Dixiecrats was to deny either major party an electoral college majority and thereby to create an opportunity to reenact another sectional compromise like that of 1877. Arguing that Truman and the national Democrats had abandoned the "true" Democratic party, the Dixiecrats sought to restore Democratic virtue by making Governor J. Strom Thurmond of South Carolina and Governor Fielding Wright of Mississippi the Democratic nominees of the southern state parties. Only in Alabama, Louisiana, Mississippi, and South Carolina did state party executive committees place the Thurmond-Wright ticket under the Democratic label, and those were the only four states the Dixiecrats carried. The southern electorate cast Democratic ballots, regardless of whether Truman or Thurmond headed the ticket (although in Alabama the choice was relatively easy since the names of Truman and Alben W. Barkley were not permitted on the ballot). In 1952 southern conservatives switched tactics and championed the campaign of General Dwight D. Eisenhower. The purpose of the Eisenhower campaign was to expand southern influence by demonstrating to northern liberals that southern whites could not be taken for granted. In fact, the Republican candidate did carry four southern states. Perhaps the logical outcome of all of this was the 1960 presidential election when, in Alabama, voters elected a slate of Democratic electors, five of whom were pledged to vote for the national Democratic party ticket and six of whom were pledged to vote against the national Democratic party ticket.

The Supreme Court's *Brown* v. *Board of Education* desegregation decision of 1954 further inflamed the southern leadership and intensified southern defensiveness. Southern state leaders launched a campaign of massive resistance to desegregation, and the bulk of the southern congressional delegation signed the Southern Manifesto, which commended such action. Increasingly, the southern revolt from the National Democratic party, which had begun as an elite movement, became a popular reaction. Flared tempers, frayed nerves and sometimes violent confrontations marked the course of southern politics. In rapid-fire order during the early 1960s, blacks launched a South-wide sit-in movement that led ultimately to the Civil Rights Acts of 1964 and 1965. In *Baker* v. *Carr* (1962) the Supreme Court required reapportionment of legislative districts.

Republicans challenged Democrats in state politics as the one-party system proved unable to contain such volatile conflicts. Voters flocked to the polls; in the 1968 presidential election, for the first time in the twentieth century, a majority of the potential electorate in the South cast ballots.

Ultimately, tempers cooled. Southern whites, having experienced desegregation during the years following the Civil Rights Act of 1964, eventually came to accept it, at least on a token level. Reapportionment, the end of disfranchisement, and the decline of the one-party system destroyed the foundations of the old order, while southern blacks became an important factor in politics. As a result the fiercer defenders of the social and political status quo suffered a decline in both electoral support and popular prestige. In the backwash of the turmoil and racial demagoguery that had marked southern politics during the 1950s and 1960s, the 1970 southern elections swept in a wave of moderate political leaders, many of whom were relatively young and most of whom were newcomers to state office.

The acceptance of desegregation in the South, the decline of the southern Old Guard in Congress, and, indeed, the decline of the liberal coalition in the North brought an abatement to the long struggle between North and South, or at least shifted its focus. In 1976 most of the northeastern states supported a Deep South resident in the presidential election, as did all but one of the southern states. Four years later, ten of the eleven southern states rejected native son Jimmy Carter in the 1980 presidential election to support a western conservative. In the 1980 election, Republican candidates won four of the seven Senate races in the South, thereby creating a southern senatorial delegation of eleven Democrats, ten Republicans, and one Independent. The Democrats still held a commanding 69-39 majority of the southern seats in the House of Representatives, but clearly the days of the yellow dog Democrats had passed.

During the tumultuous and sometimes violent conflict that centered in the 1960s, southern politics passed through a transformation of fundamental magnitude. The old system has collapsed; yet the outlines of its replacement remain unclear. Within this context the essays in this book take on particular significance. Several books published in the early and mid-1970s examined the disruption of the old political order,[7] but a more fundamental question concerns the new political system in the South and its place in American party politics. In 1978 the first Citadel Symposium on Southern Politics delved into various aspects of this issue. From that Symposium evolved *Party Politics in the South*, edited by Robert P. Steed, Laurence W. Moreland, and Tod A. Baker. In the introduction to that work, William C. Havard noted its contribution to the study of southern politics "during a time of great fluctuation in voter participation, factional and party identification, and partisan electoral alignments."[8] This comment would be equally applicable to the essays that follow.

The second Citadel Symposium on Southern Politics was held in March 1980, and selected papers from that conference provide the basis of this volume. The following fourteen essays are divided into three sections focusing on ideology, party politics, and the relationship between mass and elite behavior in the South. Each of them, either directly or indirectly, investigates the overall theme of the volume; that is, the extent to which the South retains its historical political distinctiveness. These studies develop this theme from a variety of perspectives and utilize a rich diversity of data and research techniques. Collectively, they help to illuminate the complexity of southern politics.

NOTES

1. V. O. Key, Jr., *Southern Politics in State and Nation* (New York: Vintage Books, 1949), p. 229.
2. Raymond H. Pulley, *Old Virginia Restored: An Interpretation of the Progressive Impulse, 1870-1930* (Charlottesville: University of Virginia Press, 1968), p. ix.
3. George Brown Tindall, *The Disruption of the Solid South* (Athens: University of Georgia Press, 1972), p. 47.
4. Key, *Southern Politics*, p. 3.
5. David M. Potter, *The South and the Concurrent Majority* (Baton Rouge: Louisiana State University Press, 1972), pp. 67-68.
6. Donald B. Johnson and Kirk H. Porter (comps.), *National Party Platforms, 1840-1972* (Urbana: University of Illinois Press, 1973), p. 435.
7. William C. Havard (ed.), *The Changing Politics of the South* (Baton Rouge: Louisiana State University Press, 1972); Numan V. Bartley and Hugh D. Graham, *Southern Politics and the Second Reconstruction* (Baltimore: The Johns Hopkins University Press, 1975); Earl Black, *Southern Governors and Civil Rights: Racial Segregation as a Campaign Issue in the Second Reconstruction* (Cambridge, Mass: Harvard University Press, 1976); and Jack Bass and Walter DeVries, *The Transformation of Southern Politics: Social Change and Political Consequence Since 1945* (New York: Basic Books, 1976).
8. Robert P. Steed, Laurence W. Moreland, and Tod A. Baker (eds.), *Party Politics in the South* (New York: Praeger, 1980), p. xv.

PART I:

IDEOLOGY IN SOUTHERN POLITICS

INTRODUCTION

The Editors

Throughout much of this nation's history the South has been widely considered to be the country's most distinctive region — distinctive politically, socially, economically, and culturally. For years this perceived distinctiveness contributed to sustained research interest in the South and, consequently, to the production of a large body of literature on the region.[1] The general theme is illustrated clearly in V. O. Key, Jr.'s landmark 1949 study, *Southern Politics in State and Nation*, which emphasized that the politics of the South at mid-century differed markedly from the politics of the remainder of the nation.[2] Key, however, suggested that this distinctiveness might be eroded as postwar economic and social developments served to move the South more into the mainstream of American life. As Numan V. Bartley points out in the General Introduction to this volume, during the past three decades the South has undergone many of the changes that Key (and others) foresaw, and, in fact, the theme of change has joined that of distinctiveness in much of the recent research on the region.[3]

In light of these changes in southern political, economic, social, and cultural life, some writers have suggested that regional distinctiveness in the United States has come to an end as even the South has become increasingly assimilated into a broadly-based national culture. John Shelton Reed has aptly summarized this viewpoint in the following words:

The South, runs the refrain, is disappearing: the region is well on its way to becoming "almost indistinguishable from any other region of the country." As usual, journalists have announced this development more colorfully than have social scientists. Harry Ashmore has written *An Epitaph for Dixie*; while *Esquire* magazine, proclaiming that "the

3

South is over," describes for its readers "some of the ways the cracker crumbled." But scholars have also contributed (although more cautiously) to the development of this belief. Leonard Reissman, writing in a symposium with the title "Urbanization and Social Change in the South," has observed that the titles of most recent monographs and symposia on the South have emphasized the South's "emergence," its "transformation," in a word its *change* — another way of saying its increasing resemblance to the rest of the United States.[4]

On the other hand, some writers have maintained that the South has retained much of its regional character, so much so that its regional characteristics still clearly define an identifiable "southernness" in culture, in politics, and in social life. For example, Bartley, while recognizing increasing similarities between the South and the rest of the country, argues that this does not necessarily imply a decline in its political sectionalism;[5] and Reed, while acknowledging that change has taken place, maintains that the South still differs from the non-South in such cultural respects as the attachment of its people to the local community, the importance of fundamentalist religious beliefs, and the acceptance of violence as a part of daily life.[6]

In short, much of the scholarly attention paid to the South in recent years has focused on the interrelated features of regional distinctiveness, regional change, and the degree to which the South has retained those characteristics with which it has long been associated. This volume, framed within the context of the debate over continued southern distinctiveness, presents new research exploring three aspects of contemporary southern political attitudes and behavior. Taken together, these essays provide information pertinent to understanding the extent of southern assimilation into national cultural, social, and political patterns.

The chapters in Part I focus attention on the nature of ideological and issue concerns in the region. The first two, "Ideology in the South: Meaning and Bases Among Masses and Elites" by Jerry Perkins and "A Microanalytic Return to the Mind of the South" by Robert E. Botsch, examine the attitudes of selected subgroups of southerners and provide information on the nature of southern ideological and issue positions. These serve to set the stage for the regional comparisons presented in the next two chapters, "Southern Conservatism 1956-1976" by Earl W. Hawkey and "Sources of Political Intolerance: The Case of the American South" by Ted Jelen. Perkins explores and compares the attitudes of a political elite (210 members of the General Assembly) and a sample of the population in one southern state (Georgia) in an effort to identify some components of southern thinking on designated political matters. Botsch, employing a technique used with great success by such scholars as Robert Lane, presents an in-depth analysis of the belief systems of a small group of southern blue collar workers, and, while the results are limited in their general application, he advances some highly suggestive and useful conclusions about the nature of the contemporary mind of the South. The chapters by Hawkey and Jelen are much broader, since they are based on data for the entire region; in addressing the question of southern ideological distinctiveness, they offer regional comparisons on selected issues. Hawkey finds evidence of regional convergence on certain issues and continued differences on others. Interestingly, he suggests that in those areas where regional distinctiveness has lessened it has resulted more from a movement by nonsoutherners toward the attitudes of southerners than from a movement of southerners toward the attitudes of nonsoutherners. Finally, Ted Jelen investigates essentially the same question through an examination of attitudes toward deviant subgroups. He finds that in the specific topic areas selected, regional differences are still quite significant.

In short, these four chapters offer a range of data differing in scope and method and addressing different aspects of the same broad theme essential to understanding whether the South retains its ideological distinctiveness.

NOTES

1. As John Shelton Reed points out, the South stands as the most common exception to the American rule, and this contributes to its being the most studied region in the world. Reed provides an extensive bibliographical listing of research on the South in support of this contention. On this point, see John Shelton Reed, *The Enduring South: Subcultural Persistence in Mass Society* (Chapel Hill: University of North Carolina Press, 1972), p. 1. See also the bibliographies of material on the South in William C. Havard (ed.), *The Changing Politics of the South* (Baton Rouge: Louisiana State University Press, 1972); and in Numan V. Bartley and Hugh D. Graham, *Southern Politics and the Second Reconstruction* (Baltimore: Johns Hopkins University Press, 1975).

2. V. O. Key, Jr., *Southern Politics in State and Nation* (New York: Alfred A. Knopf, 1949).

3. The theme of change in the South is central to most of the chapters in Havard, *The Changing Politics of the South*, but it is summarized most effectively in Chapter 1 of that work. See also Bartley and Graham, *Southern Politics and the Second Reconstruction*; and William C. Havard, "Introduction," in *Party Politics in the South*, eds. Robert P. Steed, Laurence W. Moreland, and Tod A. Baker (New York: Praeger, 1980), pp. x-xvi. A number of the essays in this book address the theme of political change in the region as well.

4. Reed, *The Enduring South*, p. 1; Reed's references in this quotation are to Harry Ashmore, *An Epitaph for Dixie* (New York: Norton, 1957); Joseph B. Cummings, Jr., "Been Down Home So Long It Looks Like Up to Me," *Esquire* (August 1971): 84; Leonard Reissman, "Social Development and the American South," *Journal of Social Issues* 22 (January 1966): 102; Thomas D. Clark, Jr., *The Emerging South* (2d ed.; London: Oxford University Press, 1968); Robert B. Highsaw (ed.), *The Deep South in Transformation* (University, Alabama: University of Alabama Press, 1964); Allan P. Sindler (ed.), *Change in the Contemporary South* (Durham: Duke University Press, 1963); Raymond W. Mack (ed.), *The Changing South* (Chicago: Transaction Books, 1970); and John M. Maclachlan and Joe S. Floyd, *This Changing South* (Gainesville: University of Florida Press, 1954).

5. Numan V. Bartley, "The South and Sectionalism in American Politics," *Journal of Politics* 38 (August 1976): 239-257.

6. Reed, *The Enduring South*. For additional arguments that the South retains some of its traditional distinctiveness, see also Havard, *The Changing Politics of the South*, Chap. 1; and Bartley and Graham, *Southern Politics and the Second Reconstruction*, Chap. 8.

1

IDEOLOGY IN THE SOUTH: MEANING AND BASES AMONG MASSES AND ELITES

Jerry Perkins

The use of ideological symbols to describe political processes is widespread in American politics. For journalists, politicians, and many academic observers ideological categorization represents a convenient summation of political acts and actors. Ideology has been particularly useful to describe the most fundamental of democratic activities, the linking of voters and politicians through elections. If the complex world of politics can be cast in terms of overarching, explanatory symbols, both prospective representatives and the represented can act in a commonly understood frame of reference to maximize their benefits.[1]

Ideological correspondence or the lack thereof between leaders and followers can be employed to explain political events. Interpretation of "liberal" representational behavior may be grounded in estimations of the liberal inclinations of those represented. Or, defeats of particular candidates may be said to result from an inconsistency between representative and the represented, as in "he's too liberal for his constituency." Similarly, laments about the failure of the electoral process may be grounded in perceptions of continued ideological misrepresentation.

While ideological shorthand is widespread, its use is perhaps most conspicuous in conversation and writing on the American South. Histories of the region are replete with liberals, progressives, conservatives, populists, and the like.[2] In the South, as in the nation, questions sometimes focus on the nature of the ideological linkage between representatives and the represented. Often it is less a process or calculation than it is a kind of unspoken consensus arising out of cultural solidarity. Thus, it has been said that the region is inherently conservative.[3] Others, particularly indigenous liberals and outside observers, have noted that ideological correspondence between southern leaders and followers may not be accurate. The extreme view is that of William G. Carleton, who,

6

over 30 years ago, claimed that southern conservatism was a myth and that the public opinion of the region is really liberal.[4] Other more measured views, including that of V. O. Key, essentially agree with Carleton in principle if not in emphasis: southern opinion has not been as conservative as leadership behavior, at least insofar as governmental intervention in economic life goes.[5]

It is true that survey evidence illustrates a convergence between the South and the nation on economic issues, if not on noneconomic issues such as racial integration and tolerance.[6] It is also true that leadership in Washington has been shown to have been conservative relative to the behavior of Democrats from other regions,[7] although in the aftermath of civil rights, the hegemony of the old guard is thought to be waning as new Democratic representatives align with their party more than with regional tradition.[8]

While the scope of both southern political change and attendant scholarship is impressive, many questions emerge about the rather easy generalizations on both the old and new southern politics. In the absence of comparable measures of individual attitudes or behavior, how can we compare the ideology of southern leaders and followers? Are there in fact interrelated sets of opinion that can be understood in ideological terms among either leaders or followers? If there is ideology, or perhaps ideologies, how do southern leaders and followers compare? What are the sources of southern ideology?

This paper addresses key aspects of the meaning of southern ideology. In so doing, it ignores the question of how conservative the South is, relative to other regions. Instead, employing survey data from the mid-1970s, the measurement of southern ideology is addressed in one southern state by: (1) comparing patterns of issue and ideological self-labels among elites and mass; (2) examining the degree to which mass and elite opinion can be described as consistently ideological; and (3) exploring the bases of ideological thought among elites and mass.

CONFLICT AND IDEOLOGICAL RESPONSE

Among both elites and mass, ideological symbols and thought can provide cognitive and evaluative guides to the social order and disruptions therein. From the perspective of assessing the meaning of ideology in any population, two subjects must be addressed: the nature of conflict, and the population's ability to respond and give order to that conflict.

Sources of Southern Conflict

The history of southern politics is rich with drama and complexity. If there is any order to that history it is perhaps focused on the twin themes of racism and defense of the agrarian society. Southern racism is well known. Resistance to black equality has persisted through several sociopolitical periods. Electoral devices, political alignments, and violence have been used against blacks.[9]

Apart from race, however, the agrarian tradition can be a source of conservative resistance to change. The economic modernization of the region through industrialization and urbanization has not been readily accepted by southern defenders of tradition. The virtues of personalism, place, and tradition are deeply imbedded in southern regional consciousness, as are the fears of mass, industrial society. Thus, as Everett Carll Ladd, Jr., points out, southern alignment with the national Democratic Party can be seen at least in part as a defense against the business nationalism of the Republican Party.[10]

The southern agrarian and racist traditions have, however, produced other than conservative tendencies. Traditional justifications of status and place have been couched in the context of the deprivation and poverty of small farmers and workers, both white and black. Socioeconomic disparities in the old South between landed elites and the many at the margin of economic life have given rise to periodic challenges to traditional dominance in the form of populist revolts.[11]

The combination of race and class conflicts has provided the South with a particularly volatile mix. The division of poor whites and blacks by racist appeals is well known, and class politics has often become race politics with the turn of events and the passage of time.[12]

Against the agrarian and racial backdrop of resistance, the South has modernized in this century. Industrialization and urbanization have proceeded apace. That which transpired in the North in a previous generation became reality in the South.[13] Northerners moved in to help man the new industrial, corporate order, and the South has begun to produce its own urban middle class. In politics and society, the new industrial elite is "progressive" relative to the ways of old. Courthouse politics is challenged. Good government and bureaucratic efficiency are promoted, and they in turn promote the cause of business in the region. Republicanism, first in national politics and then in the local arena, becomes an alternative for the new urban middle class to the traditional Democratic ways.[14]

Though there are sources of conflict between old agrarian elites and new urban elites, there are common conservative aspects. Both see government as limited in terms of socioeconomic welfare. Both, however, do see a positive governmental role in the maintenance of order and stability.

The new economics, however, has not obliterated the old racism. Survey research and voting studies suggest a blending of new and old conservatisms. Besides the racial antipathies of the white working class, there is the presence of both economic and racial conservatism among white-collar whites of the region, according to Norval D. Glenn.[15] Thus, while many have hoped for the emergence of class-based politics,[16] others have estimated that race-based politics is still close to the surface, even if it is not as obvious as it was in the past.[17]

Ideology as Attitude Constraint

The degree to which southern citizens organize their thoughts in response to southern history and the degree to which there are shared elite-mass notions on the proper role of government are matters of importance. Scholarship on the American population has produced two divergent if not incompatible views of what to expect. First, there is Philip Converse's contention that elites have ordered sets of constrained attitudes, but masses do not.[18] Converse's theory is rooted in the very simple assumption that interrelationships among attitudes reflect a central constraining force, and the mass attitudes are very loosely if not randomly connected. Second, there is the claim that over the past 20 years the degree of attitudinal constraint and ideological self-awareness in the American population has heightened.[19] Sources of increased restraint are thought to result from higher political interest, increasing sophistication, and a changing political environment.

Revisionist thought on attitude constraint, however, has not gone without challenge. What might be called "revision of the revisionists" has emphasized that methodological shortcomings[20] and peculiarities of particular statistical techniques[21] have exaggerated if not produced the new results.

For many observers, the failure to find more ideological consistency in the population is frustrating. Some suggest that there is really ideology in the population, but we have not yet tapped it, or that we may not be able to calibrate it with a common measure because each person's belief system may be unique to his/her particular experience and context.[22] Doubtlessly, survey research does overlook and/or obscure many individualized belief systems. That is, it is likely that there is order and meaning to a larger part of the population than suggested by national surveys. Yet, to overly emphasize this is to miss a central concern, which is: to what degree are there common frames of reference understood by both masses and elites? To assume Converse's position is not to deny the existence of thought in the mass. His position does, however, say a great deal about the difficulty of linking mass and elite opinion through elections.

The initial assumption guiding this research is that while both southern masses and elites share political and historical experience, overarching ideological summaries of that experience may be more extensive in the elite owing to their more intense involvement in the political process.[23] This may particularly be the case with summary labels like liberal and conservative.

Bases of Ideology

Estimating the causes of southern ideology is to some degree dependent on how many "dimensions" are thought to exist. If we assume the simple notion of a left-right continuum and consistency between elite and mass in the ideological space, southern history suggests several hypotheses. Most obvious would be the assumption that southern blacks more than whites would be liberal. In terms of status, if modernization is the chief force and the South is becoming more like the old industrial North, upper status elements should provide the sources of conservatism. Relatedly, Republican partisan identification should be linked to conservatism. If the cities change faster than the countryside, we would expect rural residence also to be related to resistance to change, particularly among rural whites on racial matters. With respect to generations, the old would have ideas formed in an earlier time and should therefore be more conservative than the young. Finally, religion may have some bearing on this issue in the South. Benton Johnson suggests that fundamentalism is linked to more conservative value orientations among southerners.[24]

DATA AND METHODS

Interviews with General Assembly members in Georgia, and a statewide sample of Georgia's population constitute the basis for this analysis. Both sets of interviews were taken in 1974. First, early in the year, 210 of 236 legislative representatives responded to trained interviewers. Shortly thereafter, a comparable instrument was administered to an area probability sample of 500 Georgians.

The preponderance of the two questionnaires weighed on legislative procedure and representation. Several items, however, relate specifically to the questions at hand. First, both instruments addressed ideological self-identification by asking first if the respondent thought of himself/herself as a liberal, moderate, or conservative; if the respondent said yes, s/he was then asked which of the three labels was an accurate description. A second set of terms related specifically to issues. Respondents were asked if they thought government should do more, the same or less than is currently being done on the following seven issues:

1. maintaining law and order
2. ensuring that blacks and other minority groups get fair treatment and equal opportunity
3. stopping the sale of pornographic material
4. seeing to it that women get fair treatment and equal opportunity
5. protecting consumer rights
6. improving the economic position of the poor
7. making sure industry doesn't damage the environment.

"Do more" responses on items 1 and 3 are viewed as conservative, and these items were reverse coded to be consistent with the remaining five areas where a "do more" response is thought to be liberal.

In addition, race, religion, and age were obtained on each individual. The party affiliation of General Assembly members was taken from the official records and the party identification of the population sample was ascertained by asking the standard questions. Finally, both respondent universes were classified as to urban or rural residence by determining if they lived in one of the standard statistical metropolitan areas of the state.

In terms of population characteristics, three status indicators — education, occupation, and income — are available for the general population only. One population characteristic, that of race, varies between the two populations as it is used here. Because there was only a handful of black representatives in the General Assembly at that time, the proportion of black representative constituencies is used in place of the respondent's race. Beyond questions of limited numbers, this would seem to be a justified procedure on the grounds that the proportion of voting blacks in one's district would bear upon opinion, either through the process of candidate selection or in anticipation of maintaining one's representative seat.

The analysis proceeds at several levels. First, simple marginal comparisons of General Assembly members and the population are made. Second, attitude consistency is analyzed two ways: by factor analysis and by determining the proportion of each population with ideologically consistent answers. Third, scale scores from the factor analysis and ideological self-identification are regressed on the major population categorized following the hypotheses articulated above.

FINDINGS

Distribution on Issues and Ideological Identification

TABLE 1.1
PERCENTAGE GIVING CONSERVATIVE RESPONSES[a]

Government involvement in:[b]	General Assembly	Georgia Population	Statistical Significance
Assuring law and order	75	92	$p < .05$
Helping Minorities	61	45	$p < .05$
Stopping Pornography	58	65	n.s.
Helping Women	33	40	n.s.
Protecting Consumers	25	19	n.s.
Helping the Poor	45	37	n.s.
Protecting the Environment	55	29	$p < .05$
Average % Conservative	50	41	—

[a]A conservative response on law and order and on pornography is a "do more" response. On all remaining issues, "do the same" and "do less" responses are combined to produce the percentage conservative.

[b]For the full wording of the questions see the text.

n.s.: Not statistically significant.

Source: Compiled by the author.

By comparing responses of the General Assembly and the population sample, V. O. Key's speculation that southern representatives are more conservative than their constituents can be assessed, at least within the context of one state at one point in time. Table 1.1 contrasts the proportions with conservative responses to the seven issues in the assembly and the population. On four of the seven — minorities, consumers, the poor, and environment — the assembly members are more conservative than their constituents. In only the cases of aiding minorities and protecting the environment are the magnitudes of difference substantial. The remaining three issues — law and order, pornography, and women — produce higher conservative responses in the population than in the assembly. Of the latter three, the only significant difference is in the area of doing more to ensure law and order, although both samples are overwhelmingly in favor of doing so. In terms of being on opposite sides of majority/minority cutting points, only two issues are so divided: minorities and the environment.

Viewed in terms of overall ideological direction, Free and Cantril's description of the American population as "operationally" liberal would generally apply to the Georgia population as well.[25] The Georgia population shows a net conservative direction only on law and order and on pornography. The General Assembly members reflect the population pattern on these two issues and add an overall conservative balance on minorities and the environment. Thus, while not an overwhelming set of differences, the political elite does appear on these issues to be slightly more conservative than the population.

As Table 1.2 shows, the slightly more conservative nature of the General Assembly is reflected in ideological self-identification as well. Also consistent with Free and Cantril's national findings is the higher number of self-identifying conservatives than liberals in the Georgia population, even though that same population is operationally liberal on most issues.

TABLE 1.2
IDEOLOGICAL SELF-IDENTIFICATION

	General Assembly	Georgia Population
Liberal	7	10
Moderate	55	26
Conservative	32	25
don't know/doesn't apply	6	39
	100%	100%
N =	(210)	(500)
p < .05		

Source: Compiled by the author.

However, the most important evidence emerging from Table 1.2 is not the overall ideological direction, or differences therein, but the relative degree to which the two populations are willing to adopt an ideological label. Of the whole mass sample, 39 percent are filtered out by the question asking if they have ever thought of themselves in such terms or don't know which one when they are asked directly. This substantial percentage is contrasted with the 6 percent figure in the General Assembly.

The inclination to identify with an ideological position appears to be primarily a function of education and, to a lesser extent, race. The highly educated are more likely than those of low education to say they have thought of themselves in ideological terms (r = .25). Whites more than blacks identify (r = .16), although this is at least in part the result of whites having a higher education than blacks (r = .25). Partialling out the effect of education reduced the race association to .09.

Attitude Constraint

The question of attitude constraint has been approached in two ways. One approach is to look at constraint in *individual* terms by determining the proportion of individuals who are consistent.[26] In so doing the standard of consistency is that of the investigator who imposes his/her idea of what is the "correct" combination. A second approach, used by Converse and many others, is to use correlational and factor analysis, and in so doing, emphasize issue *pairs in the aggregate* rather than individuals. Both approaches are used here. The first, that of looking at consistent individuals, is further modified by including also the *number* of issues on which an individual has a response. Therefore, high constraint measures both the direction and the *scope* of an individual's responses. The latter is necessary because it is obvious that we would not want to give a high score to an individual who is consistent but only answers two questions. This individual clearly should be distinguished from another who answered five questions and was consistent on all.

The ideological self-identification question is a good example of the potentially different effects of the two methods. Should it be included, the high number of nonclassifications in the mass population would automatically lower the constraint of mass relative to elite where constraint is approached from an individual perspective. This would not be true with respect to correlational analysis where inter-item correlations would simply be cast on the available data for all pairs, thereby lowering the base N. In that individual constraint between self-identification and the issue items could not possibly be high in the mass by the standards employed here, the balance of the analysis will consider ideological self-identification separately from the issue items. In effect, this provides more opportunity for the general population to be highly constrained in individual terms, and it maintains a higher number of cases for the factor analysis.

In terms of constraint among individuals, high attitude constraint is defined as an individual who answered six or seven of the items in a direction consistent with political-world expectations about the proper direction. By these standards, 15 percent of the General Assembly are highly consistent in a liberal direction and 14 percent are highly consistent in a conservative direction. The total, then, of "highly" consistent attitudes in the assembly is 29 percent. In the population, 8 percent is consistently liberal and 10 percent is consistently conservative. Thus, the total scoring high on consistency in the population is 18 percent, some 11 percentage points lower than the General Assembly.

While this result is consistent with other findings, two cautions should be forwarded. First, the magnitude of difference is not large. This is possibly due to the fact that there is no filter question on the issue items as there is in much of the established national research. Presumably, if there were a filter (as in the ideological self-identification question) asking if the respondent had any interest in the issue, there would be fewer of the mass who said yes and therefore a smaller number of individuals who were constrained. This consideration would lead the observer to expect *more* differences between the two samples. A second qualification, however, would lead to an expectation of *less* difference. Marginal distributions are important. If there is a distribution approaching the extreme — as there is on the law and order question in the mass — then there are fewer individuals who could possibly score in a highly constrained manner, because the "liberals" would have a difficult time being consistently liberal given the fact that over 90 percent of the sample favored a conservative response on law and order. Generally, because the distributions for all questions were less extreme in the General Assembly than in the population, this possibility should not be discounted.

While the employment of correlation-based technique to study attitude constraint does have some weaknesses, there are clearly some strengths as well. Perhaps the strongest is that of discerning the underlying patterns through factor analysis. In so approaching the topic, no assumptions are made about the correct direction of association; instead direction and clustering of items is empirically determined. Additionally, the number of dimensions can also be assessed by this technique. As Stimson points out, factor analytic results may vary across studies according to the number of items, but it is useful for comparing two groups in the same study.[27] In the case at hand, if either of the two groups is highly constrained, that group should produce fewer factors than the less constrained group. Judging from previous evidence, we would expect that the General Assembly attitudes would produce fewer factors than the general population.

The expectation is *not* borne out, as Tables 1.3 and 1.4 illustrate. In both the General Assembly and in the population, two factors are produced for the seven items. Further, the items composing the factors are exactly the same across both sets of respondents. Ensuring law and order and stopping pornography constitute a factor, the weaker of the two, and is labeled "morality."

TABLE 1.3
FACTOR MATRIX FOR TWO ATTITUDE DIMENSIONS
(In the General Assembly)

| Items[b] | Factors[a] | |
	Socioeconomic Liberalism-Conservatism	Morality
1. Law and Order	−.01	.83
2. Pornography	.03	.84
3. Minorities	.71	.06
4. Women	.65	.10
5. Consumers	.63	.10
6. Poor	.68	−.15
7. Environment	.59	−.07
Eigenvalue	2.16	1.45
Percent of Variance	30.9	20.6

[a]The correlation matrix from which the factors are extracted is as follows (with non-significance designated by a *):

	Minorities	Pornography	Women	Consumer	Poor	Environment
Law and Order	.02*	.38	−.03*	.02*	.05*	.03*
Minorities		−.04*	.31	.35	.32	.32
Pornography			−.03*	−.02*	.09*	.03*
Women				.31	.35	.19
Consumers					.26	.22
Poor						.29

[b]For full item wording see text.

Source: Compiled by the author.

The remaining five items — those on minorities, women, consumers, the poor, and the environment — form a factor, and this factor is labeled "socioeconomic liberalism-conservatism." The differences between the two groups are only matters of degree. Law and order and pornography, while forming an independent factor in the population, do have moderate loadings on the first factor as well. In the General Assembly the morality factor is somewhat more distinct than in the general population in that the two items composing it have high loadings on morality and loadings close to zero on socioeconomic liberalism-conservatism.

As for the meaning of the two factor division, the empirical results are not incompatible with what we might expect. While the items are few in number, the morality factor represents one in which the moral behavior of the population

TABLE 1.4
FACTOR MATRIX FOR TWO ATTITUDE DIMENSIONS
(In the Georgia Population)

	Factors[a]	
Items[b]	Socioeconomic Liberalism-Conservatism	Morality
1. Law and Order	−.20	.72
2. Pornography	−.34	.65
3. Minorities	.67	.24
4. Women	.70	.07
5. Consumers	.58	.05
6. Poor	.69	.27
7. Environment	.67	−.09
Eigenvalue	2.36	1.09
Percent of Variance	33.7	15.5

The correlation matrix from which the factors are extracted is as follows (with non-significance designated by a *):

	Minorities	Pornography	Women	Consumer	Poor	Environment
Law and Order	.07*	.24	.05*	.06*	.02*	.10
Minorities		.07*	.41	.18	.43	.30
Pornography			.16	.11	.10	.19
Women				.25	.34	.34
Consumers					.32	.32
Poor						.28

[b]For full item wording see text.

Source: Compiled by the author.

is of concern. On the other hand, the five-item factor is clearly a standard liberalism-conservatism question about government intervention to either protect disadvantaged groups or to intervene to protect the environment.

From a southern perspective, the most important evidence presented here is that there is a standard liberal-conservative dimension and that government aid for blacks falls on that dimension. It is of course true that a general government aid question is perhaps different or "easier" to fit with the other items than school integration, which perhaps would form a separate dimension. But, mild as the question may be, blacks are not a separate domain for either the mass or the elite.

From a methodological perspective, why is it that almost exactly the same factor patterns were found, contrary to expectations? Doubtlessly, methodology has a role. Unlike many national questions, all used here were cast under the same general theme. The fact that all questions were in effect "joined" by a common reference to government action may make it easier for a mass population to be consistent.

Some support for this general explanation might be indirectly given by the self-identification question, which is cast in a different format. Placing it in a factor analysis as an eighth item produces different results for the General Assembly than for the general population. Self-identification in the assembly is strongly loaded on both factors; in the population the two factor pattern remains, but self-identification is very weakly loaded on both. And, adding self-identification reduces the number of respondents in the analysis by almost 40 percent, leaving the better educated users of the terms, people we would expect to more closely link labels and issues.[28]

The same results can be seen in correlations between self-identification and two factor scores in both populations. In the General Assembly ideological self-placement is moderately correlated with socioeconomic liberalism-conservatism ($r = .36$) and with morality ($r = .30$), while in the general population the comparable correlations are weak in both cases (rs = .14 and .04).

Bases of Ideology

The two sets of factor scores and liberal-conservative self-identification were regressed on the independent variables thought to be associated with ideological cleavage in the South. The results, which are shown in Tables 1.5 and 1.6, warrant one overriding generalization: in neither the General Assembly nor the population do the variables explain a great deal of the variance in ideology, although the assembly regressions are certainly more impressive than those of the population. While all these equations are significant for the assembly, only socioeconomic liberalism-conservatism is significant for the population. The proportions of variance explained in the assembly for liberalism-conservatism, morality, and self-identification are .12, .14, and .27 respectively. In the same order the population proportion of variances explained are .22, .07, and .06. Thus, there is a reversal on the liberal-conservative factor and self-identification: more of the population variance is explained in the former, the only significant equation for the population, and less in the latter, relative to the General Assembly.

As for the contributing variables, race emerges as important in the expected direction on all three equations in the General Assembly and in two of three equations in the population. In all cases, blacks or proportion of the district black contributes to liberal scores. The heaviest such incidence is on ideological self-identification of assembly members where the beta of −.44 is clearly the overwhelming figure to emerge from the regression.

TABLE 1.5
MULTIPLE REGRESSION OF INDICATORS OF IDEOLOGY
(For General Assembly Members[a])

	Beta	Simple r	Statistical Significance
A. Socioeconomic Liberalism-Conservatism:			
% BIK of Constituency	−.30	−.31	p < .05
Rural-Urban Const.	−.09	−.16	n.s.
Age	.08	.08	n.s.
Religion	.02	.03	n.s.
Party Affiliation	.02	.03	n.s.
$R = .34 \quad R^2 = .12$[b]			
B. Morality:			
% BIK of Constituency	−.25	−.21	p < .05
Age	.23	.24	p < .05
Party Affiliation	−.12	−.12	n.s.
Religion	.05	.01	n.s.
Rural-Urban Const.	−.05	−.21	n.s.
$R = .37 \quad R^2 = .14$[b]			
C. Liberal-Conservative Identification:			
% BIK of Constituency	−.44	−.48	p < .05
Religion	.14	.13	p < .05
Rural-Urban Const.	−.11	−.19	n.s.
Party Affiliation	.09	.13	n.s.
Age	.07	.05	n.s.
$R = .52 \quad R^2 = .27$[b]			

[a]Code for rural-urban constituency is 0 for rural and 1 for urban; for religion, 0 for nonfundamentalist and 1 for fundamentalist; for party, 1 for Democrat and 2 for Republican. Factor scores range from low (liberal) to high (conservative).
[b]R^2 is the proportion of variance explained by the equation.
n.s.: Not statistically significant.

Source: Compiled by the author.

Status factors in the general population contribute little, but their effect is generally in the expected directions. Those of higher education, income and occupational status are more conservative on the first factor, liberalism-conservatism, and on ideological self-identification, although it must be emphasized that these contributions are negligible on the whole. Only income makes a significant contribution in the first factor. On morality higher status is (insignificantly) associated with liberalism.

TABLE 1.6
MULTIPLE REGRESSION OF INDICATORS OF IDEOLOGY
(For the Georgia Population[a])

		Beta	Simple r	Statistical Significance
A.	Socioeconomic Liberalism-Conservatism:			
	Race	−.35	−.43	$p < .05$
	Income	.15	.28	$p < .05$
	Urban-Rural Residence	−.10	−.16	n.s.
	Age	−.10	−.18	n.s.
	Party Identification	−.06	.10	n.s.
	Education	.04	.14	n.s.
	Occupation	.01	.19	n.s.
	Religion	−.02	−.05	n.s.
	$R = .47 \quad R^2 = .22^d$			
B.	Morality:[b]			
	Age	.23	.23	$p < .05$
	Religion	.07	.09	n.s.
	Race	−.06	−.01	n.s.
	Education	−.06	−.13	n.s.
	Income	.05	−.01	n.s.
	Occupation	−.04	−.05	n.s.
	Party Identification	.03	.02	n.s.
	Urban-Rural Residence	.03	.02	n.s.
	$R = .26 \quad R^2 = .07^d$			
C.	Liberal-Conservative Identification:[c]			
	Race	.16	.18	$p < .05$
	Age	.14	.08	$p < .05$
	Party Identification	.07	.09	n.s.
	Urban-Rural Residence	−.06	−.09	n.s.
	Education	.05	.07	n.s.
	Occupation	.04	.12	n.s.
	Religion	−.03	−.06	n.s.
	Income	.00	.08	n.s.
	$R = .25 \quad R^2 = .06^d$			

[a]Codes for race: 0 for white and 1 for Black; for urban-rural: 0 for rural and 1 for urban; for party identification: 1 for Democrat, 2 for Independent, and 3 for Republican; for occupation: 0 for blue-collar and 1 for white-collar; religion: 0 for nonfundamentalist and 1 for fundamentalist. Factor scores range from low (liberal) to high (conservative).
[b]Overall equation not significant
[c]Overall equation not significant
[d]R^2 is the proportion of variation explained by the equation.
n.s.: Not statistically significant

Source: Compiled by the author.

The presumed political carrier of new conservative ideology, Republicanism, is even less significant. Republicans in the General Assembly and in the population are marginally more conservative than Democrats, except in the assembly responses on morality where Republicans are the more liberal of the two parties.

The age of the respondent is not a good predictor generally speaking, but it is the best predictor for the population on morality and next-to-best on self-identification: in both cases older age is associated with conservatism. The results for morality in the assembly parallel the population, with age being the second most important indicator of conservatism.

Fundamentalist religious identification generally contributes a marginal amount to conservative inclinations, but only in the case of assembly self-identification is the contribution significant.

Finally, whether one resides in the city or the country doesn't appear to make a great deal of difference: in not a single instance does the rural-urban variable make a significant contribution. The associations for rural-urban are particularly weak in the population; in the General Assembly the associations are somewhat stronger with urban representatives being more liberal on liberalism-conservatism and on self-identification.

CONCLUSIONS

Bartley and Graham's conclusion to their *Southern Politics and the Second Reconstruction* includes an observation that is relevant to this conclusion: "Most Americans, North or South, appear to possess little in the way of a coherent philosophy, and therefore the group orientation of a voter has been extremely significant to political behavior."[29] Certainly, if the requirements of coherency include a descriptive label, then they are right. Little of the evidence presented here is suggestive that Georgia citizens impose a summary word on their political thought that is consistent throughout the population. To whatever degree the terms liberal and conservative have consistent meaning, it is much less shared in the general population than in the political elite.

Responses to individual issue items do, however, suggest that there is at least a modicum of attitude constraint, if not ideology, in the population. Here too, Bartley and Graham's generalization may be suggestive. The items employed contained a goodly emphasis on groups, and it may well be that "group orientations" are linked and, as noted before, the fact that the fate of groups was tied clearly in the questions to level of government activity may facilitate an overall linkage in the voter's mind.

Whether there is enough common ideological understanding between the elite and mass to effect simple links during elections is debatable. While single symbols of complex ideational elements may be missing, the similar constraints on issues do suggest a basis for common understanding of campaign appeals promoting group interest or deriding excessive government involvement. The fact that a second domain — that pertaining to morality — emerged from the limited set of questions may, however, militate against assuming an overly simplistic single dimension notion of public opinion.

Whatever the measuring of ideology, the limited evidence presented here does suggest that southern orientations toward blacks may not constitute a dimension apart from all other issues. In the Georgia General Assembly specific support for blacks may fall below a majority, but this overwhelmingly white institution clearly does not isolate blacks from other recipient groups in terms of attitude structure. And the Georgia population, viewed as a whole, groups issues in a similar way.[30]

Even if blacks are no longer a unique focus in public opinion, race is still a dominant feature of southern political life from another perspective. Simply put, the most obdurate opinion division is that between the races. Interestingly, the relevance of race for the members of the General Assembly may be higher than for the general population. Although few legislators were black when the data for this study were gathered, white representative opinion would appear to be substantially linked to the incidence of minority population in the home districts. And, the association between proportion of district black and liberal sentiments of representatives is a dramatic reversal of old-time southern politics. Black voting is not without effect.

The emergence of blacks has not, however, provided grounds for rejecting V. O. Key's speculation about the conservative nature of southern representation. The Georgia General Assembly is somewhat more conservative than the general population, although the disparity is probably not as wide as existed when Key made his observations. The sources of the existing discrepancy were not a topic for this paper, but Key's speculation about the conservative bias being the result of differential participation rates between the rich and the poor has found support in a more recent national investigation[31] and would be a particularly interesting line of inquiry in a southern setting.

NOTES

1. Anthony Downs, *An Economic Theory of Democracy* (New York: Harper, 1957); see also Donald Stokes, "Spatial Models of Party Competition," in *Elections and the Political Order*, eds. Angus Cambell et al. (New York: Wiley, 1966), pp. 161-179.

2. Numan V. Bartley and Hugh D. Graham, *Southern Politics and the Second Reconstruction* (Baltimore: The Johns Hopkins University Press, 1975); see especially p. 22, where the authors define these terms in advance of their study.

3. See the arguments of what might be termed a southern "Burkean" conservative: James Jackson Kilpatrick, "A Conservative Political Philosophy," in *The South,* ed. Monroe L. Billington (New York: Holt, Rinehart, and Winston, 1969), pp. 111-118.

4. William G. Carleton, "The Conservative South — A Political Myth," *Virginia Quarterly Review* 22 (April 1946): 179-192.

5. V. O. Key, Jr., *Public Opinion and American Democracy* (New York: Alfred A. Knopf, 1967), p. 102.

6. Robert S. Erickson and Norman R. Luttbeg, *American Public Opinion* (John Wiley & Sons, 1973), pp. 174-175, 200-201.

7. Duncan MacRae, *Dimensions of Congressional Voting* (Berkeley: The University of California Press, 1958); and W. Wayne Shannon, "Revolt in Washington: The South in Congress," in *The Changing Politics of the South*, ed. William C. Havard (Baton Rouge: Louisiana State University Press, 1972).

8. Jack Bass and Walter DeVries, *The Transformation of Southern Politics* (New York: New American Library, 1972), pp. 369-391.

9. For a description of these processes, see V. O. Key, Jr., *Southern Politics in State and Nation* (New York: Alfred A. Knopf, 1949).

10. Everett Carll Ladd, Jr., *American Political Parties: Social Change and Political Response* (New York: W. W. Norton & Company, 1970), p. 217.

11. William C. Havard, "From Past to Future," in *The Changing Politics of the South*, ed. William C. Havard (Baton Rouge: Louisiana State University Press, 1972), pp. 704-706.

12. See the classic treatment of this phenomenon from a national perspective: E. E. Schattschneider, *The Semi-Sovereign People* (New York: Holt, Rinehart, and Winston, 1960), Chapter 5.

13. William C. Havard, "The South: A Shifting Perspective," in *The Changing Politics of the South*, ed. William C. Havard (Baton Rouge: Louisiana State University Press, 1972), p. 25.

14. For an extensive description of this process and the emergence of Republican identification and voting, see the aggregate voting analysis of Louis M. Seagull, *Southern Republicanism* (Cambridge, Mass.: Schenkman Publishing Company, 1975). For a discussion of social and attitudinal bases of southern Republicanism, see Jerry Perkins, "Bases of Partisan Cleavage in a Southern Urban County," *Journal of Politics* 36 (February 1974): 203-214; and Jerry Perkins, "Southern Partisan Change in National Politics," *Politics 1974* 5 (March 1974): 75-91.

15. Norval D. Glenn, "Class and Party Support in the United States: Recent and Emerging Trends" *Public Opinion Quarterly* 37 (Spring 1973): 1-20.

16. See the comments of Key, *Southern Politics in State and Nation*; and Donald R. Matthews and James W. Prothro, *Negroes and the New Southern Politics* (New York: Harcourt, Brace, and World, 1966), p. 475.

17. Bartley and Graham, *Southern Politics and the Second Reconstruction*.

18. Philip E. Converse, "The Nature of Belief Systems in Mass Publics," in *Ideology and Discontent* ed. David E. Apter (New York: The Free Press, 1964), pp. 206-261.

19. Stephen E. Bennett, "Consistency Among the Public's Social Welfare Policy Attitudes in the 1960's," *American Journal of Political Science* 17 (August 1973): 544-576; Norman Nie and Kristi Anderson, "Mass Belief Systems Revisited: Political Change and Attitude Structure," *Journal of Politics* 36 (August 1974): 540-591; Norman Nie, Sidney Verba, and John Petrocik, *The Changing American Voter* (Cambridge, Mass.: Harvard University Press, 1976); Bruce Campbell, *The American Electorate* (New York: Holt, Rinehart, and Winston, 1979); Gerald Pomper, *Voter's Choice* (New York: Dodd Mead, 1975).

20. The literature on this subject has rapidly proliferated over the past five years. For examples of the debate see: Norman Nie and James Rabjohn, "Revisiting Mass Belief Systems Revisited: Or, Doing Research is Like Watching a Tennis Match," *American Journal of Political Science* 23 (February 1979): 139-175; and John Sullivan, James Piereson, George Marcus, and Stanley Feldman, "The More Things Change, The More They Remain the Same: Rejoinder to Nie and Rabjohn," *American Journal of Political Science* 23 (February 1979): 176-186.

21. George Balch, "Statistical Manipulation in the Study of Issue Consistency: The Gamma Coefficient," *Political Behavior* 1 (Fall 1979): 217-242.

22. See the conclusions of Stephen Earl Bennett, Robert Oldendick, Alfred J. Tuchfarber, and George Bishop, "Education and Mass Belief Systems: An Extension and Some New Questions," *Political Behavior* 1 (Spring 1979): 53-72.

23. Stimson's finding that high "ability" groups think in constrained ways forms the basis for this expectation. See James A. Stimson, "Belief Systems: Constraint, Complexity, and the 1972 Election," *American Journal of Political Science* 19 (August 1975): 393-417.

24. Benton Johnson, "Ascetic Protestantism and Political Preference in the Deep South," *American Journal of Sociology* 69 (January 1964): 359-366.

25. Lloyd A. Free and Holley Cantril, *The Political Beliefs of Americans* (New York: Clarion Books, Simon & Schuster, 1968).

26. For this approach, see Hugh LeBlanc and Mary Beth Merrin, "Mass Belief Systems Revisited," *Journal of Politics* 39 (November 1977): 1082-1087.

27. Following James A. Stimson, principle component factor analysis with varimax rotation was employed.

28. The correlations between liberal-conservative self-identification and the issue items were (with a * designating nonsignificance):

Law and Order	The General Assembly	The Georgia Population
Law and Order	−.25	.03*
Minorities	.28	.06*
Pornography	−.22	−.07
Women	.25	.11
Consumers	.23	.08
Poor	.13	.12
Environment	.21	.06*

29. Bartley and Graham, *Southern Politics and the Second Reconstruction*, p. 195.

30. While it was not within the scope of this paper, it is a logical possibility that a factor analysis on whites only might produce a different pattern, with such a subgroup pattern being overridden by the 25 percent black component of the sample. A cursory look at this, however, suggests the same overall factor pattern for whites in the state.

31. Sidney Verba and Norman H. Nie, *Participation in America* (New York: Harper & Row, 1972).

2

A MICROANALYTIC RETURN TO THE MIND OF THE SOUTH

Robert E. Botsch

. . . if it can be said there are many Souths, the fact remains that there is also one South. That is to say, it is easy to trace throughout the region . . . a fairly definite mental pattern, associated with a fairly definite social pattern — a complex of established relationships and habits of thought, sentiments, prejudices, standards and values, and associations of ideas. . . .

(W. J. Cash, *The Mind of the South*, p. viii.)

INTRODUCTION

Scholars and laymen alike have long felt there to be something distinctive about the South beyond its being a less developed area of the United States and all that means in terms of social, economic, and political characteristics. Since Cash created his classical composition on the content of the southern mind in 1940, many other students of the South have followed suit. Cash remains the standard of comparison. Specifically, Cash saw southerners as differing from their economic peers in other regions with respect to pride in region and family, the tendency to swiftly and violently react to affronts to ego, to act more out of emotion and attachment to false romantic values than from rational analysis, to be fiercely individualistic, to have a narrow sense of social obligation, to oppose social change, and to hold deep-rooted values of racial prejudice.[1]

More recent works have probed for many of these same attitudinal traits. Drawing upon mass survey data, John Shelton Reed has argued that several aspects of the southern mind have persisted and endured the inevitable grinding of our mass culture, mass consumption society. Reed found a local particularist

and individualist orientation remaining in the South that could not be statistically explained by socioeconomic factors.[2] This narrow orientation was further
manifested, supported, and promulgated by a particularly strong devotion to
family and family sponsored values.[3] Family and church combined to promote
fealty to conservative social values. "Whatever behavior may actually be, the
approved morality in the South is an austere one. . . . the evidence seems to indicate no substantial decrease in Southern religious peculiarity in the recent past
and no prospects for a decrease in the near future."[4] The behavior that Reed
found, as reflected in attitudes toward corporal punishment, hunting, and the
ownership and use of firearms, was characterized as particularly violent. ". . . it
was the most violent region in an increasingly violent nation."[5] In sum, Reed
found several of those values and attitudes delineated by Cash in 1940 to be in
existence well after the turn of the mid-century.

Political scientists are concerned with these attitudes because of what they
portend for the politics of the South. William C. Havard has been one among
many political observers to note that peculiar southern attitudes have been the
foundation for the distinctive party system that has existed in the South.
Because southerners have been more concerned with social and moral issues
than with class based economic issues, the political party structure has not
functioned to express and resolve economic issues to the degree that it has in
the rest of the nation.[6] Havard also pointed to the "deeply ingrained spirit of
frontier independence and rural individualism" that had been so poignantly
described by Cash as being partially responsible for drawing southern whites to
George Wallace's attack on centralized and intellectualized government.[7]

In an important work focusing on the relationship between southern attitudes and southern voting behavior, Numan Bartley and Hugh Graham compiled
an impressive quantity of precinct data in support of their contention that, as
of the mid-1970s, racial antagonisms continued to be a barrier to the common
economic concerns of southern working class whites and blacks. They saw blacks
and working class whites rallying around opposing candidates whenever racial
and social issues were raised in a political campaign. They concluded that
"hysteria on the part of a considerable number of southern politicians and racial
fears on the part of many white voters drove a wedge between blacks and less
affluent whites, much as in the 1890's. With prosperity increasing and memories
of the Great Depression fading, many rural and lower income whites saw themselves threatened more by social change than by economic exploitation. . . .
white southerners had accepted desegregation but not much more than that."[8]

Not only did Bartley and Graham find racial and social issues to divide
blacks and whites, they also saw a trend in survey data showing a decline in
support for economically liberal welfare measures on the part of working class
whites, the issue area around which the races had previously shown a strong
common interest.[9] Thus Bartley and Graham paint a picture of both stability
and change in southern attitudes. They see a continuance of racial antagonisms
that will find political expression. They see any changes in expressed racial

attitudes as only superficially important. Social conservatism is another stable coloration of the southern mind, a coloration that has increased in political salience as government has become more involved in social planning. Finally, they see a darkening in white working class sentiments on issues involving economic redistribution, a change that increases the consistency of contrast between the races.

Th central question of this paper is whether several of these distinctively southern attitudinal traits continue to exist in the minds of a small group of young southern blue collar workers, and how attitudes are changing, if at all. Specifically, an in-depth interviewing approach will be used to explore the minds of ten white and five black workers to answer the following questions.

1. Is there any indication from their attitudes that there has been movement away from economic liberalism, and are whites distinctively more conservative than blacks?

· 2. Do these men retain an orientation toward life that is individualist in character?

3. Are their religious beliefs fundamentalist in nature and are these beliefs related to social conservatism?

4. Are they prone to violence in their personal lives and likely to accept violence as a legitimate form of political action?

5. What is the quality and depth of any racial prejudice that is uncovered?

METHODOLOGY

The small sample in this study is composed of 15 southern furniture factory workers who have spent their lives living in the same small town in central North Carolina. All held jobs that would be classified as blue collar nonsupervisory. They ranged from 18 to 33 years of age when the interviews were taking place in the winter of 1977. Their mean hourly wage was $3.73.

The town of about 15,000 in which they lived is typical of many southern towns. Created as an agricultural center, it first experienced industrial growth after the Civil War as textile factories began to spring up all over the South. Today its two main industries are textiles and furniture. Both share many common characteristics. They tend to be decentralized industries with many small and marginal companies in a highly competitive market. Both are labor intensive and mostly nonunionized. Wage structures are quite similar. In 1974 the average hourly wage for both industries in North Carolina was identical at $3.57.[10] In both, the skill levels required for most production jobs are moderate so that the labor market is practically interchangeable. Indeed, many of the men in our small sample have worked in both industries.

The sample is a quota sample by two factory settings (large and small), by race, and by job categories (all major departments are represented).

The interviews totaled more than 75 hours and the transcripts more than 1,600 double-spaced, typed pages. We covered a wide variety of subjects in the conversations, from feelings about family to ideas about how democratic clubs and organizations should be run. Most of the 157 questions were open-ended, but over 24 standard attitudinal scales were utilized.

The methodology employed in this report is a combination of content analysis and impressionistic interpretation. For each attitudinal area of interest, relevant passages from the transcripts for each of the respondents were located and compiled. From these new subsets of the original transcripts, each respondent was further categorized by his positions on component attitudes. For example, in the area of violent orientation, each man was scored according to his beliefs about corporal punishment, capital punishment, the ownership and use of firearms, problems with and how they express their tempers, fighting to protect ones honor, political violence, and that all important "other" category that allowed further insight into personal values. After seeking trends and making interpretations, each of the men was categorized as high, medium, or low in each major area so that the "southernness" of their outlooks could be summarized.

Obviously, the size of the sample and the empirical inexactitude of the methods employed make inductive generalizations improper. However, the depth of probing, multiple approaches to attitudes, and establishment of interpersonal trust that was possible in a small group intensive approach overcome some of the problems inherent in survey research. We may discover new hypotheses involving context and interpretation that might later be tested through survey methods. The respondent is also less likely to be intellectually intimidated by friendly conversations than by all too often academic sounding survey questions asked on doorsteps or over the telephone. Social scientists have learned a great deal from researchers such as Robert Coles and John Dollard, who came to *know* society by learning what it looked like through the eyes of individuals.[11] This report represents a modest effort to continue in that tradition.

FINDINGS

Economic Liberalism

This area has been of great interest to those political observers who harbor liberal hopes for the South. Contrary to the popular stereotype of the economically conservative antigovernment southern redneck, historians and political scientists have long observed that the white lower classes in the South have favored government actions that are redistributionist in nature. From support of populist political candidates in the late 1800s, through Huey Long in the 1920s and 1930s, to support of George Wallace in the 1970s, lower class whites in the South have been attracted to statements flavored with economic liberalism such as that made by Wallace in 1970. "The affluent super-rich in this country are more dangerous than the militants. . . . Citizens' power will right the wrongs perpetrated against the middle class and the lower class in the United States. . . . No government is administered according to the objective and intent of the Founding Fathers . . . unless it is administered for the weak, the poor, and the humble as well as the powerful."[12] V. O. Key's analysis of southern public opinion was that economically conservative politicians were more a result of low participation rates by working class whites (and blacks) than a reflection of their economic attitudes.[13] Other students of southern public opinion and voting behavior, such as Chandler Davidson, Donald Matthews, and James Prothro, have also found that working class southerners are much more liberal on economic matters than is generally assumed.[14] In a separate chapter in this volume, Earl Hawkey observes from relatively current public opinion data that lower status southerners are no more conservative, and perhaps even less conservative than their nonsouthern counterparts, on the key economic welfare issues of government guaranteed jobs and government sponsored health care programs.[15] In light of Bartley and Graham's contrary thesis of working class white/black divergence on economic welfare issues, let us examine the attitudes of this small group of young workers seeking possible explanations for these different findings.

Looking first to their responses to standard survey questions about government action with respect to jobs, health care, school finance, energy, and housing, we find an almost uniform liberal response. All ten whites and four of the five black men tended to agree more than disagree with the liberally worded statements. Only Lewis, a young black veneer machine tender who comes from a very authoritarian family and distrusts almost everyone including the government, gave an almost uniformly conservative response to these standard items. His own personal problems with housing and oil bills led him to call for slight government involvement in these two areas, but he stressed that government should only have "a little something" to do with them — "just a part, not completely dominant."

Blacks and whites did not differ in their pattern of answers to these questions nor was there any distinct cluster of blacks when the group was arranged according to overall summary scores.

In examining the open-ended portions of our discussions, we find a similar picture. After all the relevant passages had been coded as either economically liberal or conservative, we find that six of the ten whites took the economically liberal position more than two-thirds of the time. Eddie, one of the better paid workers who briefly worked as a supervisor in the finishing department, believes that a free market approach would be the best way to deal with energy, wants less government regulation of farmers, and tends to blame the poor for their poverty.

> *Eddie:* The biggest part of (poverty) originally was their fault and then circumstances just gathered on them and then it got out of control.

I would say that nine out of ten that really was classified as poor could really have done something about it years before.

A more typical response was volunteered by Dave, a white molding machine operator who expressed great sympathy for the poor, sick, and elderly. He was asked if he thought the government would be going *too* far on national health care in making all doctors government employees and placing them on fixed wages.

> *Dave:* No, I don't. Because they's a lot of people that, say, below average pay of what average people get paid that has to go to the doctor and just really can't afford paying it all theirself. I think, it wouldn't break my heart if they put doctors on government pay — not a bit!

Once again blacks were fairly evenly spread among the whites in the percentage of their volunteered opinions supporting government action to bring about greater material equality. Only Lewis, consistent with his conservative score on the standard survey items, voiced more conservative economic values than liberal.

We might conclude then, that these young workers generally take economically liberal issue positions, contrary to the observations of Bartley and Graham. However, when we carefully examine their explanations, the content of their beliefs, and the limitations they place on them, we uncover some supporting evidence for Bartley and Graham's findings.

First, blacks and whites explain their rationalized economic self-interests somewhat differently. Both races blame the rich, the wealthy, the corporations, the upper classes, and company owners for their economic woes. But blacks also blame whites for a perceived lack of economic opportunity. Rick, a bitter black Vietnam veteran who willingly displays his battle scars, feels that blacks are not told about jobs that have any real promotional opportunities and are shunted into dirty, low paying, low security types of jobs. Few of the whites would agree. In fact, most of them see blacks as having better promotional opportunities than they as a result of affirmative action programs, and therefore consider blacks as well as the rich as threats to economic advancement. The role the government has played in promoting affirmative action programs is greatly resented. That resentment is focused as much on blacks as on government. Paul, an articulate white forklift driver who favors price and wage controls and took a liberal integrationist position on most issues, offered one of the best expressions of this resentment. After talking about not minding if his children were in a school that was 90 percent black, he revealed a source of great ambivalence.

> *Paul:* I have mixed feelings so far as race. I feel it is a good idea to try to get things together right. I feel we should give 'em all the chances we've been giving them. (But) I don't dig the way they've taken it. You give em equal rights and now it seems to me that they want more than

equal rights. . . . you give one a job. All right, he's going to get the same money and everything. Well, soon he might want more money and more favors . . . in some cases they demand more favors. . . . If a man's going to have equal rights with me, that's fine, and everybody gets along with each other. There's no reason why all of this "I want more" and "I want your job!"

Might we merely conclude that these are the rationalizations of racists? When we examine the attitudes of these men on racial matters we shall see that their racial attitudes cannot be so simply explained. However, Paul's statement does point to a second limitation on the fervor of the men for government intervention in the marketplace. Their economic liberalism is mitigated by individualist values that permeate and flavor almost every corner of their mental orientation toward life. Government intervention is viewed as legitimate when an individual has proven himself as morally worthy of government aid. Proof of moral worth rests upon a demonstration that one has exhausted all other individual means of survival. For these men, the key phrase in the survey question about whether the government should provide jobs is the image that this should only be done for "everyone who wants to work." How does one prove that one "wants to work?" Terry, a white casefitter (adjusting drawers and doors to open properly) with a very unstable job history himself, spoke for most of the others, including the blacks, when he stated that anyone should be willing to take *any* job available before asking the government for direct financial support, and that for the most part, there have always been some kind of jobs available around town.

In the view of several of the whites, it is this moral standard that has been violated by blacks. Kevin, a 20 year old white sanding machine operator who obtained his present position because the company softball team needed a good player, clearly expressed the sentiment that blacks are generally morally undeserving of government help. He, as Terry, emphasized that the government should only help if the person "really can't find 'em a job." When he was later asked if whites try to get ahead more than blacks, he added that "a black person, if they had the chance, they would draw off the government. They wouldn't work at all if they didn't have no other way, you know."

The two policy areas where these men exhibit the greatest support for liberal social welfare measures are health care and aid to the elderly. Combining the two elicited even greater approval.

Every man save conservative Lewis supported the ideal of government funded health insurance, and 70 percent even argued for placing doctors on fixed government salaries. All but three of the men understood that the focus of Medicare is on the old, and all of them, including even Lewis, enthusiastically praise the program.

> *Lewis:* I think that's a pretty good thing, Medicare. I think that's all right. I feel like no matter how technologically advanced you get, or,

how socially far you advance, I feel like there is still a need to take care
of the old people. I feel like that should be a major concern.

The only complaints expressed were that the present programs are inade-
quate. Junior, an angry and hostile casefitter who has had many health problems
of his own, thinks Medicare doesn't pay enough to adequately cover costs. Jim,
one of the older workers in the sample who has periodically met failure in his
attempts to realize vocational alternatives to the factory, became passionate in
his indictment of the present system.

> *Jim:* I believe we've let down our elderly people. . . . Not only
> financially, but as far as feelin' they're really worth something. . . . And
> they still have that look of despair, like "who's gonna take care of me?
> Why am I here anyway?" and I believe that it's the fault of the govern-
> ment many times that these people don't have enough money to live
> on. . . . (Maybe) they've got a pill to take every day and it costs $25 a
> month to get them pills. That leaves 'em $15 and they've gotta eat!

This strong advocacy of improved health care programs for all and of greater
support for the elderly was explained in a way that is consistent with their
concept of individualism. A person who is ill is seen as unable to care for himself
by definition, and therefore temporarily exempt from the moral requirement of
self-support. Moreover, for most of these men, health care is a matter of right
rather than merit. Only one or two mentioned health care as something one
earns in return for hard work. Most regard the ill and the old as exempt from
life's competitive race.

We discussed the possibility of total equality in pay, of rewarding everyone
in the same amount regardless of what job they did. Though virtually all of the
men felt there should be relatively greater equality than now exists, nearly all
rejected the idea of total equality outright as a violation of meritocratic principles and of incentives for hard work. The four even willing to consider the
idea exhibited scant enthusiasm. John felt it would be "beautiful" to take some
things from the rich and give to the poor. But when we consider his sarcasm
directed at his peers in the working class who are "too sorry to even work in a
pie factory — just eatin' pies," we might doubt that he would find the equal
giving as "beautiful" as the taking.

Thus the pattern of attitudes we find is rather consistently in the liberal
direction with two important and related caveats. First, government programs
must not violate norms of individual self-sufficiency. As working men struggling
to achieve a few middle class comforts, their sympathy lay with the working
poor and programs focused upon them. Second, when economic liberalism is
defined in a racial context as opposed to a class context, it runs into double
trouble. Liberal affirmative action programs not only resurrect half buried
prejudices, but also violate meritocratic norms. The end result of what these
men would view as ethnic entitlement programs is reinforced negative stereotypes

and hostility directed toward the favored groups. These caveats may explain some of the conservative chords heard by Bartley and Graham in an otherwise liberal biracial harmony.

Individualism

We have already observed the preeminent role played by individualist values in attitudes on economic welfare issues. In the sense of honoring and pursuing self-reliance, the men fully embrace this traditional southern value. The behavioral component of this attitude is consistent with the cognitive component. Each struggles to persist in the hope that his family will reach the illusive goal of middle class material affluence, and each gains a real measure of pride and self-respect in frequently failing ventures. Being unable to afford that which they create while on the job, they build their own furniture while off the job. They also construct additions onto their existing small houses, when they can afford to vacate mobile homes. They are their own mechanics, and most can redeem a dented fender. Our conversations about their creative ventures were among the most animated. But when they attempt to transform this do-it-yourself handiwork into profit-making enterprises, the inevitable result seems to be debts and lost seniority at the job to which they return. However, I would guess that even if they knew they would fail again, Brent would have another go at photography, Melvin at auto bodywork, Jim at drywall finishing, and Albert at carpentry.

This strong need for self-reliance that was exhibited by 13 of these men was inherited from their parents. It seems so strongly held and openly embraced that the next generation will find it bequeathed to them. Even though many harbored great resentments toward parents, they almost universally admired their struggles for survival. Jim, who rarely speaks to his father, fondly recalled once when his dad was out of work and the family out of money. "A guy came up and asked him if he could lay brick and he had never laid a brick in his life and he said 'yes.' And the building's still there!"

In addition to self-reliance, there are other attitudes closely related to the general idea of individualism. One is volunteerism. Those who adhere to this value strongly prefer individual voluntary actions over compulsory group actions in solving problems. The exercise of compulsion restrains the expression of individual spontaneous impulse. For obvious reasons, the degree to which volunteerism is embraced limits the practical application of economic welfare programs, regardless of how much they are desired in the abstract, because all such programs inevitably involve some form of official compulsion.

Several topics in the conversations were designed to elicit beliefs about volunteerism. We discussed the use of force by government, the best ways to solve whatever problems they saw as pressing, and the kinds of activities in which ideal good citizens would participate. Based on these portions of our conversations, about a third of the small group were judged to be at each extreme.

Six of the men advocated the desirability of voluntary action in dealing with almost all social and economic problems. Eddie, for example, thinks voluntary conservation could solve the energy crisis if only the government would really ask us to make the effort. Junior also advocated volunteerism across almost all issues, including the draft and taxes. Roy, who spends his days spray finishing furniture, portrayed the ideal good citizen as a community-oriented, frequent volunteer, like a member of the jaycees. Lewis, the black conservative, was consistent with his overall antigovernment philosophy in arguing that voluntary citizen action should be used against pornography.

> *Lewis:* I don't think that the government should have to crack down on it. I think that the people . . . should have enough morality about them then to not let that stuff be circulated. I think that's something that should be taken care of on an individual basis. . . . I think Mr. Smith and his neighbors ought to go up there and say, "Hey, look. I don't want my kids seein' this stuff in the stores. How about if you stop printing this stuff?" Then (if that doesn't work), I think things, well, wherever he buys his gas at, they shouldn't sell him gas. : . . I'm not going to sell him any either, cause I got a fourteen year old daughter. When he goes to the grocery store, they tell him, "Well, your money isn't any good here," you know.

The four men at the other extreme might certainly be credited for being a bit more realistic in their plans of action, even if one does not approve of their goals. Mark, a 19 year old upholstery trainee, assumed an extreme position on many issues. He strongly supported unions and recognized the necessity of compulsion for union success, a rare insight among these men who were generally sympathetic to but naive about unions.[16] He also strongly supported school integration and again recognized that compulsion was necessary to achieve integration — even to the point of school busing. This economic and racial liberal is a moral conservative, but his means are consistent. When it comes to pornography and alcohol, he wants the government "to put military rules over things like that." The other three, if not as intense as Mark, were just about as consistent. Jim, Paul, and Rick all explained the necessity for government coercion in terms of some concept of public interest. Jim spoke of the good for the greater number, Paul of the good of the country, and Rick agreed, adding that sometimes coercion may even be legitimately exercised against the majority.

> *Rick:* (Force) all depends on whether it is for the good of the country — for the good of democracy. . . . Well, see, our Constitution — I *believe* in our Constitution. I really think we got one of the best. . . . Even though when they do force people to do things they're not ordinarily forced into doing, especially if it's for the benefit of the economy of the country — our democracy as a whole — I think it's all right. . . . That's what we elect our lawmakers for. . . . (Integration)

was forced because they figured that by integration it would upgrade both the black man and the white man. And which it does. . . . When you upgrade both people, then all their aims, anything they're after, they're going to be competitive. They're going to have more incentitive (sic).

Those five who took the vast middle ground seemed to oppose the principle of forced compliance, but found various reasons of self-interest and practical necessity to approve specific applications of force for such purposes as the draft, paying for needed government services through the income tax, and in a couple of cases even to insure racial equality.

A second attitude that is closely related to the general concept of individualism is particularism, itself a multifaceted concept. As noted at the outset, John Shelton Reed's sifting of public opinion data revealed an enduring allegiance and devotion in southerners to family, community, and region.[17] W. J. Cash's pre-World War II exploration of the southern mind discovered a failure to generalize from particular individual circumstances to broad relationships. This failure of analysis was further tainted by a narrow sense of social responsibility beyond self.[18] Therefore, in evaluating evidence of particularism, we shall be seeking several qualities: regional, community, and family orientations, an ability to reason in complex general terms, and expressions of concern beyond individual daily experiences.

Less than a third of our small sample are particularistic in orientation on all counts. The four white men who are have never been able to break away from family and community attachments, despite the experience of travel in the military. Two of these three failed to complete their terms of military service. Junior was discharged under less than honorable conditions, after being caught home with his family AWOL. Roy found himself unable to support his large family on military pay and received a hardship discharge. All of these men were so wrapped up in their own personal problems that conversations inevitably drifted back to their own peculiar worries and fears.

> *Question:* What are the major problems facing North Carolina?
> *Junior:* Well, our economy. . . . We're really in worse shape cause Carter said if anybody got the rebate, it'd be this state first due to the lot of textile plants close down and furniture plants down to two or three days a week. . . . But a lot of people get the rebate back and they turn right around and they go in debt over their head and they know it. And they just don't seem to care. They figure, well, they keep it six or seven weeks and let it go back. Which to me, I made the same mistake. I know better now. I was married to the other wife and I worked two jobs for two years — liked to kill me, but I wanted the money. I tried to have more than I could afford. I just got in over my head. I ended up losing it all. And I'm still regretting it to this day cause I've

still got bad credit and it'd take quite a bit of money to get me out of. I've tried to straighten some of it out. Then me married again and everything to pay and I just don't have it to straighten out. Course I know it's still my fault. . . .

Junior's comments illustrate another similarity among these four particularistic men. They all tend to explain complex social problems in terms of simple singular causes. For Junior it is human laziness. For Melvin, the youngest member of the group, most problems are caused by people being "smart," meaning "wise guys" looking to verbally abuse others. Roy and Terry simply don't engage in social analysis beyond discussions of material wants. Terry would never discuss problems facing the country because "I'm happy-go-lucky and things like that really don't bother me personally."

On the other hand, about two-thirds of the sample (nine of the workers) displayed few if any of the traits of particularism. They saw the relationship between their own personal concerns and general national problems and analyzed those relationships in fairly logical ways. Brent, a black furniture packer, saw his own feelings toward the town where he lives as an example of the general tendency of most people to favor ones own community. He and others, such as Kevin and Paul, saw the relationship between their own economic standing and the class interests of the two major political parties. Even though they were sometimes insecure in their discussions, they displayed a range of concerns from the relationship between education and alternative routes to success, to the multiple factors that affect the economy that in turn affect their own job security. They are cosmopolitan in their orientations even though some of them have never ventured far from home. Kevin doesn't know whether North Carolina is the best state in which to live "because I haven't been around that much." More typically, they have experienced life elsewhere and are quite realistic about the drawbacks of their own community and region, and offer few accompanying defensive rationalizations.

The one area where most of the men displayed a particularistic orientation was in their devotion and allegiance to their families. All of the men, save Rick and Brent who are lonely bachelors, center all social activities around family and for the most part seem to experience emotionally rewarding returns. Though the norms espoused by parents are often accepted, allegiance to value systems is much less universal in this small group than emotional bonds and physical responsibilities. Roy, one of the very poorest in this generally unaffluent group, explained that happiness for him is found in his wife and family of eight children. "Well, a lot of people, money makes them happy. But it wouldn't really make me happy — just having a family though, and someone that cares about you, you know." Judging from the rest of my conversation with Roy, this sentiment, though it certainly must be taken with a grain of salt, runs deeper than a mere rationalization.

Religious Fundamentalism and Moral Conservatism

The persistence that Reed found in the peculiar religious beliefs of southern-ers were less than obvious in this small group. In terms of strong religious convictions about dress, gambling, card playing, literal interpretation of the Bible, and formal membership in religious sects, only three of the men in the small group exhibited any fundamentalist tendencies. Only Mark could be considered extreme both in terms of formal ties and convictions. Jim and Junior regularly attend fundamentalist churches but reject many of the stereotypical views. None of the other men attend any church regularly.

Though there is little direct evidence of formal fundamentalist ties, moral convictions on a wide variety of social issues reflect a fundamentalist heritage. The moral prohibitions are strongest in the area of pornography. Eight volun-teered grave concerns about societal deterioration in sexual morality. Solutions ranged from Lewis's individual volunteeristic approach to Mark's call for official government repression. One of the weaknesses in survey data is gauging intensity. Little doubt remained after listening to Jim and a few of his peers concerning their intensity.

> *Jim:* I think there could be censorship. . . . I drove up in front of the convenience store on Central Street one night and they had the *Playboy* centerfold stretched out on the window! Here's my wife in the car, and this girl ain't got on a stitch — layin' there with her legs pulled apart, you know. . . . I mean, there's kids walking around and every-thing else. . . . they stretched out on the counter, where you pay for the chewing gum. . . . I believe we could do it the same way we do liquor referendums. If concerned citizens get together and say, "Man, we're gettin' tired of this stuff". . . . How can you expect your children to have clean minds when you put nothin' but filth in front of 'em? Maybe you don't, but you can't go with your kid every day and hold his hand and say, "Don't look at that, son."

Other areas command less than majority moral concern among this small group. About a third expressed apprehensions about increased drug usage. Three voiced disapproval of alcohol consumption, though only Mark would reimpose prohibition. Two of the same three and another were outraged at restrictions on religious training in schools. Lewis, the black conservative, was especially enraged at communist teachers undermining God and country.

> *Lewis:* That brings to mind the time this teacher, a communist teacher — you know, it used to be a time when you had to salute the flag in school, hold your hand to your heart — this teacher didn't make her class do that. In fact, she tole all her students to put their head down on the desk and close their eyes and say, "God, grant us some candy." See, little kids, right? She's a communist, takin' advantage of

'em. Say, "Now open your eyes," and there wasn't anything there. And she told 'em to do it three times and there wasn't anything there. And then the fourth time she says, "Oh, comrade," or something, "send us some candy." And when they had their eyes closed, she went around to all the desks and laid candy on their desks. So she says, "See, your God didn't do anything for you, we did." And cause, that's because she's allowed to operate, you know. Those were young kids who were at an impressionable age, and sometimes you can even find twenty or thirty year old people that are still impressionable, you know. They didn't have their own views, they haven't made up their minds about things yet. And if they let a communist run around loose . . . he goes with what they tell him.

Lewis also harbored intense hatreds for homosexuals and those who advocate women's liberation. He defined liberals and conservatives by views on homosexuality. Needless to say, he saw himself as no liberal.

Beyond this brief listing, there was little evidence of social conservatism. In fact, six were openly libertarian on matters of alcohol and sex. Four were even able to evoke a bit of passion in their defense of libertarianism, but none were a serious match for the likes of Lewis, Jim, or Mark. Most of these workers simply had no strong feelings one way or the other on alcohol, prayer in schools, homosexuality, and women's lib.

Even though half of these men remember parents who were active and faithful in fundamentalist churches, the transmission of habits of membership and conviction proved to be far from perfect. The generational transfer seems most efficient in attitudes on sexual matters and least effective in formal membership ties.

The intensity with which these values are held becomes an important consideration in predicting political behavior. Were these men to participate in politics (only five voted in 1976), those who hold the conservative positions on these social issues seem more likely to apply a moral measuring stick than those who hold the more libertarian views. Jim and Kevin, both of whom voted for Carter, partially based their judgment on moral evaluations. The other three Carter voters who were more libertarian explained their vote almost entirely on grounds of economic self-interest. Thus, even though moral conservatism may be declining, it could yet have significant political impact. One could argue that the political appeals and successes of moral conservatives such as Jesse Helms and Ronald Reagan among these men is circumstantial evidence consistent with this conclusion.[19]

Orientation Toward Violence

Were we simply to examine the orientations of these 15 workers to violence along the same dimensions used in public opinion studies and by Reed in his portrait of enduring southern traits, our conclusion would be simple and straight-forward.[20] Virtually all of these men have experienced corporal punishment, believe in its application at home and school, oppose gun control in almost any form, and support capital punishment. In fact, Terry, one of the few who opposed capital punishment, did so on the grounds that it was too easy a way out for the criminal. These opinions, though they may be indicators of more ego centered attitudes, are much more superficial than the violence that Cash found so deeply ingrained in the southern mind. Cash found southern violence to be an expression of romantic hedonism that was entangled in concepts of easily wounded pride and honor — what Cash called "techiness" — was often casual in nature, contained a touch of cruelty and gave notable satisfaction to participants and onlookers.[21]

In order to ferret out these traits, which are housed in the back rooms behind the front porch opinions of survey research, I talked with these men at some length about their tempers, fighting, and other interpersonal conflicts they had experienced. Almost half the sample reported having serious problems in controlling their tempers. Many associated their own tempers with the use of alcohol, but underlying even this simple explanation was a theory of human nature that is grim at best. Even most of those who have no personal temper problems see man as greedy and selfish and unable to control his base instincts without the imposition of some strong external authority. For them, total freedom would lead to indiscriminate rape and looting. This view of human nature is one more piece of evidence that their fundamentalist heritage of original sin has not been totally lost over the generations. Reported incidents of their own techiness ranged from Paul, who yells and throws things, to hostile Junior, who told of angry encounters with the police, nurses at the hospital, and his family at home.

> *Junior:* I got a little irritable at my wife over not giving the baby's medicine to her on time. I guess since this is the first child I have ever really had, I am just too watchful and wanting her to get well so bad and she's been sick so long, I just lost my temper. I knocked holes in the bedroom wall and door. I grabbed her by the arm and more or less squeezed her arm pretty hard and kind of forced her into the living room. I said, "you better give her the medicine." I was looking at her probably like I could kill her.

A third of the sample spoke of fighting as a matter of honor. Junior holds grudges for decades, only recently "beating the boy's ass" who had whipped him in grammar school. "I knowed one of these days I'd get even and when the time come I did." John, one of the older black men in the group, bears across his face the jagged scar of a knife fight. He has experienced several short stays in jail for fighting as a matter of honor. He even justifies the murder of police on grounds of personal honor.

John: I believe (police) are not properly trained. You see when you are going to arrest another grown-up, unless he's giving you a hassle — if he's giving you a hassle you got a job to do and you supposed to do it to the best of your ability — but just letting that uniform be the boss — I mean you're supposed to respect the uniform, I know that's true — but just because you've got it on, (that) don't say you got to misuse another grown-up. He got pride too. That's the reason why you got to kill someone, because he don't feel like he was treated right. It's just the way of approaching a person. You can approach someone and get them peaceable. You can't approach one and get him wrong, and he will *have* to do somethin' to you.

Several of these men are ready for fights in almost any social situation. Terry remembered an incident that had happened years earlier at a dance in which his claim that he was not seeking trouble failed to square with the evidence.

Terry: There was this dude that was dancing and this other dude came over and started arguing with him. Another dude came over and broke a beer bottle and said he was going to cut my throat. Well, I took that as pretty serious, so I came out from under my shirt with a logging chain and swung at him. I didn't know if I would hit him or not, but I wrapped it around his throat. Well, he hit the floor, bleeding and all and I thought I had killed him. Well, I took off out of there and I never did hear anymore so I guess that I didn't kill him.

Terry may well pass his logging chain on to his children, since he feels the most important thing he should teach them is to learn to protect themselves and "not to let other people run over them."

Not only was violence frequent, it was enjoyable and casual. Melvin enjoys playing football on weekends because it allows him to express his aggressive instincts. "I like football because it's rough. I don't like other games like baseball. I like games where you grab somebody and throw them down." Albert, a 26 year old materials handler with a four year old daughter, matter-of-factly related what seemed to him to be an everyday event in which he shot some neighborhood dogs.

Albert: Well, I had a little problem. I had dogs in the neighborhood, barking dogs. What I did was call the dogcatcher, and they'd always tell me was (to) "go talk to your neighbors, whoever own the dog, tell him about the dog, tell him what he doin'," this and that. "And if he didn't do nothin', give us another call." So I did that a couple of times and nothin' happened. So what I did, when the dogs started again, I just got my rifle down from the wall and killed a few around the neighborhood. It's quieter now.

About a third of our small group seem to generalize the acceptability of violence in their own personal lives to the political level, where violent tactics are seen as another legitimate and effective means of problem solving. Several thought the police should use more forceful tactics in dealing with lawbreakers. Eddie, though he disapproved of the Ku Klux Klan's positions on race, felt the Klan was performing a useful social function when they "used to, you know, kinda look after different things . . . maybe a man running around on his wife, maybe a man not treating his family right, something like that where maybe they could step in and the way they were doing it was like they wanted to throw a scare into it." Eddie's only objection to these tactics was the wearing of hoods. "If I was going to talk to a man, I'd rather talk to him face to face." Consistent with the lynching tradition of his forefathers, Jim called for vigilante action in dealing with capital offenders who hide behind the Constitution to avoid their just deserts. On this matter he is even willing to go against his church, a very strong statement from a young man who seems deeply committed to religion.

> *Jim:* I believe in capital punishment. That may be wrong. I don't know where the Baptists stand on this, but I don't really care cause even if they were against it I would still be for it. I feel that there could be more retribution made for victims. Say this man's been crippled for life and someone ought to pay. . . . And what does the criminal get? Only a few years at most! . . . Eventually the normal American citizen is going to get fed up and there is going to be a revolution — maybe even a violent revolution — like vigilantes maybe. People will get hurt. It's up to the people to say what's wrong and then do something about it. Can't blame it on the law enforcement officers because they're doing the best they can. Police hands are tied to the Constitution laws often.

Jim had earlier spoken of another revolution in which working people would rise up and demand better wages and working conditions. Brent presented an argument for political violence aimed at economic betterment on grounds of simple efficacy.

> *Brent:* Now all bad things from the start with dudn't mean that they won't have a good ending. As a matter of fact . . . like if I were to go downtown (to city hall) and try to get something done, uh, something changed, and go in with a nice suit and tie on, and talk real nice to the people, they would probably give me some nice sugar coated words and tell me to "go to hell," more or less. But if I were to go downtown with a couple of shades on and a nice beard and everything, a couple of brickbats in my hand and tore up a couple of windows and turned over some desks, they would get on the phone and start callin'.

The techniness that Cash associated with the southern mind and the inclination toward violence that Reed inferred from his analysis of survey data were found to exist in significant degrees within the value structures of about half of our small sample. The other half may have inherited regional views on child rearing practices, gun control, and capital punishment. This is of political significance in and of itself. But beyond that they seem to be free of traditional southern techniness.

Racial Prejudice

Because the purpose of this exploration of the minds of young southerners is to suggest future political implications, we must be very careful to delineate the relationship between whatever prejudice is found and its political consequences. At the outset, we noted Bartley and Graham's thesis of continuing racial antagonisms that make any black/white political alliance both impractical and impossible for the forseeable future. The literature on racial prejudice suggests that some types of prejudice may be greater barriers than others. "Folkways prejudice," which is little more than an etiquette system of learned stereotypes, speech patterns, and forms of address, might possibly be treated as secondary to economic self-interests, if those interests were made clear. However, "functional prejudice" that is centrally held within the value structure and closely associated with ego and self-identity, is a much more formidable obstacle to the would-be leaders of any biracial political coalition.[22]

Looking first at the more superficial signs of prejudice, the holding of negative racial stereotypes, we find that racial prejudice persists in the minds of most of these southern white workers. Roy came closest to total freedom from prejudice. His only prejudiced sentiments were opposition to interracial marriage for himself personally and an expressed concern over the possibility of his own children being in a racial minority in school. Despite this, he vowed that his children should attend the school nearest to his home, which has a high proportion of blacks in attendance, rather than be bused to a school across town in an all white neighborhood. He could also conceive of love conquering his apprehensions about interracial marriage. The rest of the white men expressed folkways prejudice in a number of ways. For the most part, they centered around the stereotype of the lazy shiftless black. We uncovered some of these feelings in our earlier discussion of the perceived failure of blacks to prove themselves morally worthy of government aid. A few expressed ambivalence over the consequences of school integration and a few feared blacks taking over white churches and white neighborhoods.

A content analysis of all statements pertaining to racial relations was accomplished for each of the 15 men. There were significant differences between the races. Half of the whites fell below the 50 percent mark in their percentage of statements supporting an integrated society, while only one black had less than 83 percent of his references advocating integration.

On the other hand, most of the segregationist expressions were without passion and conviction. Many were made with a great deal of compunction. Jim, for example, painfully wrestled with the conflict between his expressed belief in racial equality and his disapproval of black student conduct in public schools until he was able to resolve it in terms of a need for greater discipline. He sounded not unlike many nonsouthern white middle class suburbanites. Paul was "sorry to say" that he disapproved of interracial marriage. Many of these young men have numerous daily contacts with blacks and find most to be quite satisfactory. Incidents of social interaction and interracial friendship were frequent. Many came close to passion in defending norms of integration in the more public realms of life, such as school and work. They show evidence of moving beyond what Bartley and Graham considered minimal acceptance of integration.[23] When asked to render his view of the most ideal race relations if he had the power to mold them in any way he pleased, Jim spoke with both thought and conviction.

> *Jim:* As far as churches and stuff like that, I cannot understand why churches do not allow blacks to come in and worship. And I believe if we would have grown in a culture where blacks and whites worshipped together, I don't believe you could, in your conscience, I don't believe you could worship with a man on Sunday and hate 'em on Monday. Interracial churches would be good. . . . I guess another thing would be more black people owning businesses, and operatin' them, having a business mind about 'em, and knowin' how to operate a business. I think that's where black people have been held back a lot. . . . I think if you had a community, you should have blacks and whites ownin' stores.

Gordon Allport suggests a tripartite test for functional prejudice: avoidance of members of the outgroup, assuming a threat orientation, and the spontaneous injection of racial slurs into irrelevant contexts.[24] A third of the white men qualified as functional racists on at least one of these three tests. Melvin constantly volunteered irrelevant comments about his dislike for "niggers"; Dave makes it a point to avoid blacks as much as possible except when he must work with them; and Junior feels threatened both in his neighborhood and in sexual matters with regard to his children. These three were also at the bottom of the list in their support for an integrated society.

The words of these men construct a complex prejudicial portrait that indicates stability, change, hope, and warnings. These young white men, if they may be taken as omens of the future, trade in the seemingly timeless terminology of southern bigotry. Yet they have gone beyond mere acceptance of the fait accompli of integration and defend its more public applications in terms of basic human right. Most are not chained to racial fears and hatreds that threaten their center of being. Many are aware that the social class to which they belong is composed of both races and want more from life than existing a half step above working class blacks in the social scheme of things. But they also express a deep concern that the national government has unfairly altered the rules of competition in life to give undeserved advantages to blacks in jobs and promotional opportunities.

Recent national election returns offer only faint hope that shared economic class interests will define the electoral choices and bring southern whites and blacks together. The circumstantial evidence seems to be supportive of Bartley and Graham's prediction that the choices will be defined more in terms of social issues and racial resentments about the proper role of government than on economic class advancement. Politicians of the Democratic Party would do well to heed the advice of James Clotfelter and William Hamilton, who suggest that a biracial populist political coalition is yet a practical political possibility if leaders would "emphasize the general benefit of social programs, trying to avoid code words that say, 'blacks only,' . . . identify new targets for attack, more rationally chosen, to replace blacks . . . talk fair government employment practices . . . jobs and prices and taxes, not race . . . see that you get a fair share of government benefits — hard work *does* pay off, there is justice for whites as well as blacks."[25] Such a thematic platform could command a strong majority among these young working men of the South.

CONCLUSION

The orientations of these 15 young working class southerners toward the traditional southern values that have been discussed in this chapter are summarized in tabular form.

Each worker is identified by name and race and is scored as high, medium, or low for each attitude we have discussed. A "southernness index" was computed for each individual and the men were ordered by index score from the most southern, Junior, with a perfect score of 1.0, to Paul, who achieved a score of only 0.21. (See the table for an explanation of how these indexes were computed.) It is noteworthy that Paul fell to last place, since he is the only member of the group with parents born outside the South — some testimony of continued parental influence. As more families migrate to the sunbelt, there will be more and more Pauls, who consider themselves southerners even though they are less southern in attitudes. The other immediate noteworthy feature in this summary table is that blacks and whites are fairly evenly dispersed in the table — discounting racial attitudes, all must be considered southern in mind as well as in origin.

An examination of the summary indexes for the group on each attitude reveals a pattern of stability as well as possible change from past sketches of the southern mind. Of course, we must tread most cautiously here as our own data are not comparative with respect to time or place.

If the white working classes of the South are becoming less liberal on economic matters, it is a movement that is only partial and highly issue selective, if these men may be taken as at all typical. The economic liberalism index for the whites in the group is .75, virtually the same as that of the blacks. Their scores on standardized economic liberalism scales were also similar. All of these

TABLE 2.1
SOUTHERN VALUE ORIENTATIONS

| Respondent | (race) | Individualism | | | | Social Conservatism | Violent Orientation | Racial Prejudice | Individual Index* |
		Economic Liberalism	Self-reliance	Volunteerism	Particularism				
Junior	(W)	H	H	H	H	H	H	H	1.00
Melvin	(W)	M	H	H	H	M	M	H	.79
Terry	(W)	H	H	M	H	M	H	L	.71
John	(B)	H	H	M	M	L	H	**	.67
Jim	(W)	H	H	L	L	H	H	M	.64
Eddie	(W)	M	H	H	L	M	H	M	.64
Albert	(B)	H	H	H	L	L	M	**	.58
Lewis	(B)	L	H	H	L	H	M	**	.58
Roy	(W)	H	M	H	H	M	L	L	.57
Dave	(W)	M	H	M	M	L	M	H	.57
Kevin	(W)	M	H	M	L	M	M	M	.50
Brent	(B)	H	H	M	L	L	L	**	.42
Mark	(W)	H	M	L	L	H	L	L	.36
Rick	(B)	H	M	L	L	L	M	**	.33
Paul	(W)	M	H	L	L	L	L	L	.21
Group Index*		.77	.90	.57	.33	.43	.53	.45	

* *Note:* each index was computed as follows. H's (highs) were coded as 1; M's (mediums) as .5; and L's (lows) as 0. The sum of codes for each respondent and each category was then divided by the total number of possible entries for that respondent or category. For example, for Melvin this index was (.5 + 1 + 1 + 1 + .5 + .5 + 1) / 7 = .79.

**Insufficient response.

Source: Compiled by the author.

44

young men are moderately redistributionist in policy orientation. What seems to have changed is not their own values, but rather the injection of new kinds of issues (i.e., the issues surrounding affirmative action programs) in the liberal agenda that makes them *appear* to have shifted in the conservative direction.

Areas of apparent stability in attitude include the maintenance of a strong obligation for self-reliance and, to a lesser extent, a volunteeristic approach to life and a tendency to express oneself and solve problems through violence. In the latter two areas, a determination of the continued peculiarity of the South must await a more comparative analysis because, while these attitudes are present in significant strengths and numbers, they are far from universal.

Some changes may well be taking place in the remaining three areas. Though we uncovered significant racial antipathy, we also found several hopeful signs for future race relations. Many of these men are beginning to explain social problems in nonracial terminology that does not simply employ socially acceptable code words.

Second, though many of these men are social conservatives, there was also an element of libertarianism in their beliefs. The black subsample was particularly libertarian. Seven of the ten whites were at least moderately liberal on some moral issues. But moral issues continue to have political potency. Two of the three whites who did go to the polls in 1976 partially explained their votes for Carter in terms of conservative moral rationales. In his analysis of southern political tendencies, William C. Havard argued that resistance to political organization is partly explained by the fact that most working class southerners are merely one generation removed from the independence of the farm.[26] The fact that half of these men are merely one generation removed from actively fundamentalist homes means that some conservative moral values are likely to remain. For their own children we may someday find a quite different picture. This generation has already done some backsliding from the values and practices of their parents.

Finally, a particularistic localistic orientation to life is discernible, but barely. To be sure, their social lives and concerns are centered about family, but their concerns and consciousness extend beyond family, community, and region. Most think in national terms and are capable of fairly complex analysis, once we are able to break through fears of verbal and intellectual inadequacy. They are certainly not confident, self-assured, participant-oriented citizens, but they are thoughtful citizens. Contrary to Reed's analysis, the mass media and formal education may be beginning to have some notable impact on these young southerners.[27] The war, not the one between the states but one between North and South on the other side of the globe, is also responsible for this change, for it was the young working class men of the South, black and white alike, who did more than their region's proportional share of fighting, bleeding, and dying in Vietnam. They saw other parts of the country, other cultures, other regions of the world, and other ways of approaching life and problems. Though some, such as Roy and Junior, retreated home largely unchanged, most who returned will never be the same. Nor will their children. They returned from a nation's first defeat in war to a region that had known defeat before. This second defeat may also have vanquished some regions in the southern mind to which W. J. Cash, were he here, would gladly bid adieu.

NOTES

1. W. J. Cash, *The Mind of the South* (New York: Vintage, 1941), pp. 439-40.

2. John Shelton Reed, *The Enduring South* (Chapel Hill: University of North Carolina Press, 1972), pp. 33, 43.

3. Ibid., p. 85.

4. Ibid., pp. 69, 79.

5. Ibid., p. 55.

6. William C. Havard, "The South: A Shifting Perspective," in *The Changing Politics of the South*, ed. William C. Havard (Baton Rouge: Louisiana State University Press, 1972). pp. 702-3.

7. Ibid., p. 698.

8. Numan V. Bartley and Hugh D. Graham, *Southern Politics and the Second Reconstruction* (Baltimore: Johns Hopkins University Press, 1975), pp. 186, 189.

9. Ibid., p. 195.

10. Bureau of Labor Statistics, *Employment and Earnings, States and Areas, 1939-1978* (Washington: U.S. Government Printing Office, 1980).

11. See, for example, John Dollard, *Caste and Class in a Southern Town* (Garden City, N.Y.: Doubleday Anchor Books, 1937); and Robert Coles, *Migrants, Sharecroppers, and Mountaineers* (Boston: Little, Brown, and Company, 1967).

12. James Clotfelter and William R. Hamilton, "Beyond Race Politics: Electing Southern Populists in the 1970's," In *You Can't Eat Magnolias* eds. H. Brandt Ayres and Thomas Naylor (New York: McGraw-Hill, 1972), p. 152.

13. V. O. Key, Jr., *Public Opinion and American Democracy* (New York: Alfred A. Knopf, 1961), pp. 103-5.

14. See Chandler Davidson, *Biracial Politics* (Baton Rouge: Louisiana State University Press, 1972), p. 218; and Donald R. Matthews and James W. Prothro, *Negroes and the New Southern Politics* (New York: Harcourt, Brace, and World, 1966), pp. 397-8.

15. See Earl Hawkey, "Southern Conservatism 1956-1976" in this volume, pp. 48-72.

16. For detailed examination of these workers' views on unions, see Robert Botsch, "You Can't Have It Both Ways – The Difficulties of Unionization in the South," *Perspectives on the American South, An Interdisciplinary Annual, Volume One*, eds. Merle Black and John Shelton Reed (New York: Gordon and Breach, 1981), pp. 173-86.

17. Reed, *The Enduring South*, p. 35.

18. Cash, *The Mind of the South*, pp. 46-7, 76-7.

19. An analysis of precinct data in the town in which this study was done shows that in a predominantly white working class precinct, Reagan ran well ahead of Ford in 1976 and even commanded a slim majority. Senator Helms won reelection in 1978 against economic populist John Ingram. Helms was 5 percent more competitive in the same precinct that had given Ingram an overwhelming majority in 1976, when he ran against an economic conservative for State Insurance Commissioner in a race that raised few moral issues.

20. Reed, *The Enduring South*, pp. 45-55.

21. On this point, Cash notes that: "One of the notable results of the spread of the idea of honor, indeed, was an increase in the tendency to violence throughout the social

scale. Everyone high and low was rendered more techy. And with the dual almost rigidly bound to that techniness at the top, everybody's course was fatally mapped out. . . . (violence) was the only quite correct, the only really decent, relief for wounded honor — the only one that did not imply some subtle derogation, some dulling and retracting of the fine edge of pride, some indefinable but intolerable loss of caste and manly face." (Cash, *The Mind of the South*, pp. 52, 75-6, 125).

22. See Richard F. Hamilton, *Class and Politics in the United States* (New York: John Wiley and Sons, 1972), pp. 408-9; James W. Loewen, *The Mississippi Chinese* (Cambridge, Mass.: Harvard University Press, 1971), p. 105; and Gordon Allport, *The Nature of Prejudice* (Garden City, N.Y.: Doubleday Anchor Books, 1954), pp. 11-12.

23. Bartley and Graham, *Southern Politics and the Second Reconstruction*, p. 189.

24. Allport, *The Nature of Prejudice*, pp. 15, 50, 373-4.

25. Clotfelter and Hamilton, "Beyond Race Politics," pp. 156-8.

26. Havard, *The Changing Politics of the South*, p. 727.

27. See Reed, *The Enduring South*, pp. 84-7.

3

SOUTHERN CONSERVATISM 1956-1976

Earl W. Hawkey

The South has for some time been almost universally considered a conservative region.[1] The basis of this appellation has centered on the question of race. For longer than other regions the South attempted to preserve a segregated institutional life when such formal structures had been abandoned elsewhere. The very fact that the South was primarily agricultural and rural while the North was more industrialized (modernized if you will) nurtured this image. Certainly the politicians it elected to Congress had a very distinct tradition of conservatism.[2] As part of the "Conservative Coalition" Southern congressmen and senators became infamous for delay and resistance to integration. Talk of Southern Bourbonism fairly reeked with the aroma of conservatism. Writing in 1968, Kevin Phillips saw an emerging Republican majority in the South as Southern conservatives (obviously a majority) realigned themselves with the conservative Republican party — their true home.[3] Bartley and Graham in their work on Southern politics during the Second Reconstruction seemingly agree with this assessment when they conclude, "The Republican sweep of the South in 1972 may well have reflected a quite traditional southern triumph, under a new partisan label, of her more dominant social conservatism over her game but historically outweighed populism."[4]

Yet, few authors have taken the time or the effort to more closely examine these assertions of conservatism, or to consider this aspect of Southern culture

*The data utilized in this paper were made available by the Inter-University Consortium for Political and Social Research (ICPSR). The data for the American National Election Studies were originally collected by the Center for Political Studies of the Institute for Social Research, the University of Michigan. Neither the original collectors of the data nor the Consortium bear any responsibility for the analyses or interpretations presented here.

over time. One of the few works to focus on Southern ideology and its time-bound quality is, *Transformations of the American Party System* by Ladd and Hadley.[5] In a chapter entitled, "First Rendings: The Case of the South" the authors state,

> The 1970's picture of the South as the most conservative region of the country leads frequently to the notion that it has always been "to the right." This tendency to impose the present upon the past is furthered by the recognition that majorities of southern whites historically have proved reactionary on civil rights.[6]

They go on to argue that the New Deal struck a responsive chord in the radical agrarian tradition of the South, and that the modern conservatism of the South can be seen as a reversal of past trends rather than a reassertion of old ones. The authors see the South's racial traditions as the exception to its generally liberal social philosophy rather than as a typical example of its conservatism.

Time, then, is an important consideration in regard to the ideological distinctiveness of the region — especially in the 1970s. A great deal of the interest focused on the South has tended to look at the development of Republican voting in that region.[7] The obvious tendency is to see this as a sign of, if not increased conservatism, at least the reassertion of a distinctive conservative tradition in the South. However, it could be argued from other facts that the South may be involved in a reduction rather than an extension of its conservative tradition. For one thing, the distinct racial institutions of the South (the basis for much of the speculation concerning Southern conservatism) have given way in much of the region. Indeed, it has recently come to light that Northern school districts are far less integrated than Southern ones.[8] True, the majority of this integration is the result of legal compunction. But whatever its source, it was designed to break down the barriers of racial traditionalism in society. In addition, as the South changes economically and demographically — becoming more prosperous and urban, and less poverty stricken or rural — the major pillars of Southern conservatism would seem likely to crumble and a firm foundation for interest group liberalism laid.[9]

Hence, we must look at three different questions. First, is the South uniquely and consistently more conservative than the North when the two regions are compared? Second, is this difference between the regions, if found, simply the result of demographic differences? That is, are the regional differences consistent for all socioeconomic groups and residential classifications? Third, has there been convergence between the two regions as the South continues to become more like the North economically and socially? Obviously, the answer to the second and third questions is contingent upon finding significant differences between the two regions at the aggregate level. Yet, even when we find no important differences it is still important that we control for socioeconomic status and residence. The simple aggregate comparison of regions is not fine enough a discriminator in exploring cultural phenomena. We wish to understand the dynamics of the situation not only between the regions, but also *within* them.

CONSERVATISM DEFINED

Before launching into such an investigation, we must consider the meaning of the term "conservatism". As McClosky has noted, "Because it is a key term in the language of political conflict, choked with emotive connotation, 'conservatism' has naturally evoked controversy over its meaning."[10] Mainly relying on the works of Edmund Burke, McClosky then goes on to list the major elements of the conservative outlook. First, the conservative mind tends to see man as selfish and ruled by individual desires rather than being innately altruistic. Second, society is seen as complex, organic, and built up over time in such a way that governmental intervention to change naturally occurring societal norms is to be avoided. Third, the need for public order must be accorded primacy over individual civil liberties and the rampant individualism which will naturally tend to push society toward anarchy.

In a more recent philosophical discussion of conservative ideology Noel O'Sullivan defines it succinctly as, "A philosophy of imperfection, committed to the idea of limits, and directed toward the defence of a limited style of politics."[11] Thus, O'Sullivan sees three main aspects of the conservative philosophy as primary. First, conservative thought is a philosophy of imperfection. That is, perfect government is impossible because its building block, man, is basically a flawed being. While various conservative thinkers may see different sources of this flawed character, all see man and his works as incapable of perfection. Second, O'Sullivan notes that conservative ideology is, "committed to the idea of limits." Because man is by nature an imperfect creature, there are very definite limits on his ability to affect society. It is impossible to set all social wrongs right, and man must come to accept imperfection both in society and in himself since his ability to change this situation is strictly limited. This idea of limits is carried into the realm of politics as well. That is, conservative thought is dedicated to a limited style of politics. Changes sought by political means must be piecemeal and incremental rather than comprehensive. Since massive change will never result in the perfect society anyway, the conservative ideologue advises restraint and care in political affairs.

Despite their somewhat divergent ways of wording matters, both McClosky and O'Sullivan move toward the same conservative ideal. Both analysts see the conservative mind as one which would have a rather dim view of human nature. Both see the conservative as being less than enthusiastic concerning governmental intervention to redress societal "shortcomings". Both formulations would see the need for order in society as primary over rampant individualism. This does not imply that conservatives hold individualism as an evil to be controlled at all costs. It is only that, like all things, individualism must be moderated somewhat if individuals are to exist peacefully in society. As part of this, both conceptions of the conservative would frown upon rapid change in the political realm.

PRACTICAL PROBLEMS

At the outset it should be said that the specific areas of ideology we will consider in this paper will be primarily the result of availability. For example, we will be unable to accurately gauge Southern attitudes toward rapid social change except indirectly. We will not extensively consider attitudes toward blacks or integration in this paper. What we hope to do is look at aspects of Southern conservatism other than racial attitudes. While it could be argued that racism is simply one manifestation of a conservative culture, I do not believe that this is logically or analytically true. While conservatism and racism may be closely linked and generally coexistent, there is no logical reason for their connection. In fact, one thing we wish to consider is whether Southerners tend to be conservative in areas other than race. As has been previously noted, Southern racial relations have been almost universally accepted as proof of Southern conservative culture. Is this a valid inference? In other words, is there sufficient connection between racial attitudes and general conservative attitudes that it can be said that Southern political culture is conservative in nature? While not the primary focus of this paper, our work here will shed some light on this question.

Before moving on to discuss specific areas of conservative thought, there is one objection we must deal with. This is the question of whether the mass public has an ideology or simply an unconnected aggregate of attitudes. Is our search for conservative ideology existing in mass publics a search for the proverbial will-o'-the wisp? Philip Converse in "The Nature of Belief Systems in Mass Publics" argues that an organized and bound ideological orientation is common only to the political elites.[12] Mass publics, he argues, tend not to have, ". . . wide ranging yet highly integrated belief systems."[13] Some recent research has tended to cast doubt on the Converse thesis.[14] As Nie and Anderson have noted, most of the studies discounting the existence of firm belief systems among mass publics are based on data derived from the 1950s. Yet, "American politics in the 60's and early 70's were not the same as those of the 1950's."[15] Nie and Anderson, among others, argue that integrated mass belief systems do exist and have been in far greater evidence since 1960 than previously. There is, according to the authors, evidence for a fairly strong intercorrelation of beliefs among political issues along a conservative-liberal array. This area of research, however, is still producing a significant amount of controversy with arguments both supporting Nie and Anderson, and contradictory findings supporting the Converse thesis.[16]

This paper will not focus specifically on this problem. Instead, we will focus on individual questions and look for evidence of strong and consistent differences between the levels of conservatism in the North compared to the South. The controversy is really somewhat beside the point for the purposes espoused by this presentation. What we are looking for are the North-South differences and the reduction or expansion of these differences over time. As such, we are looking at gross features of the mass public, both North and South, and will not deal with microlevel processes.

The data used in this paper consist of the election-year studies conducted every two years since 1956 by the Survey Research Center at the University of Michigan. The national sample was divided into two regional groups. The South consists of the 11 states of the Old Confederacy. The North consists of the rest of the country and includes not only the states of the Northeast and the Midwest, but also those of the West and Far West.

Within each region, respondents were further divided by socioeconomic status and residence. The socioeconomic status (SES) variable is a composite measure derived from a respondent's family income, education, and the head of the households occupational prestige. In each year respondents were classified into a high, medium, and low category for each of these three variables. High was approximately the top 30 percent of the national population, medium was the middle 40 percent of the population, and low was the bottom 30 percent of the population. High SES respondents were then defined as those who were in the "high" category on two or more of the criteria variables (income, education, and occupation). Low SES respondents were those in the "low" category on two or more of these variables. The middle SES category contained the rest of the respondents. The residence variable (metropolitan, suburban, or rural) was derived from the Inter-University Consortium for Political and Social Research (ICPSR) "belt code" variable from 1964-1976. Previous to that time a different coding scheme was used and the author attempted to approximate the "belt code."

In the course of looking at regional differences in conservatism we hope to look at two different kinds of questions. The first type of question will be general in nature and not tied to current political controversies. In this category will be an individual's general conservative loyalty. The second type of question will be more specifically tied to current political controversies. Among these will be three questions dealing with the role of the government in guaranteeing the well-being of its citizens, two questions dealing with governmental actions to guarantee law and order, and two questions on extraordinary actions for the extension of civil rights to groups in society. By looking at this wide variety of topics, we hope to identify certain general trends, and then see how these predispositions are translated into politically relevant attitudes.

A dilemma faced in the regional comparison we have proposed is how to deal with the black subsample. One way is to simply exclude blacks from consideration and compare Northern whites to Southern whites. Yet, a difficulty with this solution is that we are not then comparing the regions, but only a subgroup within the two regions. Hence, it does not fully describe the reality of the situation. While such a procedure could have been justified when an overwhelming percentage of Southern blacks were denied an active role in politics, this justification has come to be less and less defensible. For this reason blacks were not excluded from our tables and graphs. Instead, they were treated as part of the valid regional sample. Separate runs were performed comparing Northern whites to Southern whites. Where this control procedure results in a significantly different interpretation of facts, this will be noted.

GENERAL CONSERVATIVE LOYALTY

Do Southerners tend to see themselves as more conservative than Northerners? One self-assessment measure is the Survey Research Center's (SRC) ideological placement question in which respondents are asked to place themselves on a seven point Likert-type scale ranging from extremely conservative to extremely liberal. Unfortunately this question was only included on the interview forms since 1972. Hence, we shall use a derived measure which is available from 1964 onward. Respondents were asked to rate, on a standard "feeling thermometer" scale, how favorably they saw "liberals." Potential responses ranged from 0 (least favorable) to 97 (most favorable). For each respondent the feeling thermometer value for "liberals" was subtracted from the value for "conservatives" to form an ideological score ranging from −97 to +97. These scale values were then recoded into a standard tripartite classification of respondents into liberals (−97 to −11), moderates (−10 to +10), and conservatives (+11 to +97). The reason both questions were used was to identify and compensate for those who may dislike (or like) both ideological extremes. Such people more logically should be placed in the moderate category rather than at either extreme. As a test of the validity of the derived ideological measure we cross-correlated the results of the seven point Likert scale of ideology in 1972, 1974, and 1976 with our derived measure for those years. The two variables were highly correlated with Gamma values of +.78, +.75, and +.69 respectively (other measures of association are also fairly high). Hence, we move on to look at the regional differences over time.

Figure 3.1 shows the percentage of respondents, by region, who are classified as conservatives. Throughout the time period a slightly higher proportion of Southerners have been so classified. It is interesting to note that the widest differences between the two regions occurred during the presidential election years of 1964 and 1972. Both were unusual in that a leading presidential aspirant identified himself (or was identified) with an extreme ideological position. In 1964 Barry Goldwater was the self-proclaimed "conservative" candidate and carried several Southern states. In 1972 McGovern was identified by the Nixon administration as a dangerous radical and was soundly defeated

Figure 3.1
PERCENTAGE CLASSIFIED AS CONSERVATIVE
(By the Derived Ideological Scale)

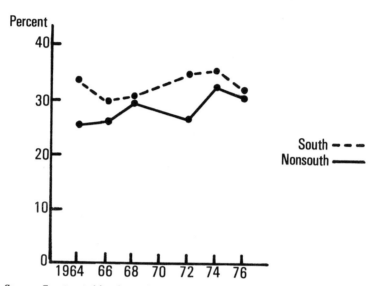

Source: Constructed by the author from ICPSR data.

in November both in the South and elsewhere. In more normal circumstances there appears to be relatively little difference between the North and the South in the percentage who identify themselves as sympathetic to the conservative cause. True, the South is consistently higher in conservatism, but the North appears to be catching up. A linear regression was performed on the datapoints for each region. The results of this procedure confirm an upward drift in conservatism for both regions. The non-Southern slope (0.41) was larger than that of the South (0.17), indicating that the North was slowly converging with the South. This is precisely the reverse of what was expected since it is the South which is converging with the North demographically and socially. The regions do appear to be becoming more alike, but this trend is the result of Northern change and transformation.

This unusual pattern indicates that the belief that a change in demographics will herald a change in regional attitudes may be misplaced.[17] The reason for this becomes clear if we subdivide our regional samples into discrete socioeconomic and residential groups. In terms of socioeconomic status the greatest difference between the regions occurs for those of high or medium SES. The original expectation was that the South might be different (i.e., more conservative) because of its unique demographics (the higher proportion of poor people). But the data in Table 3.1 show the reverse of this pattern. In 1976

TABLE 3.1
PERCENTAGE CLASSIFIED AS CONSERVATIVE
(Controlled for Socioeconomic Status and Race)

	Socioeconomic Status		
	High	*Medium*	*Low*
Total Sample:			
Nonsouth	35%	28%	29%
	(144)*	(193)	(63)
South	53%	27%	22%
	(45)	(55)	(26)
Whites:			
Nonsouth	36%	29%	32%
	(142)	(188)	(58)
South	55%	31%	30%
	(45)	(53)	(20)

*( ) – Number of respondents.

Source: Compiled by the author from ICPSR data.

(and other years as well) Southerners of lower SES were *less* conservative than Northerners of similar circumstance. This pattern remains even if we control for race by looking only at whites.

Similarly, while we might have hypothesized that the South would be more conservative because of its relatively large percentage of rural dwellers, this is not the case. In 1964 there was very little difference between Northern and Southern ruralities in terms of the percentage who identified with the conservative cause. The largest differences between North and South occurred for those of metropolitan and suburban residence. From 1964 through 1976 rural residents continued to differ by only a few percentage points in ideological orientation (except in 1972 when a rather large gap existed). Hence, it is the convergence between Northerners and Southerners of metropolitan and suburban residence which accounted for the convergence observed between the regions in Figure 3.1. In fact, by 1976 Northerners of metropolitan residence tended to be more conservative than Southerners who lived in metropolitan areas. There was no significant difference between Northerners and Southerners of suburban residence. In 1976 only Southerners of rural residence were more conservative than the Northern group in that category. Still, the difference was relatively small (33 percent North, 37 percent South). Additional analysis indicates that one of the reasons for the continued difference between ruralities is the rather large outmigration of Southern blacks from rural areas. Since blacks tend to be less conservative than whites, this outmigration has produced a slightly more conservative population in the rural areas of the South.

In summary then, Northerners and Southerners, on the whole, have tended not to be greatly distinctive in terms of conservatism. The largest differences that did occur were in 1964 and 1972 and are probably connected to short-term political factors. Northerners and Southerners have also tended to become more and more alike in conservative loyalty. Yet, this convergence is primarily the result of the North becoming more conservative rather than the South becoming less so. Within the South, the higher socioeconomic groups have tended to be significantly more conservative than Northern high socioeconomic groups. On the other hand, Southerners of lower SES have either differed little from their Northern counterpart, or have tended to be less conservative. The data also indicate that rural Southerners are generally not the source of Southern conservatism since they also tend to differ relatively little from Northerners of similar residence.

SOCIAL WELFARE POLICY

The first substantive area we will look at is that of social welfare. There are three attitudinal items under this general heading. First, since 1956 respondents have been asked in various ways whether the government should guarantee a job and good standard of living to anyone who wishes to work. Second, respondents were asked whether the federal government should subsidize medical care (1956-1968) or run a comprehensive national health insurance program (1972-1976). Finally, the subjects were asked whether the federal government should provide financial aid to local school districts. There is an underlying dimension to all of these questions in that all three tap respondents' attitudes toward the government's role in certain areas that have traditionally been private (or in the case of the last, local) areas of concern. All three also deal with the government giving some monetary benefit to individuals either directly or indirectly. Finally, all deal with the government's role in providing certain basic necessities of life (a job, health care, and an education).

Table 3.2 gives the aggregate percentage of respondents in the two regions who gave the more conservative response to each of the questions in this section. The percentages for each time period are not necessarily comparable with each other since there are significant question wording differences between the interview schedule used in the 1950s, 1960s, and 1970s. Nevertheless, the regions are comparable within each time period. As can be seen, the difference in the percentage of conservative responses is generally not very large (6 percent or less). For the question on guaranteed job and standard of living the South tends to be slightly less conservative than the North during all three decades. For the question on health care the South is less conservative during the 1950s, about equal to the North in the 1960s, and slightly more conservative than the North

TABLE 3.2
PERCENTAGE GIVING CONSERVATIVE RESPONSE
(On Social Welfare Questions)

	Guaranteed Job			Health Care			Educational Aid		
	1956-60	*1964-68*	*1972-76*	*1956-60*	*1964-68*	*1972-76*	*1956-60*	*1964-68*	*1972-76*
Nonsouth	32% (1099)*	62% (2663)	46% (2273)	30% (638)	37% (1653)	41% (1050)	25% (828)	62% (2712)	**
South	26% (302)	61% (791)	43% (718)	25% (198)	37% (478)	47% (372)	25% (279)	67% (910)	**

* ( ) – Number of respondents.
**No comparable question asked.

Source: Compiled by the author from ICPSR data.

in the 1970s. It should be noted, however, that the question asked in the 1970s taps a slightly different issue area than the question used in the 1950s and 1960s. In regard to the question on school aid, there is no real difference between the regions during the 1950s, and the South is only slightly more conservative than the North in the 1960s. In aggregate there appears to be little evidence that the South is or was significantly more conservative than the North on these three social welfare issues.

This picture is not greatly altered even if we compare only non-Southern whites to Southern whites. For instance, in 1976 there was no significant difference in the percentage of Northern and Southern whites who felt that the government should not involve itself in guaranteeing individuals a job and a good standard of living (52 percent and 51 percent respectively). This illustrates very clearly the general lack of substantial difference between the two regions in social welfare policy.

When controlling for socioeconomic status and residence, we found patterns very similar to those previously reported. Southerners of high SES tended to be more conservative than Northerners in that category, while those of lower SES tended to be less conservative or very similar to non-Southerners in that category. For instance, Table 3.3 gives the percentage of respondents in 1976 who felt that the government should not become involved in guaranteeing everyone a job and who opposed national health insurance. As can be seen, there appears to be a significant class differential in the responses. The most conservative sectors of the Southern population are those of high to moderate socioeconomic status. This pattern appears throughout the data (with a few exceptions) and across the entire time period of the study. Also similar to the presentation of general trends, we found that Southern rural areas were not consistently more conservative than Northern ones. If anything, they tended to be significantly less conservative than Northern areas — especially during the 1950s. In 1976, 46 percent of rural Southerners opposed the government guaranteeing everyone a good job and standard of living while 48 percent of rural Northerners did so. In 1956, on a different question probing the same issue, 40 percent of non-Southern ruralities opposed the government guaranteeing jobs for everyone who wished to work, while 22 percent of Southern ruralities did so.

In summary, there appear to be few significant differences between the North and the South in regard to the three social welfare issues considered. At certain times and for certain questions Southerners appear to be slightly less conservative than Northerners. At other times they appear to be slightly more conservative than Northerners. Taken in aggregate, it can hardly be said that a firm conservative stance is taken by Southerners, as distinct from that taken by non-Southerners, in social welfare issues. The only evidence of such a conservative culture appears for Southerners of higher SES. This unique subculture within a subculture was most pronounced during the 1950s. Yet, it continues even up through 1976. It also seems a mistake to conclude that Southerners of rural residence are more conservative than Northerners of similar circumstances. If anything, the opposite appears to be true.

TABLE 3.3
PERCENTAGE GIVING CONSERVATIVE RESPONSE ON GUARANTEED JOBS
AND HEALTH CARE QUESTIONS
(Controlled for Socioeconomic Status and Race)

	Guaranteed Job			Health Care		
	Socioeconomic Status			Socioeconomic Status		
	High	Medium	Low	High	Medium	Low
Total Sample:						
Nonsouth	61%	49%	40%	49%	44%	34%
	(269)*	(384)	(113)	(205)	(344)	(100)
South	68%	44%	24%	57%	53%	29%
	(65)	(108)	(30)	(54)	(118)	(35)
Whites:						
Nonsouth	61%	51%	44%	50%	45%	35%
	(263)	(362)	(108)	(202)	(323)	(90)
South	72%	48%	36%	60%	56%	40%
	(63)	(100)	(25)	(54)	(103)	(28)

*( ) – Number of respondents.

Source: Compiled by the author from ICPSR data.

LAW AND ORDER

One of the major political issues that emerged during the late 1960s and early 1970s was that of law and order. Sparked by a rash of urban riots and an increased rate of crime during the period, the need for law and order was certainly a flashy topic for any candidate to speak on. Scammon and Wattenberg labeled it as part of the new "social issue" that they felt would predominate in the 1970s.[18] Two questions in particular are appropriate to this issue area. In the first of these, subjects were asked whether the protection of individual rights or the control of crime should be given paramount emphasis. The second question asked respondents whether the problems of urban unrest should be solved by an emphasis on programs to fight poverty and urban decay, or whether (the other end of the scale) force should be used to quell urban disturbances. We will deal with the percentage of respondents in both regions who tend toward the "crime control" end of the scale.

It is hypothesized that conservatives will opt for a "crime control" point of view as opposed to a civil libertarian one. The reason for this is the conservative's concern for order and limited political activity. To a person with such values, it is obviously more important to control the criminal excesses of the few who threaten the safety of society than to be excessively concerned with the rights of the individual. This would be true in both the riot situation and the calmer atmosphere of a formal criminal proceeding. This does not mean that the conservative is not cognizant of civil liberties and rights, it just means that rampant individualism must be repressed where it could do harm to the safety of society.

Figures 3.2 and 3.3 show the percentage of respondents who took the more conservative position on each of the questions under consideration. The regional differences for the first question, once again, appear to be fairly small, but the South is consistently more conservative than the North. Yet, in 1976 some 41 percent of Northerners and 52 percent of Southerners took the more conservative position on the question. The widest gap between the two regions was in 1974, when the difference in response was some 8 percentage points. This appears to be an unusual difference since there is a smaller gap in 1972 and 1976.

The results of the second question indicate a somewhat larger and more consistent difference between the two regions than found in the first question. In fact, the gap averages some 11 percentage points across the eight-year period. The smallest gaps occurred in 1968 and 1976. The slopes of both trend lines are negative, indicating a slight reduction in the number of individuals prescribing force as the solution to urban problems. This is different from the previous question where the slopes of the region lines were positive, indicating an increase in conservative sentiments. Part of the difference in the two questions could be the lessening relevance of the riot question and the continued importance of the crime issue. By the middle 1970s the long hot summers so familiar in the

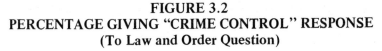

FIGURE 3.2
PERCENTAGE GIVING "CRIME CONTROL" RESPONSE
(To Law and Order Question)

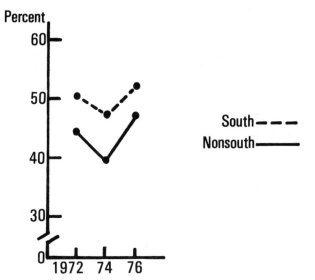

Source: Constructed by the author from ICPSR data.

late 1960s and early 1970s were a thing of the past. Large scale demonstrations and rioting declined in intensity throughout the 1970s. This decline in relevance is probably reflected in the patterns observed.

While the trends of response for the two questions are somewhat different, in one regard they are quite similar. When controlling for socioeconomic status the greatest differences between the regions is found for those of high or medium SES. Southerners of lower SES tend to be either less conservative than Northerners of similar status, or only slightly more conservative than them. Rather dramatic proof of this for the first question is shown in Figure 3.4. This bar graph shows the percentage of respondents in each socioeconomic category who gave the crime control response. Note that an increasing percentage of Northerners at each socioeconomic level gave the more conservative response, while for Southerners there is a slight decline for the first step and a dramatic decline for the second. This pattern recurs, albeit in a somewhat more restrained form, even if we only compare Northern whites to Southern whites. Hence, the drop cannot be simply attributed to the concentration of blacks in the lower socioeconomic category in the South.

When we control for SES the responses to the second question are similar. In 1976 for those of higher SES, some 30 percent of Southerners and 20 percent of Northerners felt that force should be used to quell urban unrest. For those of

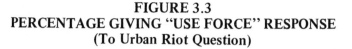

FIGURE 3.3
PERCENTAGE GIVING "USE FORCE" RESPONSE
(To Urban Riot Question)

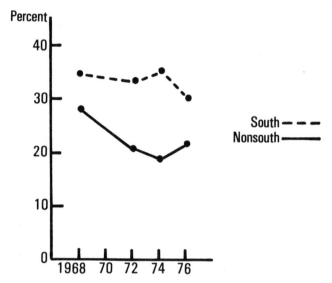

Source: Constructed by the author from ICPSR data.

FIGURE 3.4
PERCENTAGE GIVING "CRIME CONTROL" RESPONSE
(Controlled for Socioeconomic Status)

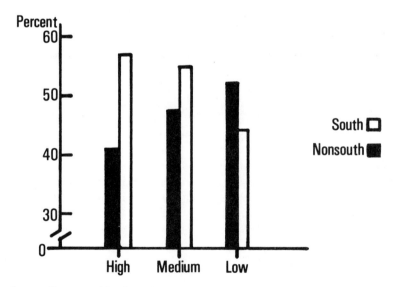

Source: Constructed by the author from ICPSR data.

lower SES in the same year, 27 percent of Northerners and only 20 percent of Southerners gave the same response. The picture is somewhat clouded if we simply look at whites in 1976. However, whites of lower SES still differ less from their Northern counterpart than do whites of higher SES in the percentage who give the "crime control" response.

We find no consistent patterns when controlling for residence. Southern ruralities are not the least conservative element in Southern politics when compared to similar Northerners, but neither are they consistently the most conservative. For the first question, where the regional differences are marginal to begin with, the residence subcategories also differ only marginally. On the urban unrest question the aggregate differences between North and South are larger, but there tend to be no consistent patterns when controlling for residence. Hence, residence does not appear to be a very relevant factor in explaining the differences between the regions in this issue area.

EQUAL RIGHTS AND AFFIRMATIVE ACTION

Two other issues of import during the 1970s have been the extension of equal rights to women and the role of the government in encouraging affirmative action programs for women, blacks, and other minority groups. Both questions deal with the further extension of civil rights first agitated for in the 1970s. In the case of women, it is the extension of civil rights rhetoric and reasoning to a group in society that has consistently been discriminated against. Although women could not really be described as a minority group, they do suffer from many of the same handicaps that have been placed on blacks. Affirmative action was a program instituted to benefit both women and blacks by calling for an active seeking out of previously discriminated against candidates for jobs and educational opportunities.

The wording of the two questions is generally in line with the discussion above. The first question asks whether women should be treated equally with men, or whether they belong primarily in the home. The second question asks whether the government should act to aid minorities and the underprivileged to improve their place in society, or whether they should simply get ahead on their own. In both cases the figures presented will show the percentage of respondents who believe women belong in the home or the percentage who believe minorities should get along on their own.

It is hypothesized that conservatives will tend to feel that women should maintain their traditional role of homemaker. This supposition goes back to the conservative mentality of preserving social norms which have grown up over long periods of time. In fact, Janet Boles, in her analysis of legislative action on the Equal Rights Amendment, has noted the tendency of this issue to become entangled in the more general liberal-conservative conflict.[19] In a similar vein, conservatives are hypothesized to feel that minority groups should rise in society by their own exertions rather than the intervention of government. To the conservative such intervention is an unwarranted disruption of societal norms and is likely to fail anyway.

Figure 3.5 shows the percentage of Northerners and Southerners who felt that women belong in the home. There is generally only a small difference between the two regions. In 1976, for example, some 23 percent of non-Southerners and 30 percent of Southerners took the conservative position on women's roles. The gap was approximately the same in 1972, while in 1974 the gap between the two regions was insignificant. The two regions are also quite similar over time. The trend line for both regions was downward from 1972 to 1976, indicating a lessening in conservatism. In sum, the two regions do not tend to differ very much in regard to women's roles. This is true even if we only consider the white subsample.

There is a wider gap between the regions on the aid to minorities question. The largest difference occurs in 1972 (8 percentage points) and the smallest in 1974 (4 percentage points). This convergence is primarily due to an increased conservatism on the part of Northern respondents (slope of 0.4). This parallels the findings for some of the questions presented earlier. Rather than the expected convergence of the South with the North, we instead see a convergence of the North with the South.

FIGURE 3.5
PERCENTAGE GIVING "WOMEN BELONG IN HOME" RESPONSE
(To Equal Rights for Women Question)

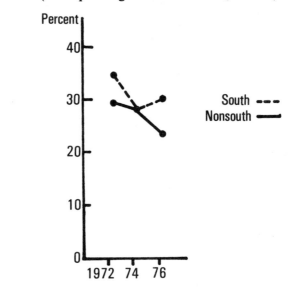

Source: Constructed by the author from ICPSR data.

FIGURE 3.6
PERCENTAGE RESPONDING "MINORITIES SHOULD GET ALONG ON THEIR OWN"
(To Aid for Minorities Question)

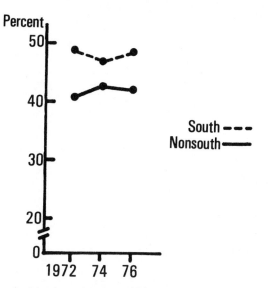

Source: Constructed by the author from ICPSR data.

As might be expected, the differences between the two regions on this question are somewhat understated because of the inclusion of blacks. Yet, even if we exclude blacks from consideration, the time trends are the same. There is an increase in the conservatism of the North on this question and a slight decrease on the part of the South (Northern slope is 0.55 and the Southern slope is −0.42).

In controlling for the socioeconomic status of each region the same patterns that emerged earlier are found. The greatest differences between the regions is found for those of higher SES. Southerners of lower SES either differ little from their Northern counterparts, or are less conservative than them. This trend can be seen in both questions. For instance, on the women's rights question in 1976, 12 percent of Northerners of high SES and 26 percent of Southerners of high SES felt that women belong in the home. This is a difference of some 14 percentage points. In that same year, 31 percent of non-Southerners of low SES and 36 percent of low SES Southerners picked the more conservative response (a 5 percent gap). This same pattern recurs even when we only look at the white subsample. The gap between North and South for whites of high SES is 12 percent and the gap for whites of low SES is 5 percent.

Table 3.4 shows the results of controlling for SES on the question of minority aid in 1976. The gaps between the two regions do differ somewhat if

TABLE 3.4
PERCENTAGE OPPOSING GOVERNMENT MINORITY AID
(Controlled for Socioeconomic Status)

| | Socioeconomic Status | | |
	High	Medium	Low
Total Sample:			
Nonsouth	39%	45%	38%
	(175)*	(372)	(107)
South	52%	53%	34%
	(53)	(135)	(44)
Whites:			
Nonsouth	39%	46%	44%
	(172)	(351)	(103)
South	54%	60%	51%
	(51)	(125)	(37)

*( ) – Number of respondents.

Source: Compiled by author from ICPSR data.

we look only at the white subsample. Yet, whether we look at the total sample or only at whites, in the South the lowest rate of conservatism on this question is for those of lower SES. This cannot be said of the non-Southern sample. Thus, we find quite a different distribution of opinions in the two regions along economic lines.

There is a difference between the two questions when we control for residence patterns. On the women's rights question the greatest conservative response is found among ruralities in both regions.

Figure 3.7 presents the 1976 percentage of those who felt that women belong in the home. The interesting thing to note is that Southerners of metropolitan and suburban residence tend to be more conservative on women's roles than Northerners of similar status. For ruralities, there is no significant difference between the two regions. This pattern is preserved even when controlled for race. In fact, for whites, Southern ruralities tend to be slightly less conservative than non-Southern ruralities on this question.

A different pattern obtains for the question of minority aid. The largest differences in response between the regions are found for those of rural residence. In 1976, 37 percent of Northern metropolitan dwellers and 39 percent of Southern metropolitan dwellers opposed government aid to minorities. In that same year 44 percent of Northern ruralities and 52 percent of Southern ruralities opposed aid. The gap was significantly larger if we looked only at the white samples.

FIGURE 3.7
PERCENTAGE OPPOSING EQUAL RIGHTS FOR WOMEN
(Controlled for Residence, 1976)

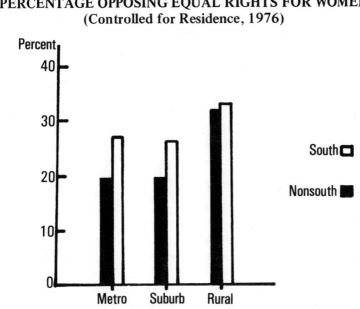

Source: Constructed by the author from ICPSR data.

To summarize, we have found that Northerners and Southerners tend not to differ significantly in terms of their presuppositions on women's roles. In the area of government support for minorities, the South does tend to be more conservative than the North — especially if we confine our sample to whites. In both cases the largest differences between the regions occurs for those of higher SES with smaller gaps for those of lower SES. For both questions rural dwellers tend to be more conservative than metropolitan or suburban residents. Yet, in the question on women's roles the smallest gap between the regions was for rural respondents. On the question of minority rights, the largest gap was for rural residents. The reason for this difference is not clear. Yet, it seems likely that specifically injecting race into the question may have caused the dichotomy. Also, the self-reliance ideal may well be much more alive in rural areas than urban ones.

SUMMARY AND CONCLUSIONS

Laying a blanket indictment on the South as representative of a distinct conservative political culture generally is not justified. Conservatism is a many splendored thing and does not appear to be confined to one region or to one group of people. In certain areas of opinion and at certain times Southern attitudes have been less conservative than Northern attitudes. In other areas Southern public opinion could be characterized as more conservative than that in the non-South. However, only in a relatively few areas is the North-South differential consistent and sufficiently large that one would expect significant policy preference differences.

It also appears to be a mistake to attribute Southern conservatism to the rural and less economically privileged sectors of the South population. Generally, the greatest differences between the North and the South appear for those of higher socioeconomic status and metropolitan-suburban residence. Only in matters of law and order or affirmative action are Southern rural areas distinct from Northern rural areas in the conservative direction. Yet, even in these two instances, the economic aspects of opinion are still present. The higher socioeconomic status groups diverge most sharply in the conservative direction while the poor diverge less sharply. If we confine ourselves to simply looking at the white sample, this pattern still obtains. It is true that among whites the relative response difference between the high and low socioeconomic status respondents is reduced considerably. Yet, the validity of looking only at the white sample in trying to explain Southern uniqueness is to be questioned more and more. It may well have been representative of reality before the Voting Rights Act of 1965 and for a period of time after that. Yet, the Southern electorate and Southern public officials are no longer all white. The proper comparison today is the entire Southern population — both blacks and whites — with the entire Northern population. In most cases where there was evidence of convergence between the two regions, it seemed to be due mainly to changes in Northern opinion rather than changes in Southern attitudes. This is contrary to what was expected and bodes ill for those who see change in Southern demographics as heralding radical changes in public opinion.

The question of convergence aside, we have some additional problems to address. The first of these is the reason for our finding that more privileged Southerners tend to be more conservative than their non-Southern counterparts, while Southerners of lower SES tend to either be less conservative, or only slightly more conservative than their Northern counterpart. I believe three hypotheses can be advanced to explain this pattern. The first of these explanations is sociological in character and argues that a conservative culture, if it does exist, would be seen primarily among the most privileged groups. In this sense the elite are the repositories of a common political culture which is only imperfectly translated and handed down to the masses in society. This process would be clearly visible in the greater boundedness to elite ideology as opposed to mass belief systems, much as Converse and others have found.[20] Hence, the regional differences should be clearest for the elite since it is only among this group that you find a firm ideology.

The second, and not incompatible explanation for the phenomenon we have found, is historical in nature. This explanation would derive from the fact that the one group least changed over the years in Southern life is the elite. Because of their social position and their great advantages of money and education, they were little affected by the social ferment of the Second Reconstruction and the civil rights struggle. This elite can easily avoid desegregation by moving to economically exclusive areas or by placing their children in private schools. Such avoidance measures were not available to those lower on the socioeconomic scale who cannot afford to flee from the civil rights struggle. The privileged have not been a part of the urban migration and have not been pushed out of agrarian life by new economic realities as many of the poor were. In sum, they are the group least affected by recent Southern history. Being the least affected by social change, we can expect evidence of a unique conservative culture to be most obvious in this group. There is some evidence to support this thesis in that the greatest volubility and change in response across time is found for those of moderate and low SES. In 80 percent of the cases, the greatest absolute change over time in relation to the North occurs for those of medium and lower SES.

There is yet a third possible explanation for the patterns found. This argument is also historical in nature and has been previously set forth. The patterns of economic conflict could be the result of long-standing Southern political patterns. The radical populist-agrarian tradition of the South is strong and has been commented on again and again by observers of Southern politics. According to this hypothesis we would expect to find evidence of this tradition among the poor and the rural dwellers of the South. Indeed, we do see such evidence in the area of social welfare. Yet, this radical tradition has also had its antithesis in the South. Racial prejudice, crosscutting the economic conflict inherent in populism, was used again and again by Southern politicians to put down what they considered radical politics. In fact, we find that social welfare issues and law and order/affirmative action issues do tend toward opposite patterns when controlled for residence. There is still evidence of economic conflict of the populist type in these questions, yet, the pattern is extremely weak when the electorate is restricted to the more prosperous whites. The North-South differences observed today are simply the vestiges of this pattern still remaining in the South. However, racial pleas have become less effective and, hence, less widely used because of the expansion of the Southern electorate. As poor whites and blacks have come to register and vote, the effectiveness of racial appeals has diminished.

All three explanations advanced for the patterns found seem reasonable, given the data and the historical context. Yet, working together they also provide us with a possible explanation for another phenomenon in Southern politics. The skeptic could well argue that our data must be in error. How could a relatively nonconservative region elect so many conservative politicians to represent them in Congress and elsewhere? Yet, the translation of a general opinion into a vote for a particular candidate is neither simple nor direct. The result of an election is, to a very great extent, decided by the candidates available for election. In Southern politics this was particularly restricted by the one-party character of the region. Even when a choice was available, it was likely to be a choice among conservatives rather than a choice between distinct ideological positions. The recruitment of candidates in the American political system (both North and South) usually occurs among the more privileged classes. Politicians are recruited from the elite of American society — from those with high occupational prestige, with broader educations, and with higher incomes. As can be seen, this is precisely the group in Southern politics which tends to be relatively more conservative than those of lower socioeconomic status. When one is confronted with a choice between two conservatives, a conservative will be elected. In a similar way the Southern elites controlled political office by restricting electoral choice to an unrepresentative group of politicians. This was even easier to accomplish when one party controlled the electoral system.

It would also be a mistake to assume that this process was completely successful. In fact, there have always been mavericks in Southern politics who have followed the radical agrarian tradition. Such individuals, it should be noted, have also been mavericks within their own party. They have usually depended on extremely personal campaign organizations rather than the established ones. The important point is that the Longs, the Watsons, and the Folsoms of the South have gotten and kept electoral support despite the so-called conservative tradition in Southern political life. In almost all such cases attempts to defeat them have used racial appeals to crosscut their vital agrarian roots. Such a strategy was a common ploy used time and again in Southern politics. Sometimes it did not work and the Southern elite were successful in restricting the available candidates.

All of this is by way of introduction to the final point we must consider — the future of Southern politics. At this time that future is somewhat cloudy, but I believe two considerations are paramount. First, while there is a certain positive side to Southern development and growth, there is a negative side to it as well. Social thinkers who see Southern development as a precursor to the development of a Southern liberal culture are warned by our analysis that such is not likely to be the case. With increasing urbanization and wealth in Southern life, the basis of the agrarian-populist tradition is also threatened. As the old South passes away, so do some of its benefits as well as its drawbacks. The populist-agrarian tradition in the South has been a positive social force not only in the South, but for the entire nation. Its death may well herald an increase in the ideological distinctiveness of the South rather than its reduction. Because of the significant time lag involved in such a process, however, that result is not likely to show itself for some time.

But, to a greater extent such an outcome is also dependent on other, national trends. The ideological ethos of the South relative to the North is likely to depend on the type of issues which occupy center stage in American politics. As we have seen, certain types of issues seem to tap Southern distinctiveness while others do not. If American public discussion revolves around such issues, we can expect to see a significant North-South differential in opinion. If, however, social welfare issues once again take center stage in American politics, we can expect the South to differ relatively little from the North in public opinion. The South would then become more and more integrated into the national political tradition and we could speak of the Southerner as an American rather than as a Southerner.

NOTES

1. For example see, Carole E. Hill, "Anthropological Studies in the American South: Review and Directions," *Current Anthropology* 18 (June 1977): 309-314; Howard Zinn, *The Southern Mystique* (New York: Simon and Schuster, 1964); Numan V. Bartley, *The Rise of Massive Resistance* (Baton Rouge: Louisiana State University Press, 1969) esp. pp. 237-250; Lewis M. Killian, *White Southerners* (New York: Random House, 1970); M. Stanton Evans, *The Future of Conservatism* (New York: Holt, Rinehart, and Winston, 1968); and James J. Kilpatrick, "A Conservative Political Philosophy" in *The South: A Central Theme*, ed. Monroe L. Billington (New York: Holt, Rinehart, and Winston, 1969) pp. 109-118.

2. W. Wayne Shannon, "Revolt in Washington: The South in Congress" in *The Changing Politics of the South*, ed. William C. Havard (Baton Rouge: Louisiana State University Press, 1972) pp. 637-687.

3. Kevin P. Phillips, *The Emerging Republican Majority* (New Rochelle, N.Y.: Arlington House, 1969).

4. Numan V. Bartley and Hugh D. Graham, *Southern Politics and the Second Reconstruction* (Baltimore: Johns Hopkins University Press, 1975), p. 200.

5. Everett C. Ladd and Charles D. Hadley, *Transformations of the American Party System* (New York: W. W. Norton & Co., 1975).

6. Ibid., pp. 129-130.

7. Phillips, *Emerging Republican Majority;* and Bartley and Graham, *Southern Politics and Second Reconstruction*, are two examples.

8. Ray C. Rist (ed.), *Desegregated Schools: Appraisal of an American Experiment* (New York: Academic Press, 1979), pp. 4-5.

9. An example of this type of assumption is found in John C. McKinney and Linda B. Bourque, "The Changing South: National Incorporation of a Region," *American Sociological Review* 36 (June 1971): 399-412.

10. Herbert McClosky, "Conservatism and Personality," *American Political Science Review* 50 (January 1958): 29.

11. Noel O'Sullivan, *Conservatism* (New York: St. Martin's Press, 1976), p. 12.

12. See generally the discussion in Philip E. Converse, "The Nature of Belief Systems in Mass Publics," in *Ideology and Discontent*, ed. David Apter (New York: Macmillan, 1964).

13. Ibid., p. 255.

14. Norman R. Luttbeg, "The Structure of Beliefs Among Leaders and the Public," *Public Opinion Quarterly* 32 (Fall 1968): 398-409; Norman H. Nie and Kristi Anderson, "Mass Belief Systems Revisited: Political Change and Attitude Structure," *Journal of Politics* 36 (August 1974): 540-487; and Steven R. Brown, "Consistency and the Persistence of Ideology: Some Experimental Results," *Public Opinion Quarterly* 34 (Spring 1970): 60-68.

15. Nie and Anderson, "Mass Belief Systems Revisited" as reprinted in *Controversies in American Voting Behavior*, eds. Richard Niemi and Herbert Weisberg (San Francisco: W. H. Freeman, 1976), p. 97.

16. Perhaps most recent among those supporting Converse is, Herbert M. Kritzer, "Ideology and American Political Elites," *Public Opinion Quarterly* 42 (Winter 1978): 484-502.

17. The same thesis is seen in, Norval D. Glenn, "Recent Trends in White-Non-white Attitudinal Differences," *Public Opinion Quarterly* 38 (Winter 1974-75): 596-604.

18. Richard M. Scammon and Ben J. Wattenberg, *The Real Majority* (New York: Coward, McCann and Geoghegan, 1970).

19. Janet K. Boles, *The Politics of the Equal Rights Amendment* (New York: Longman, 1979), pp. 170-171.

20. Converse, "Nature of Belief Systems in Mass Publics"; and Kritzer, "Ideology and American Political Elites."

4

SOURCES OF POLITICAL INTOLERANCE: THE CASE OF THE AMERICAN SOUTH

Ted Jelen

"If there be any among us who would wish to dissolve this Union or to change its republican form, let them stand undisturbed as monuments of the safety with which error of opinion may be tolerated when reason is left free to combat it."

Thomas Jefferson
First Inaugural Address

It has long been suspected that there exists a distinct "Southern approach" to the art of politics. The political distinctiveness of the American South has been noted by observers as diverse as Alexis de Tocqueville[1] and V. O. Key[2]. Even setting aside the pervasive question of race relations, analysts of Southern political life have observed profound differences in the Southern styles of political leadership, citizen participation[3], and tolerance toward nonconformists.[4]

For a number of years, it has been suggested that the South is about to undergo substantial political change. The election of Jimmy Carter is often taken as evidence of fundamental change in Southern political life:

. . . the Deep South sent men to national political prominence whose views were Old South segregationist, far more conservative than the vast majority of the national Democratic Party. But the South matured. It matured in the 1970s, as a newer and more moderate breed of Democrat was permitted to rise in the South, men like Carter and Reubin Askew in Florida, and Dale Bumpers in Arkansas, and others; and the South also matured as blacks were registered to vote.[5]

The purpose of this paper is to examine the extent of the South's political "maturation." In particular, I intend to investigate the stability and change of

Southern attitudes toward nonconformists (in this study, defined as atheists, communists, and homosexuals). It has long been known that Southerners tend to be less tolerant toward nonconformists than are Northerners, and that these differences persist when the effects of demographic variables are controlled. In this study, I plan to address three questions: First, have regional differences regarding political tolerance persisted into the 1970s and 1980s? Second, assuming that such differences still exist, to what factors might these differences be attributed? Finally, what are the prospects for long-term secular change in patterns of Southern intolerance? Is it the case that politically relevant changes in Southern life extend to attitudes toward nonconformists, or is the higher incidence of Southern intolerance due to the influence of more fixed factors?

DATA AND METHOD

Data were taken from the General Social Survey conducted by the National Opinion Research Center, for the years 1972-1978. This was a series of national probability samples, with a total of 10,625 respondents.[6]

The sample was divided into Southern and non-Southern categories[7] (see Appendix B). Indexes were constructed to measure tolerance toward atheists, communists, and homosexuals. The construction of the indexes is described in Appendix A. It should be noted that, while each of the three groups is a highly unpopular one in the United States, members of each group were depicted performing activities which are not only legal, but which might fairly be regarded as protected by the First Amendment of the Constitution. Members of these three groups were described as giving speeches, writing and distributing books, and teaching in colleges or universities.

After the tolerances responses for each group were crosstabulated by region of residence, the relationship was controlled for the effects of income, education, urbanization, religious fundamentalism (see Appendix C), and race. Finally, path analyses were conducted on each of the tolerance indexes, in order to assess the joint effects of these exogenous variables.

RESULTS

Regional Differences Between Southerners and Non-Southerners Still Exist

As Tables 4.1-4.3 clearly show, the relationship between tolerance and region reported by Stouffer[8] (1955, pp. 115-123) and Prothro and Grigg[9] persists into the 1970s. There exists a fairly strong relationship between tolerance and region, regardless of whether respondents are asked about atheists, communists, or homosexuals. Clearly, whatever demographic changes have taken place in the South over the past decade, they have not altered this aspect of Southern political culture.

TABLE 4.1
REGION[a] BY TOLERANCE TOWARD ATHEISTS[b]
(percent)

	Tolerant	Intolerant	(N)
Non-Southern	64.2	35.8	(4914)
Southern	44.3	55.7	(2291)

Tau B = .19
Gamma = .39
p < .01

[a]See Appendix B
[b]See Appendix A

Source: Compiled by the author from NORC data.

TABLE 4.2
REGION BY TOLERANCE TOWARD COMMUNISTS[a]
(percent)

	Tolerant	Intolerant	(N)
Non-Southern	58.1	41.9	(4762)
Southern	41.3	58.7	(2221)

Tau B = .16
Gamma - .33
p < .01

[a]See Appendix A

Source: Compiled by the author from NORC data.

TABLE 4.3
REGION BY TOLERANCE TOWARD HOMOSEXUALS[a]
(percent)

	Tolerant	Intolerant	(N)
Non-Southern	65.3	34.7	(3796)
Southern	46.2	53.8	(1780)

Tau B = .18
Gamma = .37
p < .01

[a]See Appendix A

Source: Compiled by the author from NORC data.

When Considered Separately, No Demographic Variable Accounts for Regional Differences

Differences between the South and the North with respect to political tolerance persist when the effects of income, education, or race are controlled. As Tables 4.4-4.6 show, the basic relationship is almost completely impervious to the effects of these three variables. Further, although the relationship between region and tolerance is affected by urbanization and religious fundamentalism, Southerners remain less tolerant than Northerners across all categories of the latter two variables.

Although Education Does Not Explain Regional Differences, the Level of Educational Attainment is the Strongest Single Predictor of Political Tolerance

As the path models in Figures 4.1-4.3 illustrate, education has the strongest effect on tolerance of any of the variables considered. This, of course, is scarcely a surprising finding, and again confirms those reported by Prothro and Grigg[10] and Stouffer[11]. Although there is a moderate tendency for Northerners to be better-educated than Southerners (see Appendix D), the path models show that this effect virtually disappears when the effects of race, religious fundamentalism, and income are considered.

Religious Fundamentalism Appears to Account for Regional Differences Better than Any Other Explanatory Variable

Although the predictive power of the path models in Figures 4.1-4.3 is not impressive, the models do suggest that the distinctiveness of the South with respect to political tolerance can best be explained by the high incidence of religious fundamentalism in that region (see Appendix D). When the effects of the other variables considered are controlled, there still exists a moderately strong relationship between religious fundamentalism and tolerance toward atheists, communists, and homosexuals.

There are two distinct paths to be considered. First, even where the effects of educational attainment are controlled, fundamentalism is still related (negatively) to tolerance. It seems entirely likely that this relationship can be explained by reference to the distinctive characteristics of Protestant fundamentalism. It has been argued that freedom of thought and expression is desirable since (among other reasons) one may learn from confronting opposing viewpoints.[12] This educative impact of thought and discussion is likely to obtain even when the opposing perspective is partially or wholly in error. Apparently, tolerance for opposing viewpoints requires a certain degree of skepticism concerning the validity of one's own views.

TABLE 4.4
RELATIONSHIP BETWEEN REGION AND
TOLERANCE TOWARD ATHEISTS
(With Controls)

	Income		
	High	*Medium*	*Low*
Tau B	.11	.17	.15
Gamma	.26	.36	.31

	Education		
	High	*Medium*	*Low*
Tau B	.14	.14	.19
Gamma	.35	.31	.40

	Urbanization		
	Metro	*Urban*	*Rural*
Tau B	.09	.17	.25
Gamma	.21	.37	.51

	Fundamentalism		
	Irreligious	*Non-fundamentalist*	*Fundamentalist*
Tau B	.30	.08	.15
Gamma	.71	.21	.36

	Race	
	White	*Black*
Tau B	.18	.20
Gamma	.37	.40

Source: Compiled by the author from NORC data.

TABLE 4.5
RELATIONSHIP BETWEEN REGION AND
TOLERANCE TOWARD COMMUNISTS
(With Controls)

	Income		
	High	*Medium*	*Low*
Tau B	.13	.15	.12
Gamma	.29	.31	.25

	Education		
	High	*Medium*	*Low*
Tau B	.16	.13	.11
Gamma	.36	.29	.25

	Urbanization		
	Metro	*Urban*	*Rural*
Tau B	.09	.14	.22
Gamma	.20	.29	.45

	Fundamentalism		
	Irreligious	*Non-fundamentalist*	*Fundamentalist*
Tau B	.24	.09	.11
Gamma	.56	.22	.26

	Race	
	White	*Black*
Tau B	.17	.17
Gamma	.33	.32

Source: Compiled by the author from NORC data.

TABLE 4.6
RELATIONSHIP BETWEEN REGION AND
TOLERANCE TOWARD HOMOSEXUALS
(With Controls)

	Income		
	High	*Medium*	*Low*
Tau B	.14	.15	.17
Gamma	.33	.32	.34

	Education		
	High	*Medium*	*Low*
Tau B	.15	.12	.18
Gamma	.36	.27	.39

	Urbanization		
	Metro	*Urban*	*Rural*
Tau B	.09	.16	.27
Gamma	.21	.33	.53

	Fundamentalism		
	Irreligious	*Non-fundamentalist*	*Fundamentalist*
Tau B	.23	.08	.11
Gamma	.57	.20	.27

	Race	
	White	*Black*
Tau B	.18	.20
Gamma	.37	.38

Source: Compiled by the author from NORC data.

FIGURE 4.1*

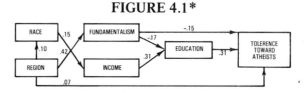

$R^2 = .19$ (proportion of variance explained).

Source: Compiled by the author from NORC data.

FIGURE 4.2*

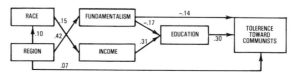

$R^2 = .16$ (proportion of variance explained).

Source: Compiled by the author from NORC data.

FIGURE 4.3*

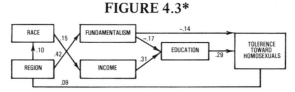

$R^2 = .18$ (proportion of variance explained).

Source: Compiled by the author from NORC data.

*All figures reported in Figures 4.1-4.3 are path coefficients. Coefficients which are less than .10 have been deleted. In all cases, the effects of urbanization and occupational prestige were reduced to inconsequential levels when the effects of the above variables were controlled.

It is fairly easy to see why Mill's argument regarding the value of free thought and expression might not be well received among fundamentalists. In the first place, the notion of "fundamentalism" entails a literal reading of the Bible[13]. Religious fundamentalists apparently hold that there exists a system of belief which is both infallible and unambiguous. Although this conclusion must remain very tentative until more direct evidence can be considered, it may be the case that fundamentalists believe that there is little or nothing to be gained by interaction with people who do not accept the central tenets of the Creed. Secondly, it is an important tenet of most Christian belief that religious beliefs are held as a matter of faith, rather than as a matter of conviction. This tendency appears to be most prominent in fundamentalist denominations.[14]

Consequently, it may be the case that the stimulus to reason that interaction with nonbelievers might entail may not be highly valued by members of fundamentalist congregations. The Creed, apparently, is not a subject to be disputed or debated, but is rather a universal and unchanging guide to human conduct.

Finally, the extent to which religious fundamentalists regard religious belief and its implications (or a lack of religious belief and its implications) as self-regarding or private behavior is questionable. Given the fact that atheists, communists, and homosexuals are all regarded as serious violators of the Creed, it may be the case that fundamentalists believe that it is difficult to live "a Christian life" (in particular, to raise children in a "Christian manner") in a world in which alternative and subversive beliefs are easily available. Given the certainty with which many fundamentalists hold their beliefs, and the importance attached by Christians to personal salvation, it is hardly surprising that the commitment to a system of religious belief often supersedes a commitment to an abstract principle such as "freedom of expression."

Religious fundamentalism also appears to exert an influence on tolerance through the intervening effects of education. The path models presented in Figures 4.1-4.3 show that fundamentalists typically represent lower levels of educational attainment than do nonbelievers or non-fundamentalists. Although this may, in part, reflect the lower socioeconomic status of fundamentalists, the relationship between income and religious fundamentalism is very small and statistically insignificant. An alternative speculation, which is supported by Figures 4.1-4.3, is that fundamentalist parents may make a deliberate decision not to expose their children to alternative and potentially subversive beliefs by sending them to college. College may be regarded as an experience in which students are forced to confront alternative beliefs and values.[15] Given the emphasis which fundamentalists place on faith as a means to salvation, it would not be surprising to learn that many fundamentalist youths choose not to have such an experience.

Again, it is important to emphasize that these explanations of the relationship between religious fundamentalism and tolerance are extremely tentative and speculative. Unfortunately, the data do not permit more direct tests of the hypotheses put forth above. It would also be a mistake to overlook the impact which economic variables such as income have on tolerance, when educational attainment is viewed as an intervening variable. However, it is the case that Southerners do not differ greatly from Northerners with respect to either income or education. Consequently, it is unlikely that either of these economic variables explains very much in the way of regional differences (see Appendix D).

Southern Fundamentalists May Impart Politically Relevant Cues to Other Southerners

It must be noted at the outset that this last result pushes speculation to its outer limits. The data, unfortunately, do not permit any direct test of a "contextual effects" hypothesis. However, with these reservations noted, it is a fact that fundamentalists constitute a majority of the population in the South, and people with such religious beliefs are in a small minority in the North (see Appendix D). It is not implausible to suppose that Protestant fundamentalists may dominate Southern social life to such an extent that they may impart politically relevant attitudes and information to non-fundamentalist Southerners.

Although direct tests of this hypothesis are impossible, the data do permit a couple of suggestive, albeit indirect, analyses. Consider first Tables 4.7-4.9 which show the effects of region on political tolerance when the effects of religious

TABLE 4.7
REGION BY TOLERANCE TOWARD ATHEISTS
(percent)

	Irreligious		
	Tolerant	*Intolerant*	*(N)*
Non-South	92.5	7.5	(362)
South	68.0	32.0	(97)
Tau B = .30			
Gamma = .71			
p < .01			

	Non-fundamentalist		
	Tolerant	*Intolerant*	*(N)*
Non-South	62.8	37.2	(3776)
South	52.7	47.3	(917)
Tau B = .08			
Gamma = .21			
p < .01			

	Fundamentalist		
	Tolerant	*Intolerant*	*(N)*
Non-South	53.2	46.8	(297)
South	34.9	65.1	(1005)
Tau B = .15			
Gamma = .36			
p < .01			

Source: Compiled by the author from NORC data.

TABLE 4.8
REGION BY TOLERANCE TOWARD COMMUNISTS,
WITH CONTROLS FOR RELIGIOUS FUNDAMENTALISM
(percent)

| | *Irreligious* | | |
	Tolerant	*Intolerant*	*(N)*
Non-South	86.2	13.8	(349)
South	63.6	36.4	(99)
Tau B = .24			
Gamma = .56			
p < .01			

| | *Non-fundamentalist* | | |
	Tolerant	*Intolerant*	*(N)*
Non-South	56.5	43.5	(3656)
South	45.7	54.3	(898)
Tau B = .09			
Gamma = .22			
p < .01			

| | *Fundamentalist* | | |
	Tolerant	*Intolerant*	*(N)*
Non-South	46.9	53.1	(292)
South	34.1	65.9	(1063)
Tau B = .11			
Gamma = .26			
p < .01			

Source: Compiled by the author from NORC data.

fundamentalism are controlled. What is most striking about each of these tables is that the relationship between region and tolerance is strongest for those who profess no religious preference, and is weakest for religious non-fundamentalists. Possibly, this is due to the fact that non-fundamentalists receive social support for their more tolerant beliefs through interaction with their coreligionists. Put more simply, perhaps the experience of attending church with people with similar beliefs serves to insulate non-fundamentalists from the dominant fundamentalist culture. Nonbelievers, who may lack frequent public opportunities to interact with one another, and to affirm their nonreligious beliefs, may also lack

TABLE 4.9
REGION BY TOLERANCE TOWARD HOMOSEXUALS,
(percent)

	Irreligious		
	Tolerant	*Intolerant*	*(N)*
Non-South	89.0	11.0	(301)
South	68.6	31.4	(86)
Tau B = .23			
Gamma = .58			
p < .01			

	Non-fundamentalist		
	Tolerant	*Intolerant*	*(N)*
Non-South	65.0	35.0	(2860)
South	55.2	44.8	(710)
Tau B = .08			
Gamma = .20			
p < .01			

	Fundamentalist		
	Tolerant	*Intolerant*	*(N)*
Non-South	49.6	50.4	(240)
South	35.8	64.2	(878)
Tau B = .12			
Gamma = .28			
p < .01			

Source: Compiled by the author from NORC data.

such social insulation. Consequently, nonbelievers may be more susceptible to the political consequences of religious fundamentalism in the South, even as they reject the religious foundations of these political attitudes.

Evidence that religious fundamentalists dominate social life in the South can be found in Table 4.10. Table 4.10 shows the religious affiliation of those people who were raised by nonreligious parents. This table is interesting for a couple of reasons. First, it demonstrates that a lack of religious belief is a relatively unstable personal characteristic. Almost two-thirds of children raised as nonreligious eventually "get religion" of some sort. Table 4.10 also shows that,

TABLE 4.10
RELIGIOUS AFFILIATION OF THOSE RAISED AS
NONBELIEVERS
By region

	Irreligious	*Non-fundamentalist*	*Fundamentalist*	*(N)*
Non-South	37.8	53.5	8.7	(172)
South	37.0	20.4	42.6	(54)

Source: Compiled by the author from NORC data.

while relatively few Northern children with a nonreligious upbringing become fundamentalists, a great many Southern children with similar backgrounds assume a fundamentalist faith. Again, this suggests that nonreligious people may acquire the beliefs and attitudes of the denominations which are locally dominant.

DISCUSSION

In his classic work *Southern Politics*, V. O. Key predicts that the economic changes which the South has experienced will strongly influence Southern political behavior:

> Apart from its effects on the race question, urbanization is, of course, an accompaniment of other changes of profound consequence for politics behavior. . . . Labor organizations in recent years have exerted a rapidly increasing influence . . . industrial and financial interests . . . have a fellow feeling with Northern Republicanism.[16]

When this prediction is viewed in retrospect, it becomes apparent that substantial political change has taken place in the American South, and that many of these changes can be attributed to the effects of urbanization and industrialization. It would, of course, be a grave mistake to underestimate the effects of such demographic transformations.

However, the analyses presented in this paper suggest that there are limits to the political consequences of economic development. Three decades have elapsed since Key's work was published, and yet the South still retains a distinctive regional character regarding tolerance toward nonconformists. Moreover, the data indicate rather clearly that the main source of regional differences is the large number of Protestant fundamentalists inhabiting the South. Fundamentalism, for reasons which need to be explored much more fully, appears to exert an influence over political tolerance which is independent of the effects of economic variables.

If this is the case, it seems likely that Southerners will be less tolerant than Northerners for some time to come. Religion seems to be a characteristic which is fixed very early in an individual's lifetime, and is highly resistant to change. Most people seem to retain the religious preference of their childhood ($r = .80$ when nonbelievers are excluded). Consequently, there is no reason to expect a decline in religiosity (and therefore, intolerance) even in the face of rapid economic development. Since the effect of religious fundamentalism on tolerance persists across all levels of education, income, and urbanization, political change in the South will probably be tempered by the effects of religion.

As is typical in our discipline, this study has raised more questions than it has answered. The finding that religious fundamentalism has a moderately strong effect is not surprising, as fundamentalism has been found to exert an influence over other politically relevant attitudes, such as party preference,[17] authoritarianism,[18] and racial prejudice.[19] What is needed is further research into the political character of religious commitment. Might fundamentalism represent an authoritarian or anti-democratic ideology, or is intolerance an essentially random response to the threatening attitudes of nonbelievers? In particular, it would be most interesting to investigate the effects of religious preference on attitudes toward education, as well as religious differences between higher education in the North and South. Further, much more work is needed on the hypothesis that Protestant fundamentalists alter the context of politics in the South. Accounts of the political and religious attitudes of friends, family, etc., as well as content analyses of local media might be quite helpful in confirming or discrediting this contextual hypothesis.[20]

In summary, this study has suggested a promising avenue for further research in the distinctive character of Southern politics. Since I am primarily interested in the prospects for long-term change, I have relied on fairly crude demographic indicators. More directly subjective (or "in-depth") accounts of the effects of religious preference on political attitudes are needed before the tentative conclusions presented here can be regarded as definitive.

APPENDIX A

Construction of the Tolerance Indexes

The tolerance indexes were constructed from the following questions:

"There are always some people whose ideas are considered bad or dangerous by other people. For instance, somebody who is against all churches and religion . . ."

"If such a person wanted to make a speech in your community against churches and religion, should he be allowed to speak, or not?"

"Should such a person be allowed to teach in a college or university, or not?"

"If some people in your community suggested that a book he wrote against churches and religion should be taken out of your public library, would you favor removing this book, or not?"

These three items form a Guttman scale with a reproducibility of .91, and a scalability of .76.

"Now, I should like to ask you some questions about a man who admits he is a communist."

"Suppose this admitted communist wanted to make a speech in your community. Should he be allowed to speak, or not?"

"Suppose he is teaching in a college. Should he be fired, or not?"

"Suppose he wrote a book which is in your public library. Somebody in your community suggests that the book should be removed from the library. Would you favor removing it, or not?"

These three items form a Guttman scale, with a reproducibility of .90, and a scalability of .77.

"And what about a man who admits that he is a homosexual?"

"Suppose this admitted homosexual wanted to make a speech in your community. Should he be allowed to speak, or not?"

"Should such a person be allowed to teach in a college or university, or not?"

"If some people in your community suggested that a book he wrote in favor of homosexuality should be taken out of your public library, would you favor removing this book, or not?"

These three items form a Guttman scale with a reproducibility of .90, and a scalability of .76.

For each group (atheists, communists, and homosexuals) an index was formed, adding the number of "intolerant" responses. A respondent was coded as "tolerant" with 0 or 1 intolerant responses, and as "intolerant" with 2 or 3 intolerant responses.

All relationships reported in this paper are robust and consistent across a number of cutting points.

APPENDIX B

The region variable was coded as follows:

Non-South: Maine, Vermont, New Hampshire, Massachusetts, Connecticut, Rhode Island, New York, New Jersey, Pennsylvania, Wisconsin, Illinois, Indiana, Michigan, Ohio, Minnesota, Iowa, Missouri, North Dakota, South Dakota, Nebraska, Kansas, Montana, Idaho, Wyoming, Nevada, Utah, Colorado, Arizona, New Mexico, Washington, Oregon, California, Alaska, Hawaii.

South: Delaware, Maryland, West Virginia, Virginia, North Carolina, South Carolina, Georgia, Florida, Kentucky, Tennessee, Alabama, Mississippi, Arkansas, Oklahoma, Louisiana, Texas.

APPENDIX C

The religious variable was coded as follows:

Nonbelievers: No religious preference.

Non-fundamentalists: Catholic, Jewish, Baptist (non-Southern), Methodist, Lutheran, Presbyterian, Episcopalian, Congregationalist, Friends, Quaker, Unitarian, and Universalist.

Fundamentalists: Southern Baptist, Churches of God, Churches of Christ, Assemblies of God, Free Methodist, Free Will Baptist, Eden Eveangelist, Nazarene, Christian Reform, Church of God in Christ, Church of God in Christ Holiness, Disciples of Christ, Evangelical, Evangelical Reformed, Four Square Gospel, Church of the Latter-Day Saints, Mormon, Mennonite, Pentecostal Church of God, Pentecostal, Pentecostal Holiness, Reformed, Reformed United Church of Christ, Reformed Church of Christ, Salvation Army, Seventh Day Adventist, United Church of Christ, Disciples of God, Evangelical Covenant.

Categories were compiled by the author from the following sources: Gallup Opinion Index, 1977, "Religion in America, 1977-78," Report No. 145. See also Benton Johnson, "Ascetic Protestantism and Political Preference," *Public Opinion Quarterly* 26 (September 1962): 35-46; and David R. Morgan, "Morality and Politics: Testing the Linkage with Referenda Voting," paper presented at the annual meeting of the Southwest Social Science Association, Ft. Worth, Texas, March 29-31, 1979.

APPENDIX D
RELATIONSHIP OF REGION TO RELIGIOUS FUNDAMENTALISM, INCOME, EDUCATION, AND RACE
(percent)

	Fundamentalism			
	Irreligious	Non-fundamentalist	Fundamentalist	(N)
Non-South	8.8	84.3	6.9	(6492)
South	4.6	42.7	52.7	(3204)
Tau C = .40				
Gamma = .76				
p < .01				

	Income			
	High	Medium	Low	(N)
Non-South	38.7	31.0	30.0	(5679)
South	27.8	32.0	40.2	(2705)
Tau C = .12				
Gamma = .20				
p < .01				

Note: In all tables, high income is any income of $15,000 per year or greater, medium income is any income between $8,000 and $14,999 per year, and low income is any income less than $8,000 per year.

	Education			
	High	Medium	Low	(N)
Non-South	32.5	35.8	31.7	(7183)
South	26.9	28.3	44.7	(3431)
Tau C = .11				
Gamma = .19				
p < .01				

Note: In all tables, high education is any college experience, medium education is a high school graduate, and low education is anything less than a completed high school education.

	Race		
	White	Black	(N)
Non-South	91.3	8.7	(7150)
South	82.0	18.0	(3434)
Tau B = .13			
Gamma = .39			
p < .01			

Source: Compiled by the author from NORC data.

90

NOTES

1. Alexis de Tocqueville, *Democracy in America*, ed. Phillips Bradley (New York: Vintage Books, 1945), I, p. 211.

2. V. O. Key, Jr., *Southern Politics in State and Nation* (New York: Alfred A. Knopf, 1949), pp. 3-4.

3. Philip E. Converse, "On the Possibility of Major Political Realignment in the South" in *Elections and the Political Order*, eds. Angus Campbell et al. (New York: John Wiley and Sons, 1966), pp. 212-44.

4. Samuel A. Stouffer, *Communism, Conformity, and Civil Liberties* (New York: John Wiley and Sons, 1955), pp. 115-123; and James W. Prothro and Charles M. Grigg, "Fundamental Principles of Democracy: Bases of Agreement and Disagreement" in *Empirical Democratic Theory*, eds. Charles F. Cnudde and Deane E. Neubauer (Chicago: Markham Publishing Company, 1969), p. 234.

5. Martin Schram, *Running for President: The Carter Campaign* (New York: Stein and Day, 1977), p. 363.

6. Data for this study were taken from James Allan Davis, *General Social Surveys, 1972-1978: Cumulative Data* (machine-readable data file). Principal investigator, James A. Davis; Associate Study Director, Tom W. Smith; Research Assistant, C. Bruce Stephenson. Chicago: National Opinion Research Center [producer], 1978; New Haven, Connecticut: Roper Public Opinion Research Center, Yale University [distributor]. 1 data file (10,652 logical records) and codebook (340 pp.). I would also like to thank Leonard Cormier, Robert Cizewski, and Robert Schneider for valuable comments and assistance.

7. In order to preserve the anonymity of some rural responses, states of residence were recorded into regional groups (*General Social Surveys, 1972-1978 Codebook*, p. 228). Consequently, it is impossible to decompose region into specific states, even though this might be desirable for certain purposes.

8. Stouffer, *Communism, Conformity, and Civil Liberties*, pp. 115-23.

9. Prothro and Grigg, "Fundamental Principles of Democracy," p. 243.

10. Ibid.

11. Stouffer, *Communism, Conformity, and Civil Liberties*, p. 90.

12. John Stuart Mill, *On Liberty* (London: Oxford University Press, 1975), p. 65.

13. Gallup Opinion Index, "Religion in America, 1977-78," Report No. 145 (Princeton: The Gallup Poll, 1977).

14. Rodney Stark and Charles Y. Glock, *American Piety: The Nature of Religious Commitment* (Berkeley: The University of California Press, 1968), pp. 42-43.

15. Stouffer, *Communism, Conformity, and Civil Liberties*, p. 127.

16. Key, *Southern Politics*, pp. 673-74.

17. Benton Johnson, "Ascetic Protestantism and Political Preference," *Public Opinion Quarterly* 26 (Spring 1962): 35-46; and Benton Johnson, "Ascetic Protestantism and Political Preference in the Deep South," *American Journal of Sociology* 69 (January 1964): 359-66.

18. W. Edgar Gregory, "The Orthodoxy of the Authoritarian Personality," *Journal of Social Psychology* 45 (May 1957): 217-32.

19. Joseph R. Feagin, "Prejudice and Religious Types: A Focused Study of Southern Fundamentalists," *Journal for the Scientific Study of Religion* 4 (Fall 1964): 3-13.

20. The data supporting these speculations must, of course, be interpreted with great care. While Tables 4.7-4.9 support the notion of a "contextual effect," it remains the case that nonbelievers are more tolerant than non-fundamentalists. While Table 4.10 is free of such ambiguity, it should be noted that the marginals are so small as to render any conclusions extremely tentative.

PART II:

PERSPECTIVES ON
SOUTHERN PARTY POLITICS

INTRODUCTION

The Editors

For approximately a century, the continuing control of the South's political system by the Democratic party has been widely regarded as the most distinctive aspect of southern politics.[1] The demise of the Republican party in most parts of the South can be traced back to the 1890s, when a combination of events interacted to increase support for the Democratic party at the expense of the Republican party. For one thing, the national Republican party's interest in cultivating southern support waned as the central concerns of the political agenda shifted from those associated with slavery, rebellion, and reconstruction to those associated with industrialization and related economic development.[2] Additionally, southern white leaders undertook a conscious effort to restore white supremacy to the region through the enactment of Jim Crow laws such as the poll tax, the white primary, and the literacy test designed to disfranchise black voters, and through the establishment of a one-party system which would presumably diminish the temptation to court black votes considered to be a constant danger in a competitive two-party system.[3] These efforts were largely successful, and the Republican party soon withered. From roughly the turn of the century until the years following World War II, the Democratic party's dominance of southern politics was virtually absolute, with the major exception being the string of highland Appalachian counties extending from southwestern Virginia to northeastern Alabama, where Republican party control seemed almost to equal that of the Democratic party elsewhere in the region.[4]

In the postwar South this feature of the region's political system has changed substantially. The same social, economic, political, and cultural developments which have altered other aspects of southern life have clearly eroded traditional party patterns in the region and have begun to bring an end to the Democratic Solid South.[5] In conjunction with these changes the debate over continued southern distinctiveness has extended to the South's political party system. Some investigators have concluded that realignment along the lines that mark national party conflict has occurred (or is occurring) in the South, others have concluded that dealignment is the key direction of the southern party system, and still others have argued that the developments are mixed, with some pointing toward realignment, some pointing toward dealignment, and some pointing toward the continuation of Democratic one-partyism, at least in some parts of the region.[6]

The chapters in this section examine the contemporary party system in the South to help ascertain whether the larger societal changes of the past three and a half decades have brought the region fully into the national party system. The first three chapters present information about the nature of Republican and Democratic party politics in the South, both historically and currently. Collectively, "Durable Democratic Factions in Southern Politics" and "Republican Party Development in the South: The Rise of the Contested Primary" by Earl and Merle Black and "Party Competition in the South's Forgotten Region: The Case of Southern Appalachia" by C. David Sutton investigate selected aspects of the southern party system addressing such matters as the nature of party factionalism, the development of Republican party support, and the nature of the political party system in that smaller part of the region having a long history of persistent Republican strength. They thereby provide a foundation for the more specific analyses of the last three chapters of this section, which relate to whether the southern party system remains clearly distinct from the national party system. The lead chapter in the second part of this section, "The End of Southern Electoral Distinctiveness" by Paul Allen Beck and Paul Lopatto, examines mass presidential voting patterns in the South from 1952 to 1980, and suggests that there is evidence that the regional party distinctiveness of past years has begun to disappear. The final two chapters, "Presidential Activists and the Nationalization of Party Politics in Virginia" by Alan Abramowitz, John McGlennon, and Ronald Rapoport and "Southern Distinctiveness and the Emergence of Party Competition: The Case of a Deep South State" by Tod A. Baker, Robert P. Steed, and Laurence W. Moreland, investigate this thesis further by examining data on state political party activists in a Rim South state (Virginia) and a Deep South state (South Carolina). Using data on comparable sets of party activists drawn from questionnaires administered to delegates to the 1980 state conventions (for both parties in each state), these chapters investigate whether the party changes seen by Beck and Lopatto at the mass voting level are extending as well into the ranks of organizational activists. Although the data base for these two chapters is similar, the approaches employed are different. Abramowitz, McGlennon, and Rapoport present a descriptive comparison of Democratic and Republican leaders along a number of dimensions of activity, party orientations, candidate support patterns, and issue positions in an effort to find evidence of realignment of the Virginia party system. Baker, Steed, and Moreland also pursue an investigation of party change and realignment, but they also seek to find if there are vestiges of southern distinctiveness in the South Carolina party system. They address two general questions: (1) is there evidence in the attitudes of South Carolina party elites of significant change in the state party system away from the traditional pattern of one-partyism in the state, and (2) if there is such evidence, do any elements of the traditional party system remain?

In combination, these six chapters offer a sweeping view of past and present political patterns in the South. While they do not provide a completely comprehensive picture, they do provide useful information to suggest some general answers to the basic question, "Is the southern political party system now integrated into the national party system or does it retain its clearly different historical characteristics?"

NOTES

1. See, for example, V. O. Key, Jr., *Southern Politics in State and Nation* (New York: Alfred A. Knopf, 1949), chaps. 1, 13-22. The impact of the one-party system in the South is addressed throughout Key's analysis, and many of the unique features of southern politics are clearly linked to one-partyism. For additional information relevant to this point see, among others, V. O. Key, Jr., *Politics, Parties, and Pressure Groups* (5th ed.; New York: Crowell, 1964), chap. 9; and Malcolm E. Jewell and David M. Olson, *American State Political Parties and Elections* (Homewood, Illinois: The Dorsey Press, 1978), chap. 2.

2. Everett Carll Ladd, Jr., *American Political Parties: Social Change and Political Response* (New York: Norton, 1970), chap. 4, esp. pp. 157-158; Richard Jensen, "Party Coalitions and the Search for Modern Values: 1820-1970," in *Emerging Coalitions in American Politics*, ed. Seymour Martin Lipset (San Francisco: Institute for Contemporary Studies, 1978), pp. 11-40; James L. Sundquist, *Dynamics of the Party System: Alignment and Realignment of Political Parties in the United States* (Washington, D.C.: The Brookings Institution, 1973), chap. 6; and J. Morgan Kousser, *The Shaping of Southern Politics: Suffrage Restrictions and the Establishment of the One-Party South, 1880-1910* (New Haven: Yale University Press, 1974).

3. Ladd, *American Political Parties*, pp. 136-140; Key, *Southern Politics*, chaps. 25-30, *passim*; Key, *Politics, Parties, and Pressure Groups*, pp. 232-235; and Kousser, *The Shaping of Southern Politics*, passim.

4. Key, *Southern Politics*, chap. 13; and Jewell and Olson, *American State Political Parties and Elections*, pp. 24-25.

5. A large literature addresses the changes which have taken place in the South's party system. Among the more useful materials are Avery Leiserson (ed.), *The American South in the 1960's* (New York: Praeger, 1964); Samuel D. Cook, "Political Movements and Organizations," *Journal of Politics* 26 (February 1964): 130-153; Allan P. Sindler (ed.), *Change in the Contemporary South* (Durham: Duke University Press, 1963); Bernard Cosman, *Five States for Goldwater* (University, Alabama: University of Alabama Press, 1966); Donald S. Strong, "Further Reflections on Southern Politics," *Journal of Politics* 33 (May 1971): 239-256; Sundquist, *Dynamics of the Party System*, pp. 245-274; Numan V. Bartley and Hugh D. Graham, *Southern Politics and the Second Reconstruction* (Baltimore: Johns Hopkins University Press, 1975); William C. Havard (ed.), *The Changing Politics of the South* (Baton Rouge: Louisiana State University Press, 1972); Jack Bass and Walter DeVries, *The Transformation of Southern Politics* (New York: Basic Books, 1976); Bruce A. Campbell, "Change in the Southern Electorate," *American Journal of Political Science* 21 (February 1977): 37-64; Paul Allen Beck, "Partisan Dealignment in the Postwar

South," *American Political Science Review* 71 (June 1977): 477-496; Louis M. Seagull, *Southern Republicanism* (New York: Schenkman, 1975); Alan I. Abramowitz, "Ideological Realignment and the Nationalization of Southern Politics: A Study of Party Activists and Candidates in a Southern State," paper presented at the 1979 annual meeting of the Southern Political Science Association, November 1-3, 1979 (Gatlinburg, Tennessee); and Robert P. Steed, Laurence W. Moreland, and Tod A. Baker (eds.), *Party Politics in the South* (New York: Praeger, 1980), esp. the "Introduction by William C. Havard" and the editors' conclusion, "Postscript: The Future of Southern Party Politics."

6. See Sundquist, *Dynamics of the Party System*, chap. 12; Beck, "Partisan Dealignment in the Postwar South"; and the essays in Steed, Moreland, and Baker, *Party Politics in the South*, esp. chaps. 5-7 and the conclusion.

5

SUCCESSFUL DURABLE DEMOCRATIC FACTIONS IN SOUTHERN POLITICS

Earl Black and Merle Black

In his landmark study of Democratic factionalism in the American South, V. O. Key, Jr. defined a faction as "any combination, clique, or grouping of voters and political leaders who unite at a particular time in support of a candidate. Thus, a political race with eight candidates will involve eight factions of varying size. Some factions have impressive continuity while others come into existence for only one campaign and then dissolve."[1] Although the political significance of factions has been widely appreciated since the publication of *Southern Politics*, in retrospect remarkably little research has been directed to the comparative analysis of factions in American state politics. Scholars who have examined factions have typically followed Key's lead in differentiating three varieties of intraparty competition based on the number of factions seeking a particular office and the distribution of the (first) primary vote between the factions: unifactionalism, where a single faction receives a substantial majority of the entire vote; bifactionalism, where the vote is divided more or less evenly between two factions; and multifactionalism, where the vote is split between three or more factions.[2]

While accepting the utility of Key's categories for detecting patterns of factional competition from one state to another, we suggest that a new approach, one based on the comparative analysis of factions rather than factional systems, will contribute to an improved understanding of the role of factions in American electoral politics. In this chapter we shall introduce a typology of factions in American state politics, analyze southern Democratic primaries for governor in light of this typology, and offer a comparative perspective on those few southern Democratic factions that have been both long-lived and highly successful.

A TYPOLOGY OF FACTIONS IN AMERICAN STATE POLITICS

Considerations of factional durability and factional success strike us as fundamentally important in assessing the significance or insignificance of particular factions. With regard to factional durability, it is essential to separate factions that persistently seek nominations for major office from factions that are manifestly short-lived. There is no commonly accepted standard for factional durability, but a factional lifespan in excess of one decade seems an appropriate benchmark. Hence a faction that contests a particular office over a period of time exceeding 10 years will be described as a *durable* faction, while a faction that lasts for a decade or less will be called a *transient* faction. To the extent that durable factions are present in primary elections, elements of continuity exist within the intraparty battle; and knowledgeable voters, if they choose to do so, can evaluate the participants in terms of the past performance of durable factions as well as the current promises of the candidates. The theoretical significance of durable factions lies in their potential for serving as positive or negative reference groups for well-informed voters, linking the past to the present.

Our second dimension for classifying factions concerns the degree of political success achieved by different factions. It is useful to know which factions won nominations and which factions failed, and three categories of factional success will be distinguished. Winning renomination to a major office is a criterion of political success widely accepted in American politics. Consequently, a faction that wins the nomination for a specified office at least twice (for an office with a four-year term) or at least three times (for an office with a two-year term) will be defined as a *successful* faction. A faction that is victorious only once (for a four-year term) or only once or twice (for a two-year term) will be designated a *moderately successful* faction; and a faction that fails to capture any nomination will be referred to as an *unsuccessful* faction. The appearance of a successful or moderately successful faction in a primary campaign gives voters so inclined an opportunity to hold officeholders accountable for their past performance.

A cross-classification of the two dimensions (see Table 5.1) produces six types of factions within each major party: successful durable factions, successful transient factions, moderately successful durable factions, moderately successful transient factions, unsuccessful durable factions, and unsuccessful transient factions. Our typology, it should be emphasized, is designed to facilitate comparative analysis of intraparty politics in the American states generally. All state parties that nominate through primaries, whatever their competitive status as parties, have intraparty histories that can be analyzed in terms of the relative importance of the various types of factions.

DEMOCRATIC FACTIONS AND THE SOUTHERN GOVERNORSHIP

Since the American South has long been recognized as a region in which factions of the Democratic party were extremely significant units of electoral

TABLE 5.1
A TYPOLOGY OF FACTIONS IN AMERICAN STATE POLITICS
(Based on Durability and Success)

	Factional Durability	
Factional Success	*Durable*[a]	*Transient*[b]
Successful[c]	Successful Durable Faction	Successful Transient Faction
Moderately Successful[d]	Moderately Successful Durable Faction	Moderately Successful Transient Faction
Unsuccessful[e]	Unsuccessful Durable Faction	Unsuccessful Transient Faction

[a]Competes for a particular office for a period of time exceeding ten years.
[b]Competes for a particular office for a period of time of ten years or less.
[c]Wins the nomination for a particular office at least twice (for an office with a four-year term) or at least three times (for an office with a two-year term).
[d]Wins the nomination for a particular office only once (for an office with a four-year term) or once or twice (for an office with a two-year term).
[e]Never wins the nomination for a particular office.

Source: Compiled by the authors.

politics, it is appropriate that we examine the types of factions that have contested the Democratic nomination for governor in the South. "The legend prevails," Key observed, "that within the Democratic party in the southern states factional groups are the equivalent of political parties elsewhere. In fact, the Democratic party in most states of the South is merely a holding-company for a congeries of transient squabbling factions, most of which fail by far to meet the standards of permanence, cohesiveness, and responsibility that characterize the political party."[3] By and large the adjectives Key selected to evoke the evanescent nature of Democratic factions at mid-century — "multifaceted, discontinuous, kaleidoscopic, fluid, transient"[4] — continue to portray accurately the most common mode of Democratic faction in the region. Based on a review of state newspaper accounts of Democratic primaries for governor, and an examination of secondary sources in light of the preceding criteria, we have identified and classified 438 Democratic factions active in southern gubernatorial politics from 1920 through 1980.[5] Table 5.2 reports the percentage distribution of the types of factions for the Deep South (Alabama, Georgia, Louisiana, Mississippi, and South Carolina), the Peripheral South (Arkansas, Florida, North Carolina, Tennessee, Texas, and Virginia), and the South. Unsuccessful transient factions constituted 65 percent of the Deep South factions, 73 percent of the Peripheral South factions, and 70 percent of the

TABLE 5.2
PERCENTAGE DISTRIBUTION OF FACTIONAL TYPES
(In Democratic Primaries, for Governor, 1920-1980)

Type of Faction	Deep South	Peripheral South	South
Successful Durable Faction	5	4	5
Successful Transient Faction	2	4	3
Moderately Successful Durable Faction	7	4	5
Moderately Successful Transient Faction	17	15	16
Unsuccessful Durable Faction	3	0	2
Unsuccessful Transient Faction	65	73	70
Totals	99%	100%	101%
Number of Factions	(183)	(255)	(438)

Source: Compiled by the authors.

southern factions. These were factions that briefly ventured into electoral politics, were rebuffed by the primary voters, and soon disappeared. Nearly 90 percent of all the southern Democratic factions were transient, a finding wholly in accord with Key's emphasis on the region's endemic "disorganization of political leadership."[6]

Yet as Key and others have recognized, from time to time factions with considerable staying power have been established in the South. No more than a tiny minority (5 percent) of the Democratic factions qualified as successful durable factions, the type of faction that most clearly represents continuity in intraparty politics. However, when the factional types are compared according to the proportion of gubernatorial nominations they managed to win (see Table 5.3), it is apparent that the small number of successful durable factions fared very well. Successful durable factions won nearly as many Democratic nominations for governor between 1920 and 1980 (38 percent) as did the moderately successful transient factions (39 percent). Moreover, in a majority of the southern states successful durable factions won more nominations than any other type of faction. They dominated Democratic primaries in Tennessee and Virginia, obtained more than half of the nominations in Alabama and Louisiana, and won a plurality of the contests in North Carolina and Georgia. Only in Florida, Texas, and South Carolina were successful durable factions unable to win appreciable percentages of the nominations. Moderately successful transient factions, the type of faction that most approximates the stereotype of the short-lived southern Democratic faction among factions that achieved any degree of success, accounted for a majority of the nominations in South Carolina and Florida, and for a plurality of the nominations in Arkansas and Mississippi. A

TABLE 5.3
PERCENTAGE OF WINNING DEMOCRATIC NOMINATIONS
FOR GOVERNOR
(By Factional Types, 1920-1980)

Political Unit	Type of Faction					
	SDF	STF	MSDF	MSTF	Total	N^a
Tennessee[b]	81	0	0	19	100	16
Virginia	79	0	0	21	100	14
Alabama	53	0	13	33	100	15
Louisiana	50	21	7	21	100	14
North Carolina	44	13	6	38	100	16
Mississippi	38	0	19	44	100	16
Georgia	35	18	18	29	100	17
Arkansas	28	11	17	44	100	18
South Carolina	13	0	13	73	100	15
Texas	6	53	6	35	100	17
Florida	0	24	12	65	100	17
Deep South	38	8	14	40	100	77
Peripheral South	38	17	7	38	100	98
South	38	13	10	39	100	175

Key: SDF = Successful Durable Faction; STF = Successful Transient Faction; MSDF = Moderately Successful Durable Faction; MSTF = Moderately Successful Transient Faction; N = Number of Nominations

[a]Calculations exclude nominations involving an incumbent governor seeking a second two-year term.

[b]States are ranked (highest to lowest) according to the percentage of nominations won by successful durable factions.

Source: Compiled by the authors.

unique pattern prevailed in Texas, where the leading type of faction was the successful transient faction. In that state a series of successful transient factions headed by Allen Shivers, Price Daniel, John Connally, and Dolph Briscoe virtually monopolized the post-1950 Democratic nominations for governor.

The results of Table 5.3 suggest that the transience of southern Democratic factions has been exaggerated. Durable factions secured almost half of the gubernatorial nominations contested over the past six decades, a magnitude of success that is at least partially inconsistent with Key's emphasis on the prevalence of uncrystallized, impermanent factions. A conceivable explanation of our findings is that transient factions, though furnishing an abundant proportion of nominations in the years covered by Key's book, may have been considerably less successful in subsequent decades. Table 5.4, which compares the percentage of

TABLE 5.4
PERCENTAGE OF WINNING DEMOCRATIC NOMINATIONS FOR GOVERNOR
(By Factional Types)

Political Unit	1920-49 Nominations						1950-80 Nominations					
	SDF	STF	MSDF	MSTF	Tot	N^a	SDF	STF	MSDF	MSTF	Tot	N^a
Tennessee[b]	100	0	0	0	100	8	63	0	0	38	100	8
Virginia	88	0	0	13	100	8	67	0	0	33	100	6
North Carolina	75	0	0	25	100	8	13	25	13	50	100	8
Louisiana	63	0	0	38	100	8	33	50	17	0	100	6
Mississippi	50	0	13	38	100	8	25	0	25	50	100	8
Georgia	44	11	33	11	100	9	25	25	0	50	100	8
Alabama	43	0	29	29	100	7	63	0	0	38	100	8
South Carolina	29	0	29	43	100	7	0	0	0	100	100	8
Texas	14	14	14	57	100	7	0	80	0	20	100	10
Arkansas	0	25	25	50	100	8	50	0	10	40	100	10
Florida	0	0	25	75	100	8	0	44	0	56	100	9
Deep South	46	3	21	31	100	39	29	13	8	50	100	38
Peripheral South	47	6	11	36	100	47	29	27	4	39	100	51
South	47	5	15	34	100	86	29	21	6	44	100	89

Key: SDF = Successful Durable Faction; STF = Successful Transient Faction; MSDF = Moderately Successful Durable Faction; MSTF = Moderately Successful Transient Faction; Tot = Total; N = Number of Nominations

[a]Calculations exclude nominations involving an incumbent governor seeking a second two-year term.

[b]States are ranked (highest to lowest) according to the percentage of nominations won by successful durable factions in 1920-49.

Source: Compiled by the authors.

nominations won by various types of factions in 1920-1949 and 1950-1980, compellingly refutes this possibility. In terms of controlling nominations for governor, the period analyzed by Key is more accurately conceived as the golden age of the durable rather than the transient faction. Between 1920 and 1949 successful or moderately successful durable factions won slightly better than three-fifths of the nominations. In addition, successful durable factions achieved far more victories in the South (47 percent) than did moderately successful transient factions (34 percent) and were the most successful variety of faction in seven out of eleven states, winning a majority of the nominations in Tennessee, Virginia, North Carolina, Louisiana, and Mississippi, and a plurality in Georgia and Alabama. Transient factions, by comparison, were far more important in intraparty politics after mid-century than they were previously. In a period characterized by the death or retirement of many leaders of durable factions, by an increase in interparty competition in many states, and by the rapid acceptance of new techniques of campaign management utilizing television to create statewide visibility for otherwise obscure politicians, transient factions managed to win nearly two-thirds of the nominations. From 1950 through 1980 moderately successful transient factions produced more victories across the South (44 to 29 percent) and won more nominations in more states (five to four) than did successful durable factions.

Since the effect of comparing factional success in 1920-1949 and 1950-1980 is to broaden and intensify rather than to reconcile the differences between our findings and those of Key, another explanation must be sought. We suggest that these alternative interpretations of the relative importance of durable versus transient factions are due to our use of discrete factions as units of analysis in contrast to Key's focus on patterns of competition between factions. Although Key was acutely sensitive to the significance of those durable factions that typically competed in unifactional or bifactional primaries, his approach led him to underestimate the presence of durable factions in multifactional settings. The ostensible free-for-all nature of many Democratic primaries in the South was mitigated by the presence of successful or moderately successful durable factions.

SUCCESSFUL DURABLE DEMOCRATIC FACTIONS

Prior to the revival of sustained interparty competition, the successful durable Democratic faction was the principal institution for injecting relatively long-term factors — the performance and policies of factions with a past and perhaps a future — into the southern electoral process. Although several of the more imposing successful durable factions (most prominently the organizations founded by Harry Byrd, Sr., of Virginia and Huey Long of Louisiana) have been the subject of extensive scholarship,[7] there has been little effort to assess the role of these factions in southern politics, especially over the three decades subsequent to Key's work.

In this section we seek to introduce a comparative perspective regarding the 19 successful durable factions that participated in southern gubernatorial politics between 1920 and 1980. (The Tennessee faction of Benton McMillin, which appeared only once after 1920, will be disregarded.) During this period no Democratic organization in Florida qualified as a successful durable faction; five of the states (Arkansas, Georgia, South Carolina, Texas, and Virginia) produced a single successful durable faction; and two such factions appeared in North Carolina and Louisiana. The largest numbers of successful durable factions were contributed by Tennessee (4), Alabama (3), and Mississippi (3). Though fairly common between 1920 and 1959 (10 to 14 successful durable factions pursued the governorship in each decade), since 1960 the number of successful durable factions has declined sharply. By the 1970s only two successful durable factions remained active (Wallace in Alabama and Faubus in Arkansas), and neither of them survived the decade.

Control of the Office of Governor

The South's successful durable factions differed considerably in their ability to control the office of governor. Table 5.5, which ranks the 19 factions according to the total number of years in which each held the governorship, clearly indicates the extraordinary achievement of the Byrd faction. Beginning with the victory of Harry Byrd, Sr., in 1925, the Byrd organization won 11 consecutive campaigns for governor during Byrd's lifetime, thus controlling the Virginia governorship for 44 unbroken years.

No other Democratic faction even remotely approached the Byrd organization's record of political domination. At a less exalted level, four successful durable factions (O. Max Gardner's "Shelby Dynasty" and Furnifold M. Simmons' machine in North Carolina, the Huey and Earl Long faction in Louisiana, and Theodore Bilbo's faction in Mississippi)[8] managed to win the governorship of their states for periods of approximately 20 years. Defeated only twice, the Shelby Dynasty was the only successful durable faction aside from the Byrd organization sufficiently cohesive and effective to hold the office of governor for 20 consecutive years. Though it was active for nearly as many years as its successor, the Simmons faction failed to control the North Carolina governorship with the thoroughness of the Shelby Dynasty. The Long organization structured Louisiana politics around its personalities and programs for roughly 35 years, but the Longs lost as many gubernatorial campaigns as they won and were unable to maintain consecutive control of the governorship for more than 12 years.

A third set of successful durable factions controlled the office of governor for more than 10 but less than 20 years. The leading factions in this category were the Tennessee organizations headed by Frank Clement and E. H. Crump, both of which held the governorship for 18 consecutive years. Clement and

TABLE 5.5
CONTROL OF SOUTHERN GOVERNORSHIPS BY SUCCESSFUL DURABLE FACTIONS (1920–1980[a])

Faction[b]	State	Active Period[c]	Total Years Controlled	Years of Longest Consecutive Control	Total Campaigns Attempted	Total Campaigns Won	% of Campaigns Won
Byrd	Virginia	1925-65	44	44	11	11	100
Gardner	North Carolina	1920-52	22	20	8	6	75
Simmons	North Carolina	1900-28	20	12	8	5	63
Long	Louisiana	1924-59	20	12	10	5	50
Bilbo	Mississippi	1915-43	20	8	8	5	63
Clement	Tennessee	1952-66	18	18	5	5	100
Crump	Tennessee	1926-48	18	18	12	9	75
Talmadge	Georgia	1932-54	16	10	9	7	78
Wallace	Alabama	1958-74	15	8	5	4	80
Faubus	Arkansas	1954-74	12	12	10	6	60
Graves	Alabama	1922-42	12	4	6	3	50
Peay	Tennessee	1918-30	10	10	6	5	83
Davis	Louisiana	1944-71	8	4	3	2	67
Johnston	South Carolina	1930-42	8	4	3	2	67
White	Mississippi	1931-55	8	4	4	2	50
Folsom	Alabama	1942-62	8	4	5	2	40
Johnson	Mississippi	1931-63	8	4	8	2	25
Ferguson	Texas	1914-40	7	3	11	4	36
Browning	Tennessee	1936-54	6	4	8	3	38

[a]In the case of the Simmons, Bilbo, Peay, and Ferguson factions, which made their first appearance in gubernatorial politics prior to 1920, data include the pre-1920 campaigns.

[b]Factions are ranked (highest to lowest) according to the total number of years in which the faction controlled the governorship. Ties are broken by considering the years of longest consecutive control of the governorship and, where necessary, the percentage of gubernatorial campaigns won.

[c]Reports the years of the faction's first and last appearances in Democratic first primaries for governor.

Source: Compiled by the authors.

Crump's factions differed primarily in the degree of their political success. While the Clement faction was undefeated in its five gubernatorial campaigns, Crump's organization was unsuccessful at the beginning and at the conclusion of its period of activity. The father and son faction of Eugene and Herman Talmadge in Georgia, George Wallace's organization in Alabama, the Orval Faubus clique in Arkansas, and Austin Peay's faction in Tennessee all won impressive consecutive victories and dominated the governorship in their states for briefer periods.

The final group in Table 5.5 consists of seven factions whose political success was more limited. Factions led by Jimmie Davis in Louisiana, Olin Johnston in South Carolina, and Hugh White in Mississippi all won more campaigns than they lost, yet they held the governorship for less than ten years and were unable to control the office for more than four years at a time. In contrast to the other 15 successful durable factions, the organizations of James Folsom in Alabama, Paul Johnson, Sr., and Paul Johnson, Jr., in Mississippi, James and Miriam Ferguson in Texas, and Gordon Browning in Tennessee were defeated more often than they were victorious.

Levels of Statewide Support

While comparisons of the length of factional control and the rate of factional victories provide considerable insight into the significance or insignificance of particular successful durable factions, it is also important to examine the proportion of the total primary vote obtained by each faction. What levels of statewide support were achieved by successful durable factions? A comparison of the median percentage of the vote won by the factions in contested first primaries for governor indicates that successful durable factions were generally unable to win reliable majorities of the first primary vote. The uniqueness of the Byrd organization is again apparent. Byrd candidates secured a median primary vote of 68 percent, a showing that was considerably stronger than the performance of the Crump faction (52.5 percent), the only other faction with a median exceeding 50 percent. Although part of the explanation for the impressive showing of Byrd and Crump candidates undoubtedly lies in the use of single primaries rather than dual primaries in Virginia (until 1952) and Tennessee,[9] we believe that a more important explanation for the persistent majorities won by these factions is that chief executives in Virginia and Tennessee possessed more resources with which to build and maintain their organizations than did governors in other southern states.

Median votes in the 40-49 percent range, magnitudes denoting substantial continuity of popular favor, were achieved by five highly successful factions (Clement, Peay, Talmadge, Gardner, and Wallace) and by two less successful factions (Long and Browning). Slightly more than half of the successful durable factions had medians of less than 40 percent, indicating relatively weak and inconsistent statewide support. Factions led by the Johnsons, Folsom, and Davis displayed the least degree of political strength, failing on the average to draw votes from as few as three out of every ten participants in the primaries.

Since comparisons based on measures of central tendencies may be misleading if the vote for successful durable factions has fluctuated widely over the life of the faction, and since it is possible that many of the factions may have experienced high levels of support for short periods of time, the level of factional strength requires more systematic investigation. To provide a comprehensive visual perspective on the strength of the factions over time, Figure 5.1 charts the percentage of the first primary vote received by the candidate of each successful durable faction against the proportion of the vote won by the strongest opponent of the durable faction in a given primary.

Figure 5.1 demonstrates that very few of the successful durable factions were sufficiently strong to win outright majorities of the first primary vote on a fairly regular basis. Only four factions achieved three or more first primary majorities.[10] Candidates awarded "the nod" by the hierarchy of the Byrd organization generally obtained between three-fifths and seven-eighths of the vote cast by Virginia's minute electorate, and only an uncharacteristic split within the Byrd faction in 1949 prevented it from winning consecutive majorities from 1925 through 1961.[11] (The Byrd candidate was unopposed in 1965.)

Relatively high levels of statewide support were also generated by the Crump, Faubus, and Long factions, although in each case the period of sustained majority support was shorter than that achieved by the Byrd faction. By making (in 1936) and breaking (in 1938) the governorship of Gordon Browning, E. H. Crump conclusively demonstrated to Tennessee politicians the leverage of the Memphis vote. Substantial majorities were secured by the Crump faction for its gubernatorial candidates in seven consecutive primaries between 1934 and 1946, a feat of persistent majority support exceeded only by the Byrd organization. Once defeated in 1948, however, the Crump faction never returned to power, and Crump's death in 1954 effectively terminated the organization.

Both the Byrd and Crump factions achieved their high levels of voter support without relying upon "demagogic qualities of personalities that attract voter-attention."[12] The rise and decline of the Faubus faction in Arkansas illustrates limitations probably inherent in factions that are constructed essentially around the leadership of a spectacular politician. Running in a state with a well-established tradition of limiting its governors to two consecutive two-year terms,[13] Faubus was elected to six consecutive terms from 1954 through 1964. Moreover, Faubus's last five nominations were accomplished with majorities of the first primary vote, a remarkable demonstration of sustained popularity. Unquestionably the event that solidified Faubus's standing among a majority of white voters was the governor's conspicuous and protracted hostility in 1957 to court-ordered public school desegregation in Little Rock.[14] Yet like many other flamboyant southern governors, Faubus was unable to transfer his personal

FIGURE 5.1
PERCENT OF STATEWIDE VOTE WON IN DEMOCRATIC FIRST PRIMARIES
(By Candidate of Successful Durable Faction and Strongest Opponent[a])

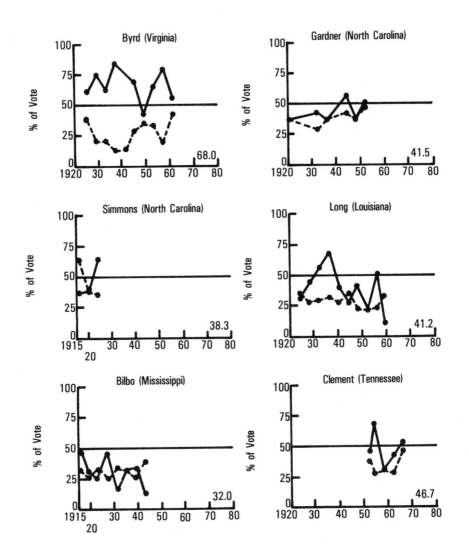

Figure 5.1 (Continued)

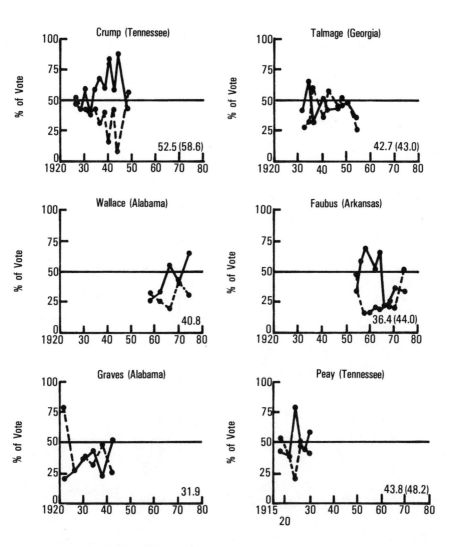

111

Figure 5.1 (Continued)

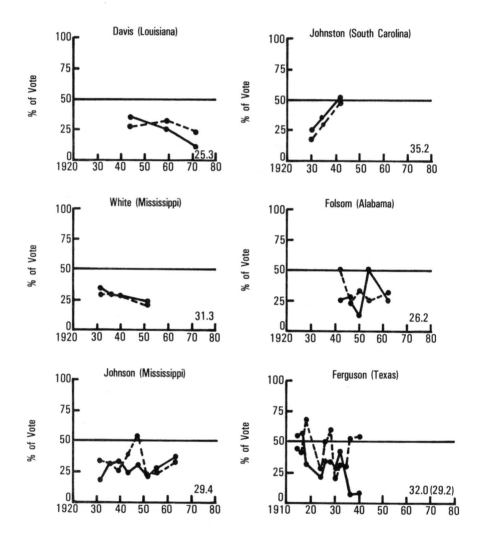

Figure 5.1 (Continued)

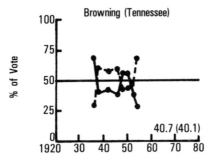

Key: Vote for candidate of successful durable faction = — ; vote for strongest opponent = - - - .

[a]The figure in the lower right-hand corner is the median percentage of the total vote won by the successful durable faction. For states with a two-year term of office for governor, the first percentage excludes and the second percentage includes the results of campaigns in which an incumbent governor sought a second two-year term.

Source: Compiled by the authors.

political strength to a designated successor. With Faubus's retirement his faction began to deteriorate, and not even the reappearance of Faubus himself as a candidate in 1970 and 1974 enabled his faction to recapture the governorship.

Huey Long's faction, the final successful durable faction that received a majority of the first primary vote on at least three occasions, won steadily increasing proportions of the first primary vote in Louisiana from 1924 through 1936, largely on the basis of a commanding personality, innovative programs, a superior organization, and the development of tangible means to reward friends and punish enemies.[15] Long's assassination in 1935, and corruption of monumental proportions associated with the administration of Long candidate Richard Leche severely damaged both the organization and its voter base, and from 1940 onward the popularity of the Long faction in first primaries was largely dependent upon Earl Long's eligibility as a candidate.

Further exploration of the charts shows that five additional factions achieved an intermediate level of statewide support by virtue of winning first primary majorities on two occasions. Although the Gardner faction in North Carolina supplied every governor elected from 1928 through 1944, the Shelby Dynasty typically encountered vigorous opposition[16] and managed to win majorities in contested primaries only in 1944 and 1952. (O. Max Gardner, the founder of the faction, was unopposed for the Democratic nomination in 1928.) In Tennessee, Frank Clement's faction was also highly successful, but it too failed to secure persistent majorities. Unlike the Crump faction in its heyday, the Clement faction won more nominations with pluralities than it did with majorities. A comparatively close bifactional cleavage prevailed in Georgia between the Talmadges and the anti-Talmadges. Although the county unit system virtually insured Talmadge victories, the Talmadge organization was never able to win consecutive landslide majorities in the manner of the Byrd, Crump, and Faubus factions. Despite George Wallace's preeminent position in Alabama politics, from his initial election as governor in 1962 until his retirement from office in 1979, the Wallace faction was supported by a majority of the first primary voters only in 1966 (when Wallace ran his wife) and in 1974 (when Wallace was eligible to run as an incumbent). Gordon Browning, winner of the 1936 Democratic nomination in Tennessee by virtue of Crump support, spent the next decade fighting the Crump organization. Browning's persistence was ultimately rewarded with majority support in 1948, but scandals in his administration contributed to the emergence of the Crump faction in 1952 as the new dominant Democratic faction in Tennessee gubernatorial politics.

None of the remaining successful durable factions were able to obtain an impressive level of popular support in first primary campaigns. Organizations led by Simmons, Bilbo, Graves, Peay, Johnston, Folsom, and Ferguson won majority support once and only once during their periods of activity in gubernatorial campaigns, and first primary majorities were beyond the capabilities of the Davis, White, and Johnson factions.

Gubernatorial Resources and Factional Domination

Between 1920 and 1980 only a small number of southern Democratic factions were sufficiently successful over an extended period of time to warrant designation as an "in" faction. Each of the political organizations headed by Byrd, Crump, Gardner, and Clement dominated the office of governor for periods exceeding the equivalent of four consecutive four-year terms. Putting aside the personalities and political skills of the leaders of these factions, what accounts for political success of this duration?

Two complementary explanations appear in *Southern Politics*. In analyzing the "tightly organized majority faction(s) within the Democratic party" that existed in Virginia, North Carolina, and Tennessee, Key argued that "In all three states Republican opposition contributes to the creation of one tightly organized Democratic faction."[17] Key's elaboration of the relationship between Republicanism and Democratic unity in North Carolina pertains as well to the dynamics of Tennessee and Virginia politics:

> The Republican contribution to Democratic discipline is plain. In those counties in which Democrats are in a minority, or must fight desperately to win local offices, leaders look to the state for aid and succor. Faced by a common threat they appreciate the necessity for concerted action under strong state leadership, and the result is a relatively cohesive state organization. It is in the counties with greatest Republican strength that the Simmons machine and its successor, the Shelby organization, found their most intense support.[18]

While agreeing with Key's generalization that "A minority locally is always far more susceptible to central control than is the local majority, which can maintain itself on the spoils of office,"[19] we suggest that Key's argument is limited in that it does not account for the success of durable factions in counties where Republicans were a distinct minority. Consistent grassroots support for the Byrd and Clement factions was by no means limited to the mountain areas of Virginia and Tennessee where Republicans were concentrated.[20]

A second, and, in our view, more significant explanation for the consecutive success of the Byrd, Gardner, Crump, and Clement factions may also be derived from Key's work. Although he neglected the topic in his most explicit appraisal of "majority" factions, in the chapters that dealt with specific states Key noted that formal powers of the governor could be used to enhance the continued political success of particular factions.[21]

Building on Key's insights, we contend that a more general explanation for the persistent victories achieved by certain successful durable factions may be found through a comparison of gubernatorial resources relevant to the development and preservation of a political organization. In the absence of complete and assessable data, we shall consider only the relationship between the appointive powers of the governor, certainly a critical resource for any politician ambitious to construct a stable organization, and the number of years in which successful durable factions maintained unbroken control of the governorship.[22]

Clearly isolated in Figure 5.2 from other successful durable factions are the Byrd, Crump, and Clement factions. Operating in states in which the governor's powers of appointment were demonstrably stronger than in other southern states, these factions retained consecutive control of the governorship for more than 15 years. By comprehensively reorganizing their executive branches in the 1920s, the states of Tennessee and Virginia created vastly expanded appointment opportunities for their chief executives.[23] In Tennessee the strengthening of the governorship preceded the rise of the Crump faction,[24] while in Virginia Governor Harry Byrd, Sr., as the principal advocate of executive reorganization, was superbly positioned to use his enhanced powers to consolidate and advance his organization.

If the history of the Byrd, Crump, and Clement factions implies that broad appointive powers — which we are essentially employing as a surrogate for a wider array of gubernatorial resources not easily measured — facilitated continued control of the governorship, the Gardner faction appears to be a deviant case. Although the appointive powers of the North Carolina governor were less extensive than those available to chief executives in Tennessee and Virginia, the founder of the Shelby Dynasty was acutely conscious of the benefits of gubernatorial resources. As governor, O. Max Gardner advocated and instituted a "program of centralization" designed to place "more power and responsibility . . . in the hands of the governor."[25] Over a period of time "the elective and appointive offices of the state administration," in particular the

FIGURE 5.2
APPOINTIVE POWERS OF SOUTHERN GOVERNORS
AND LENGTH OF CONSECUTIVE CONTROL OF GOVERNORSHIP
(By Successful Durable Democratic Factions, 1920-1980)

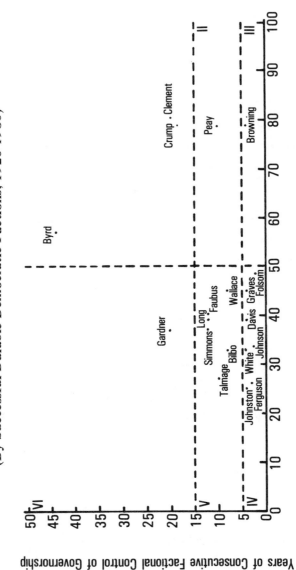

Index of Appointive Powers of the Governor

Index of governor's appointive powers constructed from data in Joseph A. Schlesinger, "The Politics of the Executive," in *Politics in the American States*, eds. Herbert Jacob and Kenneth N. Vines (Boston: Little, Brown, 1965), pp. 222-224.

"highway and revenue departments in their political activity and significance," became the key to the perpetual success of the Gardner organization.[26]

Figure 5.2 strongly indicates that sustained factional control of the governorship was related to the magnitude of the governor's powers of appointment. In most southern states the governor's power to appoint was not extensive, thus depriving governors of a significant resource for faction-building. However, in six instances (see cell V of Figure 5.2) successful durable factions that existed in an environment of weak appointive powers were able to achieve an intermediate degree of consecutive control — the equivalent of two to three consecutive four-year terms — of the governorship. The most intriguing aspect of the factions located in cell V is that five of them (Wallace, Faubus, Long, Talmadge, and Bilbo) would easily qualify for any short list of southern demagogues. Even without substantial powers of appointment, extraordinarily flamboyant personalities could occasionally dominate the politics of their states for a decade or so.

Under what circumstances, then, were successful durable Democratic factions likely to control political activity in a state for relatively extended periods of time? As Key had emphasized, states with significant traditions of mountain Republicanism produced all the factions that held the governorship for longer than 15 consecutive years. The foundations of repeated victories for the most durable of the successful durable factions lay in uniting extensive powers of gubernatorial appointment and patronage with the loyalty of Democrats residing in Republican counties. Apart from Virginia, Tennessee, and (by a narrow margin) North Carolina, one or both of these conditions did not exist in the other eight states.

CONCLUSIONS

Just as political scientists have usefully distinguished the study of parties from the study of party systems,[27] it is important for students of intraparty politics to examine, through comparative methods, factions as well as factional systems. American factional systems cannot be said to have been analyzed exhaustively in recent decades, but even less attention has been given to the comparative analysis of factions in state politics. We have sought to remedy this imbalance by creating a typology of factions grounded on criteria of durability and success. In principle this analytical framework could be applied to any state or collection of states in which nominations are determined through direct primaries.

When all factions active in southern Democratic primaries for governor are classified according to this typology and the share of nominations won by each type of faction is calculated, the findings for 1920-1949 point far less to the regional predominance of short-lived factions — results that would be anticipated from Key's interpretation of southern intraparty politics as a struggle characterized by "factional fluidity and discontinuity"[28] — than to the significance of a small number of successful durable factions. These successful durable factions, operating in the absence of genuine interparty competition, supplied an element of continuity to one-party politics. In numerous unifactional, bifactional, and multifactional settings successful durable factions functioned as points of positive or negative reference for those voters who remembered past campaigns.

Although the successful durable faction served to structure considerations of past performance into intraparty politics, we do not wish to imply that successful durable factions were effective substitutes for political parties. If the life of major American parties after the Civil War must be measured in generations, most successful durable factions stayed active in gubernatorial politics for no longer than two to three decades. Similarly, many of the successful durable factions experienced considerable difficulty in winning high levels of voter support over a series of elections. An analysis of elite-mass linkages, omitted here because of space limitations, reveals that successful durable factions typically constructed linkages to county electorates that were fundamentally narrow and transitory rather than extensive and stable.[29] Highly inferior to party in all these respects, the successful durable faction nonetheless remains important as an alternative to an intraparty politics based completely on transient factions.

NOTES

This chapter is a revised version of "Durable Democratic Factions in Southern Politics," a paper presented at the 1980 Citadel Symposium on Southern Politics. We acknowledge the helpful comments of Frank Belloni and Anne H. Hopkins at the symposium. A great deal of the archival research required to trace the history of factions was undertaken at the Library of Congress while Earl Black was a fellow of the Woodrow Wilson International Center for Scholars, and he wishes to express his gratitude to the Wilson Center for its generous support. We appreciate the efforts of Robert A. Kahn, Bruce Arbitblit, and Arlon Kemple, who assisted particular sections of the work.

1. V. O. Key, Jr., *Southern Politics in State and Nation* (New York: Knopf, 1949), p. 16.

2. For examples see, Key, *Southern Politics*, pp. 16-18, 299-302; Donald R. Matthews and James W. Prothro, *Negroes and the New Southern Politics* (New York: Harcourt, Brace & World, 1966), pp. 158-160; Malcolm E. Jewell and David M. Olson, *American State Political Parties and Elections* (Homewood, Ill.: Dorsey Press, 1978), pp. 106-118, 166-173; and Bradley C. Canon, "Factionalism in the South: A Test of Theory and a Revisitation of V. O. Key," *American Journal of Political Science* 22 (November 1978): 833-834.

3. Key, *Southern Politics*, p. 16.

4. Key, *Southern Politics*, p. 302.

5. While the names of all candidates who won at least five percent of the vote in a Democratic primary for governor in the South are available in *Guide to U.S. Elections* (Washington: Congressional Quarterly, 1975), pp. 897-908, a careful review of each primary (N = 175) is required before politicians can be assigned to the proper type of faction. We endeavored to follow each primary through two major newspapers, although in many instances, especially in the early decades covered by the study, only a single newspaper

was available. The following newspapers were used: Birmingham *Age-Herald*, Birmingham *News*, and Montgomery *Advertiser* (Alabama); Little Rock *Arkansas Gazette* and Memphis *Commercial Appeal* (Arkansas); Jacksonville *Times-Union*, Miami *Herald*, Tampa *Tribune*, and St. Petersburg *Times* (Florida); Atlanta *Constitution* and Atlanta *Journal* (Georgia); New Orleans *Times-Picayune* and New Orleans *States* (Louisiana); New Orleans *Times-Picayune* and Jackson *Clarion-Ledger* (Mississippi); Raleigh *News and Observer* and Charlotte *Observer* (North Carolina); Columbia *State* and Charleston *News and Courier* (South Carolina); Memphis *Commercial Appeal*, Nashville *Banner*, and Nashville *Tennessean* (Tennessee); Dallas *News* and Houston *Post* (Texas); and Richmond *Times-Dispatch* and Washington *Post* (Virginia).

Information gleaned from contemporary press reports was augmented by the secondary literature on the politics of each state. We did not place candidates in durable factions unless there was reasonably clear and consistent evidence in the public record to the effect that "politician X is the candidate of the Y faction" in a specific campaign. For a list of candidates who represented the successful durable factions, see Black and Black, "Durable Democratic Factions," Appendix 1.

6. Key, *Southern Politics*, p. 16.

7. J. Harvie Wilkinson III, *Harry Byrd and the Changing Face of Virginia Politics, 1945-66* (Charlottesville: University Press of Virginia, 1966); Allan P. Sindler, *Huey Long's Louisiana* (Baltimore: Johns Hopkins Press, 1956); and Perry H. Howard, *Political Tendencies in Louisiana* (Baton Rouge: Louisiana State University Press, 1971).

8. A caveat concerning the political success of the Bilbo organization should be expressed. Although candidates actively supported by Bilbo won the Democratic nomination for governor on five occasions (Bilbo himself in 1915 and 1927, Lee Russell in 1919, Hugh White in 1935, and Paul Johnson, Sr., in 1939), the latter two winners headed successful durable factions in their own right and were less clearly part of the Bilbo group than the politicians who represented the Byrd, Gardner, Simmons, and Long factions.

9. On the importance of single versus dual primaries, see Canon, "Factionalism in the South."

10. In the following grouping of factions we shall exclude, as unrepresentative of the actual strength of particular successful durable factions, majorities that were won by incumbent governors who were seeking a second two-year term. Arkansas, Texas, Tennessee, Georgia, and South Carolina used a two-year term during all or part of this period.

11. Larry Sabato, *The Democratic Primary in Virginia: Tantamount to Election No Longer* (Charlottesville: University Press of Virginia, 1977), pp. 61-62; and Wilkinson, *Harry Byrd*, pp. 92-98.

12. Key, *Southern Politics*, p. 304. Crump himself, though never a candidate for governor, enjoyed quarreling with his enemies through pungent full-page newspaper advertisements. For samples of Crump's attacks, see the Memphis *Commercial Appeal*, July 31, 1932; July 29, 1934; July 22, 1942; and July 21, 1948.

13. Key, *Southern Politics*, p. 184.

14. Thomas F. Pettigrew and Ernest Q. Campbell, "Faubus and Segregation: An Analysis of Arkansas Voting," *Public Opinion Quarterly* 24 (Fall 1960): 436-447; and Earl Black, *Southern Governors and Civil Rights* (Cambridge: Harvard University Press), pp. 99-105, 174-177.

15. T. Harry Williams, *Huey Long* (New York: Knopf, 1969); and Sindler, *Huey Long's Louisiana*, pp. 45-116.

16. Elmer L. Puryear, *Democratic Party Dissension in North Carolina, 1928-1936* (Chapel Hill: University of North Carolina Press, 1962).

17. Key, *Southern Politics*, pp. 299-300.

18. Key, *Southern Politics*, p. 223.

19. Key, *Southern Politics*, p. 65. See also pp. 66-67, 223-228.

20. For a comparative analysis of the voter bases of the Byrd and Clement factions, see Black and Black, "Durable Democratic Factions in Southern Politics," (paper presented at the second Citadel Symposium on Southern Politics, Charleston, South Carolina, March, 1980), pp. 21-23, Table 8, and Figures 5 and 6.

21. Key, *Southern Politics*, pp. 19-22, 67-68, 213, and 299-300.

22. In the absence of comparative data on the appointive powers of American governors for the entire period under consideration, we have used data presented by Schlesinger in the first edition of Jacob and Vines's *Politics in the American States* as a reasonable approximation of gubernatorial appointive powers at roughly the mid-point of our study. See Joseph A. Schlesinger, "The Politics of the Executive," *Politics in the American States*, eds. Herbert Jacob and Kenneth N. Vines (Boston: Little, Brown, 1965), pp. 222-224.

23. A. E. Buck, *The Reorganization of State Governments in the United States* (New York: Columbia University Press, 1938), pp. 219-232, 241-246; Leslie Lipson, *The American Governor from Figurehead to Leader* (Chicago: University of Chicago Press, 1939), pp. 101-102; Allen W. Moger, *Virginia: Bourbonism to Byrd, 1870-1925* (Charlottesville: University Press of Virginia, 1968), pp. 339-344; and David D. Lee, *Tennessee in Turmoil: Politics in the Volunteer State, 1920-1932* (Memphis: Memphis State University Press, 1979), pp. 38-44, 107-109, 150-154.

24. See generally, Lee, *Tennessee in Turmoil*.

25. Puryear, *Democratic Party Dissension*, p. 231.

26. Key, *Southern Politics*, p. 213.

27. See, for example, Giovanni Sartori, *Parties and Party Systems* (Cambridge: Cambridge University Press, 1976).

28. Key, *Southern Politics*, p. 305.

29. Black and Black, "Durable Democratic Factions," pp. 10-24.

6

THE GROWTH OF CONTESTED REPUBLICAN PRIMARIES IN THE AMERICAN SOUTH, 1960-1980

Merle Black and Earl Black

Few changes in recent southern politics have been more significant than the resuscitation of the Republican party. The reappearance of the South's minority party as an active challenger and frequent victor in presidential, gubernatorial, and congressional elections has stimulated an extensive scholarly literature, most of which has dealt with the measurement of competition between Democrats and Republicans. Whether aggregate data have been used to assess levels of support for Republican candidates or to explain the Republican vote,[1] or whether survey research has been employed to estimate the proportion of the voting age population identifying with the minority party, possessing favorable images, or supporting particular candidates,[2] a recurring theme has been the relative strength of the region's minority party or its candidates. This theoretical interest in patterns of interparty competition has properly guided initial research about modern southern Republicanism.

Recently, however, some observers of the southern GOP have begun to give systematic attention to patterns of elite competition within the various state parties or to emerging differences among the southern states in the relative size of Republican primary electorates.[3] The purpose of this chapter is to explore further one aspect of minority party development in the region; that is, the use of primary elections to nominate Republican gubernatorial candidates.

This chapter is a revised and expanded version of two earlier papers by the authors, "Party Institutionalization in the American South: The Growth of Contested Republican Primaries," presented at the 1973 Annual Meeting of the Southern Political Science Association, and "Republican Party Development in the South: The Rise of the Contested Primary," *Social Science Quarterly*, 57 (December 1976), 566-578. We wish to thank Arlon Kemple for his assistance in research.

The rise of the contested Republican primary potentially represents an important alteration in the institutional structure of southern electoral politics. During most of the twentieth century Republican parties in the South either failed to challenge Democratic candidates for governor or waged only token campaigns. In the few instances of genuine interparty competition, Republican candidates were typically selected by state party conventions or chosen in essentially uncontested primaries that attracted few voters.[4] An example of traditional candidate selection was the recruitment of a relatively unknown college professor, John Tower, as the Republican nominee in a 1960 senatorial election in Texas. " 'I'll tell you honestly,' Tower says, 'there wasn't much of a struggle to get that nomination; the party felt a moral obligation to run a candidate against the Democratic Majority Leader, and after others had refused to run, they came to me and said, "You can articulate the party philosophy; you do it." ' "[5] Although Republican primaries characterized by pronounced elite competition *and* by high levels of voter turnout are still far from the norm in the South, in recent years competition for Republican gubernatorial nominations has intensified and, in some states, voter participation in Republican primaries has increased.

Underlying our descriptive analysis of the rise of the Republican primary is an issue of theoretical importance in American party politics. What are the consequences (if any) of vigorous interparty competition for the development of primary elections within a minority party? Using data collected for all Republican primaries and general elections for governor held in the 11 states of the South between 1960 and 1980,[6] we shall be particularly concerned with exploring the association between interparty competition and the degree of intraparty competition.

Our comparative analysis will identify three states, Florida, North Carolina, and Tennessee, as the only settings in which significant internal conflict and a sizeable expansion of the primary electorate have occurred. We shall then examine Republican primary politics in these states in more detail, guided by two main questions. First, as more voters have begun to participate in the Republican primaries, what has been the impact upon the traditional regional and demographic bases of grassroots Republican support? At one extreme, a minority party might expand its supporters by mobilizing additional voters within its original centers of strength; alternatively, a state political organization might enlarge its ranks by attracting participants from areas which provided only minimal support in the past. Empirically, most cases probably combine both patterns of party growth. We shall describe persistence and change in the demographic and regional distribution of Republican primary participants in three key southern states from 1960 to 1980.

The second major question concerns competition among Republican activists for the gubernatorial nomination in Florida, North Carolina, and Tennessee. Over the past two decades, what patterns of elite conflict have evolved among Republican aspirants for the office of governor? On the basis of the number of candidates and their share of the Republican primary vote, what have been the trends in these key states in Republican factionalism?

INTERPARTY COMPETITION AND THE RISE OF CONTESTED REPUBLICAN PRIMARIES

Our examination of the Republican primary begins with a theme introduced by Turner and developed most extensively by Key.[7] Particularly in his analysis of party competition in the American states, Key directed attention to the "bipartisan framework of intraparty politics."[8] Though his argument is subtle and qualified, Key emphasized a positive association between the competitive status of a minority party in relation to its majority party opposition and the tendency of the minority party to experience internal conflict over its nominations. As the nominating process within the minority party becomes less transparently a search for "some willing soul to make the sacrifice in the general election" and more an effort to recruit a candidate with a fighting chance to defeat the nominee of the majority party, competition for the minority party's nomination is likely to increase.[9] But if Key hypothesized a "sharper and more persistent factionalism as party strength increases," he also recognized exceptions to the central tendency of factional conflict.[10] Increases in minority party competitiveness in general elections might encourage party leaders of the minority party to suppress factional cleavages in order to conserve party resources for the subsequent general election.[11] Consequently, as the vote given to the minority party in general elections rises, a larger proportion of contested minority party primaries should be anticipated, but intense factional competition should not be expected in all primaries.

To determine whether or not Key's hypothesis applies to Republican parties in the South, it is necessary to classify Republican gubernatorial campaigns according to the level of interparty competition, as measured by the Republican vote in general elections, and according to the level of intraparty competition, as measured by the degree of conflict over party nominations. An explanation of each classification is needed before the relationship between interparty and intraparty competition can be considered.

Levels of Interparty Competition

A familiar indicator of interparty competition is the percentage of the general election vote polled by a political party, usually averaged over a number of elections. Because this study is limited to a fairly brief period of time, and because some state parties have become much more competitive within the period, individual elections rather than state averages will be the units of analysis. To convert the data to a manageable form, we shall distinguish several "levels" of interparty competition. Key suggested five electoral settings along a continuum ranging from "Strong Republican" to "Strong Democratic," but did not furnish explicit criteria to operationalize each category.[12] More recently, Olson has proposed a typology in which the percentage cutoffs for levels of competition are more explicit.[13] The categories defined below are restatements of distinctions made previously by Key or Olson, though in some instances their terminology has been modified.

Beginning with the least competitive situation for Republicans, Olson has suggested the phrase "electorally quiescent minority" to denote parties which either fail to contest elections or conduct token campaigns.[14] In this analysis any general election in which the Republican party does not offer a candidate or in which the Republican nominee receives less than 20 percent of the general election vote is classified as *quiescent*. General elections in which the Republican candidate draws between 20.0 and 44.9 percent of the vote are considered *aspiring*.[15] A *competitive* general election occurs when the Republican nominee receives more than 45 percent but less than 55 percent of the vote. Following Key's practice, it seems useful to differentiate competitive campaigns in terms of the outcome of the election.[16] Accordingly, elections in which the Republican candidate obtains at least 45 percent but less than 50 percent are treated as *challenging*, and campaigns in which the Republican nominee receives between 50.0 and 54.9 percent are described as *leaning* Republican. Finally, the Republican party is considered *dominant* in terms of interparty competition when its candidates win a minimum of 55 percent of the vote.[17] Finer distinctions could be made about the degree of Republican domination, but a single cutting point should suffice for southern Republican parties in the immediate future.

Percentage distributions of the above categories for the 68 gubernatorial general elections waged across the South between 1960 and 1980 are presented in Table 6.1. Republican parties were quiescent in approximately one-fifth of the campaigns, reached the level of aspiration in half of the contests, and were competitive with the Democrats in slightly more than one-fourth of the elections. Landslide GOP victories for the office of governor were exceedingly rare; in each of the three instances, the opposing Democrats were in a state of advanced disarray. Republican Claude Kirk's sweeping victory over Democratic candidate Robert King High in the 1966 Florida general election was assisted substantially by the refusal of many conservative Democrats to support the nominee of their party.[18] A highly publicized atmosphere of incompetence and corruption in the administration of Democratic Governor Ray Blanton doubtless contributed to the landslide election of Republican candidate Lamar Alexander in Tennessee in 1978. And John Dalton's defeat of Democratic candidate Henry Howell in the 1979 Virginia general election was aided by the refusal of conservative and some moderate Democrats to support the liberal Democratic nominee.[19]

A more detailed analysis reveals that support for Republican gubernatorial candidates has risen since the early 1960s. Minority party nominees for governor

TABLE 6.1
COMPETITIVE STATUS OF SOUTHERN REPUBLICAN PARTIES
IN GENERAL ELECTIONS FOR GOVERNOR
(1960-1980)

Level of Interparty Competition		Deep South	Peripheral South	South[a]
Quiescent	(0-19%)	38	7	19
Aspiring	(20-44%)	42	55	50
Competitive	(45-54%)	20	31	26
Challenging	(45-49%)	12	12	12
Leaning	(50-54%)	8	19	15
Dominant	(55% or more)	0	7	4
Totals		100	100	99
Number of Cases		(26)	(42)	(68)

[a]The last column does not add to 100 percent because of rounding.

Sources: Appropriate volumes of *America Votes*, edited by Richard M. Scammon. Volumes 4 and 5 published in Pittsburgh by the University of Pittsburgh Press; volumes 6 through 13 published in Washington, D.C., by Congressional Quarterly. Results for 1980 from *Congressional Quarterly Weekly Report*, 38 (November 8, 1980).

were competitive or dominant in 36 percent of the 1970-1980 general elections, compared to 25 percent of the 1960-1969 contests. Across the entire region, though, even in the decade of the 1970s, Republican gubernatorial candidates typically did not provide genuinely competitive races against their Democratic opponents.

The data reported in Table 6.1 support Havard's conclusion that consistent Republican opposition to the Democrats is more likely in Peripheral South than in Deep South states.[20] Republicans won 11 governorships in the Peripheral South from 1960 to 1980, compared to only two victories in the Deep South. Virginia easily led the South in consistent Republican success, electing GOP governors in 1969, 1973, and 1977. Two of the victorious Republicans, Linwood Holton and John Dalton, had been longtime activists in the party, while the third winner, Mills Godwin, was a former Democratic governor — with strong ties to the old Byrd organization — who had been persuaded by GOP leaders to switch parties and lead their ticket in 1973. The victories of Republican candidates have been more episodic in other Peripheral South states. The fortunes of the Arkansas GOP in the 1960s rose and collapsed with the career of Winthrop Rockefeller, and the surprise election of Frank White (another former Democrat turned Republican) in 1980 was interpreted less as grassroots support for the Republicans than as widespread dissatisfaction with the incumbent Democratic governor.[21] In Tennessee the minority party advanced from electoral quiescence in 1966 to a victory in 1970, fell to the level of aspiration in 1974, and rebounded in 1978 with a decisive victory. Texas Republicans oscillated between aspiration and genuine competition during most of the past two decades, and finally captured the governorship in 1978 behind the candidacy of a Dallas oilman, William Clements. In the remaining Peripheral South states, Florida and North Carolina, only once during the past two decades were Republicans successful in electing a governor. The emergence of energetic and popular Democratic politicians, Reubin Askew in Florida and James Hunt in North Carolina, reduced the Republican efforts to the level of aspiration.

Generally, Republican parties in the Deep South did *not* become increasingly competitive in gubernatorial campaigns between 1960 and 1980. Republicans virtually conceded the office during the reign of George Wallace in Alabama, but the competitive weakness of the minority party was even more vividly revealed when Wallace retired from politics in 1978. Businessman Fob James, a longtime registered Republican, switched his party registration to the Democrats and eventually emerged as the majority party's candidate for governor. Against the born again Democrat, the Republican challenger could attract only one-quarter of the 1978 general election vote. Republicans also failed to become more competitive in Georgia's gubernatorial races; the GOP nominees in 1970, 1974, and 1978 drew less of the vote than had the Republican candidate in 1966. The peak of popular support for a Republican gubernatorial candidate in Mississippi occurred in 1975. Gil Carmichael's impressive performance (he drew 45.1 percent of the vote) was less an expression of support for southern Republicanism than a tribute to the Republican nominee's skills as a campaigner.[22] Four years later, Carmichael's second attempt was much weaker.

Republicans were not completely shut out from gubernatorial victories in the Deep South. After wavering between quiescence and aspiration for most of the past two decades, the GOP won the 1979 gubernatorial contest in Louisiana. Against a Democratic candidate who was repudiated by all of the other losing Democratic contenders, Republican congressman David Treen slipped into office with 50.3 percent of the vote. Republican party growth appeared to be more cyclical in South Carolina. The Republican vote steadily evolved from quiescence in 1962 (no Republican candidate), to aspiration in 1966 (stimulated by Senator Strom Thurmond's conversion to Republicanism in 1964), to challenge in 1970, and to a victory in 1974 (an outcome immensely facilitated, however, by the disqualification of the original Democratic nominee). Four years of a Republican chief executive did not result in permanent gains for the minority party. Against a unified Democratic party in 1978, the Republican nominee could gather only 38 percent of the vote, the lowest vote for the party since the 1966 gubernatorial election.

Levels of Intraparty Competition

Our second classification concerns the extent to which nominations within the minority party are the product of contested primaries. First, does the party use primaries to make its nominations? Second, how much conflict has there been within the party over primary nominations? For example, where formally contested primaries have occurred, have nominations been won by candidates who clearly dominated their opposition, or have nominations involved more balanced competition? To demonstrate the emergence of the Republican primary and to summarize patterns of intraparty competition in primaries, four levels of intraparty competition will be distinguished. The first level, *no candidate*, indicates the absence of interparty, and intraparty, competition. At the second level of competition the party nominates its candidates without conducting a party primary (for example, nomination by a state party convention) or holds an uncontested primary. A third level of intraparty competition may be described as the *unifactional primary*. Here a contested primary occurs but one candidate wins a lopsided victory. Any contested primary in which the leading candidate receives more than three-fifths of the total vote is treated as unifactional. Finally, primaries may occur in which the vote is divided more evenly between two or more candidates. *Competitive primaries* are defined as contests in which the leading candidate obtains less than three-fifths of the vote. It would be possible, of course, to divide competitive primaries into bifactional and multifactional categories, but the small number of these primaries dictates the use of a single classification at this stage of Republican development.

Across the South contested primaries produced nearly half (49 percent) of the Republican nominees for governor from 1960 to 1980 (see Table 6.2).

TABLE 6.2
LEVELS OF INTRAPARTY COMPETITION FOR REPUBLICAN NOMINATIONS FOR GOVERNOR, 1960-1980[a]
(Percent)

Level of Intraparty Competition	Deep South	Peripheral South	South
No Candidate	24	2	10
No Primary/Unopposed Primary	44	38	40
Unifactional Primary	12	41	30
Competitive Primary	20	19	19
Totals	100	100	99
Number of Cases	(25)	(42)	(67)

[a]The 1979 election in Louisiana is excluded because partisan primaries had been abolished in the state. The Deep South total is thus reduced to 25, and the total for the South becomes 67.

Sources: Appropriate volumes of *America Votes*, edited by Richard M. Scammon. Volumes 4 and 5 published in Pittsburgh by the University of Pittsburgh Press; volumes 6 through 13 published in Washington, D.C., by Congressional Quarterly. For 1980 results, *Congressional Quarterly Weekly Report*, 38 (May 10, 1980, and May 31, 1980).

However, this summary figure disguises the growth of the contested primary. Table 6.3 demonstrates that the proportion of possible Republican nominations decided by contested primaries rose from 14 percent of the 1960-63 cases to 85 percent of the 1976-80 nominations. An even more revealing indicator of structural change in the southern electoral process is the increasing percentage of "competitive" primaries, contests involving two or more serious candidates. If there were no competitive primaries in the early 1960s, during the years 1972-80 more than one-third of the Republican gubernatorial nominations involved this type of intraparty conflict. Competitive primaries have occurred twice in five states (Florida, Georgia, North Carolina, Tennessee, and South Carolina) and once in three additional states (Arkansas, Mississippi, and Texas). More and more, the Republican gubernatorial nomination has been perceived by party activists as a prize to be contested rather than a burden to be avoided.

Having summarized recent trends concerning interparty competition and intraparty competition, we can now examine the relationship between our two classifications. Table 6.4 cross-tabulates levels of intraparty competition by levels of interparty competition in the general election preceding the party's nominating activities. Consistent with Key's hypothesis, intraparty competition tends to increase (gamma = +.68) as the level of Republican general election competitiveness rises. While more than half of the competitive or dominant general elections were associated with subsequent competitive primaries, only 10 percent of the aspiring and 5 percent of the quiescent general elections were followed by competitive primaries. Respectable general election campaigns, therefore, were frequently preludes to conflict over the next gubernatorial nomination of the minority party.

A comparison of our results with the work of Echols and Ranney, who recently found no relation between an increase in interparty competition and a

TABLE 6.3
CONTESTED PRIMARIES FOR THE REPUBLICAN
GUBERNATORIAL NOMINATION IN THE SOUTH

Percent of *Possible Nominations*	*1960-63*	*1964-67*	*1968-71*	*1972-75*	*1976-80*
Contested Primaries	14	29	69	54	85
Competitive Primaries	0	7	23	39	31
Unifactional Primaries	14	21	46	15	54
Number of Cases	14	14	13	13	13

Sources: Appropriate volumes of *America Votes*, edited by Richard M. Scammon. Volumes 4 and 5 published in Pittsburgh by the University of Pittsburgh Press; volumes 6 through 13 published in Washington, D.C., by Congressional Quarterly. For 1980 results, *Congressional Quarterly Weekly Report*, 38 (May 10, 1980, and May 31, 1980).

TABLE 6.4
LEVEL OF REPUBLICAN INTRAPARTY COMPETITION FOR
GUBERNATORIAL NOMINATIONS IN THE SOUTH, 1960-80
(by Level of Interparty Competition in Preceeding
General Election; Percent)

	Previous Interparty Competition Level[a]		
Present Intraparty			
Competition Level	*Quiescent*	*Aspiring*	*Competitive/Dominant*
No Candidate	20	10	0
No Primary/Uncontested Primary	60	37	24
Unifactional Primary	15	43	24
Competitive Primary	5	10	53
Totals	100	100	101
Number of Cases	(20)	(30)	(17)
Gamma = +.68			

[a]Columns sometimes do not add to 100 percent because of rounding. Because of the small number of challenging, leaning, and dominant general elections, these categories have been collapsed into a single competitive/dominant classification.

Sources: Appropriate volumes of *America Votes*, edited by Richard M. Scammon. Volumes 4 and 5 published in Pittsburgh by the University of Pittsburgh Press; volumes 6 through 13 published in Washington, D.C., by Congressional Quarterly. For 1980 results, *Congressional Quarterly Weekly Report*, 38 (May 10, 1980; May 31, 1980; and November 8, 1980).

decrease in multifactionalism within the *majority party*, suggests that the significance of interparty competition for patterns of intraparty competition may well vary according to the historical status (majority or minority) of a given party.[23] It may simply be easier to stimulate elite conflict within a minority party than to discourage a tradition of multifactionalism within a majority party. Our findings, in contrast to those of Echols and Ranney, are clearly supportive of Key's perspective. If interparty competition has apparently failed to ameliorate a fundamental weakness — excessive intraparty competition — of the majority Democratic party in one southern state, general election competitiveness has helped to remedy a characteristic deficiency — insufficient intraparty competition — of the minority Republican parties in the South.

THE SIZE OF THE REPUBLICAN PRIMARY ELECTORATES

To this point the primaries of the Republican party have been examined solely with respect to patterns of elite competition. Attention also needs to be given to the size of the minority party's primary electorate. Only if Republican gubernatorial primaries regularly attract a substantial fraction of the southern electorate can they be judged a truly integral part of the region's electoral process. As a convenient measure of mass participation in the nominating procedures of the minority party, we shall follow Key in using the ratio of the total Republican primary votes to total Democratic primary votes.[24] Though such an indicator usually understates GOP electoral strength,[25] it can be used to identify the southern states that have experienced the largest and most durable changes in the size of Republican primary electorates.

In a region historically characterized by adherence to the Democratic party in contests for state and local offices, the task of persuading voters to participate in Republican party primaries has been exceedingly difficult. Contested Republican and Democratic primaries for governor were held simultaneously on 32 occasions in the South between 1960 and 1980, and in the mean set of primaries the Republican vote was only 14 percent of the vote cast by Democrats, a telling illustration of continuing regional loyalty to the primaries of the majority party.

Republican primary electorates of considerable size have been limited to Florida, Tennessee, and North Carolina. Although Florida's Republican gubernatorial candidates were defeated in 1970, 1974, and 1978, the massive increase in the relative size of the Republican primary electorate between 1966 (12 percent of Democratic turnout) and 1970 (47 percent) represents a compelling display of grassroots strength by the minority party. Comparatively high turnouts in the 1970 (42 percent), 1974 (38 percent), and 1978 (34 percent) Tennessee primaries suggest the potential of the Republican party in that state. In North Carolina, Republican primary participation jumped from 8 percent of the Democratic vote in 1964 to 22 percent four years later. In succeeding primaries it has hovered around one-fifth of the total Democratic vote.

Elsewhere in the South mass participation in the GOP primary has been much less extensive. The Republican primary electorate has never exceeded 14 percent of the Democratic vote in Arkansas and Georgia, and in Texas it peaked at 9 percent in 1978. Only 11 Republicans voted for every 100 Democrats in the 1974 South Carolina primaries. Minuscule numbers of Republicans, relative to Democrats, have participated in primaries in Alabama, Mississippi, and Louisiana.[26] Simultaneously contested primaries did not occur through 1980 in Virginia.

Our survey of the entire South justifies the selection of three states — Florida, North Carolina, and Tennessee — for more intensive examination. Only in these states has the Republican party won general elections for governor, attracted an impressively large following of partisans sufficiently loyal to vote in its nominating primaries rather than those of the majority party, and also experienced severe intraparty strains. The modern Republican parties in Florida, North Carolina, and Tennessee stand in sharp distinction on all these characteristics to the "traditional" Republican parties in the South. An analysis of the changing bases of the Republican primary vote and of the vote for selected

Republican candidates should provide additional insight into contemporary southern Republicanism.

CHANGING DEMOGRAPHIC AND GEOGRAPHICAL BASES OF REPUBLICAN PRIMARY ELECTORATES

Our previous discussion has shown that Florida, Tennessee, and North Carolina rank highest in the South in the extent of mass participation in party primaries. Voting in Republican primaries has significantly increased in each of these states over the past two decades: Florida's Republican electorate rose from 89,686 in 1960 to 382,831 in 1978; GOP grassroots participation in Tennessee expanded from only 30,888 in 1958 to 268,620 in 1978; and Republican primaries in North Carolina attracted 63,815 voters in 1964, compared to 149,087 in 1980. The expansion of the Republican "party in the electorate" raises several questions for analysis. Within each of the states, where was participation traditionally concentrated? As new voters have entered the primary electorates, what have been the consequences for the "political centers of gravity" of the state Republican parties? Has the growth in grassroots Republicanism been uniform across a particular state, or has it been concentrated in particular regions, cities, or rural areas? A comparison of turnout in primary elections at different points in time should provide insight into the geographical and demographic bases of mass support for the rising minority party.

To assess the changing mass base of these southern Republican parties, a classification system is required which does justice to variation in Republican support across two dimensions, state geographical regions and size-of-place. It is well known from general election studies that Republican efforts in each state were stronger in some regions than in others. To determine whether participation in GOP primaries has been similarly unbalanced in the past and whether the parties are breaking out of their limited regional strongholds in recent primaries, we shall analyze the relative shares of the total Republican primary vote contributed by different regions within each state over time. The regional categories are taken from Havard's *The Changing Politics of the South*.[27] Florida is partitioned into North, Central, and South; Tennessee is classified as East, Middle, and West; and North Carolina is divided into East, Piedmont, and Mountain.

As the second dimension of our intrastate classification, we shall examine the distribution of the Republican primary vote according to three size-of-place categories; large metropolitan, medium urban, and rural. Large metropolitan counties consist of all Standard Metropolitan Statistical Areas (SMSAs) with a population in excess of 250,000. Medium urban counties include the remaining SMSAs and all counties with a city of 25-50,000; and the remaining counties are classified as rural.[28]

TABLE 6.5
THE CHANGING INTRASTATE SOURCES OF THE REPUBLICAN PRIMARY VOTE[a]
(Percent)

Florida

	1960 Region				1978 Region			
Size of Place	North	Central	South	Totals	North	Central	South	Totals
Large Metropolitan	2	49	28	78	4	32	28	65
Medium Urban	1	8	5	14	2	9	14	24
Rural	1	3	5	8	2	3	6	11
Totals	3	59	38	100	8	44	48	100
Number of Voters:	89,686/8.7 percent of total primaries				382,831/27.0 percent of total primaries			

Tennessee

	1958 Region				1978 Region			
Size of Place	East	Middle	West	Totals	East	Middle	West	Totals
Large Metropolitan	26	1	*	27	33	9	17	59
Medium Urban	*	*	*	0	2	1	1	4
Rural	69	3	1	73	23	8	7	37
Totals	95	4	1	100	59	17	25	100
Number of Voters:	30,888/4.3 percent of total primaries				268,620/25.5 percent of total primaries			

	1964 Region				North Carolina 1980 Region			
Size of Place	East	Piedmont	Mountain	Totals	East	Piedmont	Mountain	Totals
Large Metropolitan	*	25	*	25	*	34	*	34
Medium Urban	5	14	5	24	8	5	3	16
Rural	7	29	15	51	10	27	13	50
Totals	12	68	20	100	18	66	16	100
Number of Voters:	63,815/7.7 percent of total primaries				149,087/16.6 percent of total primaries			

[a]Because of rounding, some rows and columns may not give exact totals.

Sources: Official state election commission reports from Florida, North Carolina, and Tennessee.

This two-dimensional classification produces a nine-fold table for each of the states. To compare continuity and change in the sources of the Republican vote, Table 6.5 shows the geographical and demographic distribution of Republican primary voters in each of the states at two different points in time. In each case the most recent Republican primary (through 1980) for a state is compared with a contested Republican primary held approximately around the early 1960s.

In none of the earlier primaries did the Republicans attract as much as 10 percent of the total primary participants. Within this highly restricted electorate, participation in each state was highly skewed toward both a particular region and a specific demographic setting. In Tennessee nearly 95 percent of the primary voters came from the eastern counties; almost 70 percent of the Republican vote in North Carolina originated in the Piedmont; and in Florida around 60 percent of the Republican electorate was located in Central Florida. Demographically, almost 80 percent of Florida's Republicans lived in large metropolitan areas, whereas such settings provided only about a quarter of the Republican primary vote in Tennessee and North Carolina. In the latter states, grassroots Republicanism was primarily rural (over 70 percent in Tennessee and slightly more than 50 percent in North Carolina).

The center of political gravity for Tennessee Republicanism was a set of eastern rural counties, which provided 69 percent of the total primary vote. The stronghold of Florida Republicanism was utterly different; 49 percent of the GOP primary participants resided in large metropolitan areas of central Florida. In North Carolina, yet another pattern appeared. The party had two centers of strength; rural Piedmont counties (29 percent) and the large metropolitan counties of the Piedmont (25 percent). A perusal of the relevant tables also turns up areas of obvious Republican weakness in the early 1960s. West and Middle Tennessee, as well as North Florida, supplied marginal proportions of the Republican primary vote, and the party was relatively weak in East North Carolina. None of the Republican parties in the late 1950s or early 1960s had a genuinely statewide constituency.

A somewhat different pattern emerges when the Republican primaries of the late 1970s or 1980 are examined. In North Carolina, where the expansion of the primary electorate was less pronounced than in Florida or Tennessee, the hegemony of the Piedmont remained unbroken. However, a significant shift in the relative importance of the East and Mountain regions did occur, a development that has helped move North Carolina Republicanism to the right. In every Republican gubernatorial primary since 1968 (when a conservative Republican congressman, James Gardner of Rocky Mount, won the party nomination) the East counties have contributed a slightly larger share of the total Republican vote than did the Mountain counties. In North Carolina, the extension of grassroots Republicanism into the East has meant the addition of racially and economically conservative whites into GOP ranks. In terms of the demographic categories, metropolitan counties increased their share of Republican primary votes, but the typical Republican voter still resided in a rural county in 1980.

More substantial geographic and demographic change occurred in Tennessee. The East no longer monopolized grassroots Republicanism, and the party's gubernatorial candidates no longer tended to be individuals from small town or rural East Tennessee. Though a strong majority (59 percent) of the party's primary voters still resided in East Tennessee, the typical easterner was now more likely to reside in or around a large city (Knoxville or Chattanooga) than in a rural county. The East declined in importance as Republicanism spread through West and Middle Tennessee. While most of the new West Tennessee Republicanism was due to a GOP surge in Memphis, the Republicans also picked up strength in some of the rural and small town counties of the region. Middle Tennessee lagged behind the other two regions as a source of Republican primary votes, but its share of the GOP electorate had increased from 4 percent in 1958 to 17 percent 20 years later.

The major structural change in Tennessee Republicanism, however, was the increasing weight of voters living in large metropolitan areas of the state. Voters in the large metropolitan counties of Tennessee provided only a quarter of the Republican primary total in 1958 but furnished a sizeable majority (59 percent) of the vote in 1978. The shifting mass base of the primary electorate from small town and rural counties to the large cities was reflected in the residences of the leading candidates for the GOP gubernatorial nomination during the 1970s. None of the eventual nominees came from a large city in the East. Instead, Memphis provided Winfield Dunn in 1970, and Nashville contributed Lamar Alexander in 1974 and 1978. Thus the party sought to broaden its appeal beyond the original stomping grounds of rural, East Tennessee. A standard-bearer from a large city outside of this region could presumably help the party in general elections, while the traditional eastern vote would be expected to flow to the Republican candidate, regardless of where the candidate resided.

If Republican primary electorates in Tennessee and North Carolina were still disproportionately centered in a single region in the late 1970s, the growth of Republican primary voting in Florida reduced the importance of the original stronghold and dispersed Republican strength throughout Central and South Florida. The percentage of the Republican primary vote located in Central Florida declined from 59 percent in 1960 to 44 percent in 1978, while South Florida's share rose from 38 percent in 1960 to 48 percent in 1978. Most of Florida's Republicans (65 percent in 1978) still resided in large metropolitan areas, but the new trend was GOP growth in the counties with medium-sized cities.

Our comparisons of the Republican primary electorates over time reveal a diffusion of the minority party's grassroots supporters across the three states. In Tennessee and Florida the traditionally dominant region lost ground to the other two regions, while in North Carolina the Piedmont remained dominant and the East counties gained at the expense of the Mountain counties. In terms of the demography of the Republican vote, there were considerable differences among the states. Republicanism in North Carolina remained primarily a rural phenomenon, as its large metropolitan counties provided only a third of the primary vote. Florida Republicanism was still located essentially in large metropolitan counties, but medium urban and rural counties began to contribute larger shares of the total vote. The greatest change in the rural-urban division of the GOP vote occurred in Tennessee, where the large metropolitan counties displaced the rural areas as the main sources of Republican primary participants.

PATTERNS OF FACTIONAL COMPETITION

Enhanced prospects of success in general elections, as well as the expansion of the GOP primary electorates, underlie the rise of more vigorous intraparty electoral struggles over gubernatorial nominations. Key's analysis of the impact of electoral realignment (during and after the New Deal) upon many state Democratic parties outside of the South is relevant. If the phrase "southern Republican" is substituted for "Democratic" in the first sentence of the following quotation, the potential significance of Republican intraparty politics in the South becomes clear:

> As the cause of the Democratic party within the state becomes less hopeless its internal structure changes. Within the party competing centers of leadership arise. They may rest on a foundation neither more nor less substantial than the ambitions of political personalities for positions of leadership. They may be founded on quite real social, economic, geographic, or other cleavages within the membership of the party. They may be embodied in more or less formalized subparty organizations with long traditions and perceptibly contrasting policy colorations. As these characteristics develop they are paralleled by more frequent and more intense competition within the party among the continuing or transient centers of leadership. And, as these circumstances come about the politics of the state becomes more an intraparty politics and less an interparty politics.[29]

Indeed, each of the three "advanced" southern states experienced spirited Republican intraparty fights in the early 1970s over the gubernatorial nomination. Florida (1970) and North Carolina (1972) Republicans were sharply divided into two opposing factions, while the Tennessee GOP (1970) was fragmented into multiple contending factions. Relying mainly on the gubernatorial contests of the 1970s, we shall briefly analyze the emerging patterns of Republican factional competition in Florida, North Carolina, and Tennessee.

In Florida, Republican gubernatorial primaries in the 1960s had oscillated between contests dominated by a single candidate (1970 and 1966) and an election in which the vote was divided more evenly (1964). Traditional Florida

Republicans, whose stronghold was Pinellas County, were unable to generate a major candidate for the 1966 election, and into the leadership vacuum stepped a candidate from northern Florida — Claude Kirk of Jacksonville. Kirk easily won the primary and, taking advantage of Democratic disharmony, eventually scored a landslide general election victory. Governor Kirk's performance in office from 1966 to 1970 was rarely without controversy, even among his fellow Republicans, and the incumbent governor's bid for renomination was challenged by Jack Eckerd, a millionaire businessman from Pinellas County and a close political ally of the "father" of modern Florida Republicanism, U.S. Congressman William Cramer. Meanwhile, Cramer sought the GOP nomination for a vacant U.S. Senate seat. Joining forces with Republican Senator Edward Gurney, Kirk and Gurney talked Federal District Judge G. Harold Carswell into challenging Cramer. Carswell had been nominated by President Richard Nixon for the Supreme Court, but the nomination had been blocked in the Senate, and the Kirk-Gurney forces tried to exploit resentment over Carswell's fate to deter Cramer. Differences between the two factions were not based on ideology — all the candidates were conservatives — but were instead rooted in rival political ambitions. The resulting fights in both the gubernatorial and senatorial primaries turned into abrasive confrontations. Eventually each faction laid claim to a single nomination, Kirk for the governorship and Cramer for the Senate, but the intraparty resentments were so severe that both GOP leaders were defeated by Democratic candidates in the subsequent general election.[30]

Four years later, vivid memories of the fiasco of party disunity induced the GOP leadership to rally around the only candidate who apparently wanted the job — Jerry Thomas, a former Democratic speaker of the Florida state legislature. The big city Republican candidate from South Florida proved no competition against Rueben Askew, the popular incumbent Democrat. A pale revival of the fierce factionalism of 1970 occurred in 1978. Jack Eckerd again attempted to win the nomination, and his only opposition was Congressman Louis Frey, a former law partner of Edward Gurney.[31] The old Kirk-Gurney faction was in shreds. Gurney's political career had crashed several years earlier, and Kirk's standing among Florida Republicans was so dismal that he actually ran as a candidate for the gubernatorial nomination of the Democratic party! Vastly outspending his opponent, Eckerd scored an easy primary victory, but he subsequently lost the general election. As the decade drew to a close, bifactionalism had given way, at least temporarily, to unifactionalism, but again the party had not found the formula for victory in the gubernatorial general election.

Factionalism within the North Carolina Republican party has involved ideological differences as well as more routine conflicts of ambitious politicians. The party has been split between conservative (sometimes referred to in North Carolina as "moderate conservatives" or even "moderates") and ultraconservative wings. The "old guard" or traditional Republicans are composed of the moderate conservatives, whose leading spokesmen in gubernatorial politics have been James Holshouser (elected governor in 1972) and David Flaherty (nominated in 1976). The control of the party by this faction came under increasingly successful attack during the 1970s by a new group of outspoken ultraconservatives, whose acknowledged political leader was U.S. Senator Jesse Helms. When asked in 1973 if he were a "right-wing extremist," Helms replied that "Beauty is in the eye of the beholder."[32] The most important representatives of this faction in gubernatorial politics have been party nominees James Gardner of Rocky Mount in 1968 and I. Beverly ("Bev") Lake, Jr., of Wake County in 1980. Old-time Democrats who have left that party have sometimes felt at home in the Helms wing of the Republican party; indeed, both Helms and Lake changed their party registration to be eligible for a Republican party nomination.

The strongest head-on confrontation of the two wings in gubernatorial politics occurred in 1972. Gardner again sought the nomination, but was opposed by three other candidates, the most important of whom was Holshouser, a former state party chairman. The primaries were bitter personal and ideological confrontations. Gardner led in the first primary with a plurality of the vote, but Holshouser prevailed in the runoff election. The elections showed sharp differences in the grassroots support of the two factions. The factions split the Piedmont vote, with the right wing candidate drawing on the eastern and southern sections of the region, and the moderate conservative winning the northwestern and most of the large metropolitan counties of the region. Each candidate drew disproportionately from the remaining regions. Holshouser won most of the Mountain counties, while Gardner was the favorite of the growing number of registered Republicans in the state's East counties. The factions were almost equal in strength, and Holshouser eventually won by only 1,682 votes of a total of 138,050.

Both factions maneuvered for advantage during the next eight years, but at the end of the decade the ultraconservatives were in command. To be sure, Flaherty, a Holshouser ally, won the gubernatorial nomination in 1976 when conservatives were unable to agree on a candidate. The nomination had little value, though, because Flaherty was destroyed by the extraordinary strength of Democratic gubernatorial candidate James Hunt in the 1976 general election. A case can be made that the turning point in Republican intraparty politics came not in gubernatorial politics, but in the direct confrontation between Holshouser and Helms supporters in the 1976 Republican presidential primary. Ronald Reagan's upset victory of President Gerald Ford was due largely to the fundraising, organizing, and media work by the North Carolina Congressional Club, an organization created after the 1972 elections to pay off Helms' campaign debts. The original goal accomplished, the Congressional Club became active in other matters of state politics, including the Reagan challenge of President Ford. Reagan's victory not only shocked President Ford but was a devastating embarassment for Governor Holshouser. Unlike the Holshouser-Gardner contest four years earlier, the large metropolitan areas of the Piedmont swung behind Reagan, and the outcome signaled a shift in Republican politics toward the right wing as the dominant faction of the future.

The pervasive influence of the Congressional Club was even more evident in 1980. The organization actively recruited the party's eventual nominees for governor (Lake) and senator (John East) and provided strategic, tactical, and financial support for their campaigns. East was unopposed in the Republican primary and went on to defeat incumbent Democratic Senator Robert Morgan. Lake faced ineffectual opposition in the primary (in a demonstration of party unity, former governor Holshouser endorsed Lake), but was predictably defeated in the general election by incumbent Governor Hunt. At the end of the decade, the right wing seemed firmly in control of the state GOP, and the faction was enthusiastic about having a sympathetic friend in the White House in the 1980s.

While Republicans were elected governor in Florida and North Carolina only once during the period under review, Tennessee twice chose Republican chief executives (1970 and 1978). Intraparty politics for the GOP evolved from an extensive multifactionalism in 1970, to a quasi-bifactionalism in 1974, and finally to widespread party unity in 1978. All of the nominees have been associated with the brand of moderate Republicanism practiced by Senator Howard Baker, rather than a more conservative Republicanism.

The first seriously contested GOP gubernatorial primary in modern times occurred in 1970. The vote was split among four major candidates, and the winner was Winfield Dunn, a Memphis dentist who seized the nomination with only 33 percent of the vote. As in many Democratic primaries, voting was organized around each candidate's "friends and neighbors" base. Although Dunn came from a region of the state that provided only a quarter of the GOP primary vote, he had the advantage of being the *only* candidate from the West. His monolithic support in Memphis (he took 92 percent of the Shelby County vote), coupled with the fragmentation of the massive East Tennessee vote among three other rivals, gave Dunn a plurality.

In 1974, four candidates sought the Republican nomination, but a semblance of bifactionalism appeared as the top two candidates received 80 percent of the total vote. Though other top Republican officeholders did not officially endorse any candidate, the *Congressional Quarterly* reported overtones of intraparty rivalry between the state's two Republican senators, Howard Baker and William Brock.[33] The leading candidate of the moderate Republicans was Lamar Alexander of Nashville, who had close ties to Senator Baker and Governor Dunn. He had worked for Baker in Congress, served as Dunn's campaign manager in 1970, and subsequently worked as a Nixon administration aide in the White House. The more conservative candidate, who reportedly drew from Republicans more attuned to Brock's style of Republicanism,[34] was Nashville psychiatrist Nat Winston. Alexander won the primary with 46 percent of the vote and ran some 30,000 votes ahead of Winston, who received 34 percent. Analysis of the voting returns shows the close links between Alexander and the supporters of Senator Baker and Governor Dunn. More than half of Alexander's gross margin came from the Second Congressional District (particularly from Knoxville), the political stronghold of Baker, and another quarter of his lead was contributed by Republicans residing in Shelby County (Memphis), the home of Dunn. By contrast, Winston carried Brock's political base, the Third Congressional District (Chattanooga), by only about 3,000 votes. The general election was another story. In the aftermath of Watergate, 1974 was an inauspicious year for Republican candidates. Alexander was embarrassed and put on the defensive by his Democratic opponent, Congressman Ray Blanton, who reminded crowds of Alexander's former ties with the Nixon administration. Blanton easily won the election.

Undiscouraged by his defeat, Alexander again sought the nomination in 1978. Against a more conservative opponent who had managed Ronald Reagan's presidential primary bid in Tennessee in 1976, Alexander used his advantage in finances, name recognition, and organization to coast to victory with 87 percent of the vote. It was a very good year to be a Republican gubernatorial candidate in Tennessee. An atmosphere of corruption, malfeasance, and stupidity had settled permanently around the administration of Democratic Governor Ray Blanton. The situation deteriorated so rapidly — the scandal chiefly involved flagrant abuses of the pardoning power — that Republican and Democratic leaders joined to force Blanton to resign before his term expired, and Alexander took the oath of office a few days earlier than expected. The election of Alexander as governor augmented the political resources of the moderate wing of the Tennessee Republican party.

CONCLUSIONS

Though the small number of cases available for each state severely restricts our ability to compare the significance of the Republican primary from one state to another, several generalizations are possible. Between 1960 and 1980 Republican primaries for governor reached their fullest development in Florida, Tennessee, and North Carolina, states in which the minority party could either build upon geographic sectionalism (Tennessee and North Carolina) or capitalize upon an influx of migrants uncommitted to traditional one-party politics (Florida). Only in these three states was there at least one Republican primary characterized by intense elite competition and by relatively high voter participation. In a second cluster of states the primary has emerged but thus far has failed to elicit both intraparty competition and high turnout. Republican primaries in Arkansas, Georgia, Texas, Mississippi, and South Carolina have combined elite competition with low rates of turnout. In Alabama the Republican primary has been less developed, never passing beyond unifactionalism and marginal mass participation. When partisan primaries were abolished in Louisiana in 1975, the issues raised in this study were rendered moot for that state. Contested primaries did not appear at all in Virginia. In this rough differentiation of states Virginia emerges as the most prominent deviant case, the leading exception to the linkages previously developed between interparty competition and intraparty competition. Despite the election of three Republican governors, the Virginia party has consistently determined its nominees through state conventions.[35] Presumably the state's deferential political culture and the complexities of absorbing elements of the Byrd organization into the Republican party have contributed to the party's disinterest in primaries. It remains to be seen whether or not the ambitions of future Republican candidates can be reconciled so easily through elite negotiation and bargaining.

This paper has explored an aspect of southern Republicanism — the primary elections of the minority party — that has largely been ignored in the literature. Although the Republican primary generally has not met the criteria of robust intraparty competition and extensive mass participation that would make it a truly significant component of the southern electoral process, our overview demonstrates that, since the late 1960s, the contested primary has emerged as the typical means by which Republican parties have nominated candidates for governor. Given time and resourceful leadership, the Republican primary in some states may well come to rival the Democratic primary as an arena of electoral choice.[36] For students of southern politics one consequence of the rise of the minority party primary is clear: increasingly, a comprehensive analysis of electoral politics in the more "advanced" southern states will require attention not only to Democratic primaries and general elections, but also to the primaries of the Republican party.

NOTES

1. Donald S. Strong, *The 1952 Presidential Election in the South* (University, Ala.: Bureau of Public Administration, 1955); Donald S. Strong, *Urban Republicanism in the South* (University, Ala.: Bureau of Public Administration, 1960); Donald S. Strong, "Durable Republicanism in the South," in *Change in the Contemporary South*, ed. Alan P. Sindler (Durham, N.C.: Duke University Press, 1963), pp. 174-194; Donald S. Strong, "Further Reflections on Southern Politics," *Journal of Politics* 31 (May 1971): 239-256; Bernard Cosman, "Presidential Republicanism in the South, 1960," *Journal of Politics* 24 (May 1962): 303-322; Bernard Cosman, *Five States for Goldwater* (University, Ala.: University of Alabama Press, 1966); Bernard Cosman, "Republicanism in the South: Goldwater's Impact Upon Voting Alignments in Congressional, Gubernatorial, and Senatorial Races," *Southwestern Social Science Quarterly* 48 (June 1967): 13-23; William C. Havard, ed., *The Changing Politics of the South* (Baton Rouge: Louisiana State University Press, 1972); Louis M. Seagull, *Southern Republicanism* (Cambridge: Schenkman, 1975); Numan V. Bartley and Hugh D. Graham, *Southern Politics and the Second Reconstruction* (Baltimore: The Johns Hopkins University Press, 1975); and Kevin Phillips, *The Emerging Republican Majority* (New York: Anchor Books Edition, 1970), pp. 187-289.

2. Philip E. Converse, "A Major Political Realignment in the South?," in *Change in the Contemporary South*, ed. Alan P. Sindler (Durham, N.C.: Duke University Press, 1963), pp. 195-222; Donald R. Matthews and James W. Prothro, "The Concept of Party Image and Its Importance for the Southern Electorate," in *The Electoral Process*, eds. M. Kent Jennings and L. Harmon Zeigler (Englewood Cliffs, N.J.: Prentice-Hall, 1966), pp. 139-174; Donald R. Matthews and James W. Prothro, *Negroes and the New Southern Politics* (New York: Harcourt, Brace & World, 1966), pp. 369-404; E. M. Schreiber, "Where the Ducks

Are: Southern Strategy Versus Fourth Party," *Public Opinion Quarterly* 35 (Summer 1971): 157-167; John H. Kessell, *The Goldwater Coalition* (Indianapolis: Bobbs-Merrill, 1968), pp. 255-297; Douglas S. Gatlin, "Party Identification, Status, and Race in the South: 1952-1972," *Public Opinion Quarterly* 39 (Spring 1975): 39-51; Richard J. Trilling, *Party Image and Electoral Behavior* (New York: Wiley, 1976); Everett Carll Ladd, Jr., with Charles Hadley, *Transformations of the American Party System*, 2nd Edition (New York: W. W. Norton, 1978); Bruce Campbell, "Patterns of Change in the Partisan Loyalties of Native Southerners: 1952-1972," *Journal of Politics* 39 (August 1977): 730-761; Paul Allen Beck, "Partisan Dealignment in the Postwar South," *American Political Science Review* 71 (June 1977): 477-498; Charles D. Hadley and Susan E. Howell, "The Southern Split Ticket Voter, 1952-1976: Republican Conversion or Democratic Decline?" in *Party Politics in the South*, eds. Robert P. Steed, Laurence W. Moreland, and Tod A. Baker (New York: Praeger Publishers, 1980), pp. 127-151; Merle Black and George B. Rabinowitz, "American Electoral Change: 1952-1972 (With a Note on 1976)," in *The Party Symbol*, ed. William Crotty (San Francisco: W. H. Freeman and Company, 1980), pp. 226-256; and Earl Black, "Competing Responses to the 'New Southern Politics': Republican and Democratic Southern Strategies, 1964-1976," in *Perspectives on the American South, An Interdisciplinary Annual, Volume One*, eds. Merle Black and John Shelton Reed (New York: Gordon and Breach, 1981), pp. 151-164.

3. In addition to earlier work by the authors, cited in the credit notes, see Malcolm E. Jewell, "Participation in Southern Primaries," in *Party Politics in the South*, eds. Robert P. Steed, Laurence W. Moreland, and Tod A. Baker (New York: Praeger Publishers, 1980), pp. 8-32; Malcolm E. Jewell and David M. Olson, *American State Political Parties and Elections* (Homewood, Ill.: The Dorsey Press, 1978), pp. 125-176; Arlon Kemple, "Changes in Party Competitiveness and the Evolution of Intraparty Processes: The North Carolina Republican Party," Ph.D. dissertation, University of North Carolina at Chapel Hill (1979); and Arlon Kemple, "Changes in Party Competitiveness and the Evolution of the Party Role in Southern Republican Parties" (paper prepared for the 1980 Citadel Symposium on Southern Politics, Charleston, S.C., March 1980).

4. For analyses of traditional southern Republicanism, see V. O. Key, Jr., *Southern Politics in State and Nation* (New York: Alfred A. Knopf, 1949), esp. pp. 277-297, 440-442; and Alexander Heard, *A Two-Party South?* (Chapel Hill: University of North Carolina Press, 1952).

5. Stephen Hess and David S. Broder, *The Republican Establishment* (New York: Harper & Row, 1967), p. 346.

6. The South is defined as the states of the former Confederacy.

7. Julius Turner, "Primary Elections as the Alternative to Party Competition in 'Safe' Districts," *Journal of Politics* 15 (May 1953): 197-210; and V. O. Key, Jr., *American State Politics* (New York: Alfred A. Knopf, 1956), pp. 97-118. See also Jewell and Olson, *American State Parties*, pp. 131-138.

8. Key, *American State Politics*, p. 97.

9. Ibid., p. 105.

10. Ibid., p. 110.

11. Ibid., pp. 110-111.

12. Ibid., pp. 97-100.

13. David M. Olson, "Attributes of State Political Parties: An Exploration of Theory and Data," in *New Perspectives in State and Local Politics*, ed. James A. Riedel (Waltham, Mass.: Xerox College Publishing, 1971), pp. 127-129.

14. Ibid., pp. 128-129.

15. Ibid., p. 128.

16. Key, *American State Politics*, p. 99.

17. Olson, "Attributes of State Political Parties," p. 128.

18. Earl Black, *Southern Governors and Civil Rights* (Cambridge: Harvard University Press, 1976), p. 97.

19. Alan Abramowitz, John McGlennon, and Ronald Rapoport, "Voting in the Democratic Primary: The 1977 Virginia Gubernatorial Race," in *Party Politics in the South*, eds. Robert P. Steed, Laurence W. Moreland, and Tod A. Baker (New York: Praeger, 1980), pp. 81-95.

20. Havard, *Changing Politics of the South*, pp. 719-729.

21. *Congressional Quarterly Weekly Report* 38 (November 9, 1980): 3328.

22. R. Walters, "Snatching Lessons from the Jaws of Defeat," *National Journal* 7 (November 15, 1975): 1579.

23. Margaret Thompson Echols and Austin Ranney, "The Impact of Interparty Competition Revisited: The Case of Florida," *Journal of Politics* 38 (February 1976): 142-152. Echols and Ranney examine a single southern state (Florida) to test the proposition (as they read and paraphrase Key) that "Other things being equal, the higher the degree of interparty competition the more likely is the dominant party to have a bifactional rather than a multifactional structure" (p. 143). Growing Republican competitiveness in general elections for governor, the authors find, has not been associated with a discernible reduction in multifactionalism within the Florida Democratic party; their conclusion is that "Key's hypothesis is not supported by events in Florida since he published *Southern Politics*" (p. 152).

24. Key, *American State Politics*, pp. 99-102.

25. Many participants in southern Democratic primaries are weak Democrats or behavioral independents. They can be mobilized behind a Republican candidate if they experience sufficient dissatisfaction with the nominee of their nominal party. The best recent example of the (sometimes) huge gap between GOP primary and general election strength occurred in the 1978 Texas gubernatorial race. The Republican primary attracted only 158,403 voters, compared to a turnout of 1,812,790 in the concomitant Democratic primary (9 Republicans for every 100 Democrats). But the Democrats failed to unite behind their candidate, and the Republican nominee barely won the general election.

26. In 1975 the Louisiana legislature abolished partisan primaries in favor of an open primary law. *Congressional Quarterly Weekly Report* 33 (October 25, 1975): 2275.

27. Consult the analyses in Havard, *Changing Politics of the South*, pp. 92-164, 165-200, and 366-423.

28. The demographic classification for the earlier primaries was based on 1970 Census data; for the latter primaries, counties were classified according to 1975 demographic data.

29. Key, *American State Politics*, pp. 196-197.

30. For previous discussions of conflict between the Kirk and Cramer factions, see Manning J. Dauer, "Florida: The Different State," in *Changing Politics of the South*, ed. William C. Havard, pp. 144-146; and Michael Barone, Grant Ujifusa, and Douglas Matthews, *The Almanac of American Politics* (Boston: Gambit, 1972), p. 139.

31. Michael Barone, Grant Ujifusa, and Douglas Matthews, *The Almanac of American Politics 1976* (New York: E. P. Dutton and Co., 1976), pp. 176-177.

32. Washington *Post*, August 20, 1973.

33. *Congressional Quarterly Weekly Report* 32 (July 20, 1974): 1870.

34. Ibid.

35. For an analysis of Republican and Democratic convention activists in Virginia, see Alan I. Abramowitz, "Ideological Realignment and the Nationalization of Southern Politics: Party Activists and Candidates in Virginia," in *Perspectives on the American South*, Vol. I, eds. Merle Black and John Shelton Reed, pp. 83-106.

36. Ironically, this development may hinder the minority party's competitiveness in the general election, if an acrimonious intraparty struggle occurs. The 1970 governor's race in Florida offers the best example of a general election defeat which followed a closely contested Republican primary.

7

PARTY COMPETITION IN THE SOUTH'S FORGOTTEN REGION: THE CASE OF SOUTHERN APPALACHIA

C. David Sutton

In his classic study of the Southern Appalachians, *The Southern Highlander and His Homeland*, John C. Campbell concluded that the mountain country of the South was "a land about which, perhaps, more things are known that are not true than of any part of our country."[1] Robert Munn, a bibliographer of works on Appalachia, came to a similar conclusion when he observed that "a strong case can be made for the statement that more nonsense has been written about the Southern Appalachians than any comparable area in the United States."[2]

The people of the Southern highlands have been variously described as "Yesterday's People" and as "Our Contemporary Ancestors" to emphasize the obsolete nature of their values and traits. They have been portrayed as an apathetic, fatalistic, and backward people who cling tenaciously to the past and resist all new ideas and experiences. Although many writers and scholars have demonstrated the mythological nature of this image of the Southern mountaineer, a stereotyped picture of the region and its people has persisted.

According to Wilma Dykeman, more than ignorance, perversity, or whimsy was involved in the creation of these mental constructs. This picture of the mountain people had purpose and result. In her view, the image was developed and nurtured after the Civil War to explain Appalachia's general defection from the Confederacy. Dykeman argues that journalists and travel writers wittingly and unwittingly accepted and transmitted to the nation the South's viewpoint that its aristocrats had been Confederates and that its mountain cousins who had defected were backward, ignorant, and inferior. Such a stereotype of the mountaineer not only explained his defection but also served to justify later

The author wishes to express his gratitude to his colleague Joel A. Thompson and to Charles McEnerney for their assistance.

efforts to disenfranchise him and to deny him such essential services from the state as adequate roads and schools.[3]

Of course, even before the Civil War, the people of the Southern highlands perceived that their lowland governments were not especially responsive to them and indeed discriminated against them in terms of fair representation and governmental expenditures. Yet, the people from the hills probably thought of themselves as Southerners. However, during 1860-61 this natural political cleavage between lowlands and hills found new expression during the secession crisis when the highland yeomanry voted to remain in the Union and, in many cases, opted to give significant support to the Union war effort. Historian Gordon McKinney writes that both the highland people and the rest of the country came to accept the mountain vote against secession and the subsequent contributions to the Union cause as evidence of a difference between mountaineers and other Southerners.[4]

This new sense of regional identity, plus the natural cleavage between upland farmers and lowland planters with its attendant legacy of economic and political discrimination, provided favorable conditions for the establishment of the Republican party in the Southern mountains. While mountain Republicans are currently found spread throughout the Appalachian highlands, their principal concentrations are in western North Carolina, southwestern Virginia, and eastern Tennessee. Discussing the influence of these Southern mountain Republicans, V. O. Key noted that "they control local governments, elect a few state legislators, and an occasional Congressman, and sometimes even make the Democrats fearful lest they lose control of their states."[5]

This chapter seeks to analyze the voting patterns of the hill people in the states of Tennessee, Virginia, and North Carolina. Several closely related questions about these patterns have been posed. It will be helpful to array these here in the order in which they are treated in the pages that follow. First, interparty competition in the Appalachian counties will be measured to ascertain to what degree the Republican party is preeminent in the highlands. Second, the ideological cast of the mountain voter and of the traditional mountain wing of the Republican party in these three states is explored. Voting patterns in recent elections are studied to determine if mountain voters support candidates who are philosophic and racial conservatives. Finally, voter turnout for the Appalachian counties in the three states is calculated and compared to voter turnout in the nation, the South, and the states in which they lie. The results should reveal whether the people of Appalachia go to the polls and vote in significant numbers or whether they are apathetic and indifferent toward this most characteristic form of political participation.

DEFINITION OF APPALACHIA

The parts of Southern Appalachia which are included in this study consist of all of those counties in the States of Tennessee, Virginia, and North Carolina defined as Appalachian by the Appalachian Regional Development Act of 1965, as amended. The study thus encompasses 100 counties — 50 in Tennessee, 29 in North Carolina, and 21 in Virginia.

One special problem with regard to the state of Virginia should be noted. There are five "independent cities" included in the Appalachian region of Virginia. All voting and census data are reported separately for the independent cities and the counties in which they are located. To provide uniformity in the study, the author combined the voting data for these cities and the counties in which they lie.

PARTY COMPETITION IN THE APPALACHIAN COUNTIES

Until recent years, one question of fascination for historians and political scientists had been whether the South should be regarded as "solid" in most of its major political attributes. Prior to the decade of the 1950s, most political writers cited the 11 states of the Old Confederacy as representing the most complete and enduring pattern of one-party control. As V. O. Key put it: "The Civil War made the Democratic party, the party of the South and the Republican party, the party of the North."[6] In his *The Mind of the South*, W. J. Cash says that the Democratic party "ceased to be a party in the South and became the party of the South, a kind of confraternity having in its keeping the whole corpus of Southern loyalties. . . ."[7]

Cash's image of the South failed to account correctly for the diversity within the region and certainly made no allowance for the dissenting experience of Appalachia. For those outside the Appalachian region, it generally comes as a surprise to learn that the Republican party has had pockets of support scattered along the Appalachian highlands. Of course, students of Southern political history recognized the Republican strength in the highlands, but often they perceived that influence as comparable to that wielded by the Democrats in the lowlands and the blackbelt. Leonard Ritt writes that "very little research has been published on the politics of the 'Other Solid South,' — the highland areas of the southern Appalachians." He notes that while the Southern Appalachian region contains a number of counties that have traditionally voted Democratic, "the heart of the mountain area is composed of counties which were strongholds of Whiggery before the Civil War and Constitutional Unionism in 1860, and subsequently strongly Republican."[8] Jewell and Olson observe that in the Appalachian mountain areas there was very little slavery because of the terrain and consequently, there was much opposition to secession. As a result, "they became Republican, and have remained Republican to the present."[9]

Do mountaineers march dutifully to the polls and loyally vote Republican out of tradition and habit? Is the Republican party preeminent in the Appalachian counties of North Carolina, Tennessee, and Virginia? For this paper, interparty competition in the Appalachian counties of North Carolina was measured by averaging the mean percentage of the two-party vote cast for the Democratic candidates for governor from 1952 to 1976 and the mean percentage of the two-party vote cast for the Democratic candidates for president from 1952 to 1964 and from 1972 to 1976. (Because it was a three-man contest, the 1968 presidential election vote was omitted.)

The same procedure was also employed with Virginia. Six of the seven Virginia gubernatorial elections from 1953 to 1977 were used. The 1973 gubernatorial race was omitted because the Democratic party did not field a candidate. For Tennessee, only the presidential elections were used because the Republicans did not generally offer a serious contender for the governorship in the 1950s and 1960s.

While this measure of interparty competition (the average percent of the popular vote won by Democratic presidential and gubernatorial candidates) only taps one basic dimension of the variable, it does provide a rough estimate of the usual distribution of votes between Republicans and Democrats for these offices. A simple index of interparty competitiveness was constructed by establishing the following categories and definitions of counties (all numbers are presented as the county mean percentage for the elections covered):

.6000 or higher: one-party Democratic
.5500 to .5999: modified one-party Democratic
.4500 to .5499: two-party
.4000 to .4499: modified one-party Republican
.0000 to .3999: one-party Republican

By the above criteria, no Appalachian county in North Carolina qualified as one-party Democratic or as modified one-party Republican. The distribution of the Appalachian counties in North Carolina among the other three categories is given in Table 7.1. According to this classification scheme, 20 of the 29 Appalachian counties merited inclusion in the two-party category. Clearly the Appalachian counties of North Carolina do not constitute a preserve for either party but rather a region where the two parties may vie on fairly even terms for voter support.

Corroborative evidence for this finding comes from a study by Richard J. Trilling and Daniel F. Harkins. Trilling and Harkins analyzed party competition in North Carolina for five offices (president, governor, attorney general, U.S. senator, and U.S. congressman) during the period 1948 to 1974. They discovered that in the mountain counties competition existed up and down the ballot in 1948 and persisted throughout the ensuing 25 years.[10]

The results of the analysis of the interparty competition in the Appalachian counties of Virginia can be seen in Table 7.2. In that state, 10 of the 21 Appalachian counties fall into the two-party category. Only two counties can be

TABLE 7.1
THE APPALACHIAN COUNTIES OF NORTH CAROLINA
CLASSIFIED BY DEGREE OF INTERPARTY COMPETITION
(1952-1976)

Character of County Party System	(N)	Percent
One-Party Democratic	(0)	0
Modified One-Party Democratic	(3)	10
Two-Party	(20)	69
Modified One-Party Republican	(0)	0
One-Party Republican	(6)	21
Total	(29)	100

Source: Compiled by the author.

TABLE 7.2
THE APPALACHIAN COUNTIES OF VIRGINIA CLASSIFIED
BY DEGREE OF INTERPARTY COMPETITION
(1952-1977)

Character of County Party System	(N)	Percent
One-Party Democratic	(0)	0
Modified One-Party Democratic	(3)	14
Two-Party	(10)	48
Modified One-Party Republican	(6)	29
One-Party Republican	(2)	9
Total	(21)	100

Source: Compiled by the author.

classified as one-party Republican. Six counties are modified one-party Democratic. Clearly, the evidence does not suggest that most Appalachian counties in Virginia are "safe" for the Republicans.

In Table 7.3, the distribution of the Appalachian counties in Tennessee according to degree of interparty competition can be seen. Unlike the situation in North Carolina and Virginia, one does discover a significant number of "safe" Republican counties in the Appalachian portion of Tennessee. Based on their presidential vote from 1952 to 1964 and from 1972 to 1976, 23 of the 50 Appalachian counties in Tennessee merit the label "one-party Republican" and 9 are classified as modified one-party Republican. Only 7 of the 50 counties may

TABLE 7.3
THE APPALACHIAN COUNTIES OF TENNESSEE CLASSIFIED
BY DEGREE OF INTERPARTY COMPETITION
(1952-1976)

Character of County Party System	(N)	Percent
One-Party Democratic	(8)	16
Modified One-Party Democratic	(3)	6
Two-Party	(7)	14
Modified One-Party Republican	(9)	18
One-Party Republican	(23)	46
Total	(50)	100

Source: Compiled by the author.

be classified as two-party. For the Democrats, there are eight counties which may be considered safe for them in presidential voting and three which may be classified as modified one-party Democratic.

Just as earlier writers stressed the uniformity of all Southerners and the South in general, there has been a tendency to imply a certain homogeneity in Appalachia. The findings of this study cast some doubt upon this assumption. There appears to be significant variations in the degree of interparty competition in the Appalachian parts of the three states. While the Appalachian portion of Tennessee is a Republican stronghold for the most part, many of the Appalachian counties in North Carolina and Virginia are highly competitive in election after election.

Yet, one cannot deny that in all three states there exists considerable Republican strength in the mountain areas. As Key observed, the mountain Republicans provided a strong foundation on which to build a competing party in these states. Although a statewide minority, the Republicans had in the highlands "a base for the maintenance of the party and for the recruitment and training of party leaders and candidates."[11] Starting with this base of support in the mountains, the Republican party in all three states in the middle to late 1960s made determined efforts at statewide success. Today a highly competitive two-party politics at the state level exists in Tennessee, Virginia, and, to a lesser degree, in North Carolina.[12]

POLITICAL PHILOSOPHY

Perhaps no misconception of the highlander has greater political and social implications than the popular perception of the attitudes or beliefs of the mountaineer. Among the attitudes or beliefs ascribed to the Appalachian people are: resistance to social change; hatred and contempt for blacks; and conservative or reactionary political attitudes.

Describing the loyalty of the mountain people to the past, Horace Kephart observed that "their adherence to old ways is stubborn, sullen, and perverse to a degree that others cannot comprehend."[13] Jack Weller adds that while most Americans are "progressive," the outlook of the mountain culture is "regressive."[14]

As for the racial attitudes of the white mountaineer, W. J. Cash says that the mountaineer "had acquired a hatred and contempt for the Negro even more virulent than that of the common white of the lowlands; a dislike so rabid that it was a black man's life to venture into many mountain sections."[15] In the harshest judgment of all on the region and its people, the British historian Arnold Toynbee wrote that "the Appalachian 'Mountain People' at this day are no better than barbarians." Toynbee concluded that "the Appalachians present the melancholy spectacle of a people who have acquired civilization and then lost it."[16]

The notion of the Appalachian as inferior and backward still persists and is often used to explain why the mountaineer's level of living is substandard. The characteristics of the mountain people, in other words, are cited as the fundamental causes of why the people lag behind the national average in education, income, housing, and health care. This explanation of Appalachian poverty has, of course, important political and policy ramifications because the way we define problems determines how we think about solutions. As long as attention is focused on what the Appalachian is supposedly doing to himself, few questions will be asked about the economic and political arrangements or institutions that serve and affect him.[17]

Before examining whether some of these "negative" or "destructive" traits are reflected in the mountaineer's electoral choices, it is worthwhile to cite the findings of two surveys. A random sample of North Carolinians conducted in 1971 revealed that the percent of respondents who identified themselves as conservative was smallest in the Mountains (23 percent in the Mountains, 36 percent in the Piedmont, and 39 percent in the Coastal Plain counties). The percent of mountaineers who claimed to be "middle-of-the-road" or "liberal" exceeded the percentage of residents in the Piedmont or Coastal Plain counties who classified themselves in either of these categories.[18]

An earlier survey of Appalachian residents drawn from a representative sample of households in the Southern Appalachian region concluded that:

> . . . the old stereotypes that have so long guided social action in the Region no longer apply to the great majority of the residents. The Southern Appalachian people, although they may lag in their social and economic development, they are living in the Twentieth Century. To be sure, they retain the impress of their rural cultural heritage, but

for the most part their way of life, their beliefs, their fears, and their aspirations are not radically different from those of most other Americans.[19]

In the same survey, interviews were held with 379 individuals named as community leaders by respondents in the sampled localities. The survey found that the Southern Appalachian leaders are neither fatalists nor reactionaries but "are 'activists' and 'progressives' for the most part, committed to a philosophy of individual achievement and social development."[20]

But are these survey results reflected in the voting patterns of the Appalachian counties in recent elections? Do the mountain counties typically support the candidates who are the more conservative in philosophic and racial outlook? To answer these questions, the author will: (1) examine the 1964 presidential vote between Lyndon Johnson and Barry Goldwater in the Appalachian counties; (2) compare Richard Nixon's share of the presidential vote in 1960 with Goldwater's share in the region; and (3) determine George Wallace's percent of the 1968 presidential vote in the counties.

In 1964 when the people of the Appalachian counties were given a choice between Lyndon Johnson, who advocated a program of domestic legislation reminiscent of the New Deal and who signed the strongest civil rights act the nation had ever adopted, and Barry Goldwater, who voted against the 1964 Civil Rights Act and who represented the Republican party's conservative wing, a majority of the Appalachian voters in the counties in this study chose Johnson.

In North Carolina, 22 of the 29 Appalachian counties picked Johnson. He carried 15 of the counties by 55 percent or more of the vote. In Virginia, Johnson carried 17 of the 21 Appalachian counties and won 57.4 percent of the popular vote. Only in Tennessee was Goldwater able to win a majority of the Appalachian counties — 27 out of 50. Even here, however, he failed by a narrow margin to garner a majority of the popular vote, winning 49.6 percent of the vote cast in the region.

While Goldwater was perceived as leading a party of reaction, on both economic and racial issues, Richard Nixon was seen as advocating a number of progressive and dynamic new policies in the 1960 presidential election. In the Appalachian region did Goldwater receive a larger share of the 1964 presidential vote than Nixon did in 1960? In the Appalachian counties of Tennessee, Nixon won 61.2 percent of the popular vote in 1960 to Goldwater's 49.6 percent in 1964. Hence, Goldwater's percent of the two-party vote was almost 12 percentage points below what Nixon had received in 1960.

In the Appalachian counties of North Carolina, the percentage of the popular vote was 57.2 for Nixon in 1960, and 46.1 for Goldwater in 1964, or a difference of 11 percentage points. The two most Republican counties in the Appalachian area of North Carolina, Mitchell and Avery, went for Goldwater but his percent of the vote was more than 15 percentage points below what Nixon had received in 1960. In the Appalachian counties of Virginia, the popular vote was 51.5 percent for Nixon, and for Goldwater 42.6 percent, or a differ-ence of almost 9 percentage points. Goldwater clearly did not fare as well as Nixon in Southern Appalachia.

In his third-party bid for the Presidency in 1968, George Wallace attacked various federal domestic programs and made thinly veiled appeals to racist sentiments. How did Wallace's mixture of racism and anticentralization atti-tudes go over in the Appalachian region? To answer this question, the author compared Wallace's percent of the popular vote in the Appalachian counties with his percent of the vote in the state in which they are located.

While George Wallace received 34 percent of the statewide vote in Ten-nessee, he received only 26.4 percent of the vote in the Appalachian counties, or a difference of 7.6 percentage points. Although Wallace carried 47 of Tennes-see's 95 counties, only 11 of the counties he won are classified as Appalachian counties. Wallace won 23.6 percent of the popular vote in Virginia but his percentage in the Appalachian area was 16.9, or a difference of 6.7 percent. Wallace failed to carry a single mountain county in Virginia in 1968. In North Carolina, Wallace received 31.3 percent of the vote. His percentage in the Appalachian counties was 22.5, or almost 9 percentage points below his state-wide average. As in Virginia, Wallace did not capture a plurality of the popular vote in any Appalachian county of North Carolina.

The voting patterns which emerge from the elections studied above suggest that politics in the Appalachian counties are moderate. There is little support for the notion that mountain people are more susceptible than other Americans to candidates who express a conservative reactionism on social issues or make racial appeals. For the most part, one may say that the supporters and leaders of the traditional mountain wing of the Republican party in these three states have practiced a brand of moderate politics. From this wing came the candidates who provided the early challenges to Democratic hegemony at the state level.

Linwood Holton, Virginia's first Republican governor in this century, grew up as a mountain Republican. A critic of racial bias and a mild reformer on social and economic issues, Holton won the endorsement of many labor unions and black political groups in his 1969 gubernatorial campaign. In Tennessee, Howard Baker, Jr., a true son of the East Tennessee hills, blended economic conservatism with racial moderation in 1966 to become the first popularly elected Republican senator in the State's history. In 1972 James Holshouser, who came from the mountain town of Boone, became North Carolina's first Republican governor in 76 years. Described as a conservative progressive, Hols-houser put together a winning coalition of voters in the mountains and urbanized Piedmont.

Today, however, these traditional Republicans face strong challenges to their role and influence in the party they have kept alive in the hills and hollows for over a century. In North Carolina, Holshouser's ticket-mate in the 1972 election was Jesse Helms, who hailed from the eastern part of the state and who was running for a U.S. Senate seat. Helms, a former Democrat and ultraconservative, is especially strong in the traditionally Democratic areas of the Coastal Plain and the eastern Piedmont.[21] In 1976 the Helms faction of the party managed to deny Holshouser a seat as a delegate to the Republican National Convention. At present, there is a struggle between the party's old guard and Helms' group of "new" Republicans for control of the party apparatus.

In Tennessee there has also been competition between the traditional and "new" Republicans. At the 1964 state party convention the dominant Goldwater faction, despite opposition from the mountain delegates, sent a lily-white delegation to the national party convention for the first time in Tennessee Republican history.[22] Although the struggle between the two factions will likely continue in the state, the moderate wing appears to be in the ascendant with Howard Baker serving as the Majority Leader of the U.S. Senate and Lamar Alexander, a young progressive from the East Tennessee hills, occupying the governor's mansion in Nashville.

The Grand Old Party in Virginia has also been split ideologically between the two factions. Peirce writes that the new Republicans are mostly "refugees from the Democratic right, who had been nurtured in the Goldwater campaign and were as conservative on racial matters as they were on economics."[23] While the balance of power in the party in Virginia is still unclear, John Dalton, a moderate-conservative Republican from the southwestern highlands, won the governorship in 1977.

CITIZEN PARTICIPATION

The final question to which this study addresses itself is the extent of voting participation in the Appalachian counties of Virginia, North Carolina, and Tennessee. In any discussion of Southern politics, a prominent place is given to the low levels of voting in the region. Although the gap appears to be narrowing, studies of the national electorate have repeatedly found that persons from the South are significantly less likely to vote than persons living in other regions of the country.

According to many studies, a substantial portion of that deviation from the U.S. norm can be accounted for by the sociodemographic characteristics of the Southern electorate.[24] Contemporary research in voter participation has resulted in the findings that levels of voter turnout are highly correlated with socioeconomic status, income and educational levels, urbanization, and a sense of political efficacy, among others.[25] In general, Lester Milbrath finds the Southern states ranking below average on these variables. Of the South, Milbrath says: "More persons are engaged in agriculture. Industrialization is less advanced there, and income and educational levels are lower."[26]

Whether one examines census data on per capita income, families with poverty-level incomes, or median school years completed, the Border South states in this study lag behind the national averages.[27] As one might expect, the educational, income, and urbanization levels of the Appalachian counties are not only below those of the nation but, as a rule are below those of the South and of the states in which these counties lie.

Table 7.4 compares the per capita personal income in 1967 of the three Appalachian states in this study and the Appalachian and non-Appalachian portions of each state. Of the three states, only Virginia comes even close to the average per capita income of the United States. Yet, the Appalachian portion of that state shows the greatest disparity in terms of per capita income — only 58 percent of the national average. In similar fashion, Table 7.5 compares the level of educational attainment of the adult population in the nation, the three states, and their Appalachian portion. The table reveals that the three states lag behind the national average in terms of the proportion of their people completing a high school education. As with per capita income, the educational attainment levels of the people in the Appalachian portions of North Carolina and Tennessee are somewhat below their respective state's average, and in the case of Virginia's Appalachian portion, considerably below the state average.

Although there is no consensus in the literature, many writers have argued that "in most national and state elections the metropolitan areas have the largest turnouts, the small towns have the next largest, and the rural areas have by far the lowest."[28] One cannot deny the rurality of the Appalachian counties. In the 1960 census, two out of three residents of Southern Appalachia were

TABLE 7.4
PER CAPITA PERSONAL INCOME CLASSIFIED BY REGION (1967)

Area	Per Capita Dollars	Percent of U.S. Per Capita
U.S.	3,159	100
North Carolina		
Total	2,425	77
Non-Appalachian	2,455	78
Appalachian	2,308	73
Tennessee		
Total	2,397	76
Non-Appalachian	2,479	78
Appalachian	2,293	73
Virginia		
Total	2,739	87
Non-Appalachian	2,848	90
Appalachian	1,821	58

Source: Appalachian Regional Commission, *Appalachian Data Book*, 2nd ed. (Washington: April 1970), Summary Table 10, pp. 10-11.

TABLE 7.5
POPULATION 25 YEARS OLD AND OVER WHO COMPLETED
FOUR YEARS IN HIGH SCHOOL
(Classified by Region, 1970)

Area	Percent of Population
United States	52.3
North Carolina	
Total	38.5
Appalachian	36.7
Tennessee	
Total	41.8
Appalachian	40.1
Virginia	
Total	44.2
Appalachian	28.6

Source: Appalachian Regional Commission, *Appalachia – A Reference Book*, 2nd ed. (Washington: February 1979), p. 72.

classed as rural, compared with less than a third of the residents of the nation.[29] According to the 1970 census, 16 of the 29 Appalachian counties in North Carolina and 15 of the 21 in Virginia do not contain a single incorporated town of 2,500. Only in Tennessee does one find a majority of the Appalachian counties – 32 out of 50 – having some degree of urbanization as defined by the Census Bureau.

To explain the low turnout figures in the rural areas, voting scholars cite the distances and bad weather that plague the rural people and their isolation from social contacts and political discussions.[30] Appalachian mountain folk are, of course, generally perceived as being physically, socially, economically, and psychologically isolated from the center of American society.

One could continue to catalogue the supposed Appalachian traits that are negatively correlated with voter turnout. Many observers of mountain culture claim that there exists in Southern Appalachia a folk culture which consists of norms and values that differ radically from those held by middle class Americans. Dean Jaros and his colleagues who studied childhood socialization in the Appalachian region of eastern Kentucky note that "in Appalachia, in contrast to most of the rest of the United States, there is a great deal of overt, anti-government sentiment in the adult populations."[31] In *Yesterday's People*, Jack Weller lists several other traits which distinguish the Southern Appalachian from the middle class American: rejection of joining groups, feeling of exploitation by government, fatalism, perception of government as evil and the belief that anyone who goes into politics becomes corrupted, fear of those in authority, and suspicion of the outside world.[32] Obviously, these are not characteristics normally associated with conventional political participation.

One can thus sympathize with Thomas Dye's bewilderment when he ranked the 50 states according to the percentage of voting age population casting votes and discovered that West Virginia had one of the highest turnout percentages in the United States. Knowing that West Virginia's characteristics did not conform to the conventional wisdom about political participation, Dye concluded in the first edition of his *Politics in States and Communities* that voter behavior in the state defied systematic explanation. He could not understand why West Virginia voters insisted upon going to the polls in large numbers. Searching for a plausible explanation, Dye finally offered this one: "Perhaps in Appalachia politics are one form of recreation, in an otherwise drab environment."[33] Milbrath called West Virginia "an interesting anomaly,"[34] and Gerald Johnson labeled it "a deviant case."[35]

How does the voter turnout in the Southern Appalachian counties of this study compare with turnout in the nation, the South, and the states in which they lie? To answer this question, the author calculated the voter turnout in each Appalachian county for the presidential elections from 1952 to 1968.

The following procedures were used to determine turnout for each election.[36] Census information on the number of people 21 and over in each of the Appalachian counties was collected for each of the years 1950, 1960, and 1970. Then the number of persons 21 and over in the inter-census years was approximated by subtracting those 21 and over in the lower year from those in the higher year (for example, 1950 from 1960) dividing that number by 10, and then multiplying the resulting figure by the number of years the election year followed the base year (for example, 1950 in this example). Then, the estimated number of citizens 21 years old and over in a given election year was divided into the number of people in the county who voted in that year as reported in *America Votes*.

Table 7.6 provides a comparison of the presidential voting turnout figures in the nation, the South, the three Border South states, and the Appalachian counties in those states in the presidential elections from 1952 to 1968. In all three states and in all five elections, one can see that the Appalachian counties have a turnout exceeding the average turnout of the states in which they are located. In the case of North Carolina, the Appalachian counties have a voting turnout which surpasses the national average in all five elections.

As a postscript to this discussion of citizen participation, the author discovered that the two Appalachian counties in North Carolina which ranked highest in terms of per capita income, urbanization, and educational level — Buncombe (Asheville) and Forsyth (Winston-Salem) — have the lowest average voter turnout, 57.9 and 50.6 percent respectively, for the five elections. By contrast, Graham and Clay counties, which top the list of Appalachian counties in North Carolina in degree of voter participation — 86.0 and 87.7 percent respectively — have no urban populations, are among the poorest in the state, and are ranked near the bottom of the counties in educational level.

TABLE 7.6
PERCENT OF VOTING-AGE POPULATION CASTING VOTES
IN PRESIDENTIAL ELECTIONS
(Classified by Region, 1952-1968)

Area	1952	1956	1960	1964	1968
United States	61.6	59.3	63.1	61.8	60.7
South[a]	37.1	35.7	38.8	44.7	51.3
North Carolina					
Total	52.8	48.2	52.9	52.8	54.3
Appalachian	65.9	61.3	69.1	64.0	60.8
Tennessee					
Total	44.8	46.3	49.8	51.7	53.7
Appalachian	45.7	51.4	54.5	53.0	53.4
Virginia					
Total	31.7	33.5	32.8	41.1	50.1
Appalachian	37.2	43.4	41.8	46.6	55.9

[a]This is the mean (average) of the percentages of voter turnout in the 11 states of the old Confederacy.

Sources: Lester W. Milbrath, "Political Participation in the States," in *Politics in the American States*, eds. Herbert Jacob and Kenneth Vines (Boston: Little, Brown, and Company, 1965), pp. 38-39 (for percentage turnout for the states 1952-1956); and Jack Bass and Walter DeVries, *The Transformation of Southern Politics* (New York: The New American Library, 1977), p. 400 (for percentage turnout for the U.S., the South, and state totals 1960-1968).

While the characteristics of the mountain counties are those often discovered in voting behavior research to be associated with low voter turnout, one finds that some of the generalizations about political participation do not receive strong support in Southern Appalachia. Moreover, the stereotype of the mountaineer as more apathetic toward the political process than his lowland cousins is not borne out by the voting statistics. Mountain people seem to find time for voting and politics.

In summary, this chapter has attempted to break down a number of stereotypes about the voting patterns and political attitudes of the Appalachian people in North Carolina, Tennessee, and Virginia. Robert Sessions notes that "the minute we start to break down our stereotypes, at that instant we are forced to begin acknowledging that in many ways the mountaineer is not different from us, but much like us and in fact one of us."[37] When we acknowledge that the Southern Appalachian people are not radically different from other people in their aspirations, their beliefs, and their behavior, then we come to the realization that the reason the people lag behind the national average in so many areas of human need cannot be simply attributed to alleged deficiencies of the people and their culture.

NOTES

1. John C. Campbell, *The Southern Highlander and His Homeland* (Lexington: University of Kentucky Press, 1969), p. xxi; originally published by the Russell Sage Foundation, 1921.

2. Robert Munn, *The Southern Appalachians: A Bibliography and Guide to Studies* (Morgantown: West Virginia University Library, 1961), p. 1.

3. Wilma Dykeman, "Appalachia in Context," in *An Appalachian Symposium*, ed. J. W. Williamson (Boone, N.C.: Appalachian State University Press, 1977), pp. 30-32.

4. Gordon B. McKinney, "The Political Uses of Appalachian Identity After the Civil War," *Appalachian Journal* 7 (Spring 1980): 201.

5. V. O. Key, Jr., *Southern Politics in State and Nation* (New York: Alfred A. Knopf, 1949), p. 280.

6. V. O. Key, Jr., *Politics, Parties, and Pressure Groups*, 5th ed. (New York: Thomas Y. Crowell Company, 1964), p. 232.

7. W. J. Cash, *The Mind of the South* (New York: Alfred A. Knopf, 1941), p. 132.

8. Leonard Gilbert Ritt, "Presidential Voting Patterns in Appalachia: An Analysis of the Relationship Between Turnout, Partisan Change, and Selected Socioeconomic Variables," (unpublished dissertation, University of Tennessee, 1967), p. 2.

9. Malcolm E. Jewell and David M. Olson, *American State Political Parties and Elections* (Homewood, Ill.: The Dorsey Press, 1978), pp. 24-25.

10. Richard J. Trilling and Daniel F. Harkins, "The Growth of Party Competition in North Carolina," in *Politics and Policy in North Carolina*, eds. Thad L. Beyle and Merle Black (New York: MSS Information Corporation, 1975), pp. 87-88.

11. Key, *Southern Politics*, p. 285.

12. For an analysis of statewide two-party competition that developed in the Southern states from 1968 to 1978, see Alec Peter Lamis, "Southern Two-Party Politics in the 1970's," (Paper delivered at the Annual Meeting of the Southern Political Science Association, Atlanta, November 6-8, 1980).

13. Horace Kephart, *Our Southern Highlanders* (New York: Outing Publishing, 1913), p. 23.

14. Jack E. Weller, *Yesterday's People* (Lexington: University Press of Kentucky, 1965), pp. 33-35.

15. Cash, *The Mind of the South*, p. 219.

16. Arnold J. Toynbee, *A Study of History*, Vol. II (London: Oxford University Press, 1935), p. 311.

17. Stephen Fisher, "Folk Culture or Folk Tale," in *An Appalachian Symposium*, ed. J. W. Williamson (Boone, N.C.: Appalachian State University Press, 1977), pp. 20-21.

18. Schley R. Lyons and William J. McCoy, "Government and Politics," in *North Carolina Atlas*, eds. James Clay, Douglas Orr, Jr., and Alfred Stuart (Chapel Hill, N.C.: University of North Carolina Press, 1975), p. 84.

19. Thomas R. Ford, "The Passing of Provincialism," in *The Southern Appalachian Region, A Survey*, ed. Thomas R. Ford (Lexington: University of Kentucky Press, 1962), p. 34.

20. Ibid., p. 27.

21. For a map illustrating the factional cleavage in the Republican party in North Carolina in the 1972 election, see Jack Bass and Walter DeVries, *The Transformation of Southern Politics* (New York: The New American Library, 1977), p. 443.

22. Neal R. Peirce, *The Border South States* (New York: W. W. Norton & Company, 1975), pp. 305-308.

23. Ibid., p. 60.

24. Jae-On Kim, John R. Petrocik, Stephen N. Enokson, "Voter Turnout Among the American States: Systemic and Individual Components," *American Political Science Review* 69 (March 1975): 114.

25. For a summary of these findings, see Lester W. Milbrath and M. L. Goel, *Political Participation*, 2nd ed. (Chicago: Rand McNally College Publishing Company, 1977).

26. Ibid., pp. 141-42.

27. Peirce, *The Border South States*, pp. 17-18.

28. Hugh A. Bone and Austin Ranney, *Politics and Voters*, 2nd ed. (New York: McGraw-Hill Book Company, 1967), p. 45.

29. John C. Belcher, "Population Growth and Characteristics," in *The Southern Appalachian Region, A Survey*, ed. Thomas R. Ford (Lexington: University of Kentucky Press, 1961), p. 43.

30. Milbrath and Goel, *Political Participation*, pp. 106-107.

31. Dean Jaros, Herbert Hirsch, Frederic J. Fleron, Jr., "The Malevolent Leader: Political Socialization in an American Sub-Culture," *American Political Science Review*, 62 (June 1968), 565.

32. Weller, *Yesterday's People*, pp. 28-57, 161-63.

33. Thomas R. Dye, *Politics in States and Communities* (Englewood Cliffs, N.J.: Prentice-Hall, Inc., 1969), p. 68.

34. Milbrath and Goel, *Political Participation*, p. 113.

35. Gerald W. Johnson, "Political Correlatives of Voter Participation: A Deviant Case Analysis," *American Political Science Review* 65 (September 1971): 768.

36. This technique is taken from Alexander Heard and Donald Strong, *Southern Primaries and Elections 1920-1949* (University, Ala.: University of Alabama Press, 1950), p. 4.

37. Robert Paul Sessions, "Appalachians and Non-Appalachians: The Common Bond," in *An Appalachian Symposium*, ed. J. W. Williamson (Boone, N.C.: Appalachian State University Press, 1977), p. 96.

8

THE END OF SOUTHERN DISTINCTIVENESS

Paul Allen Beck and Paul Lopatto

INTRODUCTION

For more than a century the South has been *the* distinctive American region. So different were its characteristics from those of the rest of the nation, analysts have often felt it necessary to treat the South as a special case, making region an important variable in analysis.

Exceptionalism has pervaded virtually all aspects of southern life. The region's economy has deviated markedly from that of the rest of the nation, earlier in the domination of the plantation system and later in the retarded development of industrialism. Even more has been made of the distinctiveness of southern society — from its tradition of sharp racial separation to cultural mores transcending the racial sphere.[1] The South has been characterized in recent years as a separate subculture — a sort of geographically-based "ethnic group".[2]

Southern exceptionalism has been nowhere more pronounced than in politics. The Civil War and a decade of occupation by hostile military forces left deep scars in the political outlooks of southerners. An even more enduring force for isolating southerners from national political currents was the dedication of white southerners to the preservation of a dual society in which full citizenship rights were accorded only to whites.[3] From the end of Reconstruction to the eve of modern times, these forces combined to eliminate interparty competition from the region, thus eliminating a necessary ingredient of political democracy.

So important has southern political distinctiveness been that a subfield specialization in southern politics emerged among political scientists. The major impetus for this scholarly phenomenon was provided surely by V. O. Key's classic *Southern Politics*.[4] Many other works have followed in Key's wake in treating the South as a distinct political system.[5] No other region has received such treatment. No other region *qua* region is so familiar to students of politics.

After World War II the South underwent dramatic changes in its economy, its society and culture, and its politics.[6] The region experienced rapid economic growth, becoming more and more similar to the rest of the nation.[7] Also significant was the changing composition of the region's population during this period. Many southerners, especially rural blacks, left the region in search of better jobs and more fulfilling lives. Their places were taken, at least numerically, in a tidal wave of Yankee immigrants who flocked particularly to the region's periphery and its metropolitan areas. These two changes have combined to reduce southern cultural distinctiveness, although many areas of difference still remain.[8]

Political change in the South has been of earthshaking proportions. Party competition has emerged at the presidential level. In this competition, it has been the Democratic party that has been disadvantaged. The high point of southern Democratic voting in over a decade came in 1976 when the Democratic presidential nominee, himself a southerner, won the region by only the barest of margins and would not have done so without overwhelming black voter support. It would be an exaggeration to say that political competition has engulfed the region, for the Democratic party remains dominant just below the presidential level. Nevertheless, almost habitual Democratic presidential voting in the South has come to an end.

That Carter's showing in the South had its basis in black votes illustrates in dramatic fashion the other key political change which has swept the region. Blacks have been participating in southern politics in growing numbers since World War II. Their involvement exploded in the 1960s to nearly equal white levels as a result of the 1965 Voting Rights Act and federal intervention to overthrow the most blatantly discriminatory of the local voter registration practices. This participation surge has produced black elected officials and has made strictly segregationist political campaigns artifacts of the past.[9] It has also lent a new source of strength, especially in presidential politics, to the Democratic party electoral coalition.

Close observers of southern politics have been well aware of these important political changes, but rarely have they placed them in a broader perspective. Political change in the South has become a recurrent theme of contemporary studies of the region's politics.[10] With their focus on the South as a separate political system, these works have implicitly accepted the assumption of southern distinctiveness, neglecting to consider the involvement of the region in the broader currents of American politics. Yet the very findings of these studies raise questions about whether a treatment of the region in isolation is warranted. As the South has changed, it may well have become less and less distinctive as a political region. At some point — and perhaps we have reached it already — the South may cease to be a special case.

This paper deals directly with the question of southern political distinctiveness in presidential electoral behavior, traditionally a key ingredient in southern particularism. By comparing the most salient political characteristics of southern and nonsouthern electorates over the 1952-1976 period, we determine how distinctive the South remains and how much sense it makes to treat the region separately in studies of American electoral behavior.

The seeds for the present paper were sown in a previous study of southern electoral politics,[11] conducted under the assumption that the South was indeed a special case. In that article, the southern electorate, and especially its native white core, was found to be dealigning. While some of the dealignment was traceable to changing party positions on racial questions, a matter of particular significance to the region, much of the dealignment seemed explicable only in terms which applied equally to North and South — as the result of the weak partisan loyalties of new voter generations. Thus, the results of that study undercut the assumption of southern particularism which had originally justified it.

In this paper, we pursue the interest aroused by the results of the earlier study by examining three types of electoral behavior. First, we deal with partisan loyalties. How do the loyalties of southerners compare to those of the nonsouthern electorate? Similar patterns of loyalty would seem to restrict the distinctiveness of southern politics. Second, the presidential voting of the two regional groupings is compared. The overall election results are familiar, and we shall not devote extensive attention to them. Of greater interest is the question of how faithful partisans have been in supporting their party's nominee, for here is one area in which many feel that the South has grown *more* distinctive in recent times. Finally, we consider the political outlooks of southerners and nonsoutherners as of the mid-1970s: their ideological orientations, issue positions, and candidate evaluations. Do they differ in the expected ways or are they so similar as to undermine the case for southern exceptionalism?

Of course, the traditional distinctiveness of the southern electorate was not restricted to national politics. Also important was behavior below the national level, in state and local contests. Recent outcomes here suggest that *within the states* southern electoral politics remains one-party dominated. At this point, more detailed tests of changes in southern distinctiveness seem unnecessary for these contests.

Nonetheless, as V. O. Key has so wisely observed it is the organization of the region into a one-party system *for national politics* that is most important.[12] There has been extensive political competition within the region for a long time. It simply has not been *party* competition. Thus, in focusing upon electoral behavior in national politics, we deal with the critical component of southern exceptionalism — the "face" of the South toward the outside world.

The data for this study come largely from the presidential election series collected by researchers at the University of Michigan and disseminated through the interuniversity Consortium for Political and Social Research. This series provides extensive information on the political orientations of the American electorate in the presidential election years from 1952 to 1976. The samples in each year are separated into southern and nonsouthern components. The South is defined for our purposes as the 11 former Confederate states *minus Tennessee*. Tennessee was excluded from the southern state stratum in the sample frame, presumably because its enduring political characteristics make it only a marginal member of the Solid South. We would bias the southern sample if Tennessee were included. The nonsouth includes the other 39 states plus Tennessee.

THE EROSION OF SOUTHERN PARTISAN DISTINCTIVENESS

In their study of Indiana politics, Key and Munger coined the term "standing decision" to refer to the enduring voting patterns that characterized particular parts of the state.[13] Votes were conceived to be but the behavioral manifestation of voters' underlying party loyalties — loyalties which had been passed on from one generation to the next for almost a century. Working with individual-level survey data, Campbell and his colleagues at the University of Michigan revealed the psychological bases for these standing decisions.[14] They found that party attachments were analogous to group or religious identifications for many, and called these attachments "party identifications".

The foundation of southern political distinctiveness has been the overwhelmingly Democratic standing decisions or party identifications of its people. From the end of Reconstruction to modern times, almost all southerners seem to have been Democrats. The struggle between populism and industrialism that erupted in nationwide interparty conflict in 1896 was contained within the Democratic party in the South. After the Republican victory of 1896 realigned national partisan coalitions and ushered in an era of national Republican hegemony, the South remained steadfastly Democratic. Even the New Deal realignment of the 1930s, introducing a mild form of class conflict into American politics, made little mark on the South because all classes remained Democratic.

In other words, while the national electorate underwent two realignments, southerners did not vary in their standing decisions.[15] If we had survey evidence covering the years since Reconstruction, surely we would find little change in the distributions of party identification for the region. And just as surely we would find that these distributions were at all times markedly different from those for the remainder of the nation.

Survey data on party identification in 1952 probably capture well both the traditional standing decision of southerners and its divergence from that of northerners.[16] These data, presented in the first rows of Table 8.1, show a southern electorate in which Democrats outnumbered Republicans by the staggering ratio of over seven to one and Republicans were outmanned even by Independents and those without interest in partisan politics. By contrast the nonsouthern electorate was fairly evenly balanced between the two parties, with a roughly five to four ratio of Democrats to Republicans.

TABLE 8.1
REGIONAL PARTISANSHIP PATTERNS, 1952-1976
(percent)

		Democrats	Independents	Republicans	Others	(N)
1952	South	68	12	9	10	(388)
	North	41	25	32	2	(1405)
	Difference	[+27]	[−13]	[−23]	[+8]	
1956	South	62	14	15	9	(421)
	North	38	26	33	3	(1341)
	Difference	[+24]	[−12]	[−18]	[+6]	
1960	South	57	17	21	6	(489)
	North	41	25	32	2	(1439)
	Difference	[+16]	[−8]	[−11]	[+4]	
1964	South	66	19	13	3	(342)
	North	48	24	28	1	(1219)
	Difference	[+18]	[−5]	[−15]	[+2]	
1968	South	58	30	11	2	(358)
	North	42	29	28	2	(1198)
	Difference	[+16]	[+1]	[−17]	[0]	
1972	South	50	33	15	2	(676)
	North	37	35	26	2	(2025)
	Difference	[+13]	[−2]	[−11]	[0]	
1976	South	51	32	16	1	(680)
	North	36	37	25	1	(2182)
	Difference	[+15]	[−5]	[−9]	[0]	

Source: Compiled by the authors from ICPSR data.

These data make the case for southern exceptionalism in partisanship through the early 1950s. It is reasonable to suppose that the 1952 distribution of partisan loyalties in the South would conform quite closely to the distributions found at virtually any time in the preceding 75 years. It is also reasonable to suppose that the distributions for the nonsouthern electorate were always *at least* this different during the same period. Indeed, Republicans outnumbered Democrats outside the South prior to the 1930s, making regional differences probably even more substantial then.[17]

After 1952, as the succeeding rows of the table show, the case for southern partisan distinctiveness weakened considerably. While the declines in regional partisan differences are not monotonic, there is an unmistakable trend toward convergence. The regional difference in Democratic *and* Republican identifiers was almost halved by 1960 and was reduced even more later. By 1976, while differences remained, they were only a faint shadow of what they had been just two decades before.

This narrowing of regional differences was the result of changes concentrated largely in the South, as the long-standing party distribution there was "unfrozen." The ratio of southern Democrats to southern Republicans was reduced from over seven to one in 1952 to slightly more than three to one by 1976. To be sure, this was still a considerable Democratic edge, but one that was far less overwhelming than it once had been. Even more significant was the growth of political independence in the South. The percentage of Independents increased two-and-one-half fold between 1952 and the 1970s. These changes left the Democratic party with only a slender majority of the electorate by 1976.

The principal change outside the South was the growth of Independents. This growth came at the expense of both Democrats and Republicans. Proportionately greater losses were experienced by the GOP, though, and the ratio of Democrats to Republicans increased slightly from 1.3 to 1 in 1952 to 1.4 to 1 in both 1972 and 1976. Thus, as the GOP gained ground in the South, it lost ground outside of the region. At the same time the Democrats lost ground in both places.

While divergent in some respects, the patterns of change between 1952 and the 1970s in the South and North exhibit two striking similarities. First, 1964 disrupted the trend in each region. In the South the pre-1964 period was marked by steady Republican gains at the net expense of the Democrats. This growing Republicanism received the attention of perceptive analysts of southern politics,[18] but then ended. Outside of the region, on the other hand, the distribution of partisans remained remarkably stable until 1964. But neither pattern survived the early 1960s. In 1964 the nature of change itself changed in both regions.

The patterns of partisan change converged for the two regions after 1964. Both experienced Democratic losses of roughly the same magnitude through 1976. Both recorded similar gains in Independents. In these two important respects, southern distinctiveness had ended. Only in the changes in Republican identifiers after 1964 did the regions differ. Republicanism resumed its upward trek in the South after 1968, although it has not yet recaptured its 1960 high. The percentage of Republicans outside the South, by contrast, declined slightly — although the change falls well within the range of sampling error.

The unfreezing of the standing decision of the South, and the remarkable changes which have ensued from it, are the products of several separate political forces. Beck identified four such forces: Interregional population flows eroded the Democratic base in the South and increased GOP ranks.[19] The migrants who headed South in the postwar period were heavily Republican. During the same period, the South exported Democrats to the rest of the nation. A third force counteracted these changes almost entirely. At first in trickles but in a tidal wave by the mid-1960s, blacks entered southern electoral politics. By the time they had mobilized in large numbers, they were overwhelmingly Democratic in their partisan loyalties.

In large measure these three phenomena were unique to the South, lending even more support to the notion of southern exceptionalism. The impact of the migrations of "Yankees" southward and southerners northward, while sizeable in the South, was diluted in the North by the sheer size of its population. Black mobilization was restricted even more to the South, because blacks were already members of the electorate outside of the region. That these uniquely southern forces effectively cancel one another out, however, means that they can not account for partisan changes in the South and the consequent convergence of the southern and nonsouthern distributions of partisanship.

To account for the changes in the *South*, Beck turned to a fourth phenomenon — the dealignment of the native white electorate.[20] Native white southerners became 25 percent less Democratic, 22 percent more Independent, and 5 percent more Republican between 1952 and 1972. Using 1976 data in lieu of 1972 data leaves these figures virtually undisturbed. Because most of the net movement was from Democratic to Independent, the change was characterized as a dealignment — a movement of the electorate away from party loyalties into nonpartisan positions.

The peculiar behavior of native white southerners as a group, in turn, did not tell the whole story of dealignment. More insight into the nature of the change was provided by dividing this group into two parts according to age. Native whites who had entered the electorate before 1946 exhibited very little movement toward independence. Their party loyalties, developed and hardened at a time when the South was solidly Democratic, resisted change even in the face of the strong anti-Democratic forces of the postwar period. By contrast, native whites who entered the electorate after the war were by 1972 more likely to be Independents than Democrats. It is they who have been the carriers of dealignment in the South.[21]

That partisan dealignment in the South has been primarily the work of young native white southerners can be explained in terms that are uniquely southern. The "conspiracy of silence" on racial issues was broken in the postwar period. Gradually through the 1940s and 1950s and then rapidly in the 1960s, national Democratic politicians identified themselves more and more with the cause of black civil rights. Many white southerners were repulsed by the change in position of the Democratic party from protector to challenger of the region's racial traditions. This revulsion was galvanized in 1964, when most southerners first perceived the Democratic party as pro-civil rights and the GOP candidate as anti-civil rights. It was again reflected four years later in the outpouring of regional support for George Wallace. Given these strains on the *raison d'etre* for Democratic loyalties in the South, it is little wonder that they declined. What is remarkable is that this decline is accounted for almost wholly by new voters. The partisan loyalties of the older generation of native white southerners seemed immutable — a tribute to the force of habit where partisanship is concerned.

As persuasive as this explanation for southern dealignment seems to be, it is open to challenge on two grounds. First, as was shown in the earlier article, only a small part of the dealignment among native whites could be accounted for directly by rejection of the Democratic party on racial issue grounds. This left most of the dealignment open to explanation in other terms. Second, nonsouthern young people exhibited the same dealigning behavior as southern young native whites after 1964. This leads one to search for explanations which can be generalized to the entire nation rather than to one region.

That young southerners are participants in a *national* dealignment among postwar generations may be another mark of the end of southern distinctiveness. Rejection of partisan affiliations by young voters may be explained as the result of the declining relevance of New Deal politics to those who matured in the postwar period.[22] There is even good reason to believe that the rejection of the New Deal party system by today's young has parallels in rejections of earlier party systems in the third decade following every party realignment in America.[23] What is different about the contemporary dealignment is that southerners are participating in it. It seems unlikely that they were involved in earlier dealignments.

This theoretical approach requires an explicit test of southern exceptionalism: Do the party identifications of young southerners exhibit the same tendencies as those of their counterparts outside the region? Table 8.2 contains the necessary data for answering this question. It presents the partisan distributions in each region for three distinct age cohorts in 1976. The first cohort entered the electorate prior to 1946. The second entered the electorate between 1946 and 1964, the year which marks the beginning of the dealignment period. The third cohort contains the youngest voters, those whose entry into the electorate came after 1964 during the "dealignment period".[24]

These data undermine the claim of southern exceptionalism even more. For the youngest generation regional differences in partisanship are small enough to skirt the range of sampling variation. Most numerous in both regions are self-identified Independents. The next largest group among the young is comprised of Democrats, who are slightly more common in the South. Republicans finish a poor third in both regions for the post-1964 generation, with virtually the same totals in each. Dealignment is clearly the trademark of this generation in the South and in the North.

Comparisons of the older age groups show that regional differences remain substantial through 1976. The "Solid South" lives on in the party loyalties of older voters, although even they are not as Democratic as they once were. This is true for both the prewar and the 1946-1964 generations of southerners. Dealignment in the South has been carried forward almost exclusively by the youngest generation. By contrast the erosion of partisanship in the North is spread more widely, as the middle generation occupies a position about midway between the young and the old. That it was somewhat dealigned outside the South only widens the regional differences for this cohort.[25]

The contemporary American electorate bears the imprint of two different political worlds, separated by a wall of age. In 1976, the pre-1946 generation exhibited the characteristics of the old regionally-based political world. The distribution of partisanship among northerners in this age group is almost the

TABLE 8.2
PARTY IDENTIFICATION BY GENERATION, 1976
(percent)

| | Generation of Voters Who Entered Electorate . . . | | | |
	Before 1946	1946-1964	After 1964	Difference between oldest & youngest
Democrats				
South	58	52	40	[+18]
North	41	33	33	[+8]
Difference	[+17]	[+19]	[+7]	
Independents				
South	23	34	42	[−19]
North	26	38	49	[−23]
Difference	[−3]	[−4]	[−7]	
Republicans				
South	17	12	18	[−1]
North	32	28	16	[+16]
Difference	[−15]	[−16]	[+2]	
Others				
South	2	1	0	[+2]
North	1	1	2	[−1]
Difference	[+1]	[0]	[−2]	
Cases				
N for South	(294)	(178)	(205)	
N for North	(774)	(644)	(746)	

Source: Compiled by the authors from ICPSR data.

exact replica of the 1952 distribution for all northerners. The two distributions are less similar among southerners because of changes in its composition. When the comparison is restricted to native white southerners in 1952 and in 1976 (for pre-1946 cohorts only), the similarities approach those found in the North. Among older voters in 1976, in other words, we find the vestiges of two different political systems — the solidly Democratic South and a slightly Democratic but competitive North. The standing decisions of older members of the contemporary electorate show American politics as it was.

The other political world is occupied by the young and reflected most clearly in the post-1964 generation. Here we see a picture of a single national electorate in which voters seem to be responding to national rather than regional forces. At present, these national forces have a dealigning thrust.

While we cannot predict the future for sure, there is good reason to believe that the political world of the post-1964 generation is probably American politics as it will become. Already the politics of dealignment are upon us, as parties play less and less of a role in organizing either political leaders or electorates. With it has come the finale of southern exceptionalism, written in the almost equally weak partisan loyalties of young northerners and young southerners. Even if they are moved to adopt partisan loyalties later in life, it is unlikely that their movements will be in opposite directions. The time when the South was insulated from national partisan political forces, even those of realignment power, has probably come to a close.

Between these two political worlds are members of the 1946-1964 generation. They are less partisan than the older generation but more partisan than the younger group in each region. Beyond this similarity, they bear the traces of the different political systems within which they matured — southerners overwhelmingly Democratic (by a ratio of 4.4 to 1), northerners slightly more Democratic than Republican (by a ratio of 1.2 to 1). Perhaps the individual members of these generations have a foot in each of the political worlds.

We have shown that the *foundation* of southern distinctiveness — the Democratic "standing decision" of its people — has crumbled since 1952. Partially obscuring this crumbling has been the tenacious clinging of older southerners to their traditional Democratic loyalties. As the process of generational replacement operates in its inexorable way, though, these last vestiges of southern partisan distinctiveness should wither away, leaving a southern electorate which resembles its northern counterpart in terms of party loyalties. It is remarkable that in the short space of 20 years, despite considerable "drag" from the past and racial turmoil, the southern electorate has emerged from a century of isolation to become part of a national political system.

THE EROSION OF SOUTHERN DISTINCTIVENESS IN PRESIDENTIAL VOTING

It is obvious that southern distinctiveness in presidential voting had eroded long before changes in partisanship appeared. This lead-lag relationship between vote and party loyalties is not unusual and seems to have characterized periods of substantial partisan change. In the 1930s, for example, the realignment of partisan forces to favor the Democrats came only after landslide Democratic victories at the polls.

Changes in southern presidential voting patterns surfaced at the beginning of the postwar period. The States Rights bolt of Strom Thurmond in 1948 signaled deep divisions within the Democratic "coalition of the whole" in the South. Just four years later, these divisions were translated into a surge of Republican presidential voting, as many southerners voted for a Republican candidate for the first time in their lives. Another important milestone was reached in 1956, when more southerners voted for the Republican presidential candidate than the Democratic. Since then, the region has been highly competitive in presidential elections.

These changes in southern voting behavior produced a convergence of southern and nonsouthern presidential voting very early in the postwar period. Table 8.3, which presents the official popular vote totals for the ten-state South and the remainder of the nation since 1940, illustrates this quite well. In both 1940 and 1944, southerners voted over 20 percent more Democratic and less Republican than northerners. They provided the votes for the wide Roosevelt popular vote margins in those years. Regional differences declined in the 1948 contest, particularly in Democratic voting, as Thurmond siphoned off a substantial number of Democratic votes. In the next decade, regional differences in presidential voting all but vanished. By 1960 only 5 percentage points separated the Republican totals and less than 2 percentage points the Democratic totals in the two regions.

During the 1960s and early 1970s, the presidential voting responses of the two regions changed again. Beginning with the 1964 contest, the regional differences increased, but this time the Republican advantage lay in the South and rose to fully half what the previous Democratic advantage had been at its peak. Only with the "native son" Carter candidacy in 1976 did regional differences again become very narrow. These differences decreased even further in 1980. The minuscule differences that did appear seemed to have been largely a result of the differential impact of the Anderson third-party candidacy on the two regions. While Anderson did slightly better in the north than in the south, Carter did slightly better in the latter region than in the former. The appeal of Ronald Reagan seemed to be almost exactly evenly divided between the two regions.

Much has been made of these familiar changes in southern presidential voting.[26] For one thing, it was assumed early on that competitiveness at the presidential level presaged the emergence of a vibrant GOP in the region. In spite of successes at the top of the ticket, it is by now obvious that a strong Republican party has not been built in the South. The party has been unable to recruit more than a handful of attractive candidates in subnational races and has been taken over by ultraconservatives in many states.[27] It also has failed to increase by much the number of GOP loyalists in the electorate. For these reasons perhaps, it has had little success in subnational races. At this writing, the greatest hope for the GOP lies in the continued dealignment of the region's electorate.

Another common assumption has been that defecting Democrats were the major source of support for Republican presidential candidates in the South.[28] The disproportionate number of Democratic loyalists in the early part of the postwar period ensured that GOP gains came from Democratic crossovers. Low party voting rates were undoubtedly a distinguishing feature of the South in the 1950s.

Since the 1950s, though, the proportion of Democratic identifiers within the southern electorate has declined to such a point that high levels of Republican presidential voting no longer require large defection rates among Democrats.

TABLE 8.3
REGIONAL VOTING PATTERNS, 1940-1980
(percent)

		Democratic Candidate	Republican Candidate	All Other Candidates
1940	South	79.6	20.3	0.1
	North	52.4	47.1	0.5
	Difference	[+27.2]	[−26.8]	[−0.4]
1944	South	73.0	23.4	3.6
	North	51.5	48.1	0.4
	Difference	[+21.5]	[−24.7]	[+3.2]
1948	South	51.1	24.9	24.0
	North	49.3	47.3	3.4
	Difference	[+1.8]	[−22.4]	[+20.6]
1952	South	52.3	47.6	0.1
	North	43.2	56.2	0.5
	Difference	[+9.1]	[−8.6]	[−0.4]
1956	South	47.7	48.9	3.4
	North	41.1	58.6	0.3
	Difference	[+6.6]	[−9.7]	[+3.1]
1960	South	51.0	45.2	3.8
	North	49.5	50.2	0.3
	Difference	[+1.5]	[−5.0]	[+3.5]
1964	South	48.9	49.1	2.0
	North	63.3	36.5	0.2
	Difference	[−14.4]	[+12.6]	[+1.8]
1968	South	31.3	34.3	34.4
	North	45.3	45.5	9.2
	Difference	[−14.0]	[−11.2]	[+25.2]
1972	South	28.9	69.8	1.3
	North	39.5	58.6	1.9
	Difference	[−10.6]	[+11.2]	[−0.6]
1976	South	53.9	44.8	1.3
	North	49.9	49.7	2.1
	Difference	[+4.0]	[−4.9]	[−0.8]
1980	South	44.7	52.3	3.0*
	North	40.8	51.5	7.7*
	Difference	[+3.9]	[+0.8]	[−4.7]*

*Anderson vote only.

Source: Compiled by the authors. The percentages contained in this table were computed from the official elections results in the 10-state South. Votes for unpledged Democratic electors were entered in the "other" column.

The South may no longer be exceptional in the low rates of presidential party voting among its Democrats. Instead, with the emergence of a new generation of voters, whose loyalties were formed at a time when party differences were sharp, southern rates of party voting may have come to resemble those in the North.

This hypothesis concerning southern distinctiveness in party voting may be tested directly with data from the presidential election series. Table 8.4 presents the percentage of respondents within each partisan category who voted for their party's presidential nominee, for each presidential election since 1952. For purposes of comparison, the percentage of Independents voting for the candidates is also provided.

While southern Democrats have exhibited consistently less fidelity than their fellow partisans in the North, the differences are surprisingly modest

TABLE 8.4
REGIONAL PATTERNS OF PARTY VOTING, 1952-1976*
(percent)

		Democrats	*Independents*	*Republicans*
1952	South	64	15/85	100
	North	75	34/64	96
	Difference	[−11]	[−19/+21]	[+4]
1956	South	69	26/74	97
	North	76	26/74	96
	Difference	[−7]	[0/0]	[+1]
1960	South	68	32/60	90
	North	86	47/53	94
	Difference	[−18]	[−15/+7]	[−4]
1964	South	81	36/64	90
	North	92	71/29	70
	Difference	[−11]	[−35/+35]	[+20]
1968	South	60	11/61	92
	North	75	31/55	88
	Difference	[−15]	[−20/+6]	[+4]
1972	South	53	24/75	92
	North	62	35/62	94
	Difference	[−9]	[−11/+13]	[−2]
1976	South	80	45/54	89
	North	81	44/53	85
	Difference	[−1]	[+1/−1]	[+4]

*Entries for partisans are percentages of all voters voting for the candidate of their party. For Independents, the percentage voting Democratic is followed by the percentage voting Republican.

Source: Compiled by the authors from ICPSR data.

overall and very slender for a few contests. Throughout the period, even in the face of the poorly received McGovern and Humphrey candidacies, a majority of southern Democrats always supported their party's nominee. To be sure, the fidelity rates since 1964 have been buoyed by almost perfect loyalty among black Democrats, but large numbers of whites could also be counted among the party faithful in these years. It should not be surprising that the Carter candidacy rekindled the fidelity of Democratic partisans. What is surprising is that southern Democrats appear to have been as faithful in 1964. On the whole, southern Democrats were about 10 percent less faithful than northern Democrats across the entire period. While substantial, this difference is considerably less than what we had expected to find.

Regional differences in the fidelity of Democratic loyalists have been unusually low in the 1970s. McGovern was poorly received by fellow partisans in both regions in 1972, causing regional differences to narrow. In 1976 Carter received equal levels of support from Democrats in the two regions. In all likelihood, he was perceived as a national rather than regional candidate again in 1980, thus sustaining the 1976 pattern. For the moment at least, southern distinctiveness in Democratic presidential defection rates seems to have been blunted.

The voting rates of Republicans and Independents show even less regional divergence. Only in 1964 did both of these groups respond differently to the presidential candidates in the South than in the North. While Goldwater's "southern strategy" gained him the support of virtually all southern Republicans and two-thirds of the Independents, it lost him many Republicans and two-thirds of the Independents outside of the South. In all elections but 1964, regional differences in GOP fidelity were insignificant, and majorities of Independents from both regions voted Republican. Putting aside 1964 as a special case, southern Independents voted about 10 percent less Democratic than their northern counterparts from 1952-1976. A margin of this size hardly supports the case for southern exceptionalism. That it vanished in 1976 detracts even more from this case.

The Carter-Ford contest figures prominently in the convergence of regional voting patterns in recent years. Vote totals in 1976 returned to the narrow interregional differences of the 1952-1960 period, and party voting differences dropped to an all time low. Of course it is too soon to say for sure whether this was merely a temporary convergence produced by a southern presidential candidate (although Johnson failed to have a similar impact in 1964) or another sign of the nationalization of southern politics. We prefer the second interpretation. One reason is that the 1976 contest had the earmarks of a national battle. The candidates drew overall support evenly from both regions and from opposing partisans and Independents to about the same degree in each. A second reason is, of course, that the convergence of the two regions in terms of vote totals continued in 1980. For two presidential elections in a row, then, the interregional voting differences which were once such an important factor in American national politics have been all but nonexistent.

It might be argued that the nomination by the Democrats of a nonsouthern, liberal presidential candidate in the future could cause such regional differences to reappear. While a full test of this hypothesis must await the occurrence of future political events, certain evidence would argue against such a possibility. This evidence involves the lack of regional differences in terms of ideology and attitudes on policy issues which will be discussed in the next section.

We can conclude that the exceptionalism of the South has disappeared in presidential voting patterns as well as in partisanship. Regional differences narrowed greatly from 1952-1960, only to be reestablished (this time with the Republican candidates in ascendency) in the 1960s and early 1970s, but was then obliterated again in 1976. The distinctively anti-Democratic flavor to southern presidential voting in the middle years of the period may well have resulted from the pro-civil rights stance of the Democratic nominees and the willingness of the GOP candidates to make an issue of that fact. This implies that southern distinctiveness in recent years, as well as historically, has been rooted in the racial question. With the movement of racial issues off political center stage, regional differences of the magnitude of the pre-1948 period should not reappear in presidential voting. Presidential campaigns must now be waged as fully in the South as elsewhere.

THE END OF DISTINCTIVENESS IN SOUTHERN POLITICAL OUTLOOKS

Partisan loyalties and presidential votes are only two of a number of key elements in presidential politics. Positions on the issues of the day and evaluations of the candidates in terms that include but also transcend issues and party are two additional factors assigned great importance by the leading explanations of voting behavior, as well as by the popular press.[29] To these must be added political ideology, since it is so often the "coin" of political discourse. No consideration of the distinctiveness of the South would be complete without some examination of these political orientations in recent years.

While partisanship and voting have served as the major referents in discussing southern distinctiveness in the past,[30] it is often alleged that the region is more conservative than the rest of the nation when it comes to political issues.[31] Certainly southern conservatism is reflected in Congress as southern Democrats often reject their northern fellow partisans to form a "conservative coalition" with Republicans. A differential orientation toward the major party candidates is often assumed to accompany those ideological differences. Indeed, as the Democratic ties of the region were being broken in the 1950s and 1960s, it was predicted quite confidently that southerners would soon swing over to their natural ideological home in the Republican party.[32] That this has not happened provides a second compelling reason for taking a careful look at these political orientations.

Because so many discussions of the alleged distinctiveness of southerners have been couched in ideological terms, let us begin our examination with ideology. Ideology has proved to be a concept of limited value in dealing with mass political behavior, largely because few Americans seem to possess the relatively enduring systems of interrelated beliefs that constitute an ideology in the pure sense.[33] Nonetheless, a majority are able to locate themselves along a liberal-to-conservative ideological spectrum.[34] This measure of ideological self-placement will serve as our vehicle for testing the proposition of southern ideological distinctiveness.

If ever there was a basis for inferring regional differences in ideological self-placement, that basis had virtually disappeared by 1976. Table 8.5 compares southerners with nonsoutherners on ideological self-placement. The seven-point ideological scale is trichotomized here into the familiar groupings of liberal, moderate, and conservative by separating the two extreme categories from the three middle categories. The figures in the table show quite clearly that regional ideological differences fall within the range of sampling error. Northerners are only 1 percent more liberal than southerners, and just 5 percent more moderate. Southerners are only 6 percent more conservative than the rest of the nation. Differences of this magnitude hardly make the case for southern distinctiveness.

Unfortunately the ideological self-placement measure was not used in the early Michigan studies, which covered the tail end of the period during which the South was so distinctive in its partisan behavior. As a consequence, we can not know for certain whether the 1976 figures are a product of generational changes in the southern electorate or the population migrations which have played a major role in the changing face of the region. When we array ideological self-placement in the 1976 data for each of three generations separately, however, some support can be found for the latter interpretation. While ideological differences are slight in all generations, they are the least for the oldest generation in the 1976 electorate — the generation which entered politics prior to the postwar period. These findings leave a tantalizing hint that the alleged ideological gulf between regions in earlier times may well have been exaggerated.

TABLE 8.5
REGIONAL DIFFERENCES IN IDEOLOGICAL
SELF-PLACEMENT, 1976
(percent)

	Liberals	*Moderates*	*Conservatives*	*(N)*
South	11	64	25	(382)
North	12	69	19	(1526)
Difference	(−1)	(−5)	(+6)	

Source: Compiled by the authors from ICPSR data.

Because of its questionable meaning to an electorate whose main trait is often said to be pragmatism, we cannot rest our case on ideology alone. Regional differences on specific issues should be examined as well. While straightforward in principle, such an examination faces several serious problems in practice. For one thing, many political issues could be considered, and we can hardly cover all of them in this paper. An even more serious problem is that the issues of today are not always, or even often, the issues of yesterday. One need only contrast the issue questions in the 1952 and 1976 presidential election studies to recognize how ephemeral many issues are. In short, while we can identify many issues at any one point in time, few among them can be compared across a lengthy time period. Even for those issue concerns measured at two points in time, severe problems of equivalence exist. In the middle 1960s, the format of the issue questions was changed in the Michigan studies, making exact comparisons impossible. But even if the format had remained constant, the changing context of issues undermines the equivalence of the same items.

With these problems in mind, we have selected a sample of four issues to examine in the 1976 data. One of the issues reflects an enduring conflict between the two major parties in American politics since the 1930s: the matter of whether the government should guarantee jobs and a minimum standard of living. The second issue lies at the core of presumed regional differences even though it is of more recent vintage: the speed of the civil rights movement. The third issue has a foreign policy focus: should the United States give aid to nations even if they do not stand for the same things we do. While this particular wording of the question has a contemporary flavor, the basic controversy dates from at least the beginning of the Cold War. Finally, we have selected an issue of only contemporary topicality: equal rights for women. These four issues, while hardly a comprehensive set, reflect a diversity of concerns and seem fairly representative of current controversies. If southerners are distinctive in their political outlooks, they should evidence it here.

Regional differences in positions on these four issues are portrayed in Table 8.6.[35] Differences exist on each issue, but they are surprisingly small and border on statistical insignificance. This is surely not the stuff of southern distinctiveness! Indeed while southerners are more likely to elect the most conservative alternative on all four of the questions, they are also more likely to take the most liberal position on the matter of government guarantees of jobs and a standard of living. These findings join those reported by Bass and DeVries,[36] and second their conclusion that regional differences have faded. Greater issue differences may be expected, as Bass and DeVries have found, between blacks and whites within the South than between southerners and northerners.

Finally, it is of interest to compare southerners and nonsoutherners in terms of their evaluations of the presidential candidates. The 1976 comparison is particularly appropriate because it focuses upon a regional native son — the Democratic candidate, Jimmy Carter. Even if regional distinctiveness did not exist for issues and ideology, it should appear in evaluating a southern

TABLE 8.6
REGIONAL DIFFERENCES ON FOUR ISSUES, 1976
(percent)

	South	North	Difference
Government Gurantee Jobs/			
Standard of Living			
Government guarantee	27	20	(+7)
Mixed	34	45	(−11)
Each person on own	39	35	(+4)
N of cases	(505)	(1766)	
Speed of Civil Rights			
Too fast	48	40	(+8)
About right	44	52	(−8)
Too slow	9	8	(+1)
N of cases	(643)	(2030)	
Foreign Aid to Nations Unlike U.S.			
Agree	33	41	(−8)
Disagree	67	59	(+8)
N of cases	(484)	(1634)	
Equal Role for Women			
Equal role	45	47	(−2)
Mixed	33	38	(−5)
Woman's place in the home	22	15	(+7)
N of cases	(484)	(1683)	

Source: Compiled by the authors from ICPSR data.

presidential candidate if there is anything to the notion that southerners possess strong regional loyalties.[37] Table 8.7 contains the mean candidate thermometer scores registered by Carter and Ford among southerners and nonsoutherners.[38] The evaluations of Ford differed little between the regions, while, as expected, southerners were more positive than northerners toward Carter. What was not expected was the small size of the regional difference for the Democratic standard-bearer. Carter was evaluated only 6 percent more positively in the South than in the North. His margin over Ford among fellow southerners was greater but still not substantial. Southerners were more favorably disposed toward a "native son" but not to the degree we would expect from an isolated political region.

    In the interest of parsimony, we have limited our treatment in this section to the 1976 election and to samples of the several measures of ideology, the issues of the day, and well-known political figures in the land. There is little reason to suppose that regional differences are greater for the orientations we did not consider, although it is quite conceivable that they will be more

TABLE 8.7
REGIONAL DIFFERENCES IN RATINGS OF
PRESIDENTIAL CANDIDATES, 1976
(percent)

	Carter	Ford	(N)
South	69	61	(636/645)
North	63	63	(2086/2121)
Difference	(+6)	(−2)	

Source: Compiled by the authors from ICPSR data.

substantial on some of them as well as less substantial on others. As limited as our analysis has been, in other words, we believe that it reflects a basic fact of American political life by 1976: that the South was not distinctive from the North in the ideological, issue, and candidate orientations of its citizens. It was surely more distinctive in previous times.

Issues and candidate evaluations, and sometimes even ideology, are commonly referred to as short term forces in an election and contrasted with the long term force of partisan loyalty. We have already shown how the distribution of the long term force of partisanship has become more and more similar for southerners and nonsoutherners, to the point that differences in it have all but vanished among the youngest generation. The analysis of this section provides a complementary perspective: regional differences where the short term forces are concerned are insignificant as well. Given these findings, it should come as no surprise that the voting choices of the two regions differ so little. The triangulation of these three elements in mass political orientations chronicles indeed the end to southern exceptionalism.

CONCLUSION

> Though not always directly expressed, the perennial question which has nagged students of southern politics for upwards of forty years is, "How soon and under what conditions may the South's politics evolve or be brought into conformity with the national pattern?"[39]

This paper has directly addressed the question of southern conformity to national patterns in mass political behavior. Although not the whole of politics, mass orientations and behavior constitute a vital element of it. Indeed some might argue that this element defines the constraints within which the other components of politics must operate.

Where mass political behavior in presidential politics is concerned, it is clear from the findings of this study that the era of southern exceptionalism has ended. The South's mass politics now conform to national patterns. Convergence of the two regions is most obvious in the least stable aspects of political behavior — voting for presidential candidates, evaluations of those candidates, positions on issues, and political ideology. But convergence is apparent also in enduring partisan loyalties.

It is the changes in partisanship that promise to leave the lasting mark on southern politics. The party identifications of the youngest generations of southerners and nonsoutherners are very similar. By contrast the older generations reveal loyalties which conform closely to the patterns of an earlier time, when the South was solidly Democratic and the North competitive in partisan politics. These figures illustrate the tenacity with which older Americans cling to partisan loyalties developed and hardened earlier in life. They show also how change in the partisan composition of an electorate most often occurs: through the entry of new generations into politics. The generational replacement process should produce a future much different from the past, as the older generations fade from the scene, leaving American politics less regionalized and more nationalized than it has ever been.

The forces nationalizing American politics may be even stronger than this analysis suggests. As regional electorates become more similar, regional themes are likely to give way to common national appeals in presidential campaigning. Increased use of the media, especially television, in presidential campaigning certainly has accelerated this trend. Such forces reinforce, and may even promote, regional similarities. A southern president, campaigning as a national leader, can not help but intensify these tendencies.

Less clear are the conditions that have produced the end of southern distinctiveness in mass political behavior. The strength of the dealignment process among younger Americans and the election of a president from the traditional South seem the most likely proximate causes. But these proximate causes, as usual, can not provide satisfactory explanations for the phenomenon of convergence, nor for that matter can they account for their own appearance. Our search must go deeper.

As is often the case in analyzing southern politics, the search for underlying causes may be guided by the insights of V. O. Key. In his brilliant analysis of the traditional Solid South, Key identified southern racial patterns as the principal source of southern political distinctiveness.[40] He found substantial political competition in the South. What the region lacked was *party* competition. In order to preserve the "dual society," Key contended, southern whites had presented a united front to the outside for a century. The representative of the united front was the Democratic party. Whatever it meant to northerners, it stood for white supremacy in the South.

Consequently it was the South's adherence to the Democratic party in loyalty and in voting that stood for nearly a century as its most distinctive characteristic. This adherence found its basis in racial considerations. It did not depend upon the views of southerners on other matters of political controversy. For, in national politics at least, these views were kept off the political agenda by the racial question.

With the destruction of the most important features of the dual society in the postwar period, the rationale for uniform Democratic loyalties among southerners in national politics has vanished. This has freed white southerners from basing their nationally-focused political behavior upon regional considerations. Furthermore, with federal intervention to secure black voting rights, the southern electorate was leavened with large numbers of black voters, thus increasing the risk that segregationist campaign appeals would repel more voters than they attracted. As Key would have predicted, southern distinctiveness has disappeared with the end of the South's commitment to maintain a segregated order.

Even under the strongest of pressures, political change often occurs at a glacial pace. In some respects, the South has proven to be an exception to this rule. The pace of political change there has been rapid in the last 20 years. In other respects, though, the south "proves" the rule, for vestiges of the traditional South remain in the modern southern electorate and continue to affect its politics. Older southerners, as we have seen, cling to their Democratic loyalties even though the Democratic party is no longer the guarantor of southern autonomy on racial matters. Southern leadership in Congress remains tinged by the old concerns. Southern state politics still uses the Democratic party as its primary battleground. Yet these vestiges of the old order should fade with the passage of time, as the politics of dealignment engulfs the South as well as the nation.

NOTES

1. See, for example, John Shelton Reed, *The Enduring South* (Lexington, Mass: D. C. Heath, 1972).

2. See John Shelton Reed, " 'The Cardinal Test of a Southerner': Not Race but Geography," *Public Opinion Quarterly* 37 (Summer 1973): 232-240.

3. This theme is developed in detail in V. O. Key, Jr., *Southern Politics in State and Nation* (New York: Alfred A. Knopf, 1949).

4. Ibid.

5. Studies dealing with the South as a separate political system are far too numerous to list here. An excellent bibliography of them is provided in *The Changing Politics of the South*, ed. William C. Havard (Baton Rouge: Louisiana State University Press, 1972), pp. 736-738.

6. A large literature addresses the changes which have taken place in the South since World War II. See, for example, *The South in Continuity and Change*, eds. John C. McKinney and Edgar T. Thompson (Durham: Duke University Press, 1965); and *Change in the Contemporary South*, ed. Allan P. Sindler (Durham: Duke University Press, 1963).

7. John C. McKinney and Linda Bourque, "The Changing South: National Incorporation of a Region," *American Sociological Review* 36 (June 1971): 399-412.

8. See generally Reed, *The Enduring South*; and Norval D. Glenn and J. L. Simmons, "Are Regional Cultural Differences Diminishing?," *Public Opinion Quarterly* 31 (Summer 1967): 176-193.

9. The consequences of this participation surge are developed in Earl Black, *Southern Governors and Civil Rights* (Cambridge, Mass: Harvard University Press, 1976).

10. Good examples of this focus are found in Jack Bass and Walter DeVries, *The Transformation of Southern Politics* (New York: Basic Books, 1976); Paul Allen Beck, "Partisan Dealignment in the Postwar South," *American Political Science Review* 71 (June 1977): 477-496; Bruce A. Campbell, "Change in the Southern Electorate," *American Journal of Political Science* 21 (February 1977): 37-64; and Bruce A. Campbell, "Patterns of Change in the Partisan Loyalties of Native Southerners: 1952-1972," *Journal of Politics* 39 (August 1977): 730-761.

11. Beck, "Partisan Dealignment in the Postwar South," pp. 477-496.

12. Key, *Southern Politics*, pp. 315-382.

13. V. O. Key, Jr., and Frank Munger, "Social Determinism and Electoral Decision: The Case of Indiana," in *American Voting Behavior*, eds. Eugene Burdick and Arthur J. Brodbeck (Glencoe, Ill: The Free Press, 1959), pp. 281-299.

14. Angus Campbell, Philip Converse, Warren E. Miller, and Donald Stokes, *The American Voter* (New York: John Wiley and Sons, 1964), pp. 86-96.

15. James Sundquist, *Dynamics of the American Party System* (Washington, D.C.: The Brookings Institution, 1973), pp. 120-154, 183-217.

16. To simplify our analysis, we treat only partisan direction and ignore partisan intensities. Both weak and strong partisans qualify as partisans. Independents include pure Independents as well as Independents who said they felt closer to one or the other of the parties. Others are largely apoliticals but also include a handful of identifiers with third parties.

17. See the discussion in Kristi Andersen, *The Creation of a Democratic Majority, 1928-1936* (Chicago: University of Chicago Press, 1979).

18. An example of early analysis is given in Donald Strong, *Urban Republicanism in the South* (University, Alabama: University of Alabama Press, 1960).

19. Beck, "Partisan Dealignment in the Postwar South," pp. 477-496.

20. Ibid., p. 484.

21. For a useful qualification of this explanation, see Campbell, "Patterns of Change," pp. 730-761.

22. Paul Allen Beck, "A Socialization Theory of Partisan Realignment," in *The Politics of Future Citizens*, ed. Richard G. Niemi (San Francisco: Jossey-Bass, 1974), pp. 199-219.

23. Paul Allen Beck, "The Electoral Cycle and Patterns of American Politics," *British Journal of Political Science* 9 (April 1979): 129-156.

24. Initially we separated native whites from other southerners in the analysis. Because the population migrations cancel out the mobilization of blacks, however, the figures for native whites alone are little different from those for the entire southern electorate. Thus, to provide greater generalizability, we have presented the data for all southerners.

25. A generational interpretation of these partisanship trends is appropriate. When the loyalties of the three age groups are traced across the 1952-1976 period (where possible), the young emerge as much more Independent than their elders were at the same stage of the life cycle. Even if these young were to become more partisan as they aged, at past rates of "hardening" they would fall far short of the partisan levels achieved by their elders.

26. For an interesting treatment of these changes, as well as changes in party voting, using the normal vote construct, see Campbell, "Change in the Southern Electorate," pp. 37-64.

27. Bass and DeVries, *The Transformation of Southern Politics*, pp. 27-32.

28. William C. Havard, "From Past to Future: An Overview of Southern Politics," in *The Changing Politics of the South*, pp. 690-691.

29. See generally Campbell et al., *The American Voter*; and Norman H. Nie, Sidney Verba, and John Petrocik, *The Changing American Voter* (Cambridge, Mass: Harvard University Press, 1976).

30. Key, *Southern Politics*, pp. 386-528.

31. See, for example, Glenn and Simmons, "Are Regional Cultural Differences Diminishing?," pp. 176-193; and Kevin P. Phillips, *The Emerging Republican Majority* (Garden City, New York: Anchor Books, 1970), pp. 187-289.

32. Phillips, *The Emerging Republican Majority*, pp. 461-464.

33. Philip E. Converse, "The Nature of Belief Systems in Mass Publics," in *Ideology and Discontent*, ed. David Apter (New York: The Free Press, 1964), pp. 206-261.

34. Teresa A. Levitin and Warren E. Miller, "Ideological Interpretations of Presidential Elections," *American Political Science Reivew* 73 (September 1979): 751-771.

35. For the civil rights and foreign aid questions, the figures for the original categories are presented. The equality of women and government guarantee questions, on the other hand, asked respondents to locate themselves on a seven-point scale between alternative positions. In each case, we trichotomized this scale by separating the two extreme categories at either end from the middle three categories.

36. Bass and DeVries, *The Transformation of Southern Politics*, pp. 15-19.

37. Reed, " 'The Cardinal Test of a Southerner': Not Race but Geography," pp. 232-240.

38. Respondents were asked to indicate their liking for a candidate on a 100-point thermometer scale. On this scale, warmness or favorable feelings were to receive scores above 50. The score of 50 was to be reserved for neutral feelings or no feelings at all. While the thermometer scores are strongly correlated with vote, it is possible (and quite common) for both candidates to receive positive ratings from the same respondent. Thus, the thermometer difference between the candidates in the South exceeds the vote difference for the region, permitting regional favoritism even if a southerner voted for Ford.

39. Havard, "From Past to Future," p. 701.

40. Key, *Southern Politics*, pp. 665-668.

9

PRESIDENTIAL ACTIVISTS AND THE NATIONALIZATION OF PARTY POLITICS IN VIRGINIA

Alan Abramowitz, John McGlennon,
and Ronald Rapoport

Ronald Reagan's decisive victory over Jimmy Carter on November 4, 1980 concluded one of the longest presidential election campaigns in American history. By far the greatest portion of that campaign consisted of the contests for the Democratic and Republican nominations. In 1980, as in most recent presidential camapigns, the Democratic and Republican nominating conventions were largely anticlimactic gatherings which merely ratified the decisions already made in the state primaries and caucuses between January and June of 1980. Although the primaries continued to attract most of the attention of the mass media, 15 states selected some or all of their delegates to the national conventions through a system of party caucuses and conventions. The nature of the campaign in these caucus-convention states differed in several respects from that which occurred in the primary states. Probably the most important distinguishing feature of the caucus-convention system is the role played by party activists, those individuals who are willing to devote the time and effort required to attend local party caucuses and serve as delegates to the state conventions. Although there has been extensive research on the characteristics and beliefs of national convention delegates, very little is known about presidential party activists at the state level.[1] This study will examine the characteristics, political beliefs, and motivations of presidential party activists in Virginia, a southern state in which two-party competition has developed rapidly since the end of World War II.[2] We are interested in how this realignment has affected party activists and organizations in the Old Dominion.

In Virginia, as in most of the rest of the South, Jimmy Carter and Ronald Reagan were easy victors in their parties' contests for national convention delegates. At the Democratic state convention, Edward Kennedy received some support from suburban Northern Virginia as well as black support from parts of Southside Virginia. Overall, however, Kennedy's supporters were only able to elect five delegates to the Democratic National Convention compared with 59 for Carter. On the Republican side, George Bush provided the principal opposition to Ronald Reagan. Although he attracted scattered support at the Republican state convention, Bush failed to elect any delegates to the Republican National Convention. The lack of competition in both parties resulted in relatively low turnouts at most of the "mass meetings" which were held throughout the state during the spring to elect delegates to the state conventions. Since little effort was made by any of the presidential candidates to mobilize support outside of regular party channels, we expected most of the delegates elected to the state conventions to be regular party activists, rather than individuals who were motivated by factors peculiar to this contest.

Our study is based on a survey of delegates who attended the Democratic and Republican state conventions which were held in Richmond on successive weekends in June. We distributed 3000 self-administered questionnaires at each convention by placing them on the delegates' seats before the start of the main session. The questionnaires were gathered in collection boxes at the exits from the convention hall and by a crew including the authors, circulating on the floor during proceedings. We obtained 1669 usable questionnaires at the Democratic convention and 1716 at the Republican convention. In general, our sample of delegates appears to be representative of each convention in terms of candidate support and geographical distribution.[3] All of the findings presented in this paper are based on the results of the delegate survey.

WHO ARE THE ACTIVISTS?

What sorts of individuals were willing to devote the time and effort required to attend local party caucuses and serve as delegates to the state conventions? Not surprisingly, one characteristic of these activists was strong party loyalties. There has been a marked decline in party loyalties in the American electorate since the mid-1960s so that, at present, fewer than one out of four voters are strong party identifiers while two-fifths are independents.[4] However, among our sample of delegates, about four-fifths in each party were strong party identifiers while less than 8 percent were independents. Furthermore, there was almost no difference between the state and national party affiliations of the delegates. We found almost no Democratic delegates who classified themselves as Virginia Democrats but independents or Republicans in national politics. Likewise, there were almost no Republican delegates who did not identify strongly with the state as well as the national Republican party. Thus, the traditional separation between state and national partisanship which characterized Virginia politics during the Byrd era appears to have disappeared, at least among these party activists.[5]

Most of the delegates responding to our survey had been active in politics prior to the 1980 presidential campaign. Seventy-two percent of the Democratic delegates and 65 percent of the Republicans said that they had been active in all or most recent state and national campaigns. Only 7 percent of the Democrats and 12 percent of the Republicans had not been active in any recent state or national campaigns. Just over half of the Democratic delegates and three-fifths of the Republicans had been delegates to previous state party conventions and a majority of each party's delegates (55 percent of the Democrats and 53 percent of the Republicans) were members of local party committees.

As we expected, most of the delegates attending the state conventions in 1980 were regular party activists. However, very few of these delegates were professional politicians. Table 9.1 shows that only a tiny fraction of the delegates in each party held any elected or appointed political office and very few were paid campaign workers. Thus, very few of these delegates were pursuing political careers. Both conventions were dominated by amateur political activists.

Given the recent development of the Virginia Republican party, it is not surprising that almost half (46 percent) of the Republican delegates had been active in their party for less than 5 years while only 13 percent had been active for more than 20 years. Even among the Democratic delegates, however, 33 percent had been active for less than 5 years compared with 21 percent who had been active for more than 20 years. It may be difficult to sustain the involvement of amateur activists over long periods of time. As a result, there is probably a high rate of turnover among the ranks of volunteer political workers. Most of the delegates attending the Virginia state party conventions in 1980 had

TABLE 9.1
POLITICAL ACTIVITIES OF DELEGATES

	Percentage of	
Type of Activity	*Democratic Delegates*	*Republican Delegates*
Local Committee Member	55	53
Local Committee Chair	7	5
Other Local Committee Office	11	11
Congressinal District Committee Member	8	6
State Central Committee Member	5	1
State or National Elected Office	2	1
Local Elected Office	7	4
Appointed Political Office	6	7
Campaign Staff	3	2
Delegate to Previous State or National Convention	52	62

Source: Compiled by the authors.

become active since the emergence of two-party competition in the state. There were very few holdovers from the era of one-party domination.

In terms of social background characteristics, amateur political activists are generally relatively affluent and well-educated in comparison with the voting public. The skills, motivation, and disposable time required to engage in voluntary political activity are found disproportionately among the college educated business and professional classes. Table 9.2 shows that Virginia party activists were no exception to this generalization. Both Democratic and Republican

TABLE 9.2
SOCIAL BACKGROUND CHARACTERISTICS OF DELEGATES

Social Background Characteristics	Percentage of	
	Democratic Delegates	Republican Delegates
Age:		
18-29	18	15
30-39	26	21
40-49	20	21
50-59	19	24
60-69	14	15
70+	4	3
Sex:		
Female	51	47
Male	49	53
Religion:		
Protestant	78	81
Catholic	12	13
Jewish	3	1
Other, None	7	5
Education:		
High School or less	19	12
Some College	23	31
Graduated College	19	25
Post-College	40	32
Family Income:		
0-$14,999	15	9
15-$24,999	27	19
25-$34,999	22	24
35-$44,999	15	20
45-$59,999	11	15
$60,000+	11	13

Source: Compiled by the authors.

delegates were generally well-off economically and highly educated. In fact, there were only slight differences between the two parties. Almost three-fifths of the delegates in both parties were college graduates, although Democratic activists were somewhat more likely to have continued their schooling beyond college. This was partially due to the large number of teachers who were delegates to the Democratic convention. On the other hand, a somewhat larger proportion of Republican delegates reported incomes above $35,000. These relatively small differences, however, should not obscure the overriding conclusion that both groups of party activists had much higher incomes and much more schooling than the general public.

Both political parties have made special efforts in recent years to stimulate greater participation in party affairs by women and members of minority groups such as blacks and Hispanics. In the case of women, both parties appear to have been successful in Virginia. About half of the delegates in each party were female. However, there was a large discrepancy between the two parties in the representation of blacks, who make up about one-fifth of Virginia's population. Blacks comprised 17 percent of the Democratic delegates in our sample compared with only 1 percent of the Republican delegates. In this respect, at least, the conventions did reflect the social characteristics of the two parties' electoral coalitions in Virginia. With a few exceptions, the black vote in Virginia has gone very heavily to Democratic candidates in recent state and national elections.[6]

Along with its recent economic and industrial development, the South has experienced a large influx of population from the North. This in-migration, which has consisted disproportionately of skilled professionals and white collar workers, has contributed to the growth of the Republican party in many of the metropolitan areas of the South.[7] Next to Florida, among the southern states, Virginia has the largest proportion of residents who were born outside the state (approximately 37 percent according to the 1970 census). A majority (56 percent) of the Republican delegates in our sample grew up outside Virginia while two-fifths of our Democratic delegates were born elsewhere. Thus, in-migration has been an important source of new activists for both parties in Virginia, and especially for the GOP.

In addition to in-migration, another potential source of new recruits for the Republican party in the South has been the conversion of traditional Democrats who have been alienated by their party's growing liberalism. In Virginia, several prominent conservative Democrats defected to the GOP during the early 1970s.[8] In our sample, among the Republican delegates who were Virginia natives, 32 percent were former Democrats.[9] Thus, along with in-migration, conversion has been an important source of new Republican party activists in Virginia.

In addition to their involvement in party politics, many Democratic and Republican delegates had been active in other types of organizations. For these individuals, participation in politics was one manifestation of a more general pattern of civic activity. There were, however, several important differences between the types of organizations in which Democratic and Republican delegates were involved. Table 9.3 shows that Democratic delegates were more likely to be active in labor unions, teachers' organizations, conservation groups, women's rights groups, and civil rights organizations than were Republican delegates. The National Education Association, the largest teachers' organization in the nation and in Virginia, actively encouraged its members to support Jimmy Carter's reelection in 1980. Judging by our results, the NEA was very successful in getting its members elected as delegates to the Virginia Democratic Convention since more than one-fourth of the Democratic delegates in our sample had been active in teachers' organizations.

In contrast to the Democrats, Republican delegates were more likely to be active in business organizations, church-related organizations, and anti-abortion groups. The involvement of various fundamentalist Christian organizations in support of conservative Republican candidates for the presidency and other offices was a source of considerable controversy during the 1980 campaign. However, the Republican delegates in our sample were only slightly more likely than Democratic delegates to identify themselves as "born-again" Christians (32 percent vs. 26 percent) or describe themselves as "very religious" (29 percent vs. 23 percent). It does not appear that the "Christian right" had a major impact on the 1980 Virginia Republican convention. In general, the organizations represented at each convention were those which have supported the

TABLE 9.3
ORGANIZATIONAL ACTIVITIES OF DELEGATES

Type of Organization	*Percentage of*	
	Democratic Delegates	*Republican Delegates*
Labor Unions	13	2
Teachers or Educational	27	11
Other Professional	24	25
Business	16	24
Church or Religious	28	34
Women's Rights	18	4
Civil Rights	25	3
Conservation/Ecology	11	7
Public Interest	25	17
Anti-Abortion	2	11
Agricultural	9	6
Other Issue-Related	16	17

Source: Compiled by the authors.

national Democratic and Republican parties in recent years; liberal and labor organizations were well represented at the Virginia Democratic convention while conservative and business organizations were well represented at the Virginia Republican convention.

ISSUES AND CANDIDATES

Despite rather similar social background characteristics, Democratic and Republican activists in Virginia represented different types of organized interest groups. There were also sharp contrasts between their political philosophies and issue positions. A majority (58 percent) of Democratic delegates described themselves as liberals while almost 90 percent of Republican delegates described themselves as conservatives. Table 9.4 shows that Democratic and Republican delegates' positions on 13 national issues were generally consistent with their

TABLE 9.4
ISSUE LIBERALISM OF DELEGATES[a]

	Percentage of	
Issue	*Democratic Delegates*	*Republican Delegates*
Equal Rights Amendment[b]	73	21
Constitutional Amendment to Prohibit Abortions[c]	72	54
Substantial Increase in Defense Spending[c]	46	5
National Health Insurance[b]	64	13
More Rapid Development of Nuclear Power[c]	51	17
Non-Defense Budget Cuts[c]	53	22
Affirmative Action Programs[b]	72	24
Oil Price Decontrol[c]	49	23
Wage-Price Controls[b]	53	27
Increased Unemployment if Needed to Control Inflation[c]	51	28
Draft Registration[c]	30	15
Ratification of SALT II[b]	65	16
Military Presence in Middle East[c]	34	18

[a]Percentage giving liberal response + half of undecided percentage.
[b]"Favor" is liberal position.
[c]"Oppose" is liberal position.

Source: Compiled by the authors.

ideological positions. Democratic delegates were substantially more liberal than Republican delegates on all 13 issues,[10] with the greatest differences occurring on those issues on which there were clear disagreements between Jimmy Carter and Ronald Reagan, such as the Equal Rights Amendment and the SALT Treaty, or which have traditionally divided the national Democratic and Republican parties, such as National Health Insurance. The average liberalism score was 55 percent for Democratic delegates compared with 22 percent for Republican delegates. On nine domestic policy issues, the average liberalism scores were 60 percent for Democratic delegates vs. 25 percent for Republican delegates. On the four foreign policy/national defense issues the average liberalism scores were 44 percent for Democratic delegates vs. 14 percent for Republican delegates.

Although Democratic delegates were, on the average, much more liberal than Republican delegates, they were also much more divided in their issue positions than were the Republicans. If we measure intraparty agreement by the difference between the percentage of delegates on opposing sides of each issue, the average agreement score is 57 percent for Republican delegates but only 23 percent for Democratic delegates. Only on the issue of a constitutional amendment to prohibit abortion were Republican delegates more divided in their opinions than Democratic delegates. Thus, the domination of the Democratic convention by supporters of Jimmy Carter concealed deep divisions within the party on a number of important national issues. Edward Kennedy drew his support at the Virginia Democratic convention almost entirely from the liberal wing of the party while Carter delegates were about equally divided between the liberal and the moderate-conservative camps. Although Bush delegates to the Republican convention were generally less conservative than Reagan delegates, the differences between the two candidates' supporters on most issues were slight. Four-fifths of the Bush delegates expressed a favorable opinion of Reagan and three-fifths of the Reagan delegates expressed a favorable opinion of Bush. In contrast, about two-thirds of the Carter delegates expressed an unfavorable opinion of Kennedy and about the same proportion of Kennedy delegates expressed an unfavorable opinion of Carter.

Democratic delegates were much more divided than Republican delegates in their attitudes toward the candidates seeking their party's nomination as well as in their issue positions. In fact, 39 percent of Kennedy delegates indicated that they would not actively support Jimmy Carter if he received the Democratic nomination and 41 percent of Carter delegates indicated that they would not actively support Edward Kennedy. In contrast, only 2 percent of Bush delegates said that they would not actively support Ronald Reagan if he received the Republican nomination and only 18 percent of Reagan delegates indicated that they would not work for George Bush. Thus, the task of reuniting the party after the convention was bound to be much more difficult for Virginia Democrats than for the GOP.

POLITICAL STYLE AND MOTIVATIONS

The two major parties in the United States are frequently criticized for not giving voters a clear choice between alternative political philosophies. While this may often be true of the candidates who are nominated by the parties, Democratic and Republican activists in Virginia clearly did hold contrasting views on a wide range of issues. Moreover, the delegates in our study were not inclined to temporize on the issues for the sake of electoral success. About two-thirds of the delegates in each party agreed with the statement that "a political party should be more concerned with issues than with winning elections." Likewise, four-fifths of Democratic and Republican delegates agreed that "a candidate should express his convictions even if it costs him an election." A plurality of Democratic delegates (46 percent) and a large majority of Republican delegates (61 percent) also disagreed with the statement that "broad electoral appeal is more important for a political party than a consistent ideology." In general, these Virginia party activists felt that parties should take clear positions on the issues regardless of the electoral consequences. Most of these delegates were purists rather than pragmatists in their attitudes toward party strategy. For them, issues were the ends for which parties existed rather than a means to be used in pursuit of victory at the polls.

In order to explain the ideological purism of Democratic and Republican activists, we must examine their motives for becoming active in politics. With the decline of patronage as a reward for political activity, parties have had to rely increasingly on volunteer workers motivated by their enthusiasm for a cause or for a particular candidate. Among our Democratic and Republican delegates, the principal reasons given for involvement in the 1980 presidential campaign were issue concerns, support for a particular candidate, and party loyalty (Table 9.5). In contrast, very few delegates cited political career ambitions as a reason for their involvement in the 1980 campaign. Given these motivations, it is not surprising that most of these Democratic and Republican activists were more concerned with advancing their issue and ideological concerns than with winning the election. Their personal stake in the outcome of the election was minimal.

THE ACTIVISTS' VIEWS OF PARTY ORGANIZATION

A successful political party is more than a collection of individuals. It is also an organization, and it requires money, leadership, and structure. The recent success of the Virginia Republican party has been widely attributed to its organizational superiority over the Virginia Democratic party.[11] In fundraising, in computer-based information storage and retrieval, and in communications technology, the once dominant Democrats have been far out-distanced by the GOP in recent campaigns. Thus, in 1980, the Virginia Republican party reported independent expenditures of $590,000 on behalf of Ronald Reagan's

TABLE 9.5
MOTIVATIONS OF DELEGATES
(For Participation in 1980 Campaign)

	Percentage of	
Type of Motivation	Democratic Delegates	Republican Delegates
Party Support:		
Very Important	76	74
Somewhat Important	19	20
Not Important	5	6
Political Career:		
Very Important	11	6
Somewhat Important	17	11
Not Important	72	83
Campaign Excitement:		
Very Important	21	15
Somewhat Important	36	34
Not Important	43	51
Meeting People:		
Very Important:	32	27
Somewhat Important	42	42
Not Important	26	32
Candidate Support:		
Very Important	75	84
Somewhat Important	19	13
Not Important	6	3
Issue Concerns:		
Very Important	75	87
Somewhat Important	20	11
Not Important	5	2
Prestige/Visibility:		
Very Important	13	10
Somewhat Important	21	16
Not Important	66	74
Civic Duty:		
Very Important	54	54
Somewhat Important	34	34
Not Important	12	12

Source: Compiled by the authors.

presidential campaign while the Virginia Democratic party spent only $52,000 on Jimmy Carter's reelection.

Money, while extremely important, is only one measure of a party organization's effectiveness. We asked the delegates in our study to rate the overall effectiveness of each party's organization in Virginia and to evaluate their own party's performance in five specific areas: campaign assistance, issue development, intraparty communication, candidate selection, and voter communication. Both Democratic and Republican delegates rated the Republican state organization as more effective than the Democratic state organization in Virginia. Seventeen percent of Democratic delegates rated their party's state organization as "very effective," while 49 percent rated it as "fairly effective," and 32 percent rated it as "not very effective" or "not at all effective" (2 percent had no opinion). In contrast, 56 percent of Republican delegates rated their party's state organization as "very effective," 39 percent rated it as "fairly effective," and only 3 percent rated it as "not very effective" or "not at all effective" (3 percent had no opinion). While 80 percent of Democratic delegates rated the Republican state organization as "very" or "fairly" effective, only 39 percent of Republican delegates rated the Democratic state organization as "very" or "fairly" effective.

When asked how important a role their state party organization should play and how important a role it was playing in the five areas listed above, there was almost no difference between Democratic and Republican delegates' views about what role their state organization should play (Table 9.6). Both groups felt that their state party organization should play an important role in all five areas. However, Republican delegates' ratings of their organization's influence were consistently higher than Democratic delegates' ratings of their organization's influence. Democratic and Republican activists agreed about what the state party organization should be doing, but the Republicans were more likely to believe that their organization was already doing these things. Thus, the impressions of Democratic and Republican party activists were consistent with the evidence from campaign expenditures: in recent years the Virginia Republican party has apparently enjoyed a considerable organizational advantage over the Virginia Democratic party.

CONCLUSIONS

Between 1876 and 1948 Virginia supported only one Republican presidential candidate — Herbert Hoover in 1928. Between 1952 and 1980 Virginia supported only one Democratic presidential candidate — Lyndon Johnson in 1964. In presidential politics, at least, Virginia has clearly undergone a major party realignment since the end of World War II. The party activists in our study reflect the dramatic changes that have occurred in Virginia politics during this period. There is now a fairly sharp ideological cleavage between Democratic

TABLE 9.6
DELEGATES' VIEWS OF PARTY ORGANIZATION'S ACTIVITIES

Type of Activity	Percentage of Democratic Delegates		Percentage of Republican Delegates	
	Actual Party Role	Ideal Party Role	Actual Party Role	Ideal Party Role
Campaign Assistance:				
Very Important	35	82	48	82
Somewhat Important	32	15	32	15
Not Important	22	2	7	1
No Opinion	10	1	13	2
Debating Issues:				
Very Important	26	61	33	62
Somewhat Important	32	27	36	25
Not Important	33	10	18	10
No Opinion	9	2	14	3
Communication With Party Members:				
Very Important	34	82	42	82
Somewhat Important	31	15	35	16
Not Important	25	2	10	1
No Opinion	10	1	13	1
Recruiting Candidates:				
Very Important	29	70	41	73
Somewhat Important	30	23	32	20
Not Important	30	5	14	5
No Opinion	11	2	14	2
Communication With Voters:				
Very Important	33	80	41	82
Somewhat Important	27	17	34	14
Not Important	31	2	13	2
No Opinion	9	1	12	1

Source: Compiled by the authors.

and Republican activists in Virginia with a predominantly liberal Democratic party confronting an overwhelmingly conservative Republican party. The conservatives who once dominated the Virginia Democratic party have apparently either died, retired from political activity, or become Republicans. The conservative torch has been passed from the Byrd organization to the Republican party.

In-migration from the North and Democratic defections have contributed to the growth of an effective grass-roots Republican organization in Virginia.

Meanwhile, the ideologically divided Democrats have been unable to match the GOP's organizational efforts as intraparty factional strife has impeded the mounting of effective campaigns against the GOP in recent state and national elections. Even in 1980, despite Jimmy Carter's relatively easy victory at the Democratic state convention, internal divisions were evident. As an ideological moderate and a fellow Southerner, and as the incumbent, Jimmy Carter appealed to a broad spectrum of Virginia Democratic activists. In contrast, Edward Kennedy's support was confined almost entirely to the liberal wing of the party. These Kennedy delegates showed little interest in uniting behind Jimmy Carter if their candidate was denied the nomination. Moreover, although only 16 percent of the Democratic delegates in our sample supported Kennedy, his support was much greater in one section of the state which would be crucial to the outcome of the election: Northern Virginia. In November, Ronald Reagan swamped Jimmy Carter in Northern Virginia by an almost 2 to 1 margin. This was much greater than his margin of victory in the rest of the state. It seems likely that internal divisions among Democratic activists contributed to Reagan's landslide victory in Northern Virginia.[12]

In many respects, the 1980 presidential campaign in Virginia resembled the campaign in much of the rest of the country. The Republican party, dominated by conservative activists, united behind the candidacy of Ronald Reagan. Virginia Democrats, while generally backing President Carter, were divided on many national issues, and a minority of liberal activists dedicated to the candidacy of Senator Edward Kennedy remained unreconciled to the renomination of the incumbent. The Democrats were also outspent and outorganized by the GOP in the fall campaign. All of these features of the 1980 presidential election were evident in many other states. The characteristics, beliefs, and motivations of presidential party activists in Virginia in 1980 were probably similar to those of activists in other caucus-convention states.[13] In presidential politics, Virginia now resembles the rest of the nation.

NOTES

1. The literature on national convention delegates is voluminous. One of the most thorough studies is Jeane Kirkpatrick, *The New Presidential Elite* (New York: Russell Sage Foundation, 1976).

2. For a discussion of the emergence of two-party competition in Virginia, see Ralph Eisenberg, "Virginia: The Emergence of Two-Party Politics," in *The Changing Politics of the South* ed. William C. Havard (Baton Rouge: Louisiana State University Press, 1972), pp. 39-91; see also, J. Harvie Wilkinson III, *Harry Byrd and the Changing Face of Virginia Politics* (Charlottesville: University Press of Virginia, 1968).

3. Precise comparisons between the geographical distributions of the samples and the two conventions are not possible since the parties did not record actual attendance at the conventions for congressional districts. Both samples came very close to the actual propositions of delegates supporting the two major contenders in each party, as reflected by the votes cast by delegates.

4. For a discussion of this phenomenon, see William J. Crotty and Gary C. Jacobson, *American Parties in Decline* (Boston: Little, Brown, 1980), Chapter 2.

5. For a discussion of the Byrd organization, see V. O. Key, Jr., *Southern Politics in State and Nation* (New York: Alfred A. Knopf, 1949), Chapter 2. The separation of state and national partisanship was exemplified by Harry Byrd, Sr.'s traditional "golden silence" in presidential elections.

6. For evidence concerning the black vote in Virginia, see Larry Sabato, *Virginia Votes, 1969-1974* (Charlottesville: Institute of Government, 1975); and Larry Sabato, *Virginia Votes, 1975-1978* (Charlottesville: Institute of Government, 1979). Two exceptions to this generalization were Linwood Holton in his successful 1969 gubernatorial race, and Marshall Coleman in his election as attorney general in 1977.

7. See Louis M. Seagull, *Southern Republicanism* (New York: Wiley, 1975).

8. The defectors included former Democrat Governor Mills Godwin, who switched parties and was elected to the governorship as a Republican in 1973, and former Democrat State Representative George McMath, who switched parties in 1973 and served as Republican state chairman between 1976 and 1980.

9. In contrast, only 9 percent of the native Democratic delegates were former Republicans. This disparity reflects the relatively recent emergence of the Republican party in the state.

10. We defined the liberal position as favoring greater government activity to promote social and economic equality, less government regulation of personal conduct and lifestyles, and resolution of international conflicts through negotiation rather than military strength. All 13 issues showed statistically significant correlations in the expected direction with liberal-conservative identification.

11. Allan Abramowitz, John McGlennon, and Ronald Rapoport, *Party Activists in Virginia: A Study of Delegates to the 1978 Senatorial Nominating Conventions* (Charlottesville: University of Virginia Institute of Government, 1981), p. 76.

12. About two-fifths of the Democratic delegates from Northern Virginia's Eighth and Tenth Congressional Districts supported Senator Kennedy.

13. This study is part of a twelve-state comparative study of presidential party activists in 1980. In addition to Virginia, the other states included in the comparative project are South Carolina, Texas, Maine, Iowa, Minnesota, North Dakota, Colorado, Arizona, Missouri, Oklahoma, and Utah.

10

SOUTHERN DISTINCTIVENESS AND THE EMERGENCE OF PARTY COMPETITON: THE CASE OF A DEEP SOUTH STATE

Tod A. Baker, Robert P. Steed,
and Laurence W. Moreland

INTRODUCTION

Two schools of thought have developed with regard to the nature of southern distinctiveness.[1] One viewpoint, illustrated by the work of Numan V. Bartley and John Shelton Reed, bases its notion of southernness on the sectional mind — a set of attitudes, beliefs, and values that distinguish southerners from nonsoutherners. Bartley, for example, traced the evolution of white southerners from an aggregation into an ethnocultural group,[2] while Reed, in his study of southern culture, found that localism, violence, and religious fundamentalism continue to typify the southern mind.[3] Certainly, considerable weight should be given to studies of this type, if for no other reason than the findings of Nathan Glazer and Daniel P. Moynihan should make us skeptical of the capacity of the American experience to meld diverse groups into a homogeneous product.[4]

On the other hand, the arguments of the competing school are also compelling. This viewpoint, well represented by V. O. Key, Jr., and I. A. Newby, has erected its concept of southernness on foundations provided by the South's distinctive institutions — white supremacy, the one-party system, a small-town, rural society, poverty, and illiteracy.[5] It certainly seems plausible to assume that as these conditions disappear, as they have tended to do over the past 30 years,[6] the way of life they supported should also tend to disappear. As put by Newby:

It has been argued implicitly throughout this study that southernness was an ideology extruded by a distinctive way of life which grew in turn from a specific set of circumstances. If that argument is valid, southernness and thus the South, cannot long survive the destruction of the way of life . . . that expressed it and the set of circumstances that produced it. . . . [W]riters who speak hopefully of an enduring South are basing their hope not on fundamental features but on vestigial remains.[7]

This paper is not intended to resolve the debate outlined above; rather, it is designed to provide another piece of the puzzle that constitutes the perplexity of southern political life. Broadly, we seek to examine the impact on the party system of the decline of Democratic hegemony in one southern state, South Carolina. Specifically, we are concerned with the extent to which *southernness* characterizes the attitudes of white state party activists on a series of selected issues. An underlying assumption is that party activists tend to play an important role in defining their parties' functions, activities, and programs, and that, therefore, attention to party activists' attitudes is useful in understanding the party system in general. As Samuel Eldersveld has written, "The party, in one sense, is what it believes — its attitudes and perspectives, at all echelons. And what the party leaders believe may certainly determine in large part the image it communicates to the public, and the success with which it mobilizes public support."[8]

In 1949 Key found that the one-party system was a bulwark of many aspects of the traditional way of life in the South generally and in South Carolina particularly.[9] Hence, a finding that at least one party's activists expressed viewpoints that could be characterized as nonsouthern would suggest that the party system no longer tends to maintain an exclusive southern distinctiveness in South Carolina. Thus, those with nonsouthern viewpoints would be able to find an institution through which their concerns could be expressed, quite dissimilar from the traditional Democratic one-party system which institutionally provided little effective outlet for perspectives which did not coincide with the distinctively southern viewpoint.

Given the particular focus of this study, we have excluded blacks from the analysis. While the entry of blacks into southern politics since the passage of the 1965 Voting Rights Act has undoubtedly had an impact,[10] they were, for the most part, uninvolved as active participants in the area's traditional one-party system and thus were not direct contributors attitudinally to the southern mindset which helped to distinguish the South from the remainder of the nation; consequently, it is through an examination of white party activists' attitudes and perspectives that the question of continued distinctiveness can be most appropriately addressed.[11]

The activists' attitudes and beliefs to be analyzed here fall into three issue areas (each of which has been identified, as discussed below, with the distinctive southern viewpoint), military affairs, women's rights, and religious beliefs. The activists' attitudes will first be examined in terms of differences between the parties and with regard to differences between younger and older activists within each party on each individual issue. Next, an index of southernism will be constructed for each issue dimension and ultimately for all dimensions combined.

On the indexes, as on the individual issues, comparisons will be made across party lines and across age categories within the parties.

The analysis of party differences is important in ascertaining the relative southernness of the positions taken by each party. Each could take a relatively strong southern position, in which case little or no change would have occurred since the publication of Key's seminal work. On the other hand, each could take a relatively strong nonsouthern position, or one could take a southern position and the other a nonsouthern one. In the former case the parties could be thought of as changing the nature of the political choices available to the electorate, although not necessarily widening the range of those choices, whereas in the latter case they could be thought of as necessarily broadening the range of choices. The analysis of differences in attitudes between younger and older activists is based on a political generation assumption; i.e., the political climate at the time people become aware of politics tends to have an enduring impact on their political attitudes, beliefs, and behavior. Hence, differences in attitudes between younger and older activists could well point to long-term shifts in the positions of the parties.

The indexes of southernism will be constructed to clarify patterns which extend through each set of related issues; that is, we seek to determine the extent to which the activists expressed a consistency on a southern/nonsouthern dimension cutting across the three sets of issues. This should supplement the material on the individual issues and provide useful summary data.

DATA

The data for this study were derived from questionnaires administered to delegates to the state Democratic and Republican party conventions held in Columbia, South Carolina, on April 12, 1980. Of the approximately 2200 delegates in attendance at the two conventions, 1360 returned useable questionnaires for an overall response rate of 61.8 percent; the response rate for the Democratic delegates was 54.0 percent, and for the Republicans it was 70.3 percent. Within each party aggregate there was no severe imbalance from congressional district to congressional district, and across party lines each congressional district was almost equally represented, with the widest divergence being only 6 percentage points (in the Fifth Congressional District). The good response rate combined with this pattern of geographic distribution across the state provides a solid base for analyzing party activists in the state.[12]

DISCUSSION

Military Issues

As indicated above, the first issue area investigated concerns a set of military affairs issues. These include a proposal to increase defense spending even if it means cutting domestic programs, ratification of the SALT II treaty, a proposal to reinstitute draft registration, and a proposal to strengthen the United States' military presence in the Middle East.

A relatively large body of literature indicates that southerners tend to have an affinity for the military. John Hope Franklin, for example, traced the development of the military tradition in the South from 1800 to 1861,[13] and Alfred O. Hero, in his comprehensive study of the foreign policy attitudes of southerners, brought the analysis up into the post-World War II period. Southerners, Hero found, tend to have a higher esteem for military men than is the case with nonsoutherners. They are also more likely to pursue military careers and tend to have views on international affairs similar to those of military men. Finally, southerners are more apt to support the use of force in world affairs.[14] Other commentators have also pointed to the southern support for the military. For example, William C. Havard has asserted that southerners tend to be characterized by a "military-patriotic" outlook,[15] while Newby noted that southerners have tended to be more in favor of a strong American position in world affairs than nonsoutherners.[16] Finally, Charles P. Roland, writing of southern attitudes toward the Vietnam War, pointed out that ". . . southerners and their political leaders remained into the 1970s perhaps the most dedicated of all American advocates of the unilateral employment of arms, keeping alive a vestigial spirit of 'going it alone' to police the world."[17]

Thus, with regard to the four military affairs issues analyzed here, the southern position is defined as one which favors reinstituting draft registration, increasing U.S. military presence in the Middle East, increasing defense spending even at the cost of cutting domestic programs, and opposing the ratification of the SALT II treaty.

As shown in Table 10.1, a majority of the Democratic delegates took the southern position on three of the four military affairs issues while the Republicans overwhelmingly took the southern position on all four. The one issue where the Democrats took the nonsouthern position concerned ratification of the SALT II treaty, which was opposed by 88.7 percent of the Republicans but only 27.7 percent of the Democrats. However, there were some sharp interparty differences on each of the other issues as well, with the Republicans decisively registering substantially higher majorities in favor of increasing defense spending, reinstating draft registration, and increasing U.S. military presence in the Middle East. The strong suggestion here that the Republican party is the more southern of the two is borne out by the index of southernism constructed from these four issues. (See Table 10.2). On this index, 41.8 percent of the Democratic activists were classified as taking the southern position across this issue dimension, in clear contrast to the 83.5 percent of the Republican delegates so classified. Thus, while these data present evidence that there is still relatively strong support for the military within the South Carolina Democratic party, it does appear that the emergence of party competition in the state has brought about at least the potential for a change in the range of choices offered to

TABLE 10.1
ACTIVISTS' POSITIONS ON MILITARY AFFAIRS ISSUES
(Percent)

Issue and Position*	Democrats	Republicans
An increase in defense spending even if it means cutting domestic programs		
Favor	56.9	96.0
Undecided	15.7	2.4
Oppose	27.4	1.5
	100.0	99.9
N =	(350)	(696)
Ratification of the SALT II treaty		
Favor	40.0	3.8
Undecided	32.4	7.5
Oppose	27.7	88.8
	100.1	100.1
N =	(340)	(684)
Reinstituting draft registration		
Favor	66.0	82.2
Undecided	11.1	9.0
Oppose	22.9	8.8
	100.0	100.0
N =	(341)	(692)
Increasing U.S. military presence in the Middle East		
Favor	56.6	78.5
Undecided	24.6	14.4
Oppose	18.7	7.2
	99.9	100.1
N =	(341)	(688)

*The "strongly favor" and "mildly favor" responses checked by respondents on these questionnaire items have been combined to yield the "favor" percentage in this table; similarly, the "strongly oppose" and "mildly oppose" responses have been combined to yield the "oppose" percentage.

Source: Compiled by the authors.

TABLE 10.2
INDEX OF SOUTHERNISM ON MILITARY ISSUES:
INTERPARTY COMPARISONS
(Percent)

Index Position*	Democrats	Republicans
Nonsouthern	58.2	16.5
Southern	41.8	83.5
	100.0	100.0
N =	(349)	(703)

*Respondents who took the southern position on at least three of the four military affairs issues were classified as southern on this index, while respondents who took the southern position on less than three of these issues were classified as nonsouthern.

Source: Compiled by the authors.

the voters, with the Democrats being more likely to express nonsouthern viewpoints and the Republicans being more likely to express southern ones.

When age controls are introduced, the interparty patterns remain essentially unchanged. (See Table 10.3.) Moreover, an examination of each of the military affairs issues reveals that three out of four young Democrats tended to be considerably less southern than middle-aged and older Democrats. The pattern on the fourth issue, the ratification of the SALT II treaty, is not clear. For the Republicans, on the other hand, a pattern of differences by age is not so pronounced. The position of young Republicans was about the same as that of middle-aged and older Republicans on the questions of increasing defense spending and ratifying the SALT II treaty. On the other two issues, the young Republicans, while still overwhelmingly southern in orientation, were somewhat less so than their older colleagues. These observations are supported by the data showing age controls for the index of southernism on military affairs issues. (See Table 10.4.) For the Democrats 73.4 percent of the young took the nonsouthern position as compared with 50.6 percent of the middle-aged and 45.8 percent of the old. For the Republicans there is little variation by age with over 80 percent of the respondents in each age category taking the southern position. It thus appears that, insofar as these data can be used to project future developments, the Democratic party in South Carolina will tend to become less distinctively southern with regard to support for the military whereas the Republicans will remain highly supportive of the military, thereby retaining their distinctively southern orientation on this point.

TABLE 10.3
ACTIVISTS' POSITIONS ON MILITARY ISSUES
(By Age; Percent)

Issue and Position*	Democrats			Republicans		
	Y	MA	O	Y	MA	O
An increase in defense spending even if it means cutting domestic programs						
Favor	44.5	65.1	61.7	94.8	96.0	97.0
Undecided	18.8	13.8	15.0	3.4	2.6	1.2
Oppose	36.8	21.2	23.4	1.7	1.5	1.8
	100.1	100.1	100.1	99.9	100.1	100.0
N =	(128)	(160)	(60)	(174)	(347)	(171)
Ratification of the SALT II treaty						
Favor	40.1	37.0	47.3	3.5	4.8	2.4
Undecided	32.3	35.1	24.6	7.5	8.6	5.3
Oppose	27.5	27.9	28.1	89.1	86.7	92.3
	99.9	100.0	100.0	100.1	100.1	100.0
N =	(127)	(154)	(57)	(174)	(336)	(170)
Reinstituting draft registration						
Favor	52.0	73.0	78.4	77.9	82.1	87.1
Undecided	13.4	11.8	5.0	9.9	9.5	7.1
Oppose	34.6	15.1	16.7	12.3	8.4	5.9
	100.0	99.9	100.1	100.1	100.0	100.1
N =	(127)	(152)	(60)	(172)	(346)	(170)
Increasing U.S. military presence in the Middle East						
Favor	43.3	64.6	64.9	72.6	81.2	79.3
Undecided	29.1	23.2	19.3	18.1	12.8	13.6
Oppose	27.6	12.3	15.8	9.4	6.1	7.1
	100.0	100.1	100.0	100.1	100.1	100.0
N =	(127)	(155)	(57)	(171)	(345)	(169)

*For an explanation of how the responses were combined to produce the response categories in this table, see Table 10.1.

Key: Y = young (18-34)
   MA = middle-age (35-54)
   O = old (55 and above)

Source: Compiled by the authors.

TABLE 10.4
INDEX OF SOUTHERNISM ON MILITARY ISSUES:
INTERPARTY COMPARISONS BY AGE
(Percent)

Index Position*	Democrats			Republicans		
	Y	MA	O	Y	MA	O
Nonsouthern	73.4	50.6	45.8	16.6	17.6	13.4
Southern	26.6	49.4	54.2	83.4	82.4	86.6
	100.0	100.0	100.0	100.0	100.0	100.0
N =	(128)	(128)	(59)	(175)	(352)	(172)

*For the procedure used in constructing this index, see Table 10.2.
Key: Y = young (18-34)
MA = middle-age (35-54)
O = old (55 and above)

Source: Compiled by the authors.

Women's Rights Issues

The next set of issues to be examined concerns women's rights. The delegates were asked to give their positions on the proposed Equal Rights Amendment, a proposal calling for an amendment to prohibit abortions except when the mother's life is in danger, and affirmative action programs in jobs and in higher education. This last issue concerns blacks as well as women, and, in this respect, it is dissimilar from the first two; it does, however, concern women's rights and is therefore included in this discussion.

The traditional image of the southern lady has often depicted her as a creature who was a submissive wife requiring the protection of her husband, who was intuitive, nonlogical, self-denying, tactful, sympathetic, and innocent, and who, as "queen of the home,"[18] "naturally [shrank] from public gaze and from the struggle and competition of life."[19] That image was probably never completely accurate, but it has nevertheless continued to shape people's perceptions of southern womanhood. For example, Diane Fowlkes, Jerry Perkins, and Sue Tolleson Rinehart pointed out that "When the southern lady did emerge in politics — as she did in the latter part of the nineteenth century . . . — she did so with a style and flair as consistent with the myth as possible."[20] And Roland noted that "Southern women in the 1960s and 1970s harkened to the practical aspects of the Women's Liberation Movement. . . . But they did not renounce either their femininity or their southernness. They retained enough of what William Alexander Percy once called a 'morning-glory air' to make a southern Bella Abzug impossible to imagine."[21]

Hence, the southern position is defined as one which tends to look with favor on the proposal to prohibit abortion and with disfavor on the Equal Rights Amendment and affirmative action programs.

The responses to this set of issues reveal very pronounced differences between the Democratic activists and the Republican activists. (See Table 10.5.) On two of the issues (the Equal Rights Amendment and affirmative action) a majority of Democrats took the nonsouthern position while a majority of the Republicans took the southern one. This nearly occurred on the third issue as well — a clear majority (63.1 percent) of the Democrats opposed an amendment to prohibit abortions while a substantial plurality (49.5 percent) of the Republicans favored such an amendment. These sharp interparty differences are also reflected in the index of southernism constructed from these three issues. (See Table 10.6.) Over three-fourths (77.8 percent) of the Democrats gave responses

TABLE 10.5
ACTIVISTS' POSITIONS ON WOMEN'S RIGHTS ISSUES
(Percent)

Issue and Position*	Democrats	Republicans
Equal Rights Amendment		
Favor	56.4	12.9
Undecided	13.4	6.6
Oppose	30.2	80.4
	100.0	99.9
N =	(351)	(695)
Constitutional amendment to prohibit abortions except when the mother's life is in danger		
Favor	24.5	49.5
Undecided	12.4	12.4
Oppose	63.1	38.1
	100.0	100.0
N =	(347)	(693)
Affirmative action programs in jobs and higher education (for minorities including women)		
Favor	57.0	14.7
Undecided	21.1	15.6
Oppose	21.9	69.8
	100.0	100.1
N =	(342)	(681)

*For an explanation of how the response categories were combined to produce the categories in this table, see Table 10.1.

Source: Compiled by the authors.

TABLE 10.6
INDEX OF SOUTHERNISM ON WOMEN'S RIGHTS ISSUES:
INTERPARTY COMPARISONS
(Percent)

Index Position*	Democrats	Republicans
Nonsouthern	77.8	25.3
Southern	22.2	74.7
	100.0	100.0
N =	(352)	(700)

*Respondents who took the southern position on at least two of the three women's rights issues were classified as southern on this index, while those who took the southern position on fewer than two of these issues were classified as nonsouthern.

Source: Compiled by the authors.

which placed them in the nonsouthern category of this index as compared to an almost equal proportion (74.7 percent) of Republicans answering in terms which placed them in the southern category.

As was the case with the military affairs issues, controlling the data by age leaves these interparty patterns basically unchanged. (See Table 10.7.) Similarly, the intraparty patterns across age categories reveal that, as with the military issues, the young Democrats were the least southern group examined. Over two-thirds of the young Democrats took the nonsouthern position on each of the three women's rights issues as compared to half or fewer of the middle-aged and older Democrats. On the other hand, the young Republicans were somewhat more southern in their orientations on two of these issues than their older colleagues. On the third issue, young and old Republicans were somewhat less opposed to affirmative action programs than were middle-aged Republicans. On all three issues, however, the differences among these age groups were not nearly as sharp within the Republican party as they were within the Democratic party. The index of southernism on women's rights issues further clarifies the picture. (See Table 10.8.) Over 70 percent of the Democrats in each age category took the nonsouthern position, with young Democrats being the most nonsouthern. In marked contrast, over 70 percent of the Republicans in each age category took the southern position, with young Republicans being slightly more southern proportionately than either middle-aged or older Republicans. Again, as with the military affairs issues, these data strongly suggest that the South Carolina parties may become even more sharply divided along southern-nonsouthern lines in the future.

TABLE 10.7
ACTIVISTS' VIEWS ON WOMEN'S RIGHTS ISSUES
(By Age; Percent)

Issue and Position*	Democrats			Republicans		
	Y	MA	O	Y	MA	O
Equal Rights Amendment						
Favor	69.5	49.0	46.6	10.9	12.4	16.5
Undecided	9.4	18.0	10.0	5.2	7.5	5.9
Oppose	21.1	32.9	43.3	83.9	80.2	77.6
	100.0	99.9	99.9	100.0	100.1	100.0
N =	(128)	(161)	(60)	(174)	(347)	(170)
Constitutional amendment to prohibit abortions						
Favor	14.1	28.5	36.2	54.3	49.5	44.0
Undecided	10.9	12.6	15.5	11.4	14.5	9.5
Oppose	75.0	59.0	48.3	34.3	36.1	46.4
	100.0	100.1	100.0	100.0	100.1	99.9
N =	(128)	(159)	(58)	(173)	(344)	(178)
Affirmative action programs						
Favor	67.4	50.3	52.6	12.2	13.6	19.9
Undecided	15.9	22.6	28.8	20.3	12.6	16.3
Oppose	16.7	27.1	18.7	67.4	73.8	63.8
	100.0	100.0	100.1	99.9	100.0	100.0
N =	(126)	(155)	(59)	(172)	(340)	(166)

*Response categories are combined as explained in Table 10.1.
Key: Y = young (18-34)
MA = middle-age (35-54)
O = old (55 and over)

Source: Compiled by the authors.

TABLE 10.8
INDEX OF SOUTHERNISM ON WOMEN'S RIGHTS ISSUES:
INTERPARTY COMPARISON BY AGE
(Percent)

Index Position*	Democrats			Republicans		
	Y	MA	O	Y	MA	O
Nonsouthern	83.6	75.2	72.1	23.4	24.9	27.5
Southern	16.4	24.8	27.9	76.6	75.1	72.5
	100.0	100.0	100.0	100.0	100.0	100.0
N =	(128)	(161)	(61)	(175)	(350)	(171)

*For the procedure used in constructing this index, see Table 10.6.
Key: Y = young (18-34)
MA = middle-age (35-54)
O = old (55 and above)

Source: Compiled by the authors.

Religious Beliefs

Our final issue area concerns religious fundamentalism. This is, of course, not an issue in the sense that draft registration and the Equal Rights Amendment are issues. Yet, religion is important in the South[22] and, according to a number of observers, tends to support orthodox southern viewpoints. Francis Butler Simkins, for example, has asserted that ". . . orthodox Protestantism . . . is a likely explanation of why the section . . . has kept its identity as the most conservative portion of the United States."[23] Other commentators include Newby, who noted that southern religious thought has tended to reflect rather than mold secular values,[24] and Roland, who pointed out that since World War II southern churches have tended to condemn proposals for a guaranteed annual income, to denounce those northern churches which have taken up matters such as urban renewal and family planning, and to oppose condemnation of U.S. involvement in Vietnam.[25] Fundamentalism, thus, tends to be a profoundly conservative influence in the sense that it tends to support the maintenance of the status quo, i.e., southernness.

With regard to religion, therefore, the proportions of delegates with fundamentalist beliefs should be a further indicator of the degree of southernness within each political party.

On this point, the Republicans again emerged as the more southern of the two party aggregates, with 51.0 percent saying that they were fundamentalists as compared with 39.7 percent of the Democrats answering in this manner.

TABLE 10.9
RELIGIOUS BELIEFS OF PARTY ACTIVISTS
(By Age; Percent)

	Democrats			Republicans		
Beliefs	*Y*	*MA*	*O*	*Y*	*MA*	*O*
Fundamentalist	25.0	50.7	43.1	64.1	51.2	36.3
Nonfundamentalist	75.0	49.3	56.9	35.9	48.8	63.7
	100.0	100.0	100.0	100.0	100.0	100.0
N =	(120)	(150)	(59)	(170)	(336)	(157)

Source: Compiled by the authors.

However, the relative frequency of fundamentalists is much more enlightening when examined by age categories. (See Table 10.9.) For the Democrats, 25 percent of the young said that they were fundamentalists, as compared with 50.7 percent of the middle-aged and 43.1 percent of the old. For the Republicans, on the other hand, 64.1 percent of the young indicated that they were fundamentalists, as compared with 51.2 percent of the middle-aged and 36.3 percent of the old. These data indicate that the overall interparty differences on this point are largely attributable to the extremely sharp differences between the young Democrats and the young Republicans. This, in turn, suggests that if fundamentalist beliefs do help maintain orthodox southern viewpoints these age-related differences should go a long way toward illuminating the policy courses that the parties will pursue in the future.

Southernism Index

A useful way of evaluating the above data is to summarize all issues in a single index. This index is based on the two indexes constructed from the military affairs issues and the women's rights issues combined with religious fundamentalism. Such a combination yields a four-point scale ranging from zero to three. Respondents who took the southern position on all three issues were thus placed in the most southern category (three), those who took the non-southern position on all three issues were placed in the least southern category (zero), and the other respondents were placed in the remaining index positions corresponding to their respective positions on the selected issues.

As shown in Table 10.10, the interparty differences which have appeared individually on the various issues appear clearly when the issue sets are combined; the Republican delegates were again much more southern in their orientations

TABLE 10.10
SOUTHERNISM INDEX: PARTY COMPARISONS
(Percent)

Index Position	Democrats	Republicans
0 (least southern)	38.6	6.3
1	32.3	20.7
2	19.8	38.6
3 (most southern)	9.3	34.5
	100.0	100.1
N =	(334)	(695)

Source: Compiled by the authors.

than their Democratic counterparts. While over 70 percent of the Democrats scored zero or one on this index, an almost equal percentage of the Republicans scored two or three. At the extremes, almost two-fifths (38.6 percent) of the Democrats gave no southern responses on the index while over one-third (34.5 percent) of the Republicans took southern positions in all three issue areas.

These sharp interparty differences remain when the delegates are divided into age brackets. (See Table 10.11.) Moreover, as was the case in much of the earlier analyses, the young Democrats were the most nonsouthern of all the age

TABLE 10.11
SOUTHERNISM INDEX: PARTY COMPARISONS BY AGE
(Percent)

Index Position	Democrats			Republicans		
	Y	MA	O	Y	MA	O
0 (least southern)	54.1	29.7	29.8	4.0	6.3	8.1
1	28.7	34.2	35.1	18.9	18.7	26.7
2	13.1	23.2	24.6	31.4	40.5	41.9
3 (most southern)	4.1	12.9	10.5	45.7	34.5	23.3
	100.0	100.0	100.0	100.0	100.0	100.0
N =	(122)	(155)	(57)	(175)	(348)	(172)

Key: Y = young (18-34)
 MA = middle-age (35-54)
 O = old (55 and above)

Source: Compiled by the authors.

groups. For the Democrats, 82.8 percent of the young delegates scored zero or one on the index as compared with 63.9 percent of the middle-aged and 64.9 percent of the old. On the other hand, 77.1 percent of the young Republicans, 75.0 percent of the middle-aged Republicans, and 65.2 percent of the older Republicans scored two or three on this index. At the extremes, 54.1 percent of the young Democrats were classified as *least* southern while 45.7 percent of the young Republicans were classified as *most* southern. Again, these data strongly suggest that the existing interparty differences on these issues have the potential for becoming even sharper if current leadership patterns continue into the future; to the extent that this happens, the party leadership aggregates will diverge as the Democrats become more nonsouthern (at least on the types of issues examined here) and as the Republicans become more southern.

CONCLUSION

Quite obviously changes have occurred in the party systems of South Carolina and other southern states since Key published *Southern Politics* in 1949. On the basis of the South Carolina data the two parties present rather clear alternatives to the voters. In this sense the party system has come more nearly to approximate national party patterns, and with this nationalization it has lost its southern distinctiveness, at least as regards the traditional one-party system.[26]

Yet, in another and perhaps more important sense, the party system has retained important elements of southern distinctiveness. The South Carolina evidence suggests that, although the Democratic party has redefined itself in such a manner that it no longer can be thought of as the party of the South, the emergent Republican party has taken positions that place it very much in the tradition of southern distinctiveness. At least at the level of party activists, the Democrats were less supportive of the military, were strongly favorable toward the extension of women's rights, and tended to be clearly less fundamentalist. The Republicans, on the other hand, came out rather strongly in favor of the military and just as strongly against the extension of women's rights; further, consistent with traditional southernism, the Republicans tended to be more fundamentalist.

One long-time student of southern politics, Donald S. Strong, has observed the possible emergence of a new conservative coalition with regional strength in the white South and the West. This coalition, "an overwhelmingly white group," would espouse an "uncritical faith in a capitalistic free economy" with the South in particular contributing "a strong nationalistic military posture."[27] The coalition would also oppose abortion, and women who were "heavily involved in liberation would probably not be at home in this coalition."[28] The South Carolina data suggest that Strong's observation is not far off the mark, at least insofar as this state's party system is concerned. The Republican party, already racially distinctive, has demonstrated a clear tendency toward creating the kind of attitudinal and programmatic coalition predicted by Strong. Thus, it seems not unreasonable to hazard the observation that those who adhere to traditional southern viewpoints are today finding a home, ironically, in the house that Lincoln built.

NOTES

1. I. A. Newby, *The South: A History* (New York: Holt, Rinehart, and Winston, 1978), pp. 505-506.

2. Numan V. Bartley, "The South and Sectionalism in Southern Politics," *Journal of Politics* 38 (August 1976): 257.

3. John Shelton Reed, *The Enduring South: Subcultural Persistence in a Mass Society* (Lexington: Lexington Books, 1972), esp. chaps. 4-7. Also see John Shelton Reed, "To Live – and Die – in Dixie: A Contribution to the Study of Southern Violence," *Political Science Quarterly* 86 (September 1971): 429-443.

4. Nathan Glazer and Daniel P. Moynihan, *Beyond the Melting Pot: The Negroes, Puerto Ricans, Jews, Italians, and Irish of New York City* (Cambridge, Mass.: Massachusetts Institute of Technology Press, 1963).

5. See, for example, V. O. Key, Jr., *Southern Politics in State and Nation* (New York: Alfred A. Knopf, 1949); and Newby, *The South: A History*.

6. An extensive literature addresses the changes which have taken place in the South since World War II. Among the more useful materials are John C. McKinney and Edgar T. Thompson (eds.), *The South in Continuity and Change* (Durham: Duke University Press, 1965); Avery Leiserson (ed.), *The American South in the 1960's* (New York: Praeger, 1964); Samuel D. Cook, "Political Movements and Organizations," *Journal of Politics* (February, 1964): 130-153; Allan P. Sindler (ed.), *Change in the Contemporary South* (Durham: Duke University Press, 1963); Bernard Cosman, *Five States for Goldwater* (University, Alabama: University of Alabama Press, 1966); Donald S. Strong, *Urban Republicanism in the South* (University, Alabama: University of Alabama Press, 1960); Donald S. Strong, "Further Reflections on Southern Politics," *Journal of Politics* 33 (May 1971): 239-256; James L. Sundquist, *Dynamics of the Party System: Alignment and Realignment of Political Parties in the United States* (Washington, D.C.: The Brookings Institution, 1973), pp. 245-274; Numan V. Bartley and Hugh D. Graham, *Southern Politics and the Second Reconstruction* (Baltimore: The Johns Hopkins University Press, 1975); William C. Havard (ed.), *The Changing Politics of the South* (Baton Rouge: Louisiana State University Press, 1972); Jack Bass and Walter DeVries, *The Transformation of Southern Politics* (New York: Basic Books, 1976); Earl Black, *Southern Governors and Civil Rights* (Cambridge, Mass.: Harvard University Press, 1976); Bruce A. Campbell, "Change in the Southern Electorate," *American Journal of Political Science* 21 (1977): 37-64; Paul Allen Beck, "Partisan Realignment in the Postwar South," *American Political Science Review* 71 (1977): 477-496; Louis M. Seagull, *Southern Republicanism* (New York: Schenkman, 1975); Alan I. Abramowitz, "Ideological Realignment and the Nationalization of Southern Politics: A Study of Party Activists and Candidates in a Southern State" (paper presented at the 1979 annual meeting of the Southern Political Science Association, Gatlinburg, Tennessee, November 1-3, 1979); and Robert P. Steed, Laurence W. Moreland, and Tod A. Baker (eds.), *Party Politics in the South* (New York: Praeger, 1980).

7. Newby, *The South: A History*, p. 507.

8. Samuel J. Eldersveld, *Political Parties: A Behavioral Analysis* (Chicago: Rand McNally, 1964), pp. 180-181.

9. Key, *Southern Politics*.

10. Material on recent black participation in southern politics includes, among others, U.S. Commission on Civil Rights, *The Voting Rights Act: Ten Years After* (Washington, D.C., 1975); Mack H. Jones, "The 1965 Voting Rights Act and Political Symbolism" (paper presented at the 1979 annual meeting of the Southern Political Science Association, Gatlinburg, Tennessee, November 1-3, 1979); Richard L. Engstrom, "Racial Discrimination in the Electoral Process: The Voting Rights Act and the Vote Dilution Issue," in *Politics in the South*, eds. Steed, Moreland, and Baker, pp. 197-213; Richard Murray and Arthur Vedlitz, "Racial Voting Patterns in the South: An Analysis of Major Elections in Five Cities," *Annals of the American Academy of Political and Social Science* (September 1978): 29-39; Thomas F. Eamon, "Black Coalition Politics in the Post Civil Rights Era: The Election of Mayors in Two Southern Cities, 1975-1979" (paper presented at the 1980 Citadel Symposium on Southern Politics, Charleston, South Carolina, March 27-29, 1980); Vinton M. Prince, "Black Voting Strength in Mississippi: The Case of the Unreal Advantage" (paper presented at the 1978 Citadel Symposium on Southern Politics, Charleston, South Carolina, February 16-18, 1978); Donald R. Matthews and James W. Prothro, *Negroes and the New Southern Politics* (New York: Harcourt, Brace, and World, 1966); Richard Murray and Arnold Vedlitz, "The Life Cycle of Black Political Organizations: A Study of Voter Groups in Five Southern Cities" (paper presented at the 1978 Citadel Symposium on Southern Politics, Charleston, South Carolina, February 16-18, 1978); Lester M. Salamon, "Leadership and Modernization: The Emerging Black Political Elite in the American South," *Journal of Politics* 35 (August 1973): 615-646; James M. Carlson, "Political Context and Black Participation in the South," in *Party Politics in the South*, eds. Steed, Moreland, and Baker, pp. 180-196; Huey L. Perry, "Political Participation and Social Equality: An Assessment of the Impact of Political Participation in Two Alabama Localities" (paper presented at the 1978 Citadel Symposium on Southern Politics, Charleston, South Carolina, February 16-18, 1978); and Laurence W. Moreland, Robert P. Steed, and Tod A. Baker, "A Profile of Contemporary Black Party Activists in South Carolina" (paper presented at the 1981 Citadel Conference on the South, Charleston, South Carolina, April 23-25, 1981).

11. For a similar approach, see Reed, *The Enduring South*.

12. Since the state parties did not keep detailed records on the demographic characteristics of the delegates in attendance at the conventions, we cannot check our respondents' representativeness on these points.

13. John Hope Franklin, *The Militant South: 1800-1861* (Cambridge, Mass.: The Belknap Press, 1956).

14. Alfred O. Hero, Jr., *The Southerner and World Affairs* (Baton Rouge: Louisiana State University Press, 1965), chap. 3.

15. Havard, *The Changing Politics of the South*, p. 6.

16. Newby, *The South: A History*, p. 468.

17. Charles P. Roland, *The Improbable Era: The South Since World War II* (Lexington: The University Press of Kentucky, 1975), p. 90.

18. Anne Firor Scott, *The Southern Lady from Pedestal to Politics: 1830-1930* (Chicago: University of Chicago Press, 1970), chap. 1.

19. George Fitzhugh, *Sociology for the South* (Richmond: A. Morris, 1854), p. 214.

20. Diane L. Fowlkes, Jerry Perkins, and Sue Tolleson Rinehart, "Women in Southern Party Politics: Roles, Activities, and Futures," in *Party Politics in the South*, eds. Steed, Moreland, and Baker, p. 214.

21. Roland, *The Improbable Era*, p. 179.

22. See, for example, Reed, *The Enduring South*, chap. 6.

23. Francis Butler Simkins, *The Everlasting South* (Baton Rouge: Louisiana State University Press, 1963), p. 79.

24. Newby, *The South: A History*, p. 410.

25. Roland, *The Improbable Era*, pp. 128-129.

26. For an argument along these lines for the party system in another southern state, see Alan Abramowitz, John McGlennon, and Ronald Rapoport, "Presidential Activists and the Nationalization of Party Politics in Virginia," chapter 9 in this volume.

27. Donald S. Strong, *Issue Voting and Party Realignment* (University, Alabama: University of Alabama Press, 1977), p. 75.

28. Ibid., p. 76.

PART III:

LINKAGES BETWEEN THE MASS PUBLIC
AND PUBLIC OFFICIALS

INTRODUCTION

The Editors

Part III investigates one of the most difficult yet important aspects of the study of politics: the relationships between mass electorates and elected or appointed governmental elites. Whether government officials conceptualize their roles as delegates, trustees, or "politicos,"[1] the democratic model ranks as fundamental a responsive relationship of some kind between the electorate and public officials.[2] This aspect of southern politics has seldom been studied,[3] and it deserves special attention in light of the cultural and political changes which have overtaken the South in recent decades.[4] These linkage relationships are typically seen as relationships between voters and elected officials but they exist as well between appointed officials and citizens, especially citizens organized as interest groups.[5] The chapters in this section investigate the linkage relationship both between the mass electorate and elected representatives, and between citizens (and interest groups) and public officials.

These chapters also address the southern distinctiveness question by relating linkage relationships to conditions that may be, if not completely unique to the South, at least more characteristic of that region than of other regions in the United States. Even if the contemporary South should look to the casual observer to be very similar to other regions of the nation, it must still be recognized that linkage relationships are rooted in the southern historical experience which continues to set the South apart from the rest of the nation.

The cultural distinctiveness of the South historically has extended to a variety of cultural phenomena including religion, family and local attachments, and interpersonal relationships. In many instances cultural factors have impinged on political structures and practices to help produce the political distinctiveness of the region. One of the most obvious examples (and one of the most intensively investigated) has been the historical interaction between patterns of race relations and a wide range of political practices. V. O. Key, Jr., for example, saw race relations as the central ingredient in southern political distinctiveness and, for many years, practically all analyses of southern politics unavoidably dealt, at least in part, with the racial foundations of various political institutions.[6] Clearly, the nature of race relations in the region has undergone dramatic change since 1950, and, while the questions (and problems) relating to race have not been put completely to rest, they no longer occupy so central a place in the southern political fabric.[7] In light of the traditional importance of the race issue in helping to create a distinctive southern politics, a reasonable hypothesis, then, is that the erosion of the centrality of this issue should contribute to the erosion of southern political distinctiveness in general.

The first three chapters of this section address this point by examining the impact of a racially changing electorate on the behavior of elected representatives. Historically, these linkages between electorate and representative were, at least rhetorically, shaped largely by the traditional whites-only character of the Democratic party which dominated the politics of the South. However, in recent decades, especially since the passage of the 1965 Voting Rights Act,[8] the infusion into the electorate of large numbers of blacks has resulted in notable changes in the traditional relationships between voters and their legislative representatives. In "Black Political Mobilization and White Legislative Behavior," Gary Brooks examines the relationship between white representatives in the Mississippi legislature and their racially-mixed constituencies by investigating the impact of the proportion of black voters in a given constituency on the representatives' voting behavior on racially salient issues in the legislature. In "Black Public Officials and the Dynamics of Representation," Kenneth Wald and Carole Southerland examine the political problem of elected or appointed black public officials who, while representing black constituencies with at least some degree of racial consciousness, must nevertheless seek to build coalitions with whites, who constitute the bulk of public officials in a given locality. In "Assessing the Impact of the 1965 Voting Rights Act: A Micro Analysis of Four States," Mark Stern raises the unit of analysis to the national level by examining the impact of increasingly black electorates on the behavior of southern congressional representatives in roll-call votes on issues relating to black civil rights.

A somewhat different kind of linkage is explored by Marcus Ethridge in "Regulatory Policy Administration and Agency-Citizen Linkages in Southern States: Some Hypotheses and an Exploratory Analysis." Much of traditional southern politics has been characterized by informal yet powerful relationships between public officials and their publics — relationships shaped by highly personal followings and potent political organizations noted for their allegiances to particular political figures.[9] Indeed, southern history is replete with names such as Long, Byrd, and Talmadge, famous for the political dynasties they represented. Therefore, one might hypothesize that, in areas other than party politics where these highly personalized ties have been especially important, these same kinds of informal relationships would characterize other aspects of the conduct of southern politics, including the work of regulatory commissions where such informal relationships have been shown to shape both policy-making and policy-application.[10] Ethridge, however, demonstrates that the South may yet be unexpectedly distinctive, when he examines the nature of these informal relationships in the context of the regulatory movement which has generally had so much impact on the environment, the workplace, and the like.

Together, these four chapters focus on the broad relationship between culture and politics by examining selected linkages between government officials and the public within the context of racial and interpersonal interactions. The central question of the volume, the continuation or the disappearance of southern political distinctiveness, is thus addressed by these four chapters from a cultural perspective.

NOTES

1. See John C. Wahlke, Heinz Eulau, William Buchanan, and Leroy C. Ferguson, *The Legislative System* (New York: John Wiley & Sons, 1962), pp. 281-286.

2. Henry B. Mayo, *An Introduction to Democratic Theory* (New York: Oxford University Press, 1960), pp. 72-106.

3. For important research that generally examines this relationship, see Warren E. Miller and Donald E. Stokes, "Constituency Influence in Congress," *American Political Science Review* 57 (March 1963): 45-46; Charles F. Cnudde and Donald J. McCrone, "The Linkage Between Constituency Attitudes and Congressional Voting Behavior: A Causal Model," *American Political Science Review* 60 (March 1966): 66-72; and V. O. Key, Jr., *Public Opinion and American Democracy* (New York: Alfred A. Knopf, 1966), pp. 441-531.

4. See, for example, *The Changing Politics of the South*, ed. William C. Havard (Baton Rouge: Louisiana State University Press, 1972); Numan V. Bartley and Hugh D. Graham, *Southern Politics and the Second Reconstruction* (Baltimore: Johns Hopkins University Press, 1975); and *Party Politics in the South*, eds. Robert P. Steed et al. (New York: Praeger Publishers, 1980).

5. See, e.g., Susan Welch and John Comer, *Public Opinion: Its Formation, Measurement, and Impact* (Palo Alto, Cal.: Mayfield Publishing, 1975), pp. 409-423.

6. V. O. Key, Jr., *Southern Politics in State and Nation* (New York: Alfred A. Knopf, 1949), esp. pp. 533-675. Although Key's *Southern Politics* appeared more than 30 years ago, it remains the leading work of a political scientist on the politics of the South. Historians have also emphasized race as, if not the central theme of southern history, at least as an important component of southern post-Civil War politics. See, e.g., U. B. Phillips, "The Central Theme of Southern History," *American Historical Review* 34 (October 1928): 30-43. For a discussion and evaluation of Phillips' view that race has been the "central theme" of southern history and for a citation of sources relevant to such an inquiry, see I. A. Newby, *The South: A History* (New York: Holt, Rinehart and Winston, 1978), pp. 1-31, 509-512.

7. For a discussion of what some have seen as a "social revolution" with regard to race relations in the South, see, among others, Jack Bass and Walter DeVries, *The Transformation of Southern Politics* (New York: Basic Books, 1976), pp. 7-13; Numan V. Bartley and Hugh D. Graham, *Southern Politics and the Second Reconstruction* (Baltimore: Johns Hopkins University Press, 1975), pp. 136-163; William C. Havard, "The South: A Shifting

Perspective," in *The Changing Politics of the South* ed. William C. Havard (Baton Rouge: Louisiana State University Press, 1972), pp. 10-24; and Angus Campbell, *White Attitudes Toward Black People* (Ann Arbor: Institute for Social Research, 1971), pp. 147-154.

Even if race retains some salience in social relationships, it has largely disappeared from the rhetoric of southern politics; see, e.g., Earl Black, *Southern Governors and Civil Rights* (Cambridge, Mass.: Harvard University Press, 1976).

8. See, e.g., U.S. Commission on Civil Rights, *The Voting Rights Act: Ten Years After* (Washington, D.C., 1975).

9. See, e.g., Allan P. Sindler, *Huey Long's Louisiana* (Baltimore: Johns Hopkins University Press, 1956).

10. See, e.g., Marver H. Bernstein, *Regulating Business by Independent Commission* (Princeton: Princeton University Press, 1955).

11

BLACK POLITICAL MOBILIZATION AND WHITE LEGISLATIVE BEHAVIOR

Gary H. Brooks

The passage of the Voting Rights Act of 1965 and the consequent emergence of blacks as a significant electoral force constitute an important watershed in Southern political history. While the importance of this historic transition is acknowledged widely, little attention has been paid to the impact of black enfranchisement on Southern state legislatures. This study examines the relationship between black political mobilization and white legislative behavior in one Southern state in order to call attention to a promising area of research and to examine some existing hypotheses concerning the nature of the response of white elected officials to black constituents.

A great deal of the research dealing with the post-Voting Rights Act era has dealt with the effectiveness with which blacks have been able to mobilize politically,[1] or in a not unrelated vein, the ability of blacks to elect black officials.[2] The literature points to the clear conclusion that the election of black elected officials is closely tied to the existence of black electoral majorities. Few Southern whites appear ready to vote for black candidates if white alternative candidates are available.

The problem presented to blacks by the situation described above is rather obvious. There are relatively few governmental jurisdictions or electoral districts characterized by the presence of black electoral majorities. In Mississippi, the most heavily black state in the nation, only 29 of 82 counties have black population majorities, and the number of such counties has been declining steadily throughout the twentieth century.[3]

While blacks may hope to wield effective electoral control over some local governmental units, no state in the South has or appears likely to have a black electoral majority. In statewide politics, blacks are and will remain an electoral minority. Given this situation, the achievement of state policies responsive to the needs of Southern blacks depends to a great extent upon the ability of black legislators to forge coalitions with whitle legislators and/or the ability of minority black electorates to influence the voting behavior of white elected officials. The focus of this study is on the latter phenomenon.

Mississippi, with its high black population and its unusually powerful state legislature,[4] would appear to be an appropriate site for an initial exploration of the relationship between black political mobilization and white legislative response. Prior to the legislative elections of 1979,[5] only 4 blacks had been elected to the 174 member Mississippi state legislature. Until the present (1980) legislative session, the significance of black enfranchisement has been limited for all practical purposes to its impact on the behavior of white legislators.

This paper is essentially a descriptive exploration into the relationship between black political mobilization and white legislative behavior in Mississippi. As befits an exploratory outing, the central questions are basic and rather simple: What is the relationship between black political mobilization and the voting behavior of white legislators? What factors influence the nature of that relationship?

THE DATA

The relationship between black political mobilization and the roll call voting behavior of white legislators is the central concern of this analysis. Roll call votes from the 1977 session of the legislature were selected since that session represented the most recent session for which roll calls were readily available. The House of Representatives was selected as the site of the study due to the larger size of that body and due to the presence (in 1977) of a four-member black delegation in the House.

Since the principal interest of the study is the impact of black mobilization on white legislative behavior, votes on issues of particular salience to blacks would appear to be the variety of votes which would most clearly reflect the influence of black mobilization. The delineation of such issues is, of course, problematical.

From the universe of 1977 House roll calls, all votes on which at least 30 percent of the voting membership dissented from the majority position were selected for further analysis. Each of these roll calls were then examined, allowing the identification of those roll calls on which at least three of the four members of the black legislative delegation were unanimously for or against the measure. This procedure resulted in the selection of 82 roll call votes.

The use of an index constructed from these 82 roll calls as the dependent variable presents some obvious problems. The position of the black delegation may not, in all cases, be highly visible to white legislators or be taken by them as "the" black position. Some of the votes on which the black delegation cast unanimous ballots may reflect some basis of common interest or outlook other than "blackness." In addition, some of the roll calls selected may reflect sheer chance agreement on the part of a small group of black legislators.

In light of the above considerations, each of the 82 roll calls were examined carefully, and 28 roll calls which appeared to have obvious racial saliency were selected. These roll calls included votes on such measures as compulsory school attendance (the state's original compulsory attendance law was repealed in the aftermath of *Brown v. Topeka*), the disposition of the files of the defunct State Sovereignty Commission (a conduit of state funds for the White Citizens Council and an intelligence gathering unit focusing on civil rights activists), state funding formulas for primary and secondary education, methods of selecting school board trustees, appropriations for predominantly black universities, workmen's compensation, and bills related to public employee benefits and firing practices in local school districts and municipal governments.

Each of the 118 white legislators was assigned a score which represented the degree to which his votes were consistent with the position taken by the black members of the House on the 28 selected roll calls.[6] This score, referred to hereafter as the Index of Agreement with the Black Delegation (IBD), is the dependent variable in the analysis.

The measurement of "black political mobilization" encounters problems as well. Neither voter registration nor voter turnout data by race are available in Mississippi. Even if such measures were available, they would not appear to be adequate measures of the concept of black political mobilization.

The concept of black political mobilization implies more than the potential black percentage of the electorate or even the percentage of the total vote actually cast by blacks. Black political mobilization, as defined for the purposes of this study, refers to the ability of blacks to mobilize (or vote) effectively in pursuit of black interests as defined by the black community or a majority thereof. In order to obtain some rough indicator of black political mobilization in this sense, one needs a statewide race in which the majority of the black electorate had a clear preference. A statewide race is necessary in order to obtain scores for every legislative district.

The most recent statewide campaign of Charles Evers would appear to be the best available approximation of black political mobilization as defined above.[7] Evers has been without doubt the most visible and charismatic black politician in Mississippi and the only black politician with a statewide political base. Black political strategy in Mississippi for many years has been influenced strongly by Evers, who holds the office of mayor of Fayette.[8]

Unfortunately, Evers' last statewide campaign, and the race closest in time to the 1977 legislative session under examination, was his 1978 race for the United States Senate against Democrat Maurice Dantin and the eventual Republican winner, Thad Cochran. A measure of black mobilization based on 1978 election data but used as an explanatory variable with roll call data from 1977 presents an obvious conceptual difficulty. Such problems, however, are not uncommon in political analyses.

The chronological problem encountered above need not be fatal. One can with some justification argue that the percentage of the vote received by Evers in a particular legislative district in 1978 would probably not have been much higher or lower if the same election had been held in 1977. Unless the effectiveness of black electoral mobilization varies widely from year to year, the extent of black mobilization in the 1978 United States Senate race can be viewed as a reasonably reliable estimate of the degree of black mobilization in each of the districts in 1977. Given other studies which have examined the factors which inhibit or facilitate black political mobilization,[9] it would appear unlikely that mobilization rates would be substantially altered in a one year time period.

Of course, the vote for Evers is not a perfect measure, even if the chronological problem was not present. While Evers ran most strongly in areas characterized by substantial black electorates, some blacks may have voted for other candidates and some whites may have voted for Evers. The number of whites voting for Evers appears to have been quite small. Available survey data indicate that the Evers vote was approximately 95 percent black.[10]

The size of black defections from the Evers candidacy raises fewer conceptual problems. The frequent defection of black voters from black political candidacies has been pointed to by a number of observers as a major obstacle to effective black political mobilization in Mississippi.[11] This problem has been particularly severe in some of the more rural areas of Mississippi. As a result, black voters casting ballots for candidates other than Evers can be viewed as a symptom of ineffective black mobilization. For the purposes of this analysis, black voters who defected to Dantin or Cochran will be viewed in this light.

THE NATURE OF THE BASIC RELATIONSHIP

Supplied with these two measures of our central concepts, the analysis of the relationship between IBD scores (support for the positions of the black delegation) and black political mobilization (percentage of the pro-Evers vote) can begin. A simplistic expectation would be that a positive and linear relationship exists between the degree of support for the positions of the black legislative delegation and the extent of black mobilization in the districts represented by white legislators. If this expectation were correct, scores on the Index of Support for the Black Delegation (IBD) would rise in a simple monotonic manner as the vote for Evers (black political mobilization) increased across legislative districts.

A more sophisticated and complex expectation concerning the relationship between black political mobilization and support for the positions of black legislators can be found in the work of William R. Keech. Keech's rationale for a curvilinear relationship is stated in the following form:

> If we assume that federal law has guaranteed the right to vote of all Southern Negroes, and that the percent of eligible Negroes registered

is relatively uniform over the whole region, we might expect a curvilinear relationship between the percent of the electorate Negro and the payoffs of voting. Up to 30 percent of the electorate Negro the relationship would be positive because the threshold of white resistance seems to be about 30 percent of the population Negro. Between 30 and 50 percent of the electorate Negro, the relationship might become neutral or negative because white resistance will be higher in communities with larger Negro population bases. Beyond 50 percent of the electorate Negro the relationship will become positive again because . . . a Negro voting majority can overcome a lot of white resistance.[12]

A glance at the grouped data presented in Table 11.1 reveals that the form of the relationship between the percentage of the vote for Evers and the mean score of white legislators on the IBD is indeed curvilinear. As one moves from districts with black mobilization scores ranging from zero to 30 percent, mean IBD scores among white legislators decline from 59.4 percent, to 46.9 percent, to 43.7 percent. At the 30 percent Evers mark, IBD scores abruptly jump to 60.5 percent, and increase slightly to 62.1 percent in those districts in which Evers claimed 40 to 49.9 percent of the vote.

Unfortunately, it is not possible to examine mean IBD scores for white legislators in districts in which the Evers vote exceeds 50 percent. Of the five districts in which Evers polled over 50 percent of the vote in 1978, four had elected black legislators in 1975. Only one white legislator held a seat in a district which gave Evers over 50 percent of the vote. While this feature of the data stands as an important reminder of the necessity of black electoral majorities for the election of black officials (and perhaps also as a confirmation of the reliability of the Evers vote as a measure of effective black political mobilization), it makes it impossible to extend the analysis of the relationship between black mobilization and white legislative behavior to districts characterized by Evers majorities.

TABLE 11.1
MEAN IBD SCORES BY PERCENTAGE VOTE FOR EVERS

Percentage Vote for Evers	*Mean IBD Score*	*(N)*
0- 9.9	59.4	(22)
10-19.9	46.9	(36)
20-29.9	43.7	(29)
30-39.9	60.5	(22)
40-49.9	62.1	(8)

Source: Compiled by the author.

While the nature of the relationship protrayed in Table 11.1 is curvilinear, the relationship is not the curvilinear relationship specified by Keech. Keech's hypothesis predicts an upward movement in black payoffs (IBD scores) as black mobilization moves from zero to a point at which white resistance becomes more significant (to elected officials) than gains in black mobilization. Keech expects this crucial transition to occur at or around the 30 percent black mobilization level. Instead, white legislative support for the black delegation varies inversely with black mobilization as black mobilization scores move from zero to 30 percent. The Pearson r between vote for Evers and IBD scores is −.33 in the three subgroups of legislators with Evers votes below the 30 percent mark.

The curvilinear hypothesis as stated by Keech also predicts that the mean level of "payoffs" to blacks, measured in this analysis by the IBD scores, will drop in those districts in which black mobilization ranges from 30 to 50 percent, and that the relationship between black mobilization and black payoffs will be either negative or nill. The data presented in Table 11.1 clearly indicate that IBD scores become abruptly higher, not lower, in districts with black mobilization scores over 30 percent. Although the mean scores move in a manner which contradicts Keech's hypothesis, the relationship between pro-Evers votes and mean IBD scores among legislators with IBD scores ranging from 30 to 49.9 percent is consistent with Keech's expectation (Pearson r = −.06). Clearly, increases in black mobilization beyond the 30 percent mark are not strongly associated with higher IBD scores.

These initial findings point to a situation in which legislative payoffs to blacks are higher in districts in which black mobilization constitutes less than 10 percent of the total vote than in districts in which black mobilization ranges between 20 and 30 percent of the vote. A legislator with a relatively small (less than 10 percent) mobilized black electorate may find it rather easy to make some concessions to black voters without undue fear of adverse white response. Legislators in districts in which mobilized black voters constitute 20 to 30 percent of the active electorate may fear adverse white response more than the electoral sanctions of the black community. After the 30 percent mark is reached, however, blacks seem to make appreciable gains in positive white legislative response, although growth from 30 to 49.9 percent seems to provide only minimal additional gains. For whatever reason, the 30 percent mobilization point seems to mark a crucial threshold for white legislative response in Mississippi.

Keech's initial formulation contends that payoffs to blacks are a function of two factors: black mobilization and white resistance. As a result, Keech does not expect to find a simple positive, linear relationship between black mobilization and payoffs to blacks. The initial results of this work and the previous work of other scholars examining similar questions in different ways and in diverse settings seem to indicate that no such simple linear relationship exists.[13] That the findings presented here and in previous work lend support for a curvilinear relationship may be more important than the failure to find the specific curvilinear relationship posited by Keech, or the failure of scholars to find a single curvilinear function which applies in all cases.

The nature of white resistance (when it occurs and when it manages to overpower gains in black mobilization) is assumed by Keech to take a form similar to that postulated by Matthews and Prothro in their classic study of black voting in the South.[14] It should not be startling, however, to contend that such cutpoints might well be different in different times and places, or that such cutpoints may well vary with the type of issue or "black payoffs" under study.

The basic logic of Keech's curvilinear hypothesis appears sound and intuitively plausible. At some point, gains in black political mobilization will produce rapidly increasing white resistance or counter-mobilization, which may become more important or threatening to decision makers than the increases in black mobilization. As black mobilization reaches some critical threshold, black mobilization will overcome white resistance, and greater payoffs to the black community will be forthcoming. The crucial factor then becomes specifying the point at which white resistance becomes a more important factor and why.

A thorough examination of the interaction between white resistance and black mobilization is beyond the scope of this paper;[15] however, the degree of white resistance could be and probably is produced by factors other than the degree of black political mobilization. Keech's initial formulation of the curvilinear hypothesis makes two simplistic assumptions: (1) that all white constituencies respond to black mobilization in the same manner, regardless of important socioeconomic characteristics or the impact of the broader environment in which whites are embedded; and (2) that all white elected officials use the same decision-making calculus in responding to the conflicting demands of black mobilization and white resistance. Obviously, both of these assumptions are problematical.

In the remainder of this analysis, our attention will turn to the relationship between black political mobilization and black "payoffs" as measured by IBD scores, with controls added for potentially important characteristics of the white constituents of legislators, and with controls added for selected individual characteristics of white legislators. Such a procedure should allow us to see whether these variables affect the level of response to black mobilization or alter in any way the basic structure of the curvilinear relationship discovered in Table 11.1.

THE IMPACT OF WHITE CONSTITUENCY CHARACTERISTICS

As noted earlier, the level of "payoffs" to blacks may well be influenced by factors other than the level of black political mobilization. One possible confounding influence is the nature of the white constituents in a particular governmental unit or electoral district. All whites cannot reasonably be expected to respond in precisely the same manner to black political mobilization or to issues which have great saliency for the black community.

In this section of the analysis, the relationship between black mobilization and white legislative behavior will be examined by introducing controls for potentially important white constituency characteristics. The essential logic is that all whites will not respond in the same manner to a given level of black mobilization or in the same manner to a particular issue of concern to the black community. Specifically, white response will be assumed to vary with white income, white education, and the social environment (whether rural or urban) of the particular legislative district.

A good deal of evidence suggests that highly educated whites evidence greater levels of racial tolerance than whites with lower levels of education.[16] Given such evidence, one might expect to find higher levels of support for the positions of black legislators among white legislators representing districts in which the white population is relatively well-educated. In addition, white educational levels might produce a pattern of response to black mobilization significantly different from the curvilinear form discovered in the initial analysis of all cases.

Table 11.2 presents data on legislators differentiated into subgroups based on the mean educational level of whites residing in the legislative district.[17] One of the more striking features of Table 11.2 is that mean IBD scores among white legislators with more highly educated white constituents are higher at every level of black mobilization. Mississippi's white legislators representing more highly educated white constituents are indeed more supportive of the positions of black legislators than legislators faced with more poorly educated whites.

TABLE 11.2
MEAN IBD SCORES BY PERCENTAGE VOTE FOR EVERS
AND BY EDUCATIONAL LEVEL
(For Whites)

Percentage Vote for Evers	White High Education		White Low Education	
	Mean IBD	(N)	Mean IBD	(N)
0- 9.9	63.0	(13)	54.2	(9)
10-19.9	53.4	(11)	44.0	(25)
20-29.9	44.7	(18)	42.0	(11)
30-39.9	71.5	(13)	44.7	(9)
40-49.9	62.1	(8)	*	*

*No respondents in this category.

Source: Compiled by the author.

A glance at Table 11.2 also reveals that the original shape of the curvilinear relationship reported in Table 11.1 is modified in each of the two subgroups. In those districts characterized by relatively high white educational levels, mean IBD scores show an initial decline as black mobilization moves from zero to 30 percent, and an abrupt rise in scores in the 30 to 39.9 percent mobilization range group. Unlike the initial results when all districts were in the analysis, IBD scores decline from 71.5 percent to 62.1 percent as one moves from districts with 30 to 39.9 percent pro-Evers vote to those with over 40 percent but less than 50 percent of the vote for Evers.

The change in the basic shape of the original curvilinear relationship is even more pronounced among those legislators representing poorly educated white constituencies. Mean IBD scores are at their highest point in the zero to less than 10 percent pro-Evers group and demonstrate relatively little movement as black mobilization scores move from 10 to less than 40 percent. The absence of any cases in the white lower education and 40 to 49.9 percent pro-Evers groups prohibits the extension of the analysis.

In districts with poorly educated whites, payoffs to blacks appear to remain relatively constant after the 10 percent pro-Evers vote mark is reached. The apparent lack of any meaningful relationship between black mobilization and IBD scores in those districts characterized by whites with low educational levels could reflect a situation in which the level of white resistance to black demands and/or mobilization is relatively constant compared to a more variable rate of resistance more dependent upon the level of black mobilization among highly educated whites. On the other hand, these findings may not reflect differing constituency reactions but differing responses to similar patterns of white resistance on the part of legislators faced with different types of white constituencies. At any rate, it appears clear that the relationship between black mobilization and white legislative behavior does vary with the educational levels of white constituents in a particular legislative district, and that payoffs to blacks tend to be higher among legislators representing well-educated whites.

Closely related to educational differences among white constituencies are differences related to income. While income and education measures tend to vary together, they are not identical and differences found between districts classified on the basis of educational measures may be modified when districts are classified on the basis of such income measures as median family income.[18] While higher socioeconomic status whites have been found to be more racially tolerant than lower socioeconomic status whites, low income whites share many of the economic problems faced by a disproportionately poor black population. As a result, one could well formulate contradictory hypotheses concerning the influence of controls for white income. On the one hand, one might expect to find higher levels of support for the black delegation among those legislators representing relatively affluent white constituents as a result of the lower levels of racial intolerance among such whites. On the other hand, representatives from relatively low white income areas might join black legislators in supporting measures viewed as beneficial to low income citizens regardless of race.

The nature of the components of the IBD measure employed in this analysis would lead one to predict the former relationship rather than the latter. While some of the votes included on the IBD reflect economic or class interests, the bulk of the votes could be more easily conceptualized as racial or race status questions. Given the nature of the component votes constituting the IBD, one would expect to find higher levels of support from representatives with relatively affluent white constituents.

Table 11.3 indicates rather dramatic confirmation of the affluence/higher support for the black delegation proposition. At each level of black mobilization, legislators from more affluent white districts achieve higher mean IBD scores than their counterparts from less affluent white districts. Once again, the nature of the curvilinear relationship varies across the subgroups.

Among representatives from more affluent white areas, the original curvilinear relationship is still evident. Scores on the IBD decline in the zero to 30 percent range of the pro-Evers vote, jump upward at the 30 to less than 40 percent mark, and show modest increments in the over 40 percent but less than 50 percent pro-Evers group. Among lower income representatives, the pattern is rather different. While IBD scores evidence the familiar initial decline and begin climbing after the 30 percent pro-Evers mark is reached, the 30 percent pro-Evers plateau does not result in any dramatic upward surge in the tendency of legislators to support the positions of the black delegation. Similar to the findings in districts with whites of low educational levels, the mean level of IBD scores remains relatively flat as black mobilization moves from 10 to less than 50 percent. The level of support for the black delegation does not appear to have any strong relationship with black mobilization in low income white districts, particularly after the 10 percent pro-Evers mark is passed. Again, if one follows

TABLE 11.3
MEAN IBD SCORES BY PERCENTAGE VOTE FOR EVERS
AND BY MEAN FAMILY INCOME
(For Whites)

Percentage Vote for Evers	White High Income		White Low Income	
	Mean IBD	(N)	Mean IBD	(N)
0- 9.9	65.8	(11)	53.1	(11)
10-19.9	57.6	(10)	42.8	(26)
20-29.9	45.3	(17)	41.4	(12)
30-39.9	63.8	(18)	45.6	(4)
40-49.9	66.9	(6)	47.6	(2)

Source: Compiled by the author.

the logic of Keech, this could be taken as an indication that white resistance among low income whites is less variable and less dependent upon the level of black mobilization than is the case for more affluent whites. Alternatively, the findings presented in Table 11.3 could be indicative of differences in the decision-making calculus of legislators from districts with different levels of affluence rather than an indicator of varying mass responses to black mobilization.

The influence of urbanism on Southern race relations has been granted an important place in much of the relevant literature.[19] Traditionally, scholars have pointed to a more tolerant racial climate in Southern cities compared to the atmosphere in the more rural environment. The greater tolerance of urban whites has been attributed to two major factors: (1) the impersonality of urban environments which leads to a greater tolerance of or indifference to all sorts of "deviant" behavior, including violations of the traditional racial code; and (2) the socioeconomic characteristics of white inhabitants, i.e., the generally higher socioeconomic status of Southern urban dwellers relative to rural white Southerners.

Table 11.4 displays the results obtained when the analysis of black political mobilization and support for the position of the black delegation is supplemented by differentiating districts by degree of urbanism.[20] The results presented in Table 11.4 include one anomalous finding. While mean IBD scores generally are higher among legislators from urban districts, in those districts in which the percentage of the pro-Evers vote ranged from 20 to less than 30 percent, mean IBD scores are lower in urban districts (40.5) than in nonurban districts (45.2).

In urban districts, the basic shape of the original curvilinear relationship remains intact with one exception. Similar to the pattern found in high income districts, mean IBD scores decline as one moves from districts in which Evers received 30 to less than 40 percent of the vote to districts in which Evers received

TABLE 11.4
MEAN IBD SCORES BY PERCENTAGE VOTE FOR EVERS
AND BY URBAN/RURAL DISTRICT

Percentage Vote for Evers	Urban Districts		Rural Districts	
	Mean IBD	*(N)*	*Mean IBD*	*(N)*
0- 9.9	65.1	(10)	54.7	(12)
10-19.9	59.8	(8)	43.2	(28)
20-29.9	40.5	(9)	45.2	(20)
30-39.9	69.2	(9)	54.5	(13)
40-49.9	64.3	(2)	61.3	(6)

Source: Compiled by the author.

from 40 to 49.9 percent of the vote. Among nonurban districts, mean IBD scores begin climbing somewhat earlier than was the case when all districts were included in the analysis. Mean IBD scores begin to move in a simple monotonic fashion with black mobilization scores after the 10 percent pro-Evers vote mark is reached. As was the case with low education and low income subgroups, the 30 percent mobilization mark does not result in a sudden upward leap in mean IBD scores. While urban districts in the 30 to 39.9 percent pro-Evers range achieve mean IBD scores 28.7 points higher than districts in the 20 to 29.9 percent pro-Evers range, nonurban districts in the 30 to 39.9 percent range are only 9.3 points higher than nonurban districts in the next lower black mobilization subgroup.

The evidence examined here points to the conclusion that representatives from urban districts show greater support for the positions of the black delegation than do nonurban representatives from districts with similar levels of black mobilization, with one exception. This one exception, coupled with the results of the previous analyses of socioeconomic characteristics, appears to suggest that the greater levels of support found in urban areas may not be a function of urbanism per se (i.e., the greater impersonality of city life), but may be attributed more directly to the education and income differences which exist between urban and rural Mississippians. The differences in mean IBD scores are indeed much more distinct and consistent in the case of educational and income differences than is the case with the urban-rural distinction.

To this point, we have seen that the level of support for the positions of the black delegation varies with certain characteristics of white constituents and that the shape of the original curvilinear relationship also varies with these characteristics. The nature of white constituents is, of course, only one potential intervening variable which could affect the nature of the relationship between legislative payoffs to blacks and levels of black political mobilization.

THE IMPACT OF INDIVIDUAL LEGISLATOR CHARACTERISTICS

The original formulation of the curvilinear hypothesis assumed not only that all white constituents would respond to black mobilization and demands in a similar manner, but also assumed that all white decision makers would use a similar, if not identical, decision-making calculus in weighing the demands of blacks against the resistance of whites. Obviously such a simple assumption is not likely to reflect the complexities of the real political world. In this section, attention turns to the influence of individual legislator characteristics on the relationship between black political mobilization and white legislative behavior. While the range of such individual characteristics of legislators is quite substantial, this initial probe will focus on two potentially important characteristics: (1) the political "generation" of legislators; and (2) the "safeness" of a legislator's seat.

Merle Black, in an analysis of the relationship between the racial composition of congressional districts and support for voting rights legislation among Southern congressmen, found evidence that "generational" differences were associated with different responses to the presence of high black population concentrations.[21] In an earlier work, Earl Black had characterized Southern politicians first elected to office after passage of the Voting Rights Act of 1965 as a "New South generation" composed of individuals who "reached political maturity after the principle of desegregation had been settled."[22]

Following the lead provided by the "generational" concept, Merle Black found significant differences between the level of support for extension of the Voting Rights Act in 1975 provided by "New South" (post-1965) congressmen and "Old South" (pre-1965) congressmen. While the New South congressmen had been more willing to break with the traditional Southern resistance to black voting rights, "Old South" congressmen had not. According to Black, "The careers of many veteran Democrats from high black districts had been rooted in the defense of racial conservatism, and these members were not inclined to abandon long-held positions."[23]

In order to examine the possible influence of the generational factors, the analytic procedures employed previously have been repeated for subgroups of legislators differentiated both by levels of black political mobilization and by political generation. Due to the relatively high level of turnover in the Mississippi legislature, use of the pre-1965 cutpoint reduced the number of cases to such an extent as to make meaningful comparisons impossible. To overcome this difficulty and to reflect the peculiarities of Mississippi politics more accurately, the legislative elections of 1967 were used to delineate "Old South" and "New South" generations in the Mississippi legislature. This later cutpoint more faithfully portrays the transition from the racially polarized period of Mississippi politics which did not take place in a clear and unmistakable fashion until the 1971 gubernatorial and legislative elections.[24]

Table 11.5 reveals rather strong support for the importance of the generational concept. In each subgroup, legislators elected after 1967 achieve higher mean IBD scores. In addition, these differences are generally more striking in those districts characterized by relatively high levels of black mobilization. In the two groups in which Evers garnered less than 20 percent of the vote, the average difference in mean IBD scores between pre-1967 and post-1967 legislators is 5.8. In the three groups in which the Evers vote was greater than 20 percent, the average difference between pre-1967 and post-1967 legislators is 12.1.

The basic shape of the original curvilinear relationship is evident among the "New South" legislators, the only major difference being the extremely small decline in mean IBD scores as one moves from the 10 to less than 20 percent pro-Evers group to the 20 to less than 30 percent pro-Evers group. Among the "Old South" legislators, two features deserve some comments. First, the mean IBD score for the pre-1967 legislators representing districts in

TABLE 11.5
MEAN IBD SCORES BY PERCENTAGE VOTE FOR EVERS
AND BY POLITICAL GENERATION OF LEGISLATOR

Percentage Vote for Evers	New South Legislators		Old South Legislators	
	Mean IBD	*(N)*	*Mean IBD*	*(N)*
0- 9.9	60.9	(14)	56.9	(8)
10-19.9	49.0	(26)	41.5	(10)
20-29.9	48.4	(19)	34.8	(10)
30-39.9	64.3	(10)	57.4	(12)
40-49.9	68.4	(5)	51.5	(3)

Source: Compiled by the author.

which the pro-Evers vote was in the 20 to 29.9 percent range is the lowest mean score obtained by any subgroup in this analysis and represents a much steeper decline in support for the positions of the black delegation than has been previously found. Second, the "Old South" legislators evidence a drop in mean IBD score as one moves from the 30 to 39.9 percent pro-Evers group to the 40 to less than 50 percent group.

The generation of Mississippi legislators does appear to influence both the level of support for the positions of the black delegation and the basic shape of the relationship between black political mobilization and white legislative behavior. Mean IBD scores are higher for post-1967 legislators, and the essential form of the original curvilinear relationship between black mobilization and white legislative behavior is reproduced in the New South subgroup. Among post-1967 legislators, mean IBD scores are consistently lower and the original curvilinear relationship is altered in two ways: (1) the initial decline in mean IBD scores is much steeper than that found in other subgroups and in the total sample; and (2) increases in black mobilization beyond the 40 percent mark are associated with lower, rather than higher, levels of support for the positions of the black delegation.

Another dimension on which legislators differ, and one generally given considerable attention by political scientists, is the relative "safety" of a legislator's seat. As a result of the unusually severe problems in obtaining election results across time in Mississippi, the measure of competitiveness employed is based on the legislative elections of 1975. Legislators were classified as holding competitive seats if they: (1) were forced into a second primary runoff; and/or (2) failed to gain more than 55 percent of the vote in a two-candidate first primary or in the general election. The results of the analysis with legislators differentiated on the basis of this measure of competitiveness is presented in Table 11.6.

TABLE 11.6
MEAN IBD SCORES BY PERCENTAGE VOTE FOR EVERS
AND BY COMPETITIVENESS OF DISTRICT

Percentage Vote for Evers	High Competition		Low Competition	
	Mean IBD	*(N)*	*Mean IBD*	*(N)*
0- 9.9	57.2	(14)	63.3	(8)
10-19.9	46.9	(20)	46.9	(16)
20-29.9	44.1	(12)	43.4	(17)
30-39.9	58.3	(6)	61.4	(16)
40-49.9	54.2	(4)	69.9	(4)

Source: Compiled by the author.

In general, legislators holding "safe" seats scored somewhat higher on the IBD measure than legislators holding competitive seats. In three of the subgroups (zero to 9.9 percent, 30 to 39.9 percent, and 40 to 49.9 percent pro-Evers), legislators from safe districts achieved higher mean IBD scores than their counterparts from more competitive districts. In the 10 to 19.9 percent pro-Evers range, the two groups had identical mean IBD scores. In the 20 to 29.9 percent pro-Evers group, legislators from competitive districts obtained a mean IBD score a scant 0.7 higher than legislators with safe seats.

The shape of the curvilinear relationship between black mobilization and support for the positions of the black delegation found in the original analysis of all cases holds also in the subgroup of "safe" legislators, with one exception. A somewhat higher jump in mean IBD scores in the 40 to less than 50 percent pro-Evers range distinguishes the pattern of this subgroup from the original. The initial curvilinear relationship also appears virtually intact among legislators from competitive districts. In the case of these legislators, only a decline in mean IBD scores among legislators in the 40 to less than 50 percent pro-Evers category appears as a distinguishing characteristic.

Political competition per se does not seem to enhance white legislative response to black mobilization. If anything, the somewhat mixed evidence points to the opposite conclusion. Introduction of controls for the degree of competition does not appear to have a major influence on the basic shape of the initial curvilinear relationship. At best, one can characterize the findings on the impact of competition on "black payoff" levels as mixed.

CONCLUSION

This exploration into the relationship between black political mobilization and white legislative behavior in Mississippi has found additional support for the proposition that no simple linear positive relationship exists between these two variables. The nature of the relationship is curvilinear. The curvilinear relationship discovered, however, is not consistent with the expectations generated from the premises of the major theoretical work of Keech.

Other investigators using different variables and methods and examining different types of issues and political environments have also found evidence for a curvilinear relationship, but have generally not found the specific relationship posited by Keech. The overall result has been a rather unsatisfactory set of attempts to either: (1) ignore the degree to which the discovered relationship does not fit Keech's predictions; or (2) to construct *ad hoc* explanations for the lack of fit with Keech's expectations.

The major thrust of this work has been to argue that while the essential logic of Keech is quite attractive and parsimonious, Keech's original formulation makes two implicit and rather simplistic assumptions concerning the nature of white response to black political mobilization and the decision-making calculus employed by white elected officials. By examining the influence of important characteristics of white constituents and key characteristics of individual legislators, suggestive evidence has been revealed that the nature of the basic relationship between black mobilization and black payoffs is influenced by such white constituency characteristics and by such individual legislator characteristics.

Little progress, however, has been made in understanding the underlying processes which produce the curvilinear relationship revealed when all cases are included in the analysis. Here, additional research is clearly needed. A more complete analysis would need to encompass not only measures of black mobilization but also empirical indicators of white resistance independent of the black mobilization measure.

Beyond the theoretical concerns mentioned above, this paper has attempted to call attention to a potentially fruitful area of research. The political mobilization of Southern blacks following the passage of the Voting Rights Act of 1965 represents one of the most dramatic and significant changes in the history of Southern politics. Unfortunately, the impact of black political mobilization on Southern state legislatures has gone virtually unexplored. The need for single-state studies that extend across time and for comparative state analyses is particularly great. The impact of black political mobilization on Southern state legislatures represents an area of research which, if subjected to systematic inquiry, could produce knowledge of both practical and theoretical importance.

NOTES

1. See, for example, Lester M. Salamon and Stephen Van Evera, "Fear, Apathy, and Discrimination: A Test of Three Explanations of Political Participation," *American Political Science Review* 67 (December 1973): 1288-1306; Sam Kernell, "Comment: A Re-evaluation of Black Voting in Mississippi," *American Political Science Review* 67 (December

1973): 1307-1318; and Salamon and Van Evera, "Fear Revisited," *American Political Science Review* 67 (December 1973): 1319-1326.

2. See, for example, Charles S. Bullock, "The Election of Blacks in the South: Preconditions and Consequences," *American Journal of Political Science* 19 (November 1975): 727-739.

3. Black population majorities do not signify the existence of black voting age majorities. The younger nature of black populations in most areas of the South requires a black population percentage in excess of 50 percent in order to assure a 50 percent black voting age population.

4. For analyses of the dominance of the legislature in Mississippi politics, see Charles N. Fortenberry and Edward H. Hobbs, "The Mississippi Legislature," in *Power in American State Legislatures*, ed. Alex B. Lacey (New Orleans: Tulane Studies in Political Science, 1967), pp. 81-119; and John Quincy Adams, "The Mississippi Legislature," in *Mississippi Government and Politics in Transition*, eds. David M. Landry and Joseph B. Parker (Dubuque, Iowa: Kendall-Hunt, 1976), pp. 57-88.

5. In the special elections of 1979, one additional black member was elected to the Mississippi House, and the first black since Reconstruction won a seat in the Mississippi Senate. In the regular elections during the fall of 1979, the number of black legislators jumped from the previous high of six to a new modern high of 16. At the beginning of the 1980 session, the first formal Black Legislative Caucus was founded by the 16 black legislators.

6. The calculation of the Index of Support for the Black Delegation was quite simple. The number of roll calls on which a legislator did not cast a vote was subtracted from the total number of roll calls and the result was divided into the number of roll calls on which the legislator cast a vote consistent with the black delegation. The result was a percentage measure of frequency with which a legislator voted with the black delegation, controlling for abstentions and absences.

7. Previous statewide campaigns by Evers could not be used because of extensive legislative redistricting which made it impossible to reconstruct earlier votes on the basis of the legislative districts existing in 1977.

8. For a paean to Evers which is nevertheless instructive in demonstrating the central role of Evers in Mississippi black politics, see Jason Berry, *Amazing Grace: With Charles Evers in Mississippi* (New York: Saturday Review Press, 1978); see also Gary H. Brooks, "Inter- and Intra-Group Conflict in Black Politics," (unpublished M.A. thesis, Tulane University, 1971), especially Chap. 4.

9. See Salamon and Van Evera, "Fear, Apathy, and Discrimination"; Kernell, "Comment"; and James M. Carlson, "Political Context and Black Participation in the South," (paper delivered at The Citadel Symposium on Southern Politics, February 16-18, 1978, Charleston, South Carolina).

10. For results of a statewide poll, conducted by Market Opinion Research, Inc., concerning the 1978 U.S. Senate race see Jackson *Clarion-Ledger*, October 22, 1978, 1(B).

11. Lester M. Salamon, "Protest Politics and Modernization in the American South: Mississippi as a Developing Society," (unpublished Ph.D. dissertation, Harvard University, 1971), especially Chap. 8.

12. William R. Keech, *The Impact of Negro Voting* (Chicago, Ill.: Rand McNally, 1968), p. 101.

13. See Merle Black, "Racial Composition of Congressional Districts and Support for Federal Voting Rights Legislation in the American South," *Social Science Quarterly* 59 (December 1978): 435-450; Charles S. Bullock and Susan A. MacManus, "Policy Responsiveness to the Black Electorate: Programmatic versus Symbolic Representation," (unpublished manuscript); and Charles S. Bullock and Christopher Dennis, "Policy Consequences of the Mobilization of a Black Electorate in the South," (paper presented at the 1979 Annual Meeting of the Southwestern Political Science Association, Fort Worth, Texas).

14. Donald R. Matthews and James W. Prothro, *Negroes and the New Southern Politics* (New York: Harcourt, Brace, and World, 1966), pp. 115-120.

15. See Gary H. Brooks and William Claggett, "Black Mobilization, White Resistance, and White Legislative Behavior," (paper presented at the 1980 Annual Meeting of the Midwestern Political Science Association, April, 1980. Chicago, Illinois).

16. William Brink and Louis Harris, *Black and White: A Study of U.S. Racial Attitudes Today* (New York: Simon and Schuster, 1967).

17. The variable employed is the mean years of school attended by those whites over the age of 25 residing in a legislative district. Districts in which the mean years of school attended was equal to or exceeded the mean across all districts (12.0) were assigned to the high education subgroup. All others were assigned to the low education group. Educational data were obtained from 1970 U.S. Census reports.

18. Districts were differentiated on the basis of median white family income. All districts which had higher than average median white family income ($7620) were placed in the high income group. All others were assigned to the low income group. Income data were obtained from 1970 U.S. Census reports.

19. See Matthews and Prothro, *Negroes and the New Southern Politics*; and V. O. Key, *Southern Politics in State and Nation* (New York: Vintage Books, 1949), pp. 669-670.

20. Districts have been classified as "urban" if a city with a population in excess of 25,000 was located in the district. The relatively low level of urbanization is reflected in the rather low n in the urban group.

21. Merle Black, *Racial Composition*.

22. Earl Black, *Southern Governors and Civil Rights* (Cambridge, Mass.: Harvard University Press, 1976), p. 337.

23. Merle Black, *Racial Composition*, p. 447.

24. See Earl Black, *Southern Governors and Civil Rights*; and Gary H. Brooks and Walter C. Opello, "Socioeconomic Cleavages and Mississippi's New Political Era," in *South Atlantic Urban Studies, Vol. 3*, eds. Samuel M. Hines and George W. Hopkins (Columbia, S.C.: University of South Carolina Press, 1979), pp. 293-315.

12

BLACK PUBLIC OFFICIALS AND THE DYNAMICS OF REPRESENTATION

Kenneth D. Wald and Carole Southerland

"I am less interested in how many Negroes are selected for public office than in how they were selected."

— black leader[1]

INTRODUCTION

The relationship between the representative and his constituency, one of the oldest and most enduring questions in political science, provides the theoretical focus for this study of black public officials in a Southern city.

The civil rights revolution left in its wake a large and growing corps of black public officials in Southern communities. The political awakening of Southern blacks, like other social movements, has attracted attention from the scholarly community. On the shelves of any good library, the interested observer can now find books about the process of black mobilization and the effects of black participation upon the conduct of political life in the South.

Scholars have just begun to examine systematically the *consequences* of increased black representation on public policy. To some extent (and we do not overlook the many constraints operating on public officials), the policy impact of black representation will depend on the qualities and performance of the blacks who gain public office. The earliest relevant studies pointed out a high level of diversity among blacks leading the fight for equality,[2] a finding largely

The research for this paper was supported in part by a Faculty Summer Grant from Memphis State University. The support of the University does not necessarily imply an endorsement of the findings or the conclusions, which are the sole responsibility of the authors.

confirmed and amplified by subsequent empirical research.[3] Using interviews with more than 70 officials in one Southern city (Memphis, Tennessee), we seek to account for variations in the behavior of black leaders. We suggest that the behavioral differences observed among black leaders are a function of variations in the selected representation role which can, in turn, be explained by differences in the path to public office. The findings of the study testify to the wisdom of the epigraph at the beginning of the paper.

DEPENDENT VARIABLE: REPRESENTATION

One major thrust of the civil rights movement, especially in the "Black Power" phase, was an effort to place blacks in positions of public authority previously monopolized by whites. On the assumption that black interests could not adequately be served by white public officials, it was argued, blacks had to be directly involved in making and enforcing government decisions. Putting blacks in public office went beyond symbolism; it was part of a broader strategy to advance the collective interests of the black community.[4]

These efforts were based on a conception of politics which Salisbury has called the "like unto" theory of representation: "A representative must share the values that his constituents most highly prize, and . . . to do this accurately and effectively, he must be the same kind of person they are."[5] From this perspective, the task of the leader is to advance the interests of his group over competing groups. The "best interests" of the group are defined by the collective preference of its members, and such preferences should guide the official when he acts in an official capacity. To fully represent his constituents in this sense, the black official should be attuned to the concerns and needs of black people and reflect those concerns in the policy process.[6]

We will use the degree of "racial consciousness" exhibited by the black officials in this study as a measure of the extent to which they reflect the "like unto" mode of representation. Our use of this strategy is supported by the literature of black protest. The advocates of increased black representation indicated their belief that black officeholders must exhibit "racial consciousness" in their official behavior. Only if black officials perceived and evaluated issues in racial terms, only if they reacted to political developments as spokesmen for the black community, would the black population profit from increased representation. Kenneth B. Clark, the distinguished black psychologist and prominent spokesman for the electoral strategy, emphasized the need for racial awareness among black political leaders:

> If the black elected official is to be relevant and effective in the continuing and intensified struggle for racial justice, he cannot be just another politician. While he must be realistic, he cannot be expedient. His realism must be the realism of unswerving and uncompromising concern with the problem of social and racial justice.[7]

Julian Bond, an early beneficiary of the growth of political consciousness among Southern blacks, admonished other black candidates to remember that "racial self-interest, race consciousness, and racial solidarity must always be paramount in the deeds and words of the black political animal; when self-interest is forgotten, organized racism will continue to dominate and frustrate the best-organized political action of any black political unit. . . ."[8] For blacks to insist that "black politicians be strongly identified in the public mind as black politicians," it was claimed, was no different from the group strategy long pursued by America's white ethnics.[9]

To what extent do black officials exhibit race consciousness in their behavior? An examination of the available literature indicates that the level of race consciousness varies considerably among black officials. In his Chicago study, Harold Baron contrasted the behavior of two black members of the Board of Education.[10] The widow of a judge tacitly approved Board policies of *de facto* segregation while an activist businessman fought consistently against those same policies. Recognizing this diversity among black officials, several scholars have developed typologies which classify black leaders by their attentiveness to black concerns and willingness to accommodate white leadership.[11]

In the few attempts to account for these differences among black politicians, scholars have emphasized variations in the political structure of different cities. Hence, the existence of cohesive political machines is cited to explain low levels of race consciousness among black politicians in Chicago and Philadelphia, while the openness of the political structure in New York and Detroit is said to promote race-oriented black politics.[12] Yet, as the example cited in the previous paragraph should make clear, there are substantial behavioral variations among the black officials within a single city. To explain such intracity differences, we shall call attention to another factor — the manner in which the black official obtained his position.

INDEPENDENT VARIABLE: ROUTE TO OFFICE

The pressure on black public officials to articulate the frustrations which are felt in the black community[13] may well run headlong into another, even more powerful current — the organizational context. Specifically, the black official who enters the political system is likely to be confronted with inducements to abandon overt racial appeals.[14] Since whites hold a majority on most elective or appointive bodies in most American cities the black official can achieve progress most readily by forging alliances across racial lines. Success in such an environment requires tact, a willingness to compromise and the ability to convince white members that measures to help the black community will benefit the entire population. These considerations may lead the black official who wishes to accumulate influence to follow Sam Rayburn's famous dictum: "To get along, go along." Blacks who cannot adjust to such imperatives are likely to be isolated and ineffective. Each black official has to balance the prospect of effectiveness within the organization against the price of abandoning the role as militant spokesman for the black community.

How is this tension between the conflicting imperatives of race consciousness and organizational success likely to be resolved? We think this depends on how racially-conscious the black official can afford to be. Like the observers who argue that the method of securing power sets limits on the range of permissible behavior,[15] we think that route to office powerfully conditions the behavior of black officials. The ability of the black official to resist "incorporation" should vary with the manner in which the officeholder obtained his position. *Specifically, the more dependent the official is upon black support for obtaining and retaining office, the higher the level of race consciousness.*[16]

Officials from predominantly black constituencies should find it easiest to resist the tendency to minimize racial emphasis. Because the black electorate judges its representatives by their fidelity to the group's interests,[17] the black official who moderates racial appeals can be charged with neglecting the well-being of his constituents. In many cities during the recent past, ambitious challengers have defeated incumbents from black districts by outbidding them for support on racial grounds.[18] To retain the confidence of their constituents, representatives from black districts will emphasize their racial consciousness by serving as vocal spokesmen for the black community.

At the other pole of race consciousness stands the black official who owes his position primarily to whites. Most blacks in this category are appointive officials holding positions at the discretion of white officeholders who have the legal authority to staff boards and commissions. Several observers have noted that white leaders seeking out minority representatives for appointment have historically favored blacks with a known willingness to accommodate white leadership.[19] Black activists have been unanimous in their attacks on the "ceremonial Negroes" recognized as black leaders by whites, arguing that such clientage militates against the assertion of racial interests.[20] If it is true that whites have only appointed blacks who were "safe" on the race question, we should find that blacks in this category are less likely to act as black spokesmen or exhibit racial consciousness.

Between delegates from majority black districts and the officials appointed by whites, there is an intermediate stratum of black officials — individuals representing racially mixed districts. The black official from a mixed constituency has to walk a narrow line.[21] He must be sufficiently assertive of black interests to earn strong support from the blacks in the district, yet accommodating enough to retain some white votes. Excessive deference to white constituents opens up an opportunity for ambitious rivals in the black community; but if the official seems too attentive to his black constituents, he may inspire the white electors to a level of race consciousness which would imperil his career. So the black from the heterogeneous district is likely to be less race conscious than his colleague from a majority black district, but more racially-oriented than the official dependent solely upon the favor of whites.

On the basis of this reasoning, we offer two testable hypotheses:

H.1. Blacks elected to office will express higher levels of race consciousness than blacks appointed to office.

H.2. Blacks elected by predominantly black constituencies will express higher levels of race consciousness than blacks elected from racially-mixed or predominantly white constituencies.

These predictions were tested by analyzing data gathered during interviews with black public officials in Memphis, Tennessee. Like most American cities, Memphis has in recent years witnessed the development of political activity among its black citizens. Though long a vital electoral component in the political machine which dominated Memphis for the first half of the twentieth century,[22] blacks did not seriously seek public office until the 1950s. Initially unable to win city-wide office,[23] black candidates were aided during the 1960s by the adoption of district representation for most public authorities. Blacks now sit on the city council, county council, and the local school board, and have places on the Shelby County delegation to the Tennessee General Assembly. In 1974, voters in the Eighth Congressional District of Tennessee, which is located entirely within the boundaries of the city, elected a black to represent them. The movement for black representation has also affected appointment practices to boards and commissions. Most of these statutory bodies now have one or more black members. Because of the extent and diversity of black representation in Memphis, it is an appropriate context in which to test the propositions about the behavior of black public officials.

DATA AND MEASURES

The data to test the hypotheses were derived from personal interviews with black public officials in Shelby County (Memphis).[24] Of the 82 blacks holding formal positions of public authority, we successfully obtained interviews with 72 for a completion rate of 88 percent. Most of the omissions were due to illness, removal from the city, or our inability to make contact.[25] The high rate of coverage enables us to treat the black respondents as the population of theoretical interest, rather than a sample. Hence we will not report the significance tests appropriate for sample data.

The interviews, ranging from twenty minutes to over two hours, were conducted during the spring and summer of 1977 by a team of black undergraduates from Memphis State University.[26] Trained in interview procedures by the authors, the students conducted the interviews at a location chosen by the official, usually his home or place of work. The interviews, consisting of both open-ended and closed option questions, were tape recorded with the respondents' permission and coded by the authors.

We argued above that the behavior of the black official is conditioned by the extent of his dependence upon a black constituency. We first distinguished in our study between appointed (N=56) and elected officials (N=16). The elected officials were further subdivided into representatives elected from districts with at least a 25 percent white electorate (N=7) and representatives elected from districts with less than a 25 percent white electorate (N=9). These latter divisions correspond to the mixed and predominantly black constituencies discussed in the theoretical section of the paper. This division is arbitrary but not, we think, unreasonable. Our informal conversations with some of the black elected officials indicated that a district would be considered absolutely "safe" for a black candidate only when white voters comprised no more than one-quarter of the electorate. The districts we defined as majority black had an electorate which ranged from 81 to 99 percent black, with a mean of 90 percent. The mixed districts, which elected the remaining seven black officials, varied from 35 to 74 percent black, with the mean black share of the electorate at 57 percent.

To what extent do the three types of black officials constitute distinct social types? The data in Table 12.1 indicate some minor variation in social background but only on one of the variables — age — is there a drastic difference between the categories. In particular, the elected officials as a whole are significantly younger than their appointed counterparts. Rather than assume that any observed attitudinal differences between types of officials are due to the spurious

TABLE 12.1
BACKGROUND DIFFERENCES AMONG BLACK OFFICIALS
(By constituency)

	Appointed	Elected		
		Total	More than 25% White	Less Than 25% White
Percentage male	70	88	100	78
Percent with college degree and/or advanced degree	73	88	100	78
Percent in professional or business-related occupation	73	88	100	78
Mean age	51	39	37	41
Mean years in Memphis	36	31	30	33
N =	(56)	(16)	(7)	(9)

Source: Compiled by the authors.

influence of age, it seems more sensible to assume that both age and racial attitudes are related to constituency type. We know from a variety of studies that racial militance varies negatively with age.[27] White officials seeking out moderate blacks are thus going to have to find their appointees among the older blacks. And the race-conscious blacks seeking to build a power base in the black community will more than likely be young.

The theory developed above argues that variations in constituency should be associated in a systematic manner with differences in the level of race consciousness. The concept of race consciousness implies that the individual regards himself as a member of "a racial or cultural group which stands separate from or opposed to dominant groups in society."[28] Race-conscious black officials, it follows, will perceive issues from a racial perspective and favor actions popular in the black community. We assume that variations in race consciousness can be gauged by answers to survey questions administered to the officials.

How can we identify the issues which engage the attention of the black community and thus activate the constituency-representative linkage discussed above? One alternative is simply to select those issues or questions which informed observers would define as possessing racial overtones. A better method would be to develop some sort of empirical indicator of racial conflict. We chose the latter strategy by adapting a simple index of group conflict commonly employed in studies of legislative behavior. Roll-call votes are said to involve a partisan dimension when a majority of one party is aligned against a majority of the other party.[29] Similarly, for this study, a "racial question" is an issue on which the response of a majority of black officials differs from the opinions of a majority of the white officials. We obtained the necessary indicators of white attitudes by interviews with a comparison sample of white officials, conducted at the same time and under the same conditions described for the black officials.

The case for limiting attention to such cases of racial conflict is compelling. It is reasonable to expect that the black officials will disagree among themselves on many issues for the same reasons that white officials do not always see eye-to-eye — differences of philosophy, judgment, self-interest, obligations to particular constituents, etc. We are interested only in those issues on which black officials are likely to take a race-oriented position. Only on such issues is there likely to be both constituent pressure for black solidarity and strong pressure from white officials to moderate racial appeals. Our theoretical discussion spoke to the manner in which the route to office influenced the resolution of that tension.

From the lengthy interview schedule, we found several items which satisfied the selection criteria. The 10 forced-choice items on which a majority of blacks and whites took opposite sides are listed, by the magnitude of the percentage difference between races, in Table 12.2. These items tap a variety of dimensions including current policy questions (items 1, 4, 7, 8), evaluations of other public officials (2, 10), self-identified political attributes (3, 6), and questions about

TABLE 12.2
ITEMS ON WHICH A MAJORITY OF BLACK AND WHITE OFFICIALS DISAGREED

	White Officials	Black Officials	Percentage Differences
1. "Busing has hurt the quality of education in Memphis." (Percent agree)	90	24	66
2. "We'd also like to find out what you think of other public officials. Please tell me, for every name I read you, if you think *very highly* of the person or *just average* or *not very highly*. How about Ronald Reagan?" (Percent very highly)	60	6	54
3. "What political party do you usually support?" (Percent naming Democrats)	22	75	53
4. "The Supreme Court recently ruled that local communities could pass zoning ordinances which would keep out low income housing. Do you agree with that decision?" (Percent yes)	69	16	53
5. "The government is pretty much run by the big interests who ignore the public." (Percent agree)	24	74	50
6. "How would you describe your political philosophy? On most issues, are you a liberal, a moderate, or a conserative?" (Percent to the left of moderate)	9	54	45
7. "The Memphis police treat people harshly when they arrest them and afterwards." (Percent agree)	17	56	39
8. "One issue that has received a lot of attention in the papers is the proposal to consolidate the city and county governments. How do you feel about the idea? (Percent approving)	74	40	34
9. "Black people who want to work hard can get ahead just as eaily as anyone else." (Percent agree)	57	25	32
10. "How about Jimmy Carter?" – same form as question 2 (Percent very highly)	39	56	17
N =	(70)	(72)	

Note: Due to occasional missing values, the N's vary slightly from question to question.

Source: Compiled by the authors.

political efficacy (5) and black opportunity (9). Judging by the considerable differences between black and white officials, these are the kinds of issues with a racial dimension. It is on such issues, we suggest, that black officials will manifest varying degrees of race consciousness due to differences in constituency type.

ANALYSIS

The first hypothesis suggested that blacks appointed to office would exhibit lower levels of race consciousness than blacks who had been elected to their official positions. The data to evaluate that hypothesis are presented in Table 12.3. The entries in the table indicate the proportion of black officials who answered the question with the race-conscious response. We defined race consciousness as the response given by a majority of the black officials in opposition to the response indicated by a majority of the white officials.

The data in Table 12.3 strongly support the first proposition. Taking the average over all 10 items, 68 percent of the appointed officials chose the race-conscious response. The corresponding figure for the elective officials, 81 percent, confirms that elective officials are more apt than their appointed counterparts to exhibit high levels of race consciousness. Eight of the ten individual items were consistent with this interpretation. The elected blacks were more race-conscious than their appointed counterparts in their attitudes toward school busing, Ronald Reagan, restrictive zoning, police brutality, consolidation, Jimmy Carter, and their partisanship and self-described political orientation.

TABLE 12.3
ATTITUDINAL DIFFERENCES AMONG BLACK OFFICIALS
BY CONSTITUENCY
(Proportions)

	Appointed	*Elected*
1. Busing (For)	.73	.87
2. Ronald Reagan (Against)	.93	1.00
3. Party I.D. (Democrat)	.70	.93
4. Restrictive zoning (Against)	.84	.86
5. Government run by big interests (Yes)	.77	.62
6. Political philosophy (Left)	.51	.67
7. Police are harsh (Yes)	.54	.62
8. Consolidation (Against)	.51	.93
9. Black opportunity (Limited)	.75	.73
10. Jimmy Carter (For)	.52	.75
Mean	.68	.81
N =	(56)	(16)

Note: Due to occasional missing values, the Ns vary slightly from question to question.

Source: Compiled by the authors.

The appointed officials are slightly more likely to believe that black opportunities are limited and substantially more likely to believe that the government is run by a conspiracy of elites.

The confirmation of H.1 is impressive despite the small magnitude of some of the differences. It should be emphasized that we have restricted our attention to issues on which there is considerable consensus among the blacks. Technically, that means that we have minimized the variance of the responses. Under these stringent conditions, it is no small matter that eight of the ten items varied in the predicted direction.

We might speculate on the reasons for the one contrary finding, the item about "big interests" controlling political life. This seems to us less a matter of race consciousness than a question based on the recruitment experience and authority of the two types of black officials. The elected officials, who reached office through their own initiative, not surprisingly regard the political system as open to penetration. Having invested so heavily to obtain their positions, they are not likely to admit that elite control of politics renders their efforts inconsequential. Nor is it surprising that the appointed officials, who reached office through the actions of others, should be inclined to believe that an elite dominates political life. The limited scope of authority granted to many of the appointive boards and commissions probably confirms this sense of inefficacy. So on the one item which distinctly violates the predicted order to responses, there is no real challenge to the hypothesis.

The second hypothesis calls for comparing the level of race consciousness among two subgroups of elected officials. We expect higher levels of race consciousness among blacks elected from predominantly black districts (defined as districts where 75 percent or more of the registered voters are black) than blacks elected from racially-mixed or majority white districts. Because of the very small number of cases in these two groups, we have avoided spurious precision and converted the figures to ordinal measures. In Table 12.4, the group with the highest level of race consciousness is indicated with a "3" and the lowest with a "1". The data in Table 12.4 verify the prediction of H.2 for seven of the ten items. The only exceptions are attitudes toward consolidation, zoning, and Ronald Reagan, and none of the differences are particularly large. So, as predicted, the officials elected from majority black districts generally are more likely to choose the race-conscious position.

Implicit in Hypotheses 1 and 2 was the notion that race consciousness should increase in a linear fashion from the appointed officials, to those elected from heterogeneous districts, to those representatives from predominantly black constituencies. The data in Table 12.4 also speak to that prediction and they generally validate the hypothesis. The appointed officials achieve (including ties) the lowest level of race consciousness on five of the ten items. The officials elected from mixed districts place last (with ties) on four items. The officials elected from predominantly black districts, who were predicted to have the highest level of race consciousness, achieve the highest scores on six items and the lowest only on two. It is particularly worth noting that the items which

TABLE 12.4
RANK ON RACE CONSCIOUSNESS BY ROUTE TO OFFICE

	Appointed	*Elected*	
		More than 25% White	*Less than 25% White*
1. Busing (For)	1	2	3
2. Ronald Reagan (Against)	3	1.5	1.5
3. Party I.D. (Democrat)	1	2	3
4. Restrictive zoning (No)	2	3	1
5. Government run by big interests (Yes)	3	1	2
6. Political philosophy (Left)	2	1	3
7. Police are harsh (Yes)	1	2	3
8. Consolidation (Against)	1	3	2
9. Black opportunity (Limited)	2.5	1	2.5
10. Jimmy Carter (For)	1	2	3
Total	17.5	18.5	24.0
N =	(56)	(7)	(9)

Note: A "1" indicates the lowest proportion of race-conscious responses.

Source: Compiled by the authors.

order exactly as predicted include what are probably the two most volatile political issues in the black community — school busing and police brutality. Two other items of considerable day-to-day political relevance — partisanship and evaluations of President Carter — also scale according to prediction. While there is less support in the item analysis for the implicit proposition than for either Hypotheses 1 or 2, some of the more important or pressing issues do conform to the theory and the summary statistics confirm the argument.

In sum, there is considerable support for our hypotheses in the data analysis. Generally speaking, the black elected officials are more race conscious than the appointive officials and those blacks elected from predominantly black districts are yet more race conscious than blacks elected from heterogeneous constituencies. These findings suggest that route to office powerfully influences the representation role adopted by the black public official.

CONCLUSION

In our earlier discussion, we indicated that black politicians face conflicting imperatives of race consciousness and success within the organization. The pressures for race consciousness come from the black community which treats politics as an avenue to advance the interests of the community. But since black officials in most cities must work with whites who hold a majority on most elective and appointive bodies, a strong emphasis on racial issues may be counterproductive. The manner of resolving this tension, we further argued, depended on the nature of the constituency. Officials with their base in the black community could afford to adopt the "like unto" mode of representation by serving principally as spokesmen for the black community. The officials from mixed or majority white districts had much less freedom to exhibit race consciousness and, to judge by their responses to our questions, were somewhat less inclined to take the "black position" on a series of racial issues.

We can infer from these findings that the behavior of black officials is governed, at least in part, by survival values. Black politicians, like white politicians, seem to be concerned with remaining in office and thus adjust their behavior in order to win approval from their constituency. We hesitate to make this argument too boldly in causal terms because there are other mechanisms at work to account for the relationship between representation style and constituency type. Still, our findings suggest that the role adopted by public officials is in part a function of their constituency. This confirms Banfield and Wilson's observation that black politicians "generally find it necessary to be politicians first and Negroes second."[30]

These findings were derived from a study of black politics in a large Southern city. Though a large proportion of Southern blacks now live in urban areas, the phenomenon of black politics is not restricted to metropolitan areas. It was in the smaller towns of the rural South that some of the fiercest battles for civil rights were fought. Does the Memphis study speak to the situation in the Black Belt towns?

The answer would seem to depend on the meaning attached to the term "small." The reasoning advanced in framing our hypotheses assumed a situation in which blacks constituted a minority of the population and some black officials represented districts with white majorities, or at least a sizable white population. These conditions are not likely to be met in the small Southern towns where blacks outnumber whites and political issues are customarily framed in zero-sum terms. In such circumstances, black leaders have substantial voting majorities which provide a strong stimulus to race consciousness and confer a degree of immunity from the need to placate whites. If this reasoning holds, black leaders in these towns should feel less tension from conflicts between the demands of the constituency and pressures emanating from white officials.

Because electoral considerations are not the only factor in determining freedom of maneuver, the dilemma we described should not be unknown to black leaders in rural areas. Though less hampered by electoral considerations, black leaders in small towns may be more susceptible than their white counterparts to direct economic pressure and more dependent upon white capital if their plans for development are to be realized. Hence, they are not entirely free from the pressure for compromise faced by their urban counterparts.

Depending upon one's value commitments, these findings may be cheering or cause for concern. To take the optimistic tack first, the results augur well for the continuation of a politics based on bargaining and compromise. The

American democracy, it is often argued, rests on a balance among groups which avoids the kind of zero-sum conflicts which have disrupted the fabric of political life elsewhere. From this perspective, a politics of strident race consciousness, in which all issues became unbargainable, would threaten the stability of the regime. Attitudinal variations among black politicians should be welcomed because they prevent complete polarization by race. On the other hand, there has been and undoubtedly will continue to be a lively debate among observers of black America about the payoff from conventional political activity. Some critics suggest that the kind of bargaining and adjustment associated with conventional politics are unsuitable to solve the pressing problems faced by the black community. Blacks, they argue, simply cannot afford the compromises which black politicians may be forced to make. They would point to our findings as confirmation that blacks in office do occasionally find it in their interest to downplay racial themes and thus deny the black community the gains promised by representation.

Though our study does not resolve the question about the benefits of conventional political activity for blacks, we trust it contributes to clarifying the dynamics of the representation process among black officials.

NOTES

1. Quoted in Charles E. Silberman, *Crisis in Black and White* (New York: Vintage Books, 1964), p. 195.

2. See, for example, Ralph Bunche, "A Brief and Tentative Analysis of Negro Leadership," unpublished memorandum for the Carnegie Commission, available on microfilm from the New York Public Library (1940); Harold F. Gosnell, *Negro Politicians: The Rise of Negro Politics in Chicago* (Chicago: University of Chicago Press, 1935); Guy B. Johnson, "Negro Racial Movements and Leadership in the United States," *American Journal of Sociology* 43 (July 1937): 57-65; Lewis M. Killian and Charles U. Smith, "Negro Protest Leaders in a Southern Community," *Social Forces* 38 (March 1960): 253-257; and Hugh Smythe, "Negro Masses and Leaders," *Sociology and Social Research* 35 (September 1950): 31-37.

3. See, for example, M. Elaine Burgess, *Negro Leadership in a Southern City* (Chapel Hill: University of North Carolina Press, 1962); Leonard Cole, *Blacks in Power* (Princeton: Princeton University Press, 1976); James E. Conyers and Walter L. Wallace, *Black Elected Officials* (New York: Russell Sage Foundation, 1976); Donald R. Matthews and James W. Prothro, *Negroes and the New Southern Politics* (New York: Harcourt, Brace, and World, 1966); Everett Carll Ladd, Jr., *Negro Political Leadership in the South* (Ithaca, N. Y.: Cornell University Press, 1965); Lester M. Salamon, "Leadership and Modernization: The Emerging Black Political Elite in the American South," *Journal of Politics* 35 (August 1973): 615-646; James Q. Wilson, *Negro Politics: The Search for Leadership* (New York: The Free Press, 1960); and Richard Young, "The Impact of Protest Leadership on Negro Politicians in San Francisco," in *Black Liberation Politics: A Reader*, ed. Edward Greer (Boston: Allyn and Bacon, 1971), pp. 281-304, originally published in *Western Political Quarterly* 22 (March 1969): 94-111.

4. See Julius J. Adams, *The Challenge: A Study in Negro Leadership* (New York: Wendell Malliet, 1949), p. 100; *The Black Politician: His Struggle for Power*, ed. Mervyn M. Dymally (Belmont, Cal.: Wadsworth, 1971); Mathew Holden, *The Politics of the Black "Nation"* (New York: Chandler, 1973), p. 193; and Silberman, *Crisis in Black and White*, p. 195.

5. Robert H. Salisbury, *Governing America: Public Choice and Political Action* (New York: Appleton-Century-Crofts, 1973), pp. 187-189.

6. One need not accept uncritically this theory of representation. It can be argued that black interests will best be served by a politics of accommodation. A strident racial politics by black officials may well inspire a severe backlash among whites. In a predominantly white society, blacks are bound to lose every such encounter. Hence a black official who pursues accommodation may produce far more benefits for his constituents than his overtly race-conscious black colleague. Our aim in this paper is not to choose between these alternative possibilities but to indicate how black officials resolve the dilemma. We most emphatically do not wish to suggest that blacks who opt for accommodation are submissive or lacking in race pride.

7. Quoted by Dymally in his introduction to *The Black Politician*, p. ii.

8. Quoted in Julian Bond, "Black Experiences in Politics (Second Part)," in *The Black Politician*, p. 62.

9. Chuck Stone, *Black Political Power in America* (Indianapolis: Bobbs-Merrill, 1968), pp. 164.

10. Harold M. Baron, "Black Powerlessness in Chicago," *Trans-action* (November 1968): 27-33.

11. See Oliver C. Cox, "Leadership Among Negroes in the United States," in *Studies in Leadership*, ed. Alvin W. Gouldner (New York: Harper and Brothers, 1950), pp. 228-271; Matthews and Prothro, *Negroes and the New Southern Politics*; and Daniel C. Thompson, *The Negro Leadership Class* (Englewood Cliffs: Prentice-Hall, 1963).

12. Jerry Webman, "Political Institutions and Political Leadership: Black Politics in Philadelphia and Detroit," paper delivered at the annual meeting of the Midwest Political Science Association, April, 1977, Chicago, Illinois; and James Q. Wilson, "Two Negro Politicians: An Interpretation," *Midwest Journal of Political Science* 4 (November 1960): 346-369.

13. For example, see the material in *What Black Politicians Are Saying*, ed. Nathan Wright (New York: Hawthorn Books, 1972).

14. Adams, *The Challenge*, pp. 114-115; William G. Carleton, "Negro Politics in Florida: Another Middle-Class Revolution in the Making," *South Atlantic Quarterly* 57 (Fall 1958): 417-432; Holden, *Politics of the Black "Nation,"* p. 206; Ladd, *Negro Political Leadership*, pp. 135, 312-318; Silberman, *Crisis in Black and White*, p. 211; and Young, "The Impact of Protest Leadership," pp. 284 ff.

15. Among others, see Nathan Hare, *The Black Anglo-Saxons* (New York: Marzani and Munsell, 1965); Martin Luther King, Jr., *Where Do We Go From Here?* (New York: Harper and Row, 1967); Ladd, *Negro Political Leadership*, p. 10; Silberman, *Crisis in Black and White*, p. 195; Stone, *Black Political Power*, p. 162; and Young, "The Impact of Protest Leadership," pp. 287-288.

16. Three additional mechanisms probably underlie the predicted relationship between race consciousness and route to office:

(1) *Self-selection*: Young observed that San Francisco's black politicians chose constituencies compatible with their racial styles. Militants preferred a black power base so they could engage in the kind of overt race-conscious behavior which they thought necessary for political advancement. Moderates, who were uncomfortable with the overt race appeals necessary to secure election in a black district, chose to work in environments which called for interracial bridge-building. See Young, "The Impact of Protest Leadership," p. 288.

(2) *Recruitment criteria*: Appointments to boards and commissions are usually made because the individual possesses expertise or some special familiarity with problem areas. Elected officials, by contrast, seem to be chosen on the basis of their fidelity to black interests in the community. See Christopher Jennewein, "Just Why Do We Call All Those Meetings?," Memphis *Commercial-Appeal*, issue of November 20, 1977: 1G, 3G.

(3) *Visibility*: Members of appointive boards, largely isolated from public view, rarely feel pressure from the black masses. But the black elected officials are constantly in

the public eye, especially when an elective body splits along racial lines. When the conflict pits black against white, the black official is compelled to pose as the vigorous defender of his constituents. The glare of public visibility, or its absence, conditions the race orientation of black leaders.

17. Carleton, "Negro Politics in Florida," p. 422; Alexander Heard, *A Two-Party South?* (Chapel Hill: University of North Carolina Press, 1952), p. 227; and Ladd, *Negro Political Leadership*, pp. 123, 131-135.

18. Lewis M. Killian, "Leadership in the Desegregation Crisis: An Institutional Analysis," in *Intergroup Relations and Leadership*, ed. Muzafer Sherif (New York: John Wiley, 1962), p. 161; Ladd, *Negro Political Leadership*, pp. 136-143; Ernest Patterson, *Black City Politics* (New York: Dodd, Mead, 1974), pp. 17, 200-211; and Silberman, *Crisis in Black and White*, pp. 179-209.

19. Hare, *The Black Anglo-Saxons*, p. 26; Gunnar Myrdal, *An American Dilemma* (New York: Harper and Row, 1962, reprint of 1944 ed.), pp. 721, 729; Ladd, *Negro Political Leadership*, pp. 115-117, 120; and Patterson, *Black City Politics*, pp. 34-35.

20. Hare, *The Black Anglo-Saxons*, p. 24; and Stone, *Black Political Power*, p. 74.

21. Edward C. Banfield and James Q. Wilson, *City Politics* (New York: Vintage, 1963), pp. 307-308; and Young, "The Impact of Protest Leadership."

22. Kenneth D. Wald, "The Visible Empire: Tne Ku Klux Klan as an Electoral Movement," Memphis State University, unpublished manuscript, 1978; and Kenneth D. Wald, "The Electoral Base of a Political Machine: A Deviant Case Analysis," Memphis State University, unpublished manuscript, 1978.

23. Harry Holloway, *The Politics of the Southern Negro: From Exclusion to Big City Organization* (New York: Random House, 1969); and William E. Wright, *Memphis Politics: A Study in Racial Bloc Voting* (Rutgers, N.J.: Eagleton Institute Cases in Practical Politics, 1962).

24. Because we are not interested in elucidating the black power structure in Memphis, we limited our attention to blacks holding formal governmental appointments. Nevertheless, we were gratified to learn that our respondents comprise a sizeable share of the local black elite. A local newspaper polled 84 "prominent black Memphians" a few months before our survey to determine the most influential blacks in the city. Nine of the thirteen individuals who emerged on the final list of powerful blacks were included in our sample because they held some kind of public office. While we do not wish to put too much stock in such informal reputational analysis, it is nice to learn that our respondents are not unknown to the larger black community. See Joseph Weiler, "Search Concentrates on Full Political Power," Memphis *Commercial-Appeal*, issue of February 6, 1977: 1A.

25. To determine the names of black office-holders, we began with a list which appeared in one of the local newspapers. The list was updated and expanded after some determined sleuthing by two of our student assistants, Bob Childers and Marion Reynolds. See Clark Porteous, "Blacks Now Hold Many Top Elected Positions," Memphis *Press-Scimitar*, issue of February 13, 1976: 15.

26. In his earlier study of black leaders in New Orleans, Thompson reported substantial differences among his respondents due to the race of the interviewer. We thought it best, in testing a hypothesis about how black officials present themselves to other blacks, to use only black interviewers. For interviews with the white officials discussed below, we used white interviewers. See Thompson, *The Negro Leadership Class*.

27. William Brink and Louis Harris, *Black and White: A Study of U.S. Racial Attitudes Today* (New York: Simon and Schuster, 1967); Peter Goldman, *Report from Black America* (New York: Simon and Schuster, 1970); and Gary T. Marx, *Protest and Prejudice: A Study of Belief in the Black Community* (New York: Harper and Row, 1967).

28. Stanley B. Greenberg, *Politics and Poverty* (New York: Wiley-Interscience, 1974), p. 5.

29. Duncan MacCrae, Jr., *Issues and Parties in Legislative Voting: Methods of Statistical Analysis* (New York: Harper and Row, 1970), p. 183.

30. Edward C. Banfield and James Q. Wilson, *City Politics* (New York: Vintage, 1963), p. 293.

13

ASSESSING THE IMPACT OF THE 1965 VOTING RIGHTS ACT: A MICROANALYSIS OF FOUR STATES

Mark Stern

INTRODUCTION

Black civil rights, the issue that V. O. Key, Jr., defined as the core of southern solidarity in Congress,[1] has become a hallmark of southern change in the 1970s. A majority of southern House members from the 11 states of the old Confederacy supported final passage of the 1975 Voting Rights Act and the 1978 proposed constitutional amendment for full District of Columbia voting representation in Congress. In the 1960s few would have predicted such southern support for bills that strike at the symbolic heart of the traditional southern position on race relations. Intra-southern differences in congressional roll-call voting on black rights issues have now become so commonplace that studies analyzing southern roll-call votes in recent years examine the bases of both opposition and support for black rights.[2]

While the more affluent and metropolitan areas were the first to break the traditional southern line on black rights in the 1960s, in recent years the break has occurred even within some, although clearly not all, of the most traditional of southern districts.[3] Bass and DeVries,[4] Deckard,[5] Black,[6] and Stern[7] note that southern Republicans have emerged as a new base of resistance to broadened black civil rights, albeit on a set of "new" and interregionally controversial rights related issues. Antiriot bills, busing bills, legal services, corporation bills, etc., have replaced antilynching bills, poll tax bills, voting rights bills, etc., as the black rights issues. And southern Republicans are the most cohesive group of House defenders of the new status quo on these issues.

The 1965 Voting Rights Act, which is specifically directed at the states and areas most resistant to black voter participation (Alabama, Georgia, Louisiana, Mississippi, South Carolina, Virginia and selected counties in North Carolina), is seen as having an effect on southern congressional civil rights voting. Daniel,[8] Feagin and Hahn,[9] Rodgers and Bullock,[10] Bartley and Graham,[11] and Murray and Vedlitz,[12] among others, document the immediate and persistent increase in southern black voter registration and participation after passage of the 1965 Act. Cavanaugh[13] demonstrates that southern blacks in the post-Act years had higher rates of increases in voter turnout than any other major demographic group, and southern blacks over the age of 40 "are at present the only demographic group in the entire population whose turnout is rising." Black finds that southern districts with moderate proportions of blacks in the population are now likely to have congressmen who provide at least some support to black rights legislation.[14] Stern finds that even among districts with relatively large numbers of blacks, traditionally the most resistant districts to racial change, there now is support for at least some of the civil rights related issues supported by the black population.[15]

Stern and Black's studies have examined the voting records of congressmen from throughout the 11 states of the old Confederate South. They have assumed that black percent of the total population is a valid indicator of black registration and voting. We can, however, directly examine the relationship between black voter registration and civil rights voting by congressmen. There are four southern states for which 1970s black voter registration data are available: Florida, Louisiana, North Carolina, and South Carolina. We thus have available data for a state not covered by the Act (Florida) as well as states covered in whole or in part by the Act. This paper assesses the relationship between the black rights voting record of the congressmen from these four states and several indicators of potential black electoral impact on that record. For each district we examine the percentage of the black voting age population registered to vote, the black percentage of the total of all voters registered to vote, and the black percentage of the total population.[16] We examine the relative impact of each of these variables as well as other socioeconomic variables which have been shown to be related to southern congressional voting on black civil rights issues: percent of population of foreign stock, percent of population in non-metropolitan areas, median years of population education, median income of the population, median income of the non-white population, percent of population in the white collar occupations.[17] This paper also examines the use of the black population and black voter characteristics as a separate set of independent predictors of southern congressional civil rights voting.

The bills employed to measure civil rights support are shown in the appendix. These bills represent all major substantive legislation voted on during the 1965-1978 period, as well as several major amendments related to busing and school desegregation. The roll-call votes on final passage of these bills and amendments are employed to determine if the position is for or against black rights. A "pairing" is considered equivalent to a vote. Black civil rights has been the symbolic issue of southern politics. A roll-call vote or public pairing in favor of the passage of legislation in this area, no matter how it may have been preceded by procedural votes to table or amendment votes to water it down, is both a visible and antitraditional stance. In the not too distant past such a vote was an act of political suicide for most southern congressmen.[18]

FINDINGS

The socioeconomic variables and indicators of potential black electoral strength are employed in a series of regression runs as independent variables against two different indicators of civil rights support in each district: (1) the overall percentage support for civil rights in the entire period, 1965-1978; and (2) the difference in overall support comparing the years 1965-1972 to the years 1973-1978.[19] In earlier studies Stern,[20] Black,[21] and Bass and DeVries[22] find that for the South as a whole, as well as for these four states, there appears to be a distinct, positive shift in southern congressional support for civil rights in the 1970s as compared to the 1960s. The break at 1972 marks the beginning year of the congressional districts apportioned on the basis of the 1970 census. Table 13.1 shows the results of these regression runs. The variables which account for at least 1 percent of the variance explained in one or more of the regression equations are shown. The variance explained (r^2), the simple product moment correlation coefficient (r), and the standardized slope of the regression line (beta) are given for each variable.

Foreign stock in the population appears to be a strong predictor variable for black rights voting. But it is not a prediction of change in support for this issue domain. The "liberal" Miami area district, Tampa area district, and the New Orleans district held by Hale and later Lindy Boggs, account for much of the initial support for civil rights among these congressional districts. This is reflected in the importance of foreign stock, non-metropolitanism, and median income as predictor variables. Percent non-white, while not accounting for a very high percentage of the variance in civil rights voting, is a significant predictor of (negative) voting on civil rights. An examination of other variables related to black voter registration yields significant and interesting results. The percentage of the black voting age population registered to vote is a small yet positive and statistically significant predictor of overall civil rights support. It is not a statistically significant predictor of change in levels of support. Thus, districts in which higher proportions of the black population were registered to vote were more likely to support civil rights legislation, but changes in such support are not related to the black percentage registered to vote of the black voting age population. On the other hand, the black percentage of registered voters of the total of all registered voters is significantly related to both dependent variables. The black percentage of the total of all voters registered to vote is negatively related to the overall levels of civil rights support. As one would expect, lower levels of civil rights support are found in districts which have traditionally been hostile to black registration — especially where there are large

TABLE 13.1
SUPPORT FOR CIVIL RIGHTS BY CATEGORY, RELATED TO SELECTED VARIABLES

Selected Characteristics of Districts	Percentage of Votes for Civil Rights 1965-1978			Change in Percentage of Votes for Civil Rights, 1965-1972 Compared with 1973-1978		
	r^2	r	Beta	r^2	r	Beta
Percent Foreign Stock	.20**	.70**	.63	.00	−.30*	−.09
Percent Non-Metropolitan	.26	−.53**	−.01	.20	.45**	.31
Percent Non-White	.03**	−.20	.57	.02**	.27*	−.50
Median Years of Education	.03	.27*	−.15	.12***	−.58***	−.53
Median Income	.03	.43**	.35	.01***	−.41**	−.79
Median Income Non-White	.00	.45**	−.11	.01***	−.41**	.86
Black Percent of Total Registered Votes	.06**	−.28*	−.56	.04**	−.17	.72
Percent of Black Voting-age Population Registered	.02**	.31*	.36	.10**	.37*	−.04
(Total r^2 for variable)	(.66)			(.60)		

**p < .01
*p < .05

Note: The significance level of the r^2 is for its value in the full multiple regression equation.

Source: Compiled by the author.

257

numbers of blacks in the district. But a remarkable turnaround occurs in the 1970s: the net increase in congressional support for civil rights is positively and significantly related to the black percentage registered to vote of the total population registered to vote.

An analysis of the regression and correlation results in Table 13.1 shows that it is precisely the areas targeted by the 1965 Voting Rights Act — the districts which generally have high levels of non-metropolitanism, blacks in the population, and lower levels of education and income — that we find the most change in support for black civil rights issues.[23] It is in these types of districts *after* 1972 that we also find a significant proportion of the variance of the change in civil rights voting being accounted for, with a positive correlation coefficient, by the black percentage of the total registered voters. It appears that influence on this issue domain is gained by the black population in relation to their potential leverage at the ballot box in the context of their relative voting position in the population, not in the context of the black population itself. The black percentage of total voters registered is strongly correlated with the black percentage in the district population ($r = .82$), and it is moderately correlated with the percentage of blacks registered of the total black voting population ($r = .45$). Percent nonwhite in the population is also related moderately, at best, to the black percentage registered to vote of the total blacks of voting age population ($r - .26$).

Table 13.2 shows the r^2, r, and standardized slope of the regression line (Beta) for the percentage of overall votes cast for civil rights and the change in civil rights support (1965-1972 versus 1973-1978), with the black percent of the total population, the percent of the black voter age population registered to vote, and the black percent of all registered voters in each district as three predictor variables in a single linear equation.

It is clear that the variables related to black voter registration are important in explaining overall civil rights voting — more important apparently than is the black percent of the total population. The percent of all registered voters who are black is negatively related to overall civil rights support, but is positively and strongly related to changes in civil rights voting. In fact, of these three indicators of black political strength it is evident that change in southern congressional civil rights voting is related in a significant positive manner only to the black percentage of total registered voters.

An examination of a scattergram of the first-order relationship between the black percentage of the total population registered to vote and the net change in support for black rights provides us with further insight into the relationship between these two variables. Figure 13.1 shows this scattergram and selected statistics for this relationship. There is a moderately positive and statistically significant relationship evident between these two variables. However, the correlation coefficient and slope of the line for the first-order relationship between the black percentage of total voter registration and overall civil rights support in the 1965-1978 period as a whole is negative ($r = -.28$,

TABLE 13.2
SUPPORT FOR CIVIL RIGHTS BY CATEGORY, RELATED TO BLACK POPULATION AND VOTER VARIABLES

Selected Characteristics	Percentage of Votes for Civil Rights 1965-1978			Change in Percentage of Votes for Civil Rights, 1965-1972 Compared with 1973-1978		
	r^2	r	Beta	r^2	r	Beta
Percent Non-White	.04	−.20	.17	.07	.27*	−.14
Percent of Black Voting-age Population Registered	.14**	.31*	.52	.00	.09	−.11
Black Percent of Total Registered	.16**	−.28*	−.42	.08**	.37	.54
(Total r^2 for variable)	(.34)			(.15)		

**p < .01
*p < .05

Note: The significance level of the r^2 is for its value in the full multiple regression equation.

Source: Compiled by the author.

FIGURE 13.1
BLACK PERCENTAGE OF POPULATION REGISTERED TO VOTE AND PERCENTAGE NET CHANGE IN SUPPORT FOR CIVIL RIGHTS ISSUES

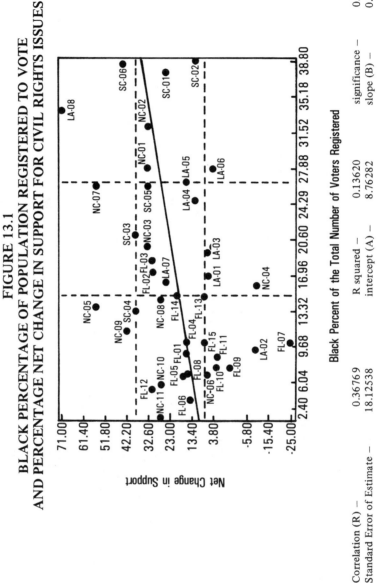

Correlation (R) –	0.36769	R squared –	0.13620	significance –	0.00977
Standard Error of Estimate –	18.12538	intercept (A) –	8.76282	slope (B) –	0.69864

Source: Constructed by the author.

260

$p < .05$, $B = -.54$), although in the post-1972 period the overall level of civil rights support and percent black is not significantly negative ($r = -.03$, $B = -.06$). The 1965-1978 result is what one would expect from the literature on the traditional South, given the strong relationship between the percentage of blacks in the population and the black percentage of the registered voters in these districts ($r = .82$).[24] Furthermore, Louisiana, North Carolina, and South Carolina, three of the four states whose delegations are in this study, fell under the auspices of the Act. Yet, the strongest positive changes in civil rights voting support is found in these states.

The extent of the overlap between the districts with higher percentages of blacks in their population and the districts which had the highest increases in support for black rights is shown in Figure 13.2. The first-order relationship between black percent in the population and the change in civil rights voting is not as strong as the first-order relationship between black percent of total voter registration and civil rights voting, but both are related in a statistically significant and positive fashion to civil rights voting. The Eighth District of Louisiana changed the most in terms of support for black civil rights, and this change occurred as Democrat Gillis Long succeeded to the seat of Democrat Speedy O. Long in 1973. This district has the second highest proportion of blacks in all of Louisiana (36 percent). Louisiana's Second District, with 40 percent black population, had the strongest overall record of black civil rights support in this state. North Carolina's Fifth, Seventh, and Ninth Congressional Districts also had high rates of change in support of civil rights in this period.

Republican "Vinegar" Ben Mizell represented the Fifth District from 1968 until his defeat by Democrat Stephen L. Neal in 1974. Civil rights support in the district shifted from zero percent to 55 percent. Clearly, the black population and black voter registration are not of extraordinary proportions in this district. North Carolina's Seventh District, the district Barone, et al. characterized as "most like the deep South" in North Carolina,[25] goes from zero percent in the early period to 55 percent in the later period, as southern conservative Democrat Alton Lennon retired in 1972. Terry Sanford supporter, Democrat Charles Rose III, succeeded Lennon in this reapportioned district which has 26 percent blacks and 7 percent Indians. The North Carolina Ninth, with 22 percent black, had Republican James Martin succeed Republican Charles Jones. Jones had been in the House since 1952. 1972 was the year of reapportionment and Jones' departure from the House. Civil rights support in this district increased from 13 percent to 55 percent. With a much higher percentage of blacks in the total population (22 percent) than the black percentage of total registered voters (10 percent), clearly this is a district where black voter political strength has yet to measure up to black population strength.

South Carolina's Sixth District is symbolic of the change brought about by black voting. Representative John McMillan spent his career in the House, as Chariman of the District of Columbia committee (1948-1972), in devotion to the pursuit of denying political rights to the population of the heavily black

FIGURE 13.2
BLACK PERCENTAGE OF POPULATION AND PERCENTAGE NET CHANGE IN SUPPORT FOR CIVIL RIGHTS ISSUES

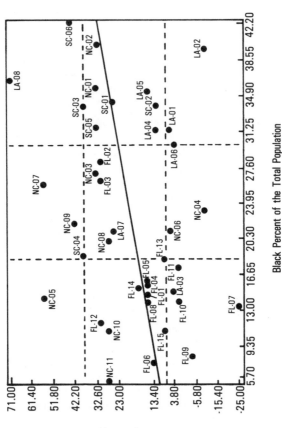

Correlation (R) – 0.26637   R squared – 0.07095   significance – 0.04882
Standard Error of Estimate – 18.78656   Intercept (A) – 9.10442   Slope (B) – 0.50542

Source: Compiled by the author

District of Columbia. And, of course, he never voted for any civil rights legislation. In 1972 John Jenrette defeated Representative McMillan in a bitter primary fight, but Jenrette was defeated in the general election by Republican Edward Young. In the 1974 general election Jenrette defeated Young. With the state's highest proportion of blacks (42 percent), and with one of the highest proportions of registered blacks among all voters, this district now has the state's best record of support for black civil rights — 44 percent. The two other South Carolina districts with relatively high rates of change in support for civil rights, the Third and Fourth, are also marked by a relatively recent turnover of incumbents. The Third had Graham Barden as its representative from 1934 to 1960 as Chairman of the Education and Labor Committee. Barden never publicly recognized the existence of black Congressman Adam Clayton Powell, even though he was the second ranking Democrat on the committee. In 1960 David Henderson succeeded Barden to this seat, and in 1976 Charles Whitley, a member of Henderson's staff, succeeded him to this seat. The Fourth district has a lower percentage of black population and black percentage of total voter registration than does the Sixth or Third Districts, but it had a change in representation in 1973 when liberal Democrat Nick Galifianakis left this seat to run (unsuccessfully) for the United States Senate, and "conservative" Democrat Ike Andrews succeeded him. Conservative or not on other matters, Andrews has moved to vote this district in a more positive direction on black civil rights.

Florida's districts are not among the most positive concerning changes in civil rights voting in the 1970s. But Florida's districts generally started off with higher levels of civil rights support than those exhibited in the districts of the three other states examined in this study. The Second, Third, and Twelfth districts of Florida did change more than any others in this state. Since 1948 Democrat Charles Bennett has represented the Third district of the Jacksonville area, and apparently he did change his vote in a more positive direction in recent years. Republican Don Fugua had represented the Second District since 1963, and he has changed in a more positive direction in the 1970s. These districts, compared to other districts in Florida, have the highest proportions of blacks in their population and the highest proportion of blacks among all registered voters. The Twelfth District meets neither of the latter conditions, but Republican J. Herbert Burke moved in a more "liberal" direction on these issues in the 1970s as his district became more like the neighboring Miami area with a constantly growing northeastern black and Jewish inmigration. In 1978 Democrat Edward J. Stack defeated Burke for this seat.

CONCLUSIONS

The areas of the South which have long been the backbone of resistance to racial change are the areas with the highest proportions of blacks in their populations. White fear was most in evidence where the potential for black political strength via the ballot box was also most in evidence. Blacks are now beginning to achieve the voting strength that has long been only potential in these areas. This study shows that congressmen from these districts are among the ones most likely to have changed their support for black rights in a positive direction in recent years. In many cases, a change in representation in these districts was followed by positive changes in civil rights support.

Jones tends to see more symbolic rather than real, substantive political change for southern blacks in recent years.[26] Black[27] and Stern[28] point out that new regional and partisan divisions on civil rights issues appeared to emerge in the 1970s as interregional education and economic factors entered the black rights issue domain. Within the South, however, the 1965 Voting Rights Act has changed the political demography that existed for a hundred years. The black percentage in the population of these congressional districts is related to the black percentage of the total voters registered in the districts, and these two variables are both independently and interdependently related to recent positive changes in southern congressional support for black civil rights.

Clearly this is a limited set of districts, a minority of southern districts, from which to draw any broad based conclusions. But these are the only southern districts for which "hard" data on black voter registration are available. This direct examination of the relationship between black voter registration and southern congressional roll-call votes on black rights issues clearly suggests that politics can be significantly altered by political action. The Voting Rights Act of 1965 substantially contributed to a basic shift in southern politics. Southern black voter registration dramatically increased as a result of the Act. And the relationship between the southern black citizen and the southern black congressmen has, in part, been altered as a result of the change in southern black voter registration.

APPENDIX

HOUSE VOTES USED FOR ANALYSIS

(66)	HR 6400.	Voting Rights Act of 1966
(66a)	HR 14765.	Civil Rights Act of 1966
(66b)	HR 10065.	Equal Employment Opportunity, 1966
(67a)	HR 10805.	Civil Rights Commission Extension, 1967
(67b)	HR 2516.	Provides protection against interference with persons exercising their civil rights, 1967
(67c)	HR 421.	Antiriot Bill, 1967
(68a)	S 989.	Federal Jury Selection, 1968
(68b)	HR 2516.	H. Resolution 1100. Resolution adopting Senate amendments to HR 2516., 1968
(69a)	HR 1035.	Bill prohibiting camping and sit-ins on public property in the District of Columbia, 1969
(69b)	HR 4249.	Voting Rights, 1969
(70a)	S 2455.	Increased appropriation for Civil Rights Commission, 1970
(70b)	HR 19446.	Emergency School Aid, to aid desegregation of public schools, 1970
(70c)	HR 4249.	Resolution supporting Senate Amendments to Bill for the extension of the Voting Rights Act, 1970
(71)	HR 7271.	Increased appropriation for Civil Rights Commission, 1971
(72a)	HR 12652.	Bill extending life of Civil Rights Commission, 1972
(72b)	HR 1746.	Equal Employment Opportunities Enforcement Act, 1972
(74a)	HR 15580.	Labor-HEW Appropriations Ashbrook (R. Ohio) amendment to prohibit use of funds for busing to integrate schools, 1974
(74b)	HR 16900.	Supplemental Appropriations Bill, Holt (R. MD.) amendment to prohibit federal government from withholding funds for lack of compliance in school desegregation, 1974
(74c)	HR 7824.	Legal Services Corporation, 1974
(75a)	HR 6219.	Voting Rights Act Amendments, 1975
(75b)	HR 10024.	Banking Regulations, anti-"redlining" requires disclosure of lending by census tract and zip code, 1975
(76)	HR 6516.	Consumer Credit Discrimination Act, 1976
(77a)	HR 6666.	Legal Services Corporation, Wylie (R. Ohio) Amendment to prohibit use of funds in cases involving school desegregation, 1977
(77b)	HR 5645.	Civil Rights Commission, increased appropriation, 1977
(78)	HR 554.	Constitutional Amendment giving District of Columbia full voting rights in Congress, 1978

Source: Compiled by the author.

NOTES

1. V. O. Key, Jr., *Southern Politics in State and Nation* (New York: Alfred A. Knopf, 1949), p. 359.

2. See, for example, Joe R. Feagin, "Civil Rights Voting by Southern Congressmen," *Journal of Politics* 34 (May 1972): 484-499; Mark Stern, "The Pro-Civil Rights Congressional Districts of the South: 1946-1972," in *Politics 74: Trends in Southern Politics*, eds. Tinsley E. Yarbrough et al. (Greenville, N.C.: East Carolina University Publications, 1974), pp. 38-50; Merle Black, "Racial Composition of Congressional Districts and Support for Federal Voting Rights in the American South," *Social Science Quarterly* 59 (December 1978): 435-450; Mark Stern, "Southern Congressional Civil Rights Voting and the New Southern Democracy," paper delivered at the annual meeting of the American Political Science Association, Washington, D.C., August 30-September 1, 1979; and Merle Black, "Regional and Partisan Bases of Congressional Support for the Changing Agenda of Civil Rights Legislation," *Journal of Politics* 41 (May 1979): 665-679.

3. Stern, "Southern Congressional Civil Rights Voting," pp. 9-10, 15-18.

4. Jack Bass and Walter DeVries, *The Transformation of Southern Politics* (New York: Basic Books, 1976).

5. Barbara Sinclair Deckard, "Political Upheaval and Congressional Voting: The Effects of the 1960's on the Voting Patterns in the House of Representatives," *Journal of Politics* 38 (May 1976): 422-423.

6. Black, "Regional and Partisan Bases of Congressional Support," pp. 665-679.

7. Stern, "Southern Congressional Civil Rights Voting."

8. Johnnie Daniel, "Negro Political Behavior and Community Political and Socio-Economic Structural Factors," *Social Forces* 47 (March 1969): 274-279.

9. J. R. Feagin and Harlan Hahn, "The Second Reconstruction: Black Political Strength in the South," *Social Science Quarterly* 51 (June 1970): 42-56.

10. Harrell R. Rodgers, Jr., and Charles S. Bullock, III, *Law and Social Change* (New York: McGraw-Hill, 1972), pp. 15-54.

11. Numan V. Bartley and Hugh D. Graham, *Southern Politics and the Second Reconstruction* (Baltimore: Johns Hopkins University Press, 1975), p. 188.

12. Richard Murray and Arnold Vedlitz, "Race, Socioeconomic Status, and Voting Participation in Large Southern Cities," *Journal of Politics* 39 (November 1977): 1064-1072.

13. Thomas E. Cavanaugh, "Changes in American Electoral Turnout, 1964-1976," paper delivered at the annual meeting of the Midwest Political Science Association, April 18-21, 1976, Chicago, Illinois, p. 12.

14. Black, "Racial Composition of Congressional Districts," pp. 435-450.

15. Stern, "Southern Congressional Civil Rights Voting."

16. The registration data are drawn from the 1975 Report of the U.S. Commission on Civil Rights. We employ percent non-white as the indicator of blacks in the population. Florida, Louisiana, and South Carolina have less than 1 percent of their non-white populations characterized by the 1978 census as other than black. North Carolina has only 1.1 percent of its 1970 non-white population characterized as other than black. See U.S. Commission on Civil Rights, *The Voting Rights Act: Ten Years After* (Washington, D.C.: U.S. Government Printing Office, 1975).

17. The socioeconomic data are drawn from 1970 census results shown in U.S. Bureau of the Census, *Congressional District Data Book, 93rd Congress* (Washington, D.C.: U.S. Government Printing Office, 1973).

18. Frank Smith, *Congressman From Mississippi* (New York: Capricorn Books, 1964).

19. *The Statistical Package for the Social Sciences (SPSS)* regression, correlation, scattergram, and crosstabulation programs were employed in this analysis. The change in

support for each district was calculated as: overall support percentage 1973-1978 *minus* overall support percentage 1965-1972.

20. Stern, "Southern Congressional Civil Rights Voting."

21. Black, "Racial Composition of Congressional Districts."

22. Bass and DeVries, *The Transformation of Southern Politics*.

23. Cf. Stern, "Southern Congressional Civil Rights Voting."

24. Utilizing the list of socioeconomic variables previously employed as predictors of civil rights voting, for a multiple regression analysis with black percentage of the total voter registration as the dependent variable, percent non-white in the population as an r^2 of .57 (p $<$ .01) with a Beta of .75. The income of the non-white population was the only other variable with a significant r^2 in this equation (r^2 = .02, p $<$ .01, Beta = $-$.46).

25. Michael Barone, Grant Ujifusa, and Douglas Mathews, *The Almanac of American Politics, 1978* (New York: E. P. Dutton, 1978), p. 636.

26. Mack H. Jones, "The 1965 Voting Rights Act and Political Symbolism: A Research Note," paper delivered at the annual meeting of the Southern Political Science Association, November 1-3, 1979, Gatlinburg, Tennessee.

27. Black, "Regional and Partisan Bases of Congressional Support."

28. Stern, "Southern Congressional Civil Rights Voting."

14

REGULATORY POLICY ADMINISTRATION AND AGENCY-CITIZEN LINKAGES IN SOUTHERN STATES: SOME HYPOTHESES AND AN EXPLORATORY ANALYSIS

Marcus E. Ethridge

Analysis of the regulatory process in Southern states has usually emphasized that it is underdeveloped and underfunded when compared with that in other states. It is suggested that administrative regulation lags behind the rest of the country both in objective terms (such as the number of state employees per 1,000 citizens and budget allocations), and in substantive terms. Quite simply, the "traditionalist" strain in Southern political culture and a relative dearth of funds are thought to result in a regulatory process which is generally ineffective because of a lack of political support and organizational capacity.[1]

There is obviously some truth in these conclusions, especially when the 50 states are compared with respect to certain objective indicators. However, the picture is too simple. The Southern regulatory process has been characterized as sluggish, inefficient, and heavily controlled by regulated interests, but Southern political support for most of the New Deal policies, for example, suggests that the regulatory process in the South is not merely a diluted, less efficient version of the process in other areas. Moreover, the particularly rapid spread of new legislative and other mechanisms relevant to regulation among Southern states indicates that the structural elements of regulatory policy-making are in a period of considerable development. The premise of this paper is that an understanding of regulatory policy administration in the South requires a more complex view than is usually contained in comparative studies of state "innovation" and state government spending patterns.

THE INFORMAL ELEMENT IN THE POLITICS OF REGULATION

Informal political linkages have been considered an important element in regulatory politics ever since the classic bureaucratic assumptions regarding politics and administration were finally rejected as unrealistic. Norton Long acknowledged both the existence and *function* of informal linkages in a landmark essay:

> It is clear that the American system of politics does not generate enough power at any focal point of leadership to provide the conditions for an even partially successful divorce of politics from administration. Subordinates cannot depend on the formal chain of command to deliver enough political power to permit them to do their jobs.[2]

Effective regulatory policy requires strong informal linkages with constituent groups. In the absence of such linkages, the influence of regulated interests will be heightened, the planning capacity of administrators is diminished, and a spirit of compromise replaces a spirit of aggressive advocacy of public purpose.[3] In the same way that a politician requires constituency support when implementing changes, a regulatory agency requires effective informal linkages.

Southern politics has always had a strong informal element. The prevalence of informal relationships in party politics led some observers to recommend a wide variety of structural changes to forge stronger patterns of responsibility, especially with regard to legislative behavior.[4] When party competition was weak or nonexistent, the important political matters were nearly always a matter of informal arrangements.[5] The absence of effective *formal* structures was often thought to be the cause of both sluggish regulatory administration and weak patterns of party competition and responsibility.

However, the special nature of Southern regulatory policy may not be a function of insufficient formal structures, but of weak *informal* linkages. This idea makes the problem considerably more complex. Regulation in the South may be different because political support for regulation is not expressed in adequate institutionalized organizational linkages, but not because of a simple lack of support. Political culture differences could help to explain why support for regulation may not be reflected in the development of an organizational base.[6] Pro-regulatory influences may be less easily transformed into public advocate organizations in the South than elsewhere because of the "traditionalist" component in Southern political culture.

There is some empirical support for the idea that extra-governmental constituencies for state regulators are relatively underdeveloped in the South. Three of the most active environmental groups — the Sierra Club, the National Wildlife Foundation, and the Isaak Walton League — were found to be smaller (relative to state population) and presumably less active in the South than in the other states.[7] The underdevelopment of such public advocate groups may not be a simple reflection of the absence of pro-regulatory attitudes among the bulk of the citizenry.

The idea that Southern regulatory administration is characterized by weak bureaucratic constituency relations is worth pursuing because it may help explain some of the formal changes being instituted. The absence of such linkages, paradoxically, may make formal changes in political and administrative structure especially important in terms of their effects on policy implementation. Two facets of this problem are explored here: legislative-administrative interactions, and citizen participation reforms.

LEGISLATIVE BEHAVIOR AND INFORMAL ADMINISTRATIVE LINKAGES

Legislative constraints on administrative decision-making are most likely to be instituted when agency-constituency relations are underdeveloped. This conclusion rests on fairly straightforward assumptions regarding the incentives of legislators. Effective oversight is not expected to occur regularly where legislators must take the interests and views of strong agency constituencies into account:

> It is likely that congressmen will sacrifice this aspect of the legislative process [oversight] to the development of mutually supportive relationships. These are variously called "subgovernments" or "cozy triangles," which consist of a (sub)committee, an agency, and an interest group.[8]

Effective agency constituencies help reduce legislative interest in oversight behavior. In the few cases in which legislators exhibit a willingness to become involved regularly in implementation-level decisions, it is likely that informal linkages are missing.

Moreover, the reelection incentives for legislators do not usually lead to strong motives for engaging in oversight. In most contexts, it is much more important for a legislator to sponsor important legislation and to provide constituent services. Constraints on time and information, along with the lack of clear incentives, are usually cited as explanations for the absence of effective legislative oversight of important implementation decisions.[9]

Instances of effective oversight, or even strenuous mechanisms to achieve it, are therefore not expected to be part of a typical legislature's relationship with the bureaucracy. If the Southern regulatory process is found to be distinctive in terms of legislative-administrative relations, it may contribute to an understanding of how informal linkages are different in these states. It can be hypothesized, on the basis of this discussion, that legislative involvement in policy implementation will be more extensive and will have more impact where informal linkages are underdeveloped.

CITIZEN PARTICIPATION AND ADMINISTRATIVE PROCEDURE REFORM

Virtually all states have enacted statutes governing the opportunities for citizen involvement in the decision-making processes of regulatory agencies.[10] While they are similar (in terms of the simple requirement for a "public hearing" when official regulations are to be adopted or changed), there is considerable variety among the statutes with regard to certain factors which are intended to expand citizen participation. In some states, agencies are not required to publish notice of their hearings for extended periods or to advertise in widely read publications. In others, the law may require agencies to publish notices of hearings in several newspapers of general circulation for 60 or even 90 days in advance of the hearing. It is expected that citizens will exert more influence over policy-making in the latter type of state.[11]

However, it can be argued that institutionalized informal linkages may also reduce the importance of these statutory reforms in terms of their impact on policy. Although the "public advocates" normally press for greater statutory reforms relating to participation opportunities, the influence of established advocate organizations may, paradoxically, be unchanged after these reforms are instituted. The effectiveness of such groups through informal channels may make the formal requirements for citizen involvement opportunities superfluous.[12]

For these reasons, reform of citizen participation procedures is not normally expected to change the regulatory process significantly. The public advocate writers that argue in favor of such reforms are thought by many administrative analysts to be exaggerating the importance of formal procedures. Where they do have such an effect, one may argue that effective informal linkages between regulatory agencies and their constituencies are lacking. In such circumstances, the choice of procedural requirements may actually have an impact on how many citizens participate in administrative hearings, since organizational linkages are not adequate to transmit information about proposed policy changes and participation opportunities.

The previous section on legislative behavior can be related to citizen participation because of the importance of informal administrative linkages to both phenomena. In states with relatively underdeveloped administrative linkages, legislative involvement in administrative decision making can be expected to be more pronounced, and citizen participation reforms can be expected to have more impact, than in other states. It should be noted that these ideas do not, in themselves, imply anything as to the *direction* of the policy consequences associated with changes in legislative involvement or citizen participation. The following section reports an empirical exploration of these issues.

THE ANALYSIS

Environmental regulation provides the substantive context for this analysis. It is especially appropriate because of the availability of data and, more importantly, because a great deal of the citizen participation and oversight literature is based on environmental policy examples and programs.[13] The basic plan of the research is to assess the impact of legislative review mechanisms and citizen participation reforms on substantive aspects of state environmental regulations.

Recent data on state standards for sulfur dioxide (SO_2) emissions are available in a form which facilitates comparative analysis. Sulfur dioxide regulation is a particularly useful context for study because all states must deal with the problem, and because it is a central component of overall air quality. Appendix 2 presents the data for all 50 states on two measures of the stringency of the standards and one measure of their complexity. Stringency refers to the actual level of SO_2 permitted by the regulation (measured in pounds of SO_2 per million BTU's heat output), while complexity is a function of the number and type of parameters included in the regulation. The complexity measure is important because it provides an additional indication of the aggressiveness of the pollution standard. For example, a regulation which only sets limits on the total sulfur contained in coal used in fuel burning installations may not be as effective in limiting emissions as a standard that limits SO_2 directly, as measured in stack gas. The simpler regulation would allow the installation to burn greater quantities of the low-sulfur coal (since its heat content is lower), and thus, total emissions would not necessarily be reduced.[14] It is necessary to assess both the complexity and the stringency of the standards in order to determine completely the "aggressiveness" of the regulation. (The criteria for rating the "complexity" of the standards is included in Appendix 2.)

Legislative Review of Regulation

The discussion of legislative-administrative relations included earlier suggests that states without effective informal bureaucratic linkages should be distinguished from other states by their more frequent enactment of oversight mechanisms and by the relatively greater impact of those mechanisms on policy. The first hypothesis can be confirmed by simply noting which states have current statutes creating a more vigorous official role for legislators in administrators' implementation decisions. The maps in Figures 14.1 and 14.2 show which states have enacted two kinds of legislative oversight mechanisms, "sunset" and legislative review of administrative regulations. Nearly all the Southern states have enacted both kinds of statutes, and while they are widespread throughout the rest of the nation, their popularity in the South is striking.

It is interesting to note that this pattern is considerably different from the more typical emulation pattern for adoption of innovative policies described by

FIGURE 14.1
ADOPTION OF STATE SUNSET LAWS*

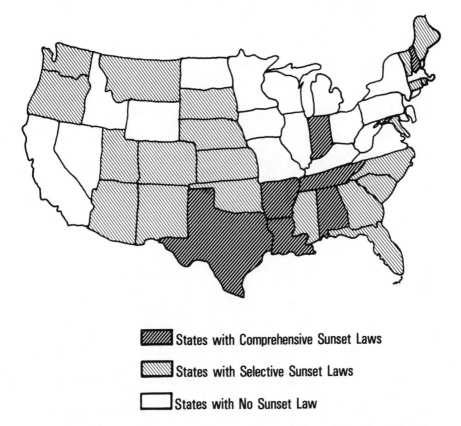

 States with Comprehensive Sunset Laws

States with Selective Sunset Laws

States with No Sunset Law

*This categorization is based on state statutes as in 1978. Alaska and Hawaii both have selective Sunset Laws.

Source: Compiled by the author.

Walker.[15] While some of the states scoring high on the innovation scale have adopted one or both of the mechanisms, these new forms of oversight are predominantly found in the states ranking in the second half on that scale. Legislative oversight statutes of this type are apparently not prevalent among the more "developed" state bureaucracies.

Using the environmental standard data, it is possible to estimate the policy consequences of the legislative rule review mechanisms and then to compare their impact in Southern states to their impact elsewhere. The rating scale in Table 14.1 was employed to compare different forms of legislative review statutes in terms of the extent to which the influence of legislative committees is

FIGURE 14.2
ADOPTION OF STATUTES ALLOWING LEGISLATIVE
COMMITTEE REVIEW OF AGENCY REGULATIONS*

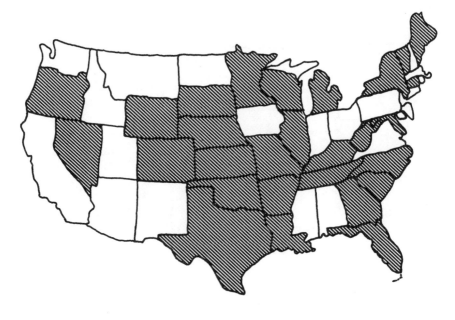

▨ States with Comprehensive Review Statute

☐ States without a Comprehensive Review Statute

*This categorization is based on state statutes as in 1978. Alaska has a legislative rule review statute; Hawaii does not.

Source: Compiled by the author.

enlarged. Each state was given a "score" on the basis of this scale. (Ratings for each state are included in Appendix 1.)

Product-moment correlation coefficients indicate that there is a fairly prominent inverse association between the strength of legislative review mechanisms and the aggressiveness of environmental regulation. Such a result is consistent with the concerns of some policy-makers and analysts who have suggested that an increase in legislative committee intrusion into the implementation decisions of administrators will lead to less vigorous regulation because it provides regulated interests with an opportunity to block or delay

TABLE 14.1
RATING SCALE FOR STATE MECHANISMS FOR LEGISLATIVE REVIEW OF REGULATIONS

no provision in statutory law	1
standing committees given advisory power	2
special joint committee with advisory power, authority to publish objections to agency rules, or power to suspend agency regulations	3

Source: Compiled by author.

TABLE 14.2
STRENGTH OF LEGISLATIVE REVIEW OF REGULATIONS AND AGGRESSIVENESS OF POLLUTION STANDARDS

	SO_2 Standards[a]		
		Strictness	
	Complexity	*Large plants*	*Small plants*
Southern states[b]	−.47	−.25	+.13
All states	−.32	−.12	−.08

[a]Since most states have separate standards for different sizes of fuel-burning installations, it was necessary to consider standards for the large and small plants separately. "Large" here means capable of producing 1000 million BTU's per hour or more; and "small" means capable of producing 10 million BTU's per hour or less. The data are compiled in J. D. Crenshaw, *State Implementation Plan Emission Regulations for Sulfur Oxides* (Research Triangle Park, N.C.: Environmental Protection Agency, 1976), pp. 13-68.

[b]The 15 Southern states used here are: Alabama, Arkansas, Florida, Georgia, Kentucky, Louisiana, Mississippi, Missouri, North Carolina, Oklahoma, South Carolina, Tennessee, Texas, Virginia, and West Virginia.

Source: Compiled by the author.

aggressive agency actions.[16] Table 14.2 presents the coefficients for all states and for the 15 states considered "Southern" for the purposes of this analysis.

For two of the three dependent variables, the Southern states exhibit a stronger inverse relationship between the aggressiveness of regulation and the strength of legislative review. (The second air standard is not significantly correlated with the review statutes in either Southern states or across all states.) Especially with regard to the important indicator of regulatory complexity, the data indicate that the institution of legislative committee review of regulations, observed to be more prevalent in Southern states, has a considerably greater impact on policy in these states. In other words, whether such a mechanism exists makes more of a difference, in terms of policy consequences, in the South than elsewhere.

Citizen Participation Reforms

Similar analytic techniques can be used to determine whether Southern regulatory processes are especially sensitive to citizen participation reforms. A prominent environmental analyst has suggested that the statutory requirements governing the duration and medium of publication of administrative hearing notices have a considerable impact on policy by determining the amount of citizen participation which occurs.[17] As noted earlier, the states vary with regard to these criteria. Each state was scored according to the following rating scale (see Table 14.3), and the scores were correlated with the stringency and complexity of the pollution standards (see Table 14.4).

The results confirm Caldwell's notion that more extensive publication requirements lead to more aggressive environmental regulation. By giving advocate

TABLE 14.3
RATING SCALE FOR STATE REQUIREMENTS GOVERNING CITIZEN PARTICIPATION IN ADMINISTRATIVE DECISION MAKING

A. Publication Medium of Notice of Hearing	
no requirement specified in statute	1
state register	2
newspaper of general circulation	3
B. Length of Notice	
fewer than 10 days or unspecified	1
10-20 days	2
21 or more days	3

Source: Compiled by the author.

TABLE 14.4
STRENGTH OF CITIZEN PARTICIPATION REQUIREMENTS
AND AGGRESSIVENESS OF POLLUTION STANDARDS

| | | SO_2 Standards | |
| | | Strictness | |
	Complexity	Large plants	Small plants
Southern States:			
Publication Medium	+.39	+.26	+.54
Length of Notice	+.13	+.38	+.11
All States:			
Publication Medium	+.04	+.18	+.17
Length of Notice	+.21	+.32	+.26

Source: Compiled by the author.

groups greater awareness of proposed changes in pollution standards, and by giving them more time to prepare their presentations, it is argued that citizen influence is significantly increased. Such reasoning assumes that the political effect of an enlarged citizen role is to counter the influence of regulated interests, thus leading to a more vigorous regulatory process. While the simple correlations do not lead inexorably to such a conclusion, they are consistent with it.[18]

It is striking that the positive relationship between the extent of reform of participation procedures and the aggressiveness of regulation is more pronounced among the Southern states than among all 50 states taken together. According to Elazar's analysis of the "traditionalist" Southern political culture, one would expect that a relatively smaller number of pro-regulatory forces are at work in the South. Moreover, the public advocate argument favoring participation reforms implies that the improved procedures will have their greatest impact where advocate groups are well-organized and able to take advantage of the opportunities created by the new requirements. The fact that the positive association between procedural reform and aggressiveness is stronger among Southern states suggests that changes in participation procedures may have their greatest impact where such groups are *not* currently effective.

INTERPRETATIONS AND CONCLUSIONS

The analysis supports the general notion that Southern state regulatory activity is more sensitive to changes in formal structure and procedure than other states. The results do not, however, lead to a simple conclusion that Southern bureaucracies are inherently less effective or aggressive than those in other states. It is argued here that the presumed absence of informal bureaucratic linkages is largely responsible for the special nature of Southern regulatory policy implementation.

For many years, administrative theorists have argued that the proper legislative role in implementation-level decisions is a matter of some contention. While it is justifiable, in terms of basic democratic norms, to advocate that legislators should control the value decisions of administrators, the proper form of legislative participation is problematic.[19] It is often argued that important disputes over policy content should, insofar as possible, be resolved in the legislative arena before implementation begins.[20] Some argue that it is even more democratic to restrict legislative participation to decisions made at that point. Especially since the new mechanisms of rule review give independent power to single committees of the legislature, doubts about the prima facie democratic legitimacy of the mechanism are reasonable. It cannot be assumed that the representativeness of the policy process is increased when legislative committee powers are expanded.

However, the ultimate value of the new mechanisms of legislative oversight is not the main issue here. The importance of the problem consists in what their adoption and consequences reveal about Southern regulatory processes. The simple fact that sunset laws and committee review statutes have been instituted in the South more than elsewhere suggests that resort to formal changes in legislative-administrative interactions is more likely in these states. Moreover, the findings show that policy implementation (measured in terms of the substance of an important air pollution standard) is more sensitive to the enactment of legislative rule review statutes in Southern than in non-Southern states. Causation cannot be assumed, of course, simply on the basis of the correlations reported here. Yet, the bulk of the existing knowledge concerning legislative-administrative relations supports the idea that these mechanisms will be enacted more readily, and have more pronounced effects, in states with underdeveloped informal linkages. The findings support such an expectation.

The fact that citizen participation reforms are found to have a greater positive effect in Southern states than elsewhere confirms and complicates this finding. When the "notice and comment" procedures are criticized for being insubstantial, the reason usually given is that the truly effective citizen participation occurs through informal consultations. Where the reform of these procedures is found to make a meaningful difference in the policies adopted by administrators, it is likely that the informal linkages between bureaucrats and their constituents have not been fully developed.

Walter Rosenbaum's analysis of an environmental controversy in Florida helps to illustrate the importance of this idea. A new airport proposal was opposed, as one might expect, by various environmental activists who were concerned about the effect of construction and aircraft traffic on certain wildlife species. A particularly insensitive politician made rather untoward remarks in response ("We'll get earmuffs for the alligators," "We'll build a place for environmentalists to catch butterflies," etc.). This attitude brought previously disinterested and unorganized citizens into the controversy on the side of the environmentalists, resulting in blockage of the airport plan.[21]

The positive implications of this study consist in what they show about the potential for bringing presumably unorganized citizens into the regulatory process in Southern states. Procedural reforms intended to promote citizen action apparently have a greater impact in the South than elsewhere, and, as in the Florida example, it may be previously uninvolved citizens that are brought into the process. If this interpretation is correct, it is possible that the overall representativeness of the regulatory policy process in the South can be increased by changes in formal structure and procedure. The more established informal patterns of influence in other states may set limits on the effectiveness of such reforms. Of course, the findings suggest that changes in formal structure or procedure which are *dysfunctional* are also more critical in the South. The most general conclusion from this research is that the formal aspects of regulation are especially important in Southern states.

Further research is necessary before we can fully understand the interesting and unique aspects of regulatory administration in Southern states. The motivation for this research is simply the idea that a region having special partisan, electoral, and legislative politics should be expected to be unique in its regulatory policy. The rapid spread of new mechanisms of legislative oversight in the South, and the fact that these and other structural changes have a greater impact on policy in the South than elsewhere, suggest that the Southern state regulatory process is, in fact, distinctive.

APPENDIX 1

STATE RATINGS ON LEGISLATIVE RULE REVIEW AND PUBLIC PARTICIPATION PROCEDURE

	Legislative Review	Publication Medium	Minimum Lead Time
Alabama	1	3	2
Alaska	3	3	3
Arizona	1	3	2
Arkansas	3	1	1
California	1	3	3
Colorado	1	2	3
Connecticut	3	2	3
Delaware	1	3	2
Florida	3	3	3
Georgia	1	2	2
Hawaii	1	3	3
Idaho	2	3	2
Illinois	2	3	3
Indiana	1	3	1
Iowa	3	2	3
Kansas	2	3	2
Kentucky	3	2	3
Louisiana	2	2	3
Maine	1	1	1
Maryland	3	3	3
Massachusetts	1	3	3
Michigan	3	3	3
Minnesota	3	2	3
Mississippi	1	3	1
Missouri	2	3	3
Montana	3	2	2
Nebraska	3	3	3
Nevada	2	2	3
New Hampshire	1	3	2
New Jersey	1	3	3
New Mexico	1	3	3
New York	1	3	3
North Carolina	1	3	2
North Dakota	1	1	1
Ohio	1	1	3
Oklahoma	3	2	2
Oregon	2	2	2
Pennsylvania	1	3	3

(contined)

Appendix 1 (Continued)

	Legislative Review	Publication Medium	Minimum Lead Time
Rhode Island	1	3	3
South Carolina	3	1	1
South Dakota	3	3	2
Tennessee	3	3	3
Texas	1	3	2
Utah	1	3	2
Vermont	2	3	1
Virginia	1	3	3
Washington	2	2	2
West Virginia	2	3	3
Wisconsin	3	2	3
Wyoming	1	2	2

Note: These scores are based on statutory law as it existed in 1976. The more recent data, used in constructing Figure 14.2, would not have been compatible with the data for the dependent variables.

APPENDIX 2

STATE SO$_2$ STANDARDS

(The states are ordered in terms of the strictness of the standard applying to large fuel-burning installations. The rating criteria for the complexity measure are listed at the end of the table.)

	Strictness (in lbs. SO$_2$/10^6 BTU's)		Complexity Score
	Large Plant	Small Plant	
Nevada	.2	.2	4
New Jersey	.3	.3	4
New York	.4	.4	3
Connecticut	.5	.5	3
Massachusetts	.5	.5	2
Pennsylvania	.6	1.0	3
California	.8	.8	3
Hawaii	.8	3.2	1
Arizona	1.0	1.0	3
Rhode Island	1.1	1.1	2
Virginia	1.1	1.1	2
Alabama	1.2	1.2	2
Indiana	1.2	6.0	2
Kentucky	1.2	4.0	2
Ohio	1.2	2.4	2
Tennessee	1.2	1.6	2
Wisconsin	1.2	1.2	2
Wyoming	1.2	5.5	3
Alaska	1.3	1.3	2
Colorado	1.3	.4	2
Florida	1.5	2.0	2
Washington	1.5	1.5	3
Delaware	1.6	1.6	1
Idaho	1.6	1.6	1
Maryland	1.6	5.5	1
Montana	1.6	1.6	2
New Mexico	1.6	1.6	3
Oregon	1.6	1.6	3
Utah	1.6	1.6	1
Vermont	1.6	1.6	1
West Virginia	1.6	1.6	2
Illinois	1.8	1.8	2
Missouri	2.3	3.2	3

(continued)

Appendix 2 (Continued)

| | Strictness (in lbs. $SO_2/10^6$ BTU's) | | Complexity Score |
	Large Plant	Small Plant	
North Carolina	2.3	2.3	2
South Carolina	2.3	3.5	2
Maine	2.4	2.4	1
Michigan	2.4	2.1	1
Minnesota	2.4	3.2	1
Nebraska	2.5	2.5	2
Arkansas	3.0	3.0	1
Kansas	3.0	5.5	2
North Dakota	3.0	3.0	2
South Dakota	3.0	3.0	2
Texas	3.0	3.0	4
Georgia	4.8	4.0	3
Mississippi	4.8	2.4	2
Iowa	5.0	5.0	2
Louisiana	5.5	5.5	2 ·
Oklahoma	5.5	5.5	2
New Hampshire	5.6	5.6	2
Mean	2.0	2.4	2.14

Criteria for Complexity Score:

regulation is in units of % sulfur in fuel	1
regulation is in units of lbs. SO_2 per unit heat output	2
regulation is in units of lbs. SO_2 per unit heat output and one other parameter	3
regulation is in units of lbs. SO_2 per unit heat output and more than one other parameter	4

Source: J. D. Crenshaw, *State Implementation Plan Emission Regulations for Sulfur Oxides* (Research Triangle Park, N.C.: Environmental Protection Agency, 1976), pp. 13-68.

NOTES

1. Daniel Elazar, *American Federalism: A View From the States*, 2nd ed. (New York: Crowell, 1972), Ch. 4. See also Ira Sharkansky, "The Utility of Elazar's Political Culture," *Polity* 2 (1969): 66-83.

2. Norton E. Long, "Power and Administration," *Public Administration Review* 9 (Autumn 1949), p. 258.

3. See Marver H. Bernstein, *Regulating Business by Independent Commission* (Princeton: Princeton University Press, 1955); James Q. Wilson, "The Politics of Regulation," in *Social Responsibility and the Business Predicament*, ed. James McKie (Washington: Brookings, 1974), pp. 135-168; and Phillippe Nonet, *Administrative Justice: Advocacy and Change in a Government Agency* (New York: Russell Sage, 1969).

4. See Citizens Conference on State Legislatures, *The Sometime Governments* (New York: Bantam, 1971).

5. V. O. Key, Jr., *Southern Politics in State and Nation* (New York: Vintage, 1949), p. 392.

6. Elazar, *American Federalism*, p. 102.

7. This was noted in a recent comparative study of environmental policy. See Lettie Wenner, "Enforcement of State Water Pollution Laws," Ph.D. dissertation, University of Wisconsin, 1971.

8. David Nachmias and David Rosenbloom, *Bureaucratic Government USA* (New York: St. Martin's, 1980), p. 54. See also Randall Ripley and Grace Franklin, *Congress, the Bureaucracy, and Public Policy* (Homewood, Ill.: The Dorsey Press, 1976), pp. 166-170.

9. See Morris P. Fiorina, *Congress: Keystone of the Washington Establishment* (New Haven: Yale University Press, 1977).

10. See "Public Interest Representation and the Federal Agencies," *Public Administration Review* 37 (March 1977): 131-154.

11. Lynton Caldwell, Lynton Hayes, and Isabel MacWhirter, *Citizens and the Environment* (Bloomington: Indiana University Press, 1976), pp. xxiii-xxv. See also Robert S. Lorch, *Democratic Process and Administrative Law* (Detroit: Wayne State University Press, 1969).

12. See Peter Woll, *Administrative Law: The Informal Process* (Berkeley: University of California Press, 1964).

13. See, for example, Lynton Caldwell, *Environment: A Challenge to Modern Society* (New York: Natural History Press, 1970); and Richard A. Liroff, *A National Policy for the Environment* (Bloomington: Indiana University Press, 1976).

14. The importance of the complexity criterion is explained in some detail in the report from which the pollution standard data were obtained: J. D. Crenshaw, *State Implementation Plan Emission Regulations for Sulfur Oxides: Fuel Combustion* (Research Triangle Park, N.C.: Environmental Protection Agency, 1976), pp. 6-7. Crenshaw also provides the conversion equations that can be used to transform standards expressed in one unit into the lbs. $SO_2/10^6$ BTU's unit for purposes of comparison.

15. See Jack Walker, "Innovations in State Politics," in *Politics in the American States*, eds. Herbert Jacob and Kenneth Vines (Boston: Little, Brown, and Company, 1971), pp. 345-387.

16. The best statement of this view can be found in Harold Bruff and Ernest Gellhorn, "Congressional Control of Administrative Regulation," *Harvard Law Review* 90 (May 1977): 1369-1440.

17. Caldwell, et al., *Citizens and the Environment*.

18. One may argue, for example, that regulated interests can be more prepared to make their presentations against vigorous standards as a result of reformed participatory procedures. In such a case, the correlations would have to be interpreted differently.

19. Bruff and Gellhorn, "Congressional Control," pp. 1423-1440.

20. In addition to Bruff and Gellhorn, good advice along these lines is provided by Jeffrey Pressman and Aaron Wildavsky, *Implementation* (Berkeley: University of California Press, 1973).

21. Walter Rosenbaum, *The Politics of Environmental Concern*, 2nd. ed. (New York: Praeger, 1977), Ch. 6.

CONCLUSION

The Editors

In many respects southern history, economics, culture, and politics have been regarded as unique. For perhaps a century most research on the region focused on these unique features; indeed, for many, this was what made the South interesting and worthy of special scholarly attention. Relatively few investigators chose to give much attention to those aspects of pre-World War II southern life which were similar to life in other parts of the country even though, as a vocal minority did try to point out, there were more similarities even then than most recognized.[1]

Over the past three decades perceptions of the South have changed because the South has changed. The growing body of literature on the region produced since World War II represents a mixed view, with some researchers still emphasizing what they see as enduring differences between the South and other parts of the nation,[2] and other investigators stressing the dramatic changes in traditional economic, cultural, and political patterns which seem to them to be erasing the South as a region clearly set apart from the remainder of the country.[3] In this, hardly anyone seriously argues that the South has not changed, but there is considerable disagreement over the degree of change and over the implications of these changes from the South vis-a-vis the non-South.

The South has long been considered a conservative region.[4] In spite of some arguments to the contrary,[5] and in the face of some recent evidence which suggests that ideological convergence between the South and the remainder of the nation has taken place,[6] this image of a conservative South has persisted. Consequently, any broad consideration of southern distinctiveness must address the question of whether the region displays conservatism to a degree which sets it apart from the rest of the country and which is consistent with its traditional character.

The four chapters in Part I offer information pertinent to such a consideration. Unfortunately for those who seek simple, clear answers, the conclusions of these four studies are not entirely congruent with each other, a consequence, no doubt, of their differing methodologies and foci. Still, taken together, they offer grounds for some tentative conclusions.

Neither Jerry Perkins ("Ideology in the South: Meaning and Bases Among Masses and Elites") nor Robert E. Botsch ("A Microanalytic Return to the Mind of the South") offers any comparative analysis across regions, but their respective chapters do provide some insight into the nature of at least certain aspects of southern attitudinal patterns. Perkins examined data on the general population of Georgia and on members of the state legislature and concluded that there was an interesting mixture of conservative and liberal attitudes. While most of the population sample who perceived themselves in ideological terms said that they were moderate or conservative, their answers to a set of specific issue items indicated that they tended to be operationally liberal. The political elites Perkins studied were somewhat more conservative than the general population, both in terms of self-assessment and specific positions on the selected issues, but even among these leaders there was not overwhelming evidence of strong and widespread conservatism. Even with the introduction of controls for race, income, education, occupation, and urban-rural residence, there was little change in the pattern. In short, Perkins found only limited support for the notion that the South is a solidly conservative region in his examination of attitudes in one Deep South state. Moreover, he found little evidence that the southerners in his study think in consistently ideological terms.

Botsch employed a different approach by conducting intensive interviews with a small sample of blue-collar workers in one North Carolina town, but his conclusions were not radically different from Perkins'. He found that these respondents were basically liberal economically, but their liberality was tempered by strongly individualistic values which hold, for example, that government aid is acceptable for those who honestly cannot take care of their needs. Beyond a fierce self-reliance, these men demonstrated only slight indications of religious fundamentalism, but their attitudes on certain subjects (such as pornography) reflected a strong fundamentalist heritage. Further, most showed an acceptance of violence in their daily lives, which seems consistent with those studies which have suggested that such a mind set is more characteristic of the South than of other regions. In the area of race relations, long considered to be the issue dimension for which the South is most strongly characterized as conservative, Botsch found that most of his respondents did in fact hold racial stereotypes of a prejudicial nature, but that this was tempered by a general acceptance of integration in the more public realms of life (e.g., school and work). In short, Botsch's data revealed both stability and change in the southern mind; areas of apparent stability were found in the acceptance of individual self-reliance and violence, while areas of possible change from the traditional image of the southern mind included these men's views on race relations and their orientations toward the local community (versus a nationalistic outlook). As with Perkins, Botsch uncovered only limited evidence of continued southern distinctiveness in the attitudinal domains he investigated.

A more direct examination was presented by Earl W. Hawkey ("Southern Conservatism 1956-1976") in his comparative study of ideology and issue orientations in the South and in the non-South from 1956 to 1976. He found that in terms of self-assessment, the South has been slightly more conservative than the non-South, but the differences were not great, and there was evidence of convergence over the past two decades as the non-South has become more conservative than it formerly was (although both have moved in a conservative direction since 1956). With regard to specific issues, Hawkey found that the South is no more conservative than the non-South on selected social welfare policy items (governmental job guarantees, health care programs, and governmental aid to education), that the South is consistently more conservative than the non-South on two law and order items (crime control and the use of force to control urban unrest), and that the South is slightly more conservative than the non-South on the questions of women's rights and affirmative action programs for women and other minorities. Interestingly, as with the self-placement question, there was evidence on a number of these questions of lessening regional differences over the past 20 years, primarily as a result of increasing conservatism in the non-South. The introduction of various controls indicated that the differences which did exist between the South and the non-South were not found consistently in all groups in these regions. For certain subgroups on certain items, nonsoutherners were more conservative than southerners, while for other subgroups on other items southerners were consistently more conservative than nonsoutherners. For example, income controls revealed that the sharpest regional differences usually occurred between those at the higher income levels while the most negligible differences occurred between those at the lower income levels. Hawkey's analysis suggested that the South was ideologically different from the non-South on at least some points, but it was not as substantially nor as consistently conservative vis-a-vis the non-South as it has been traditionally pictured. This mixed conclusion is generally consistent with the material presented by Perkins and Botsch and suggests that the South is experiencing a diminution of its ideological distinctiveness.

Of all the studies in Part I, the chapter by Ted Jelen ("Sources of Political Intolerance: The Case of the American South") offered the strongest support for an alternative conclusion. He explored comparative data concerning the tolerance of deviant subgroups and found that there were clear and consistent differences between the South and non-South. Moreover, these differential patterns still existed after the introduction of various demographic controls. This is all the more impressive because his southern data were drawn from a number of border states as well as the 11 states of the former Confederacy, a factor which might be expected to depress the conservatism apparent in the southern data. Jelen went on to link this southern intolerance of homosexuals, communists, and atheists to religious fundamentalism, a point at variance with the material in Perkins and Botsch which found no such religious link with respect to other types of issues. Jelen's focus was much more limited than the other studies, and this may account for the sharply different conclusions, but he offered strong evidence that, at least in these types of considerations, the South remains regionally distinctive.

In summary, then, these four studies suggested that the South has retained elements of its traditional conservatism, but, with the exception of matters such as attitudes toward homosexuals, communists, and atheists, this conservatism has come to be mixed with clear strains of liberalism and moderation for certain issues and for certain population groups. Perhaps the South was never as homogeneously conservative as it has frequently been depicted, especially as regards economic issues where a long history of populism among the lower classes can be identified; be this as it may, the materials examined here suggested that it is not homogeneously conservative now. The region's ideological distinctiveness has diminished and, even though an argument can be made that the South is still the South in ideological terms, this argument must be immediately followed by a list of qualifications relating to specific issues and specific subgroups, with some acknowledgement of the regional convergence that has been demonstrated by studies such as Hawkey's.

The six chapters in Part II dealt with two basic themes of southern politics. The first three chapters, those by Earl Black and Merle Black ("Successful Durable Democratic Factions in Southern Politics" and "The Growth of Contested Republican Primaries in the American South, 1960-1980") and by C. David Sutton ("Party Competition in the South's Forgotten Region: The Case of Southern Appalachia"), were historical analyses of the patterns of party competition in the South. Thus, in their chapter on the Democratic party, the Blacks focused attention on the comparative analysis of factions rather than factional systems. As a result, they arrived at conclusions considerably different from those of V. O. Key. While Key concluded that southern Democratic politics tended to be characterized by shifting, ephemeral coalitions,[7] the Blacks found a small number of successful durable factions operating in intraparty politics in the South. Hence, the one-party system was more effective in structuring choices for the electorate than has commonly been assumed.

In their chapter on the Republican party, the Blacks examined the emergence of Republican gubernatorial primaries in the South. To date they found that there are only three states — Tennessee, North Carolina, and Florida — in which there has been at least one Republican primary characterized by intense competition between members of the party elite and by a relatively high turnout. In Tennessee and North Carolina the Republican party was able to build on a mountain Republican base, and in Florida, on Republican immigration. However, the Blacks also found that since the 1960s the contested primary has become the typical means by which southern Republican parties have nominated candidates for governor. It thus can be assumed that if Republicanism gains a stronger foothold in the South, Republican primaries will begin to rival Democratic primaries as significant components of the electoral process.

Finally, David Sutton ("Party Competition in the South's Forgotten Region: The Case of Southern Appalachia") critiqued three stereotypes of the other South. He found that party competition in the Appalachian counties of Tennessee, Virginia, and North Carolina tended to be much more pronounced than has been traditionally assumed. He thus rejected the notion of southern Appalachia as a one-party Republican island. In terms of political philosophy, Sutton found that rather than being strongly conservative, regressive, and racist, southern Appalachian residents tended to be moderate in outlook. Indeed, he found that the mountain counties provided the geographical base for the moderate wing of the Republican party in Tennessee, Virginia, and North Carolina. Finally, in terms of voting participation, the Appalachian counties tended to have higher turnouts than the non-Appalachian ones. Sutton therefore concluded that the Appalachian stereotype is wrong and that there are no pronounced cultural differences between those who live in the southern highlands and those who do not.

The second group of three chapters in Part II focused attention on the maintenance or breakdown of southern distinctiveness. Paul Beck and Paul Lopatto ("The End of Southern Distinctiveness") found that since 1964 partisan dealignment has tended to characterize both the southern and nonsouthern electorates, with this tendency being particularly pronounced among young southerners. With regard to presidential voting behavior, Beck and Lopatto found a pattern of convergence between southerners and nonsoutherners, with Republican candidates exhibiting a stronger appeal in the South. Thus, southern exceptionalism has disappeared here as well. Finally, in terms of the political outlooks of southerners, Beck and Lopatto also found an end to southern distinctiveness. With regard to political ideology, southerners were no more conservative than nonsoutherners and, in terms of stands on political issues, the differences between southerners and nonsoutherners verged on the statistically insignificant.

Alan Abramowitz, John McGlennon, and Ronald Rapoport ("Presidential Activists and the Nationalization of Party Politics in Virginia"), in their study of delegates to the 1980 Democratic and Republican conventions in Virginia, tended to support Beck and Lopatto's conclusions. They found that Democratic and Republican delegates represented different types of organized interests, differed with regard to political ideology, and took conflicting stands on political issues. Thus, the parties structured choices in a manner that presented the voters with relatively clear alternatives in election contests. This, of course, also represented a break from the traditional pattern of southern politics.

While the data presented on South Carolina party activists by Tod Baker, Robert P. Steed, and Laurence W. Moreland ("Southern Distinctiveness and the Emergence of Party Competition: The Case of a Deep South State") could have been interpreted in the same manner as the Abramowitz, et al. chapter, the authors chose to base their analysis on attitudes and beliefs that could be classified as distinctively southern. As a result, they arrived at conclusions which, to some degree, modified those of the previous two chapters by arguing that the Republican party has emerged as the political institution that articulates distinctively southern viewpoints. In this sense southern distinctiveness or exceptionalism is not at an end. Thus, partisan conflict, at least in South Carolina, can be thought of, in part, as a struggle between those viewpoints which are distinctively southern and those which express nonsouthern attitudes.

Part III of this volume, which investigated the nature of the linkages between mass publics and public officials, perhaps most indirectly examined the question of southern distinctiveness, but indications of an answer may yet be discerned. Gary Brooks ("Black Political Mobilization and White Legislative Behavior") suggested that the degree to which white legislators support black legislative initiatives is related to the nature of a legislator's constituency. In his analysis of the effect of black voting on legislative behavior in Mississippi, Brooks discovered that the relationship tended to be curvilinear in a U-shaped configuration — white legislators were more likely to support issues with black salience where there were either few black votes in the constituency or where black votes were 30 percent or more of the total vote. In addition, white legislators of a "new South" political generation (those who developed political careers essentially after the passage of the 1965 Voting Rights Act) were less likely to register resistance to measures important to black legislators. These findings, although perhaps applicable to other parts of the nation, have special application for the South: unlike nonsouthern blacks, who tend to be clustered in urban areas, southern blacks are less geographically concentrated, as they are often scattered over both rural and urban constituencies, especially in the Deep South.

Kenneth Wald and Carole Southerland ("Black Public Officials and the Dynamics of Representation") examined the linkage relationship from a perspective very nearly opposite the one utilized by Brooks. They investigated the racial consciousness, not of white legislators, but of black public officials, both appointed and elected. They found that black appointed officials who owed their appointments to a political process dominated by whites expressed less black consciousness than blacks who were elected, especially those blacks elected from heavily black constituencies. Similarly, the black consciousness of elected black officeholders increased as their constituencies became increasingly black and less racially mixed.

Mark Stern ("Assessing the Impact of the 1965 Voting Rights Act: A Micro Analysis of Four States") more directly demonstrated the changes which have taken place in the South since 1965 with regard to race and politics. He showed that the 1965 Voting Rights Act, by increasing the number of black registered voters in those congressional districts often identified with very low levels of congressional support for civil rights measures and high levels of blacks in their populations, contributed to important shifts in southern politics. Congressmen in those districts in which black voter registration dramatically increased were among those most likely to have increased their support for civil rights legislation in recent years.

These three chapters supply indirect evidence on the issue of southern distinctiveness. The central thesis of V. O. Key's observations on the South in 1949 emphasized the centrality of race in southern politics, but it was racial *exclusion* that was the distinctive element of the southern political system.[8]

Here, the authors have collectively tested the effects of racial *inclusion* rather than exclusion; as such, these studies simply were not feasible in the South of 1949 and, for many southerners, they would have been unthinkable. While the South may continue to exhibit a distinctive cast of mind as a consequence of that part of its history unshared with the rest of the nation, these three chapters have suggested that the day-to-day politics of the region may not be decisively different from the politics of any other constituency facing the realities of racial diversity.

In the fourth chapter of this section, Marcus Ethridge ("Regulatory Policy Administration and Agency-Citizen Linkages in Southern States: Some Hypotheses and an Exploratory Analysis") more directly investigated the question of southern distinctiveness. Although the South has long been known for the importance of its informal or nongovernmental mechanisms for shaping social and political relations, Ethridge found that with regard to regulatory administration the South tended to lack informal bureaucratic linkages with citizens or nongovernmental entities. The result has been that formal citizen-participation mechanisms in southern states have tended to be more utilized and more effective than in nonsouthern states. Procedural reforms designed to increase citizen participation in administrative decision making have thus had more effect in the South than elsewhere.

Taken as a whole, the four chapters of Part III both diminish and support the concept of a South which is politically distinctive from the rest of the nation. The fact that blacks are no longer systematically excluded from the political process has unquestionably eroded a central element of the old one-party South. Yet, the inclusion of blacks in the political process takes place in an environment distinctive for its racial heritage unshared with the rest of the nation, and one consequence has been the ongoing interest in what impact racial inclusion might mean for southern politics; that is, on how linkages between mass publics and governmental officials are changing as a consequence of changing constituencies. Just as blacks traditionally had little effect on government, the South's tendency to rely heavily on informal relationships such as those between individual and individual and family and family, has resulted in a South distinctive from the rest of the nation in at least one important political arena, that of policy administration, where the lack of informal linkages between government and citizen has resulted in the increased effectiveness of more formal linkages. In short, in terms of how citizens relate to government, the old South may be gone, but the new South has not necessarily become a mere reflection of the rest of the nation.

The answer to the question of a continuing southern distinctiveness is not readily or clearly apparent. One consequence, undoubtedly, is that the study of the South will continue to elicit scholarly and popular interest. For regardless of what is actually happening in the region, nonsoutherners still often see the South as "different," and southerners themselves often perceive the South (and themselves) as regionally (and personally) distinctive from the rest of the nation.

But politically, at least, the South has changed greatly from even the pre-1950 South, although it is still too early to argue conclusively that the South has lost the entirety of its political distinctiveness. Indeed, some might argue that, while the South has changed, the rest of the nation has changed at least as much; and it might be argued further that the convergence course between the South and the rest of the nation, if that is what it is, has not been so much the nationalization of southern politics as it has been the southernization of national politics. This volume has perhaps contributed an additional piece in solving the puzzle of southern politics. And though the completed puzzle may suggest that the South is no longer so very different, it may well retain enough of its differences to remain the nation's most distinctive, and still the most studied, region.

NOTES

1. See, for example, Dewey W. Grantham, *The Democratic South* (New York: W. W. Norton, 1963).

2. See, for example, John Shelton Reed, *The Enduring South: Subcultural Persistence in a Mass Society* (Lexington, Mass.: Lexington Books, 1972); and Numan V. Bartley, "The South and Sectionalism in Southern Politics," *Journal of Politics* 38 (August 1976): 239-257.

3. See, for example, I. A. Newby, *The South: A History* (New York: Holt, Rinehart, and Winston, 1978).

4. See, for example, James Jackson Kilpatrick, "A Conservative Political Philosophy," in *The South*, ed. Monroe L. Billington (New York: Holt, Rinehart, and Winston, 1969), pp. 111-118.

5. See, for example, William G. Carleton, "The Conservative South – A Political Myth," *Virginia Quarterly Review* 22 (1946): 179-192; and V. O. Key, Jr., *Public Opinion and American Democracy* (New York: Alfred A. Knopf, 1967), p. 102.

6. See, for example, Robert S. Erikson and Norman R. Luttbeg, *American Public Opinion: Its Origins, Content, and Impact* (New York: John Wiley & Sons, 1973), pp. 199-205.

7. See, for example, Key's description of the party system in South Carolina in V. O. Key, Jr., *Southern Politics in State and Nation* (New York: Alfred A. Knopf, 1949), pp. 131-142.

8. Ibid., pp. 531-675.

ABOUT THE EDITORS AND CONTRIBUTORS

LAURENCE W. MORELAND (M.A., Duke University) is associate professor of political science at The Citadel. He is codirector of The Citadel Symposium on Southern Politics. He has recently coedited *Party Politics in the South* (1980), and he is currently engaged in research on state party activists and southern politics.

TOD A. BAKER (Ph.D., University of Tennessee) is professor of political science at The Citadel. A codirector of The Citadel Symposium on Southern Politics and coeditor of *Party Politics in the South*, he has published in the areas of urban politics, party activists, and political socialization. He is currently involved in research on state party activists and southern politics.

ROBERT P. STEED (Ph.D., University of Virginia) is professor of political science at The Citadel. He is a codirector of The Citadel Symposium on Southern Politics. He has done research and publication in the areas of southern political activists, the presidency, political socialization, and intergovernmental relations and has recently coedited *Party Politics in the South*. He is currently doing research on state party activists.

ALAN I. ABRAMOWITZ (Ph.D., Stanford University) is assistant professor of government at the College of William and Mary. He has published in a number of professional journals and has contributed chapters to three recently published books. He is currently doing research on party leadership and realignment in the South as well as codirecting a multi-state study on party activists.

PAUL ALLEN BECK (Ph.D., University of Michigan) is professor of government at Florida State University. He has published widely in the areas of political socialization, electoral politics, southern politics, and public policy. His books include *Individual Energy Conservation Behaviors* (1980), and his current research interests involve electoral change, public attitudes toward taxation, and the making of energy policy.

EARL BLACK (Ph.D., Harvard University) is professor of political science at the University of South Carolina. His publications include *Southern Governors and Civil Rights: Racial Segregation as a Campaign Issue in the Second*

Reconstruction (1976) and numerous journal articles on various aspects of southern politics. He is currently doing research on change and continuity in southern politics from 1920 through 1980.

MERLE BLACK (Ph.D., University of Chicago) is associate professor of political science at the University of North Carolina. He has coedited *Political Attitudes in the Nation and States* (1974), *Politics and Policy in North Carolina* (1975), and *Perspectives on the American South* (1981) and has published articles in a number of professional journals. His current research examines southern politics during the period from 1920 through 1980.

ROBERT E. BOTSCH (Ph.D., University of North Carolina) is assistant professor of political science at the University of South Carolina at Aiken. The author of *We Shall Not Overcome* (1980), his research interests include public opinion and congressional politics as well as southern politics.

GARY H. BROOKS (Ph.D., University of Kansas) is associate professor of political science at the University of Arkansas at Little Rock. He has done research and publication in public administration, political socialization, and southern state legislative politics.

MARCUS E. ETHRIDGE (Ph.D., Vanderbilt University) is assistant professor of political science at the University of Wisconsin-Milwaukee. A coeditor of *Methods in Public Administration*, his current research interests include citizen and legislative participation in policy implementation.

EARL W. HAWKEY (Ph.D. candidate, University of Missouri) is a planner in the Missouri State Division of Budget and Planning. He has done research on public opinion and education policy in Missouri and is currently engaged in a study of southern political culture with special attention to localism, racism, conservatism, and violence from 1952 to 1976.

TED G. JELEN (Ph.D., Ohio State University) is assistant professor of political science at the University of Kentucky. His research interests are primarily in the areas of religion as related to politics and voting behavior.

PAUL LOPATTO (Ph.D. candidate, Florida State University) has collaborated with Paul Allen Beck on research on American voting behavior.

JOHN J. McGLENNON (Ph.D., The Johns Hopkins University) is assistant professor of government at the College of William and Mary. His publications include work on police bureaucracy and state party activists. He is currently engaged in research on police corruption and state party leaders, and he is codirector of a multi-state study on party activists.

JERRY PERKINS (Ph.D., Emory University) is associate professor of political science at the University of Miami (Florida). He has published articles in a number of professional journals; most recently, he has coauthored two articles on women and politics in *The American Political Science Review*. In addition to his continuing interest in southern politics, he is currently doing research on religion and politics.

RONALD B. RAPOPORT (Ph.D., University of Michigan) is assistant professor of government at the College of William and Mary. He has done research and publication in the areas of comparative politics, state party activists, and the relationship between mass media and politics. His current research focuses on state party leaders and political socialization, and he is codirector of a multistate study of party activists.

CAROLE SOUTHERLAND (Ph.D., University of Wisconsin-Milwaukee) is assistant professor of political science at Memphis State University. She has done research on southern politics, race, and public officials.

MARK STERN (Ph.D., University of Rochester) is associate professor of political science at the University of Central Florida. His research has led to publication in such journals as *Phylon* and *The Journal of Politics*, and he has contributed a chapter on electoral politics to *Florida Government and Politics* (1980). He is currently doing research on congressional voting and civil rights.

C. DAVID SUTTON (Ph.D., Indiana University) is professor of political science at Appalachian State University. He has done research on public opinion and the military; his present research focuses on voting behavior in Appalachia.

KENNETH D. WALD (Ph.D., Washington University) is associate professor of political science at Memphis State University. A coauthor of *Shall the People Rule? The Democrats in Nebraska Politics, 1850-1970*, he has also done research and publication on British voting patterns, presidential debates, and the Ku Klux Klan. He is currently engaged in research projects on the changing British party system and reform politics in Memphis.